The New Naturalis

A SURVEY OF BRITISH NA

THE BROADS
THE PEOPLE'S WETLAND

The aim of this series is to interest the general reader
in the wildlife of Britain by recapturing the enquiring
spirit of the old naturalists. The editors believe that
the natural pride of the British public in the native
flora and fauna, to which must be added concern for
their conservation, is best fostered by maintaining a
high standard of accuracy combined with clarity of
exposition in presenting the results of modern
scientific research.

The New Naturalist

THE BROADS
THE PEOPLE'S WETLAND

Brian Moss

With 29 colour plates and over 140 black
and white photographs and line drawings

HarperCollins*Publishers*

HarperCollins*Publishers*
77–85 Fulham Palace Road
Hammersmith
London W6 8JB

The HarperCollins website address is:
www.**fire**and**water**.com

Collins is a registered trademark of HarperCollins*Publishers* Ltd.

First published 2001

The author asserts his moral rights to be identified as the
author of this work

ISBN 000 220163 1 (Hardback)
ISBN 000 712410 4 (Paperback)

Printed and bound in Great Britain by The Bath Press
Colour reproduction by Saxon Photolitho Ltd., Norwich

Contents

Editors' Preface

The Broads of Norfolk and Suffolk have long attracted naturalists by the diversity and interest of the flora and fauna of their wetland habitats. Indeed, their interest stimulated some of the earliest conservation plans and freshwater biology projects. The Broads have also attracted a much wider public by their virtue as an escape from everyday life to a life on water. Add to this the sensitivity of such wetland habitats to the activities of man, and we see the conflicts between conservation, land use, agriculture and tourism. In the earlier New Naturalist of 1965, the doyen of Norfolk naturalists Ted Ellis and his colleagues wrote from their exceptional knowledge of the flora and fauna of the Broads. Much has happened since then in the development of this area, and this book presents a personal approach to these developments, and to the earlier history of Broadland, equally important to the understanding of this remarkable region. The association of historical events with the evolution of Broadland habitats shows in extraordinary detail the sensitive state of the natural history we see today in Broadland, a degree of understanding which is hardly possible in other areas of the British Isles. Much of the recent knowledge comes from the study of freshwater life, the subject of the editions (1951, 1968, 1974) of the New Naturalist *Life in Lakes and Rivers*, written by T.T. Macan and E.B. Worthington. The present book brings together freshwater biology and conditions, vegetation, fauna and the recent geology into an ecological whole, all against a historical background. The author, Brian Moss, based at the University of East Anglia for many years, has been responsible for much of the new natural history which has enabled the synthesis he describes, a synthesis that is certainly relevant to threatened wetland habitats and their natural history in the wider world. The reader will soon gather and appreciate his enthusiasm and deep knowledge of Broadland natural history and of the social factors affecting its evolution. Those who know the Broads will reap very many new insights, and those who do not will, we are sure, be drawn to the natural history of the Broads by this book.

Author's Foreword and Acknowledgements

Writing this book was no chore. My impressionable teens were profitably informed by the classic New Naturalists of Pearsall, Macan & Worthington, Dudley Stamp, Turrill, Russell, Manley and Yonge and I was glad to be invited to join them. They very much celebrated the diversity of British natural history in the spirit in which the series was founded, at a time when they could take it very much for granted. Things are different now. Whereas they could write of man the curious rural inhabitant, I must attend to man the powerful, competitive species in the environment of man the creative and destructive modifier.

You will thus not find here a traditional naturalist's book, emphasising lots of species, and delighting in the appearance of this or that flower, or the habits of some spectacular bird. The flowers and the birds do not fail to move me and I indulge myself no less than many ecologists, but there are greater urgencies to which the endlessly fascinating system of Broadland should be harnessed. Nor will you find a habitat looked at through rose-coloured spectacles. I have not set out to rival the authors of coffee-table books, nor to be lauded in glossy magazines. I have deliberately used my own photographs accumulated over the years rather than the professional shots available for marketing the area. I have tried to present what a reader might realistically see.

For 30 years I have thought something about Broadland almost every day. The Broads have been a source of great pleasure, particularly at the end of a successful day coring their sediments, when one returns to the laboratory with the self-satisfaction of the successful hunter bringing home the quarry to an admiring tribe, or on completion of a good scientific paper with an internally consistent underlying theme. They have also been a source of immense frustration, when, for example, it was apparent that one or other organisation concerned with their management appeared to be no more perceptive than a well-trained coal horse lumbering on in blinkers. But then it turned out that they were not lumbering at all, but moving in a direction deliberately decided, that can be interpreted as part of the natural history of organisation man, an important feature to be factored into the story.

I worked on the ecology of the Broads intensively for 17 years and still do so at a distance. I am not a native of the area and hence not inhibited by its hierarchies and sometimes inward emphasis. I am also an academic and enjoy the proper role of academics to say what I think and not what is politically expedient or locally convenient. I hope this is a ruthlessly honest account. Among my heroines is Marion Shoard (1980, 1987). I have few heroes. If you want to know more about what I feel on issues of conservation and science and why I feel as I do, read Moss (1999a, b, 2000). I am not a born naturalist, with a boyhood of pocketed frogs nor a checklist of birds behind me. I come to the area with a broad background of environmental science, with as strong an element of chemistry and geography as of biology, and it is from all of these viewpoints that I have written this book. From the beginning, a study of the Broads epitomised the environmental sciences, which I see as the best grouping to cope with the nature of the future, whatever that might be, by the careful dissection of the past and the interpretation of the present. I am very grateful to the School of Environmental Sciences at the University of East Anglia, Norwich, and its founders, for that revelation.

I have broken several conventions. I have used the term Broadland to cover not only the core area, of National Park Status, administered by the Broads Authority, with its undrained fens, open water and grazing marshes, but to include the catchment area of the rivers also. A significant part of Broadland's problems has been enshrined in a cosy desire on the part of many of its past administrators and inhabitants to huddle into a picturesque enclave and ignore the greater world around of which the core area is just a small part. I have used the term 'Broads' in the text to refer to the lakes, the 'Broadland floodplain' to refer to the core area and 'Broadland' to the whole catchment area.

I have used common names for animals and plants wherever possible in the text, preferring not to clutter it with the Latin scientific names that are the ulti-mately necessary but immediate esotericisms of professional ecology. This may irritate some readers (it would me), but unless one is very familiar with the sci-entific names, they can be a distraction. I have given all the scientific names in the index, after the common name. Likewise, I have not given reference in the text to every statement, as this is not a paper in a learned journal. My sources are variously contained in the further reading and in the lengthy reference lists in some of that. I have tried here to tell the story of Broadland as I see it and not to write an encyclopaedia of all the published work on it, let alone all the background of environmental sciences, history and affairs that forms the con-text for the specifics of Broadland.

In quoting further reading at the end of each chapter I have eschewed unpublished documents and reports, available to those closely involved with the area, in the offices of government agencies, local authorities and the like. These are not readily accessible to the general reader yet they are very impor-tant in understanding the politics and management of the area. Many of them are reviewed by George (1992), which can be consulted on such details. The books and papers I have quoted are those freely available in public libraries, university libraries and bookshops. National grid references to all places men-tioned are given in the index. As in all considerations of place it is most help-ful, sometimes essential, to have a map to hand. Most locations can be found on the Ordnance Survey Landranger Sheet 134 (1:50000) Norwich & The Broads/Great Yarmouth or the truly excellent (as long as you are not trying to use it in a wind) 1:25000 Ordnance Survey Outdoor Leisure Map 40, The Broads.

Finally I want to thank many people – firstly those who have been part of the research on which several of the main chapters are based, or who encouraged it or who helped find the funds to carry it out. They include (in alphabetical order) Mick Bales, Hilary Balls, Claire Bennett, Ros Boar, Ian Booker, David Brewster, Aitken Clark, Bryan Clough, Carolyn Crook, Clive Doarks, David Eminson, Diana Forrest, the late Brian Funnell, Martin George, Hameed Hameed, Trish Holdway, Ken Irvine, Penny Johnes, Rick Leah, David Leeming, Jane Madgwick, Katharine Manson, Paddy Osborne, Martin Perrow, Geoff Phillips, Debby Snook, Julia Stansfield, Debby Stephen, Peter Stephens, Mark Timms, Raymond Watson, David Wilkinson and Peter Wright. It is invidious to single out any of these, but as an exception, I would like to say how much I have valued the long-term friendship of, and discussions with, Dr Geoff Phillips who has shared with me, for three decades, a passion for the Broads system and its future, who has been crucial in keeping the profile of the Broads high with his successive employers, Anglian Water, the National Rivers Authority and the Environment Agency, and who has argued with me often – and has usually been right!

Secondly, I would like to thank Dr John Wright, Centre for Ecology and Hydrology, for providing unpublished data on the invertebrate communities of the upper rivers from contracts supported by English Nature and Scottish Natural Heritage, given in Table 3.1; Alan Batley for drawing the headline drawing of Chapter 3 and Figures 4.5 and 4.6 and painting Plates 28 and 29; and Drs Martin George and Tom Williamson simply for having written two, in different ways, remarkably valuable previous texts on the Broads, which saved me much time. I would also like to thank Richard West, Katie Piper and Isobel Smales for their sensitive sub-editing and suggestions. Finally, but not least, my family, Joyce and Angharad, have been very tolerant when I disappeared to work on the book on numerous evenings and weekends. Both have shared with me the tedium of preparing the index.

Brian Moss

Part I

Hunter, Pirate, Marshman, Monk

1

The Broads, an Overview

There are three lake districts in England. The English Lake District in Cumbria is well known. It has its mountains, its large lakes, its literature drawing on Wordsworth, Southey and Coleridge, and a long history of research, which was important in formulating many of the principles of freshwater ecology. Its lakes lie like the spokes of a wheel radiating down valleys deepened by glaciers and dammed by the moraines of debris they left when they melted back.

The second lake district, the North West Midland Meres, is the least known. Its small lakes lie hidden in farmland on the great plain of silts, sands and gravels washed out from under the glaciers that had occupied the land until about 12,000 years ago and which lies in Cheshire, Shropshire and Staffordshire. Again ice had formed the lake basins, by moraine dams and in the huge holes left when fallen icebergs, buried in the debris, had melted.

Against this dramatic background of ancient ice, it is something of a paradox that the Broads, the third English lake district, have the importance that they have. A set of around 50 very small lakes linked with four rivers, on a world scale tiny, and the equally minuscule remnants of a mosaic of wetlands, they have a remarkable prominence in national sensibilities and a key role in the scientific research literature (Plate 1). Perhaps it is their association, over more than a century, with boating holidays that gives them their national affection. Perhaps it is the fame that they have had for their bird populations and for their rare plants that fixes them in the minds of naturalists. But perhaps most important is their long association with people.

The Broads were not carved by ice, or formed from volcanic eruption or gigantic movements of the Earth's crust as many of the world's lakes have been. Their origins were humble. They were dug out by medieval people for the peat that occupied what is now their basins. Peat is accumulated plant organic matter, laid down in swamps and combustible, when dried, for cooking and heating. The history of the Broads is that of the people in the area, for everything about Broadland is interwoven with the works of man and woman. This is always true to some extent of English landscapes, but in Broadland there is the added *frisson* of water. And not only fresh water but the sea and the tension that comes in a place that has sometimes been sea and sometimes land as the levels have changed and floods have invaded and receded. And that might well be sea again in the near future.

Where is this area? It lies in East Anglia, mostly in Norfolk, a little in Suffolk. The land is lowland and fertile, floored by deposits left by ice, with chalk underlying them in the west, and a sandstone known as Norwich Crag in the east. The topography is muted, sometimes rolling, sometimes with the extreme flatness of old salt marshes, now drained, which lie behind Great Yarmouth. Just as the high massif of the central fells is the anchor point of the Cumbrian Lake District, Great Yarmouth is the focus of Broadland. Into the estuary that lies behind it and that discharges through the town, Breydon

Water, run the waters of the three main Broadland rivers, the Waveney, the Yare and the Bure. In turn, on the high tide, salt water shoots for several kilometres upriver.

The rivers and the sea

The rivers (Fig. 1.1) lie in wide valleys, their former floodplains, narrowing upstream. These valleys are underlain by marine clays and freshwater peats that tell a story of alternating freshwater and marine flooding. Towards the sea the clay is thick, for this area has had only brief freshwater episodes. The lower reaches of the rivers are now totally confined to their summer channels that have been deepened and embanked, and the valleys are floored with wet pastures. These are the grazing marshes, a broad expanse, with cattle and sheep and a characteristic landscape. Formerly they were salt marshes and mud flats exposed to the sea through an opening of the estuary that was much wider than it is now.

Upstream the sea has visited only on occasion and the valleys have usually been fresh water. From edge to edge they have been occupied by productive

Fig. 1.1 The geography of Broadland. The rivers extend far into the interior of Norfolk to about twice the horizontal extent of the map. Still undrained fen and carr is stippled. The thin line to the outsides of the rivers shows the former floodplain, now mostly drained grazing marsh.

wetlands floored by the peat from which the basins of the Broads were dug. The fresh waters are mostly rich in bases such as calcium and magnesium and the wetlands are alkaline and fen-like in nature. Sometimes they are mildly acid, but not quite so much as the peat-forming bogs of the north and west of the British Isles. Originally the rivers rose each winter to inundate the valley floors, the full widths of their channels, retreating to the main channel in summer. This flood is now sometimes confined to protect property and agriculture, but many areas of still flooded fen and reedswamp remain. Their floras and associated fauna are often rich.

For millennia following the final retreat of the ice, about 10,000 years ago, this annual flood would fill lagoons, small lakes, in the wetlands flooring the valleys. These lagoons, in a sense the prototypes of the modern Broads, were shallow. They would often change shape as vegetation encroached upon them or was eroded away in a particularly high flood. The open water would have had a soft edge as the reedswamp communities gently merged into the lilies and submerged plants that characterised their bottoms. To the outside of the reedswamps, the floodplain floor would have been covered with a dense alder and sallow forest, often impassable on foot, though there were few human feet to pass.

In the open water a sparse community of microscopic plants, the phytoplankton algae, was suspended. Algae are a diverse group of many species each waxing and waning with the changes of weather and the activities of small animals grazing on them. The open water community was not productive; the nutrients it needed were soaked up in the wetlands before they could penetrate to the centres of the lagoons and this ensured a clear water, floored with charophytes (stoneworts), a group of large water-plant-like algae that do not compete well with higher plants when nutrient supplies increase.

These lagoons no longer exist; they needed the violent disturbance of flood to create them, and, with it controlled in the historic period, they have filled in with vegetation, silt and peat, leaving the bottom deposits laid down from the open water communities as buried beds in the fens. But in the medieval period, from the ninth to the thirteenth centuries, they were replaced by the man-made Broads. Human populations settled at the edges of the Broadland valleys probably from the Bronze Age onwards, though the archaeological evidence is sparse and settlement may have been much earlier. Cut in the deep peat deposits of the floodplains, the peat pits were at first relatively dry, but a wet period around the turn of the thirteenth century raised the valley water tables and they flooded.

The Broads – flooded peat workings

The high water tables prevented movement of man and domestic beast. The answer to such stranding was to create a waterway by connecting the previously isolated basins of the Broads to the rivers by channels (locally called dykes). This resulted in their remaining flooded and they could no longer be used for deep peat extraction, even when the weather later became drier. The flooded pits, much later called the Broads, were at first and for many centuries thereafter much like the natural lagoons they had replaced.

They started out rather deeper and thus resisted encroachment of vegetation and filling-in by sediment for longer. They were still relatively infertile, for the surrounding wetlands were intact and the river waters, draining catchments of

still very unintensive agriculture, brought only small supplies of those nutrients, mostly phosphorus and nitrogen compounds, that determine lake productivity. Their communities of charophytes thus flourished in the clear water
that the previous natural lagoons had enjoyed. Indeed, until the nineteenth
century, despite new channels being dug, rivers diverted, and much of the
floodplain being grazed or drained, the system probably changed little in ecological variety from that which had preceded the Bronze Age colonisation of
the area and the peat industrialisation of the medieval villages. It may even
have increased in its diversity.

The Broads were products, in a sense, of climate change, a normal feature
of Earth since its origin. But just as the climate changes we are currently
experiencing are proceeding at a much higher rate than perhaps ever before,
so too the human influences on the Broadland valleys, though continuous for
perhaps 6,000 years since the earliest settlements in the catchments, have
accelerated in the very recent period. From the start of the nineteenth
century in particular, the Broadland has become the epitome of how people
impinge on natural systems, at first enhancing them, in the sense of creating
variety, and more recently destroying them as a result of economic and cultural changes. The natural history of Broadland can no longer be just an account
of the diverse communities of a previous era, nor even just a description of the
relic gems that remain, protected by conservation legislation or sympathetic
ownership like the crown jewels in the Tower of London. It must be an account
of the interplay of man and other organisms, sometimes depressing, sometimes heartening, as degraded areas have been restored and less exploitative
attitudes have recently emerged.

First impressions

My initial view of the Broads was 30 years ago and deeply disappointing. I was
newly appointed to the University of East Anglia in Norwich and, as a freshwater biologist, it seemed preordained that I would create a research programme
in Broadland. The first visit, in spring, with the then Conservation Officer,
Peter Stephens, of the Norfolk Naturalists Trust, to one of its reserves, Barton
Broad, was cold, grey, windy, wet and generally off-putting. The water was
greenish-brown and featureless, the banks eroded, the river downstream bordered by ugly pilings, and the occasional passing pastel-coloured, fibreglass
cruiser was anything but attractive. Where was this Mecca of wildlife trumpeted in the natural history literature? It looked better as the weather improved,
but I think the view of Broadland at the landscape scale, even in summer, must
be quite disappointing for many people. It *is* a special place, but it needs some
effort and time to realise this to the full and to get behind the hype of the
tourist board and the holiday industry, and sometimes even of the Broads
Authority, which now bears many of the responsibilities for managing the area
as one of National Park quality (Table 1.1).

It is a different place from the prewar idyll of authors like Christopher
Davies, W.A. Dutt, Arthur Patterson, Arthur Ransome, Ted Ellis and John
Betjeman, and important for different reasons now. Rather than being the
epitome of charming old England, replete with intricate detail, quaint customs
and a slow pace of life, it bears the brunt of twentieth-century environmental
abuse. Most of the brutal things that can happen to fresh waters have happened somewhere in Broadland, a complex that still has some of the charac-

teristics – detail, diversity, traditional use and history – that made it a special place. Indeed, it is at least as much a special place now as one where the environmental battle is being keenly fought on several fronts and where victory, temporary at least, might occasionally be sensed.

Table 1.1 Some statistics for Broadland.

Location
Broadland lies in eastern England, with the common outlet to its rivers close to 52°34' North and 1°44' East. Most of it lies in the County of Norfolk and some of it in Suffolk. The central and lower parts of the valleys lie in Squares TG and TM of the National Grid and are covered by the 1 in 50000 Second Series (Landranger) Ordnance Survey Map Sheet 134.

Climate
The climate is slightly more continental than in other parts of Britain with long-term average maximum and minimum temperatures around 6.1 and 2.2°C in January and 20 and 13.3°C in August. Until recently, the Broads often froze in winter for a few days but ice cover was rarely prolonged beyond a week or two and in some winters there is virtually no ice cover. Sunshine-hours range from about 50 in January to 195 in July. Prevailing winds are from the north-east and long-term precipitation is from about 600 to 700 millimetres, depending on location. Evapotranspiration is about 75 per cent, of a potential 84 per cent. The catchment soils can thus be quite dry in summer. The weather is thus drier and warmer in summer than in much of Britain, but also drier and sunnier in winter.

Catchment area and main rivers
There are three main rivers, the Yare, Waveney and Bure, with catchments of 1,414, 889 and 877 square kilometres respectively so that a substantial area of East Anglia, 3,180 square kilometres, is drained. The altitude of the catchment ranges from 101 metres above, to 1 metre below ordnance datum. Much of the catchment area is arable farmed. Over their middle and lower reaches, the river gradients are about 3 centimetres per kilometre (one in more than 30,000). The annual runoff (precipitation minus actual evapotranspiration) may be as little as 46 millimetres and up to 270, and averages about 180 millimetres. Discharges are thus low, maximally of the order of 10 cubic metres per second in the Yare at its outlet and often only a few cubic metres per second in the lower reaches of the others. Flows are thus sluggish and reversed in the lower reaches at high tide in summer. Tides at Great Yarmouth range from 1.4 metres below ordnance datum to 2.0 metres above. The mean tidal range of spring tides is generally about 40 to 70 centimetres in the lower river reaches, and up to 20 centimetres in the upper reaches of the floodplain. The total river length navigable by boats other than rowing boats and canoes is 190 kilometres with about twice as much again available to rowing boats in the upper reaches. The catchment is bordered to seaward by a coastline of 33 kilometres.

The Broads
Determining the number of Broads depends on whether basins with complex shapes that were once discrete bodies are separately listed. However, a conservative count gives 47, ranging in present area from 0.7 to 173 hectares (Norton's Broad and the complex of Hickling Broad, Heigham Corner and Whiteslea, respectively). A further 11 to 20 basins may originally have existed but have now completely filled in with vegetation or have been drained. Mean depths are never more than 2.5 metres and may be less than 1 metre. The overall mean areas and depths are 20.7 hectares and 1.2 metres respectively. The mean area in 1840, calculated from the Tithe Award maps, was about 28 hectares. Overall there were 1,227 hectares of open water in the Broads in 1840 and 836 now remain. The Broads are thus very small, very shallow lakes, much potentially subject to filling in ('terrestrialisation') by vegetation.

Table 1.1 Some statistics for Broadland cont.

Official designations
The lower reaches are included in an area given National Park status and administered by the Broads Authority whilst responsibility for water quality and resources and flood defence rests with the Environment Agency. There are 23 Internal Drainage Boards promoting drainage of the floodplain and 79 places where water is abstracted for public supply. Most of these are groundwater abstractions, and seven are from the rivers and Broads. There are 96 sewage treatment works, each treating the sewage from at least 250 people or the equivalent. The length of river bearing flood defence works is 585 kilometres, with 225 kilometres tidal. Sea defences cover 14 kilometres of the coastline.

There are 83 Sites of Special Scientific Interest in the catchment, seven National Nature Reserves and nine Local Nature Reserves, seven Ramsar sites, three Special Protection Areas and four Special Areas of Conservation. Some of these designations, made under national or European legislation, refer to the same areas. There are about 65 scheduled ancient monuments.

Modern Broadland – the mosaic of habitats

A visitor will see the modern Broadland and, though its past is the key to interpreting its present, an overview of its components today is a logical place to start. Lakes and rivers are not isolated features of the landscape. The water that feeds them drains from the land, falls as rain from the atmosphere and even comes from fine droplets sucked up from the foaming sea by the winds. Water may come also from the surge of the tide up the rivers of a flat landscape. The Broadland, then, is formed from several parts. There is the catchment, the landscape of two-thirds of Norfolk and a bit of Suffolk. There are the streams that rise in the interior but widen into floodplain rivers 20 or 30 kilometres from the estuary they share in Breydon Water. There are the wetlands of the floodplains, the undrained fens and the now partly drained grazing marshes. And there is the North Sea that borders it.

The catchments of the Broadland rivers are floored by calcium- and carbonate-rich chalk rocks to the west and the Norwich Crag, a series of layers of iron-rich sands, clays, pebbles and gravels to the east. Both rocks are ancient marine deposits. The Chalk is up to 100 million years old, the Crag perhaps two million, but almost everywhere they are covered by debris washed out from the glaciers as they melted back only a little over 10,000 years ago. This 'drift' is often rich in soluble minerals, and the fallen rain easily dissolves many salts from the soils and, in places, directly from the underlying rocks. The water that moves to the streams also acquires, from living activity in the soils, a myriad of organic compounds and their pale yellow or brown colour.

The topography of Norfolk is not quite so flat as Noel Coward would have it in a famous quotation from his play *Private Lives* ('Very flat, Norfolk'), but it is by no means hilly. The streams do not rush to the sea, but flow well enough to erode material from their beds and create a gravelly channel where brown trout and grayling can spawn, and mayflies, snails, dragonfly nymphs and other invertebrates dodge the turbulence. Silt rests at the edges and plants root in it, creating underwater forests of buttercups and watercress to backcloths of iris, reed and willow.

Removal of water from the rivers for domestic supply and for irrigation of the wheat and sugar beet fields has taken a toll and the flows are lower than they naturally should be. Piggery wastes and runoff of plant nutrients from the agricultural land have led to growths of blanket weed, a dense, vigorously growing mat of the green alga *Cladophora* in place of the buttercups, and engineering to minimise risks of flooding of the surrounding farmland has eroded the charm of many stretches and destroyed the holts of the once common otter. Damage from herbicide and pesticide residues may be subtle but pervasive. But there are still stretches of river that represent a worthy stewardship (Plate 2).

Broadland floodplains

Downstream, the rivers widen and have cut their main channels in meanders that span the floodplains. Silt has been deposited in the quieter backwaters and, away from the main channel, a complex of reedswamps, fens and wet woodlands, or carrs, gives a varied tapestry as the river has dictated and as human management of the area has modified. Rooted in waterlogged soils, the plants must cope with deoxygenation of their roots. But a habitat of base-rich water from the fertile soils of the glacial drift, and equally rich silt, brings a high productivity that feeds the food webs of invertebrates, fish and birds.

Floodplain wetlands are the most productive of all world habitats and, because of the changing intricacy of water, swamp and land, some of the biologically most diverse. Here may be found, though not so abundantly as formerly, the charismatic birds and insects of Broadland – the bittern, bearded tit and marsh harrier, the swallowtail butterfly (Plate 3) and the Norfolk aeschna dragonfly.

Some undrained floodplain is left. It is a complex of plant communities (Plate 4) reflecting the past management for useful products (reed and sedge for roofing, hay and litter for stock and alder poles for building and fencing) as well as the particular chemistry of the water from place to place. Much of it has succeeded to dense alder carr as labour-intensive management by cutting has been abandoned since the Second World War. The alder carr, unless it has not been disturbed for centuries, is less valued than the open, cleared fens for it has lower diversity of plants and animals. Nonetheless it has the appeal of a jungle-like denseness, with great stools of the tussock sedge, a metre or more high, interspersed with soft peaty mud where you might easily sink to the waist.

Other areas are of commercial reedswamp, where the common reed, prized for its qualities as a roofing thatch, and a vigorous competitor, eliminates most other plants, even when conditions are not specially managed to favour it for a clean crop. Again there are special qualities – the sights of great swathes of beige stems, topped by the flags of dried seed heads rustling in the winter wind, and the bundles of reed waiting by the marshside for the thatchers to collect them.

The most diverse undrained fens, however, are those where the vegetation is regularly cut (unlike the carrs) though not every year, and where the water table is maintained high (unlike the commercial reedswamps, where dropping of the water table in winter and annual cutting favour reed dominance). In these, now the least extensive of the floodplain communities, the plant and insect diversity is at its greatest, and small and unusual plants are able to survive because the cutting removes their more vigorous taller competitors. If the appeal of the reedswamps is winter monotone, that of the fens is summer colour.

Grazing marshes and the estuary

The fertile silts of floodplain wetlands have been their undoing. If the rivers
are straightened to speed their water faster to the sea, then embanked and the
water pumped from the floodplain into their channels, the wetlands can
become dry and fertile arable land. If the drainage is less severe, a still wet grazing marshland with pastures and ditches may be produced. The lower parts of
the Broadland valleys combine in a huge and flat area behind the estuary, the
Halvergate triangle. The floodplain in the lower parts of the river valleys was
easiest to drain and the characteristic remaining wind pump towers testify to
this. They are often called windmills, but their function was not to grind grain
but to pump water. The deposits are not solely of peat, which shrinks on
drainage and wastes away, but mostly of clay near the surface from flooding by
the sea in the past. A millennium and a half ago this was partly a great salt
marsh, echoing to the cries of geese and gulls.

Clay can be drained with lesser shrinkage than peat, though it does not form
an easily workable soil. It now sustains a permanent grassland, however, and
large areas still remain as wet grazing marsh, with dykes full of plants and invertebrates, and rough grasses where wading birds may nest. The marsh is a landscape of subtle greens (Plate 5). It is dotted with cattle, penned by dykes invisible from a distance, and its fields are connected by gates with whimsical sloping sides where bridges cross the dykes. It has its greatest appeal, perhaps, in
the winter mists or the haze of a summer morning, when there is a sense of
unendingness spoilt on a clear day by the views of distant electricity pylons
strung for miles across the flat landscape.

Some parts of the Broadland grazing marshes have been much more deeply
drained and support ugly lands of uniform arable agriculture devoid of the
detail and interest of the grazing marsh. Fortunately much of the area was
saved from this in the 1980s by public protest that eventually led to legislation
creating Environmentally Sensitive Areas, first here then elsewhere in the UK,
where traditional farming practices are supported to maintain their characteristic and attractive landscapes.

The Broads

The Broadland waterway – over 190 kilometres of navigation unimpeded by
dams or locks and including the rivers, the Broads and the connecting dykes,
together with a few Broads still isolated among the undrained fens – provides
an entirely unexpected grain of detail that most visitors to Broadland do not
see. To its observers, however, this small-scale, indeed microscopic, panoply
can be more fascinating than the spectacle visible to the naked eye. Formerly
the reedswamps bordering the rivers and Broads were fronted by belts of lilies
that gradually gave way to underwater plants covering most of the bottom. This
underwater wilderness had its flocks of grazers – crustaceans only a millimetre
or two long, snails crawling over the plant surfaces cleaning them of algae,
mayfly nymphs and fly larvae. The algal communities covering the plant surfaces (the periphyton) were more diverse than all of the visible plant communities of the fens.

There were predators: dragonfly nymphs lurking in the interstices of the
stems and leaves for passing prey; bugs and beetles actively hunting, dependent for their vigorous movement on additional supplies of oxygen gleaned

from the surface and stored as bubbles held to their bodies. There was a further layer of predators in the diverse fish community – roach, bream, tench, rudd and small perch feeding on the invertebrates, pike and larger perch taking the other fish, and cormorants, heron, grebe, bittern and otters topping the pyramid. Coot and moorhen, ducks and geese waded, dabbled and honked. It was a rich community based on clear water, where suspended algae, the phytoplankton, were kept from growing both by a shortage of certain dissolved nutrients and by flocks of grazing crustaceans that nightly ventured from their refuges in the plant beds. Broadland was the epitome, in the United Kingdom, of richness of water plants and their associated animals. A former version of this New Naturalist book, written and edited by Ted Ellis in the 1950s and 1960s, rightly celebrated this.

Much of it, alas, has now gone (Fig. 1.2). The story of its loss and replacement by cloudy water, rich in algal plankton (Fig. 1.3), is an extremely interesting one, for it gives insights into how freshwater communities everywhere function and how this functioning is affected by human activities. Unravelling the mechanisms by which the clear water, dominated by large plants, has been lost, has come from co-operation between laboratories all over Europe, for it is not a problem confined to the Broads, but is worldwide. Devising ways in which the system might be managed to restore the clear water and plants has

Fig. 1.2 The edge of a Broad in 1887 and as it often is now. 'The haunt of the pike', by the Victorian photographer P.H. Emerson, shows a complex edge with reed and other plants fronted by water-lilies and submerged plants. The more recent picture, taken 100 years later, still shows reed, but nothing else. Extension of the reed into the open water is prevented by various disturbances, including swan grazing. The swans have no alternative submerged plant food.

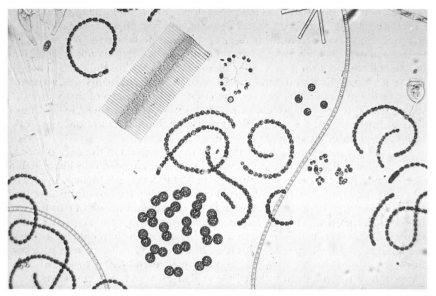

Fig. 1.3 A typical phytoplankton community will have well over 100 species, with perhaps about ten abundant at a given time, the rest awaiting conditions favourable for their increase as the seasons change.

produced a strategy that also has global value. The Broadland in its former state had international importance as a diverse wetland. Some of that importance still remains, but it has been eroded, and the significance of Broadland lies more now in its significance in environmental restoration. The Broadland is a microcosm for similar problems that wetlands face all over the planet.

The sea

There is, finally, the sea. Broadland landscapes and waterscapes, for some people, are best appreciated on clear days in winter, when wind ruffles the water surface and rustles through the reeds, when no-one else is about and the noise of motor cruisers has abated. The sea coast is like this too. The water is always brown, for it carries silt from up the coast on currents that supply the beaches with sand as they erode the cliffs to the north. The beaches (Plate 6) are long and smooth, backed by a low line of dunes topped by marram grass. There is a stark beauty about the simplicity of the parallel bands of water, beach and dune; brown, beige and yellow-green, under a sometimes blue sky.

The sea is a part of Broadland. Its levels relative to the land have changed in the past and are changing still. When the ice ceased its melt, perhaps 7,000 years ago, sea levels were high enough to create an estuary far into Broadland, where now the wetland is fresh. Two thousand years ago the same thing happened when storms destroyed a sand bar, now re-formed and the site of Great Yarmouth. The bar had occluded the estuary and kept out the sea for 5,000 years. Daily the tide still penetrates far up the Broadland rivers, taking salt water so far, but the physical effect of the surge reaches much farther, causing river water to be ponded back and to mix into the Broads. Some Broads, along the River Thurne, are modestly saline from the percolation and pumping of sea water that diffuses through the crag deposits into the inland water table; others receive shots of sea water when the tide is high and especially when weather conditions called storm surges push the tide far up the rivers.

East Anglia is steadily sinking and the relative sea level is thus rising. The land is still compensating, even after thousands of years, for the shifts in weight of the ice cover. Left to nature and without the embankments that presently separate the grazing marshes from the river, the lower parts of the Broadland valleys would now be steadily moving back to the salt marshes they naturally were at least twice in the past 10,000 years. The floodbanks are old and weak; at some high tide in the future they will break.

The sea level is also rising faster through the expansion of the mass of ocean water, as global climate warms. The warming has so far been only about half a degree centigrade, but the ocean is so huge that its level rises by a centimetre or so every year. Should we spend large sums to keep the sea out of the lower valleys with barrages, barriers or new floodbanks, or should we admit that the sea, no less than the fresh water of the rivers, is a part of Broadland and that its turn to prevail has come again? In a system where human involvement and management has been pre-eminent for centuries, there is no easy answer, just the opportunity for endless debate as we wait, tinkering here and there, to see what will happen. In this, Broadland is the epitome of all environmental problems.

The sense of place

Described so far is the view you might see from an aeroplane flying well above the level at which detail is revealed. It is an account also from an imaginary time machine whose logbooks are notes deduced from present evidence. This book will flesh these bones from the point of view of a scientist who has worked particularly on the problems of the waterway. I shall put more emphasis on some aspects than others – one writes best about what one really knows about – but the Broadland is a strongly interconnected system where a holistic view is essential. The fate of the bittern in the reedswamps, perhaps, is partly a consequence of the operation of European agricultural policies, argued out in office suites in Brussels, amplified in Whitehall and enacted in the distant arable fields around the rivers to the west. There is much information, though our understanding improves yearly as even more knowledge accumulates and our predictions have to alter as governments and ministries change policies in response to a myriad of lobbies, concerns and even whims.

At the end of it all there remains the very important sense of place. Broadland has all the elements. There is the detail. Nowhere else in England, for example, will you find a landscape dotted with so many churches with round towers of flint. The Broadland catchment has no suitable hard building stones that can be easily shaped. Only lumps of flint washed out of or mined from the Chalk were available. Flint is hard, and time-consuming to shape. Right angles are difficult to build if stones are irregular, and it has been suggested that circular towers were easier to build. This turns out to have been mere rationalisation, however; round towers were more likely a local fashion of the twelfth century, a human preference, mimicking similar fashions at the time in the closer reaches of mainland Europe.

There is also the mosaic of plant communities that make up the fens, each a consequence of water chemistry, position and past and present management. There is the interconnectedness of land and sea through the fresh waters. And

Fig. 1.4 Two prominent monasteries of Broadland. Both Norwich cathedral (left) and St Benet's Abbey (below) were greatly developed following the Norman invasion in the eleventh and twelfth centuries.

there is the long history – a minor prehistoric presence but successive waves of Roman and Danish settlement into a British community that shaped the system through digging, cutting, diversion and draining and that continues to shape it, though by the different means of policy and machinery.

There is also an aura about Broadland that you can sometimes feel. It does not always come, but when it does it comes in unexpected ways. Sit, on a November afternoon, behind the ancient choir stalls in Norwich Cathedral (Fig. 1.4), their dimly lit wood smoothed by the rubbing of countless hands and coats. You are surrounded by the great masonry of Norman pillars made of Caen stone, specially brought by boat up the Broadland rivers from France. As you hear the choir singing Fauré's Requiem on All Souls night, 2 November, remember the monks of St Benet's Abbey, whose kitchens in the tenth and eleventh centuries consumed so much peat, excavated from the pits that were to become the Broads, that the costs were worth recording in documents now held in the Cathedral library.

It can come too in the more mundane surroundings of laboratories. The patterns of chemistry in the waters have a beauty also. There has been the long day of travelling around, dipping samples from the rivers, hauling crates in and out of vans, pouring water through filters so you can separate what is dissolved from

Fig. 1.5 Concentrations of nitrate and ammonium in the inflow waters of Broadland during winter. Patterns of measurements may often reveal something of ecological processes. Inorganic nitrogen enters the Broads as nitrate or as ammonium, largely during the winter. Nitrate leaches from cultivated land, and is very abundant in the rivers flowing from the west, which drain chalk soils, and which have largely arable catchments. Ammonium is generally very scarce as it is oxidized to nitrate by bacteria. Where the streams receive water from mildly acid peat (generally underlain by Norwich Crag rocks) that has been pump-drained, however (the black areas on the map), this process is inhibited by the acidity, and ammonium, resulting from the oxidation of the drained peat, appears as a much greater proportion of the nitrogen entering the system. These peats are less productive and not so much cultivated and fertilised, so the total amount of nitrogen delivered to the Broads from them is lower than that brought in by the westward rivers. Chemical data from various publications, particularly Moss (1983). Distribution of acid peat from George (1992).

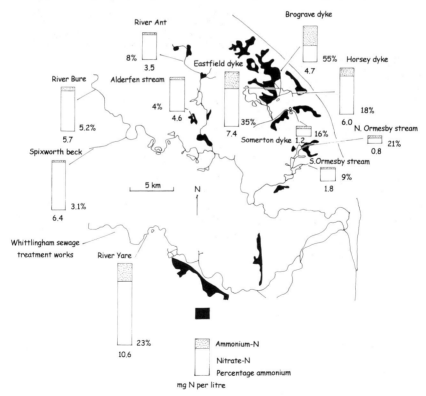

what is suspended. Now you add the reagents: phenol, sodium hypochlorite, sodium nitroprusside, sodium hydroxide and citric acid. Leave the mixture in the dark for a couple of hours and then see the intense turquoise-blue that shows the amount of ammonium ions in the water. Rich and deep in the Thurne, pale, almost absent, elsewhere. A consistent pattern (Fig. 1.5), which means something, another piece in a fascinating puzzle that this book seeks to unravel, though there is no end to it, no final solution. Environments change all the time and Broadland will too. Nature responds to change but never quite catches up. There is none of the balance of nature that romantics would wish to believe, just a continual struggle to survive that governs whole systems affected by the march of human abilities just as individual organisms subject to natural selection must meet a continually changing natural environment.

Further reading

There is a large popular literature on Broadland. Much of it is repetitive, adulatory, rose-coloured and unsatisfying for anyone wishing a real understanding. On the other hand there are some outstanding books, on which I have freely drawn in compiling this account from a different point of view. George (1992) is an authoritative and very detailed reference work on land use, ecology and conservation, whilst Williamson (1997) is a fascinating account of the history of the landscape. Ewans (1992) covers many of the issues and is particularly clear on political aspects.

The natural history of Broadland until just after the Second World War is covered in Ellis (1965), who wrote most of the predecessor to this New Naturalist book and edited the rest. There are some particularly good chapters, especially on the origin of the Broads and on vegetation, and authoritative annotated lists of major groups of organisms, which give an interesting contrast to the account that will follow in this book. Perhaps surprisingly for an official document, most of which take very little advantage of the clarity and beauty of the English language, the Broads Authority's latest edition of its Strategy and Management Plan (*Broads Plan* 1997) is a very well written and illustrated summary of the present state of the Broads, and gives an excellent account of the diversity of the problems and those solutions, at least, that are currently politically acceptable. Likewise, though written in a drier style, the Local Environment Agency Plan (LEAP), published by the Agency in 2000, gives considerable insight into the problems of water quality and resources in the area.

The early 'travel literature' on the area can be interesting reading, again for the contrasts. A long series of guides by G. Christopher Davies following his first book in 1883, and Suffling's book of 1887, give insights into the issues of the time in otherwise sometimes tedious sequences of locations to visit by boat. Dutt (1903), Wentworth Day (1967) and Manning (1980) emphasise the romance over the reality. Malster (1993) and Holmes (1998) compile photographs of Broadland from the late nineteenth and twentieth centuries.

Different insights can come from literary works. John Betjeman (1984) wrote two poems about the Broads (*East Anglian Bathe* and *Norfolk*), Arthur Ransome's children's books (*Coot Club*, 1936, and *The Big Six*, 1940) are well known. Perhaps more than anything else they convey the pleasure of messing around in boats that has been a prominent attraction of Broadland for a century or more. There are other, more tenuous, literary links (Earwaker & Becker 1998) with Norwich and Yarmouth.

2

Before the Broads

'The following data, which we have drawn up for our guidance, convey, in a brief form, the history of the Norfolk strata.

1. That the county is situate on the western side of the great chalk formation, which is the substratum of nearly all Europe.

2. It appears that this extensive marine deposit, emerging from the waters of the ocean, became inhabited by herds of elephants, together with the mastodon, rhinoceros, hippopotamus, and other tenants of the forest; the remains of which are now found imbedded in the detritus of our eastern coast.

3. That during this period, an aestuary running from north to south, must have divided the eastern part of the county from the western; and deposited its rejectamenta, which are now found reposing on the chalk in this particular tract.

4. That this aestuary existed a sufficient period of time to silt up its bed to the level of the adjacent country; and that its residuum may be seen in the brick-earth of the crag district, and to a considerable extent on each side of the same.

5. That the changes effected by the Deluge, were the disruption of the then surface, and the filling up and levelling its inequalities by the detritus; by which catastrophe the eastern side of the county was covered with a large quantity of the wreck of the lias, and the western with a similar portion of the oolitic series.

6. That at a subsequent period, and prior to the separation of this country from the continent, there existed large lakes in different parts of that which is now the county of Norfolk, and probably in that part occupied by the German ocean, lying between Norfolk and Holland. These were surrounded by extensive forests, the trunks of whose trees are found imbedded in the alluvial soil, particularly on the sea beach at Brancaster; and that these forests were inhabited by herds of deer and oxen, is apparent, from the horns and bones found buried with the trees in this deposit.

7. It also appears that the chalk was subsequently disrupted, separating this country from the continent, at the same time forming the valleys of eastern Norfolk and the drainage of the county.

8. That these valleys were afterwards occupied by the waters of the ocean, as shown in the Author's Map of Roman Norfolk, published by the Society of Antiquaries.

9. And, lastly, that the waters retreated from these valleys about the time of the Norman Conquest, leaving the county as it now appears.'

Samuel Woodward (1833)

The beginning

No human eyes saw the seascape that was the beginning of Broadland. There were eyes, but they were those of reptiles and squid-like molluscs now long extinct, living in a great sea. A constant rain of microscopic particles of lime, derived from plankton in the water, was laying down chalk sediments off the coasts of what was to become Europe. But the continent was then positioned in warmer latitudes ten degrees to the south of its present location.

It was the beginning of Broadland because the chalk sediments, compressed over 70 million years into a soft rock, and later pushed upwards by huge forces to become land, are the most ancient rocks that appear at the surface in the catchments of the Broadland rivers. They determine the basic chemistry of the Broadland waters. Yet it was a very late event in the history of the Earth. On the timescale when Earth history is compressed into one hour and now it is midnight, the chalk sea was not quite two minutes ago and human eyes have been around for less than one fifth of a second.

We have tools to unfathom the story and there have been plenty of storytellers. The early nineteenth-century geologists were clever. With only their eyes and notebooks, and later their microscopes, they had the bare outline more or less right, but in the last few decades we have added the details and put the story into a wider context of continental drifting and an Earth surface that is more turbulent than perhaps ever realised before.

John Stacy of Norwich printed and sold in MDCCCXXXIII – 1833 – the Reverend Samuel Woodward's *An Outline of the Geology of Norfolk*. A thin book, 32 small pages of text and as many again of lists of fossils and pictures of them, it includes a map of the surface geology, hand painted by a watercolourist, that closely resembles that produced by the Geological Survey of Great Britain and still sold by Her Majesty's Stationery Office (Figs 2.1 and 2.3). Woodward was a local cleric, probably of independent means, certainly with time to travel around and try to sort out the history of what was around him.

Woodward's main conclusions are quoted at the head of this chapter and there is much in them that a modern geologist would recognise but reinterpret. Chalk does underlie most of Norfolk; the climate was then much warmer and elephants *did* roam, though later than Woodward thought; a reinvasion of the sea *did* cover much of Norfolk's western surface with marine deposits – the 'rejectamenta' of the great 'aestuary'. Woodward's Deluge, to him Noah's Flood, was the melting of the ice sheets and the washout of huge amounts of clay ('the wreck of the lias'), broken chalk and sand that are the modern surface deposits. There *were* extensive forests, though not large lakes, and they did cover areas, now the bed of the North Sea, in interglacial periods when sea levels were low because so much water was bound up in the polar icecaps. And the river valleys of eastern Norfolk, where the Broads now lie, *were* invaded by the sea in historic times, with the last retreat only a few centuries before the Normans.

A little later than Woodward, Thomas Henry Huxley, the great proponent of Charles Darwin's then new theory of natural selection and evolution, now the backbone of all biology, came to a meeting of the British Association for the Advancement of Science in Norwich in 1868 to lecture to its working men. He talked 'On a piece of chalk', a familiar thing to men who might dig it out from the holes that were to be the foundations of Norwich buildings. We have the

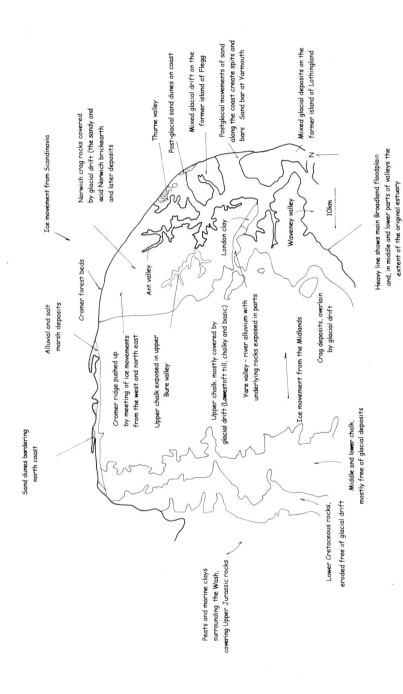

Fig. 2.1 A summary of the features of Norfolk geology that have most influenced the Broadland.

text verbatim, a literary essay turned to scientific purposes. Huxley once remarked that literature and science were not two separate things, but two sides of a single coin.

His text takes Samuel Woodward a step further. He talks of the calcium-rich microscopic plates, coccoliths and coccospheres (Fig. 2.2), that cover the cells of many marine phytoplankters – the photosynthesising, microscopic algae that fix energy in the oceans that cover over two-thirds of this planet. He refers to *Globigerina*, a single-celled protozoon animal of a group called the Foraminifera, whose cells are also surrounded by a chalky armour, the testa, with holes in it through which the cell is in contact with the water. *Forare* was the Latin for to bore or pierce, *kokkos* the Greek for a berry and *lithos* for a stone. Huxley developed his theme of the origin and age of the chalk rock, of the continuity of the process of chalk formation. But his key agendum in a Victorian age that Charles Darwin was both enlightening and spiritually destroying, was the continuity of evolution of a procession of organisms of which we ourselves are among the most recent and the most clever.

There are many details that might be added to Woodward and Huxley (Fig. 2.3), and modifications in some fairly fundamental principles governing the geology of the Earth, which came together only in the 1960s, but their understanding was considerable. The sea that laid down the chalk first covered the area that is now Broadland 135 million years ago. It was at first muddy, shallow and received sandy sediments and clays as much as chalky debris. These eventually formed, in the Jurassic period (Fig. 2.1, 2.5) the Sandringham sands and the brown carstone that outcrop in west Norfolk. But 90 or 100 million years ago, the land mass that was to become Europe started to move and to be submerged by the deepening seas that were to lay down the white Upper Chalk that forms the subsurface of half of Norfolk, the Downs of southern England and the cliffs of Dover.

Fig. 2.2 Fossils of marine organisms found in the Chalk. Left, the calcium carbonate scales (coccoliths) that cover the tiny cells of coccolithophorids, which are photosynthetic algae. Right, foraminiferans, which are small animals, up to a millimetre or two in size, covered with a test of calcium carbonate, through which strands of protoplasm extend to engulf bacteria. From Huxley (1967).

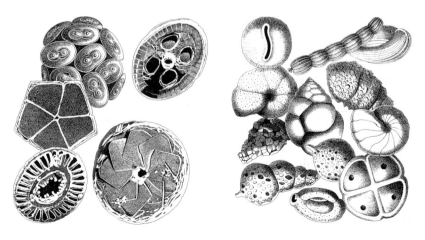

Fig. 2.3 Present understanding is always based on past investigation. In direct and indirect ways, Thomas Henry Huxley (left) and Samuel Woodward, part of whose map is shown (right), provided part of the foundation long ago for our present understanding of Broadland.

The Chalk

The sea covered most of what was to be the British Isles and the Upper Chalk is up to 400 metres thick. The coccoliths that dominate it are well preserved, which is significant. Because chalk is quite soluble, its components can become etched by the acid that results from the large quantities of carbon dioxide dissolved under pressure in deep water. In modern oceans, the sedimenting coccoliths (for they are still important components of the marine plankton) disappear in very deep water. The chalk sea, with its coccoliths undissolved, is thus thought to have been less than 600 metres deep.

This sea was large, and floored with a soft gooey sediment filled with burrowing bivalves, whose cavernous shells were probably partly floating in the goo. Its overlying waters had cephalopods and modern-looking fish, and the later dinosaurs still dominated the landmasses. Water diffusing through the chalk, then or later, deposited silicates around particles of organic matter or sponge spicules to form the tiny crystals that now make up the lumps of very hard flint found, often in horizontal layers, in the chalk. Flint was to be crucial to the development of human tool use and for building in Norfolk. Flint was the versatile plastic of our ancestors.

For 30 million years the chalk sea laid down what was to become 30 micrometres of chalk rock each year – the thickness of two coccolithophoric algal cells, one micrometre is one thousandth of a millimetre. It was a clear sea, not very productive, though many of the algae would have been consumed and their plates destroyed before they could reach the bottom. Nonetheless, 30 micrometres per year is 30 metres per million years and potentially 900 metres in the span of the later Cretaceous period which is defined by the presence of the Upper Chalk sea.

Late in the life of this sea, the Chalk began to be lifted up. The Earth's surface was in one of its periods of turmoil. The plates of the crust, which move under the colossal convection of a plastic mantle not far beneath them, were coming into collision. The Rocky Mountains were pushed up in North America, and the Alps in Europe. The forces that generated the alpine movements to the east and south of Europe lifted the Chalk, crumpled it in parts, as on the south coast of Britain, but gently tilted it in Norfolk (Fig. 2.4) so that its surface slopes down to the east and lies closer to the surface in the west.

It was a time of biological upheaval as well – perhaps for linked reasons, perhaps from some totally unconnected cause. There were major extinctions. Many families of molluscs, ammonites, belemnites, echinoderms, bryozoons and foraminiferans disappeared from the seas; but on land, the flowering plants had evolved devices that allowed them to supersede the conifers, the first mammals with placentas were appearing, reptiles were becoming less prominent and birds were diversifying. Waders and cormorants, shades of the future Broadland, were already in place.

Britain was warm and it was to be a further 40 million years before its land would have drifted as far north as at the present. At the end of the Cretaceous, a balmy chalk downland, akin to the landscapes of modern France, covered west Norfolk. As long a period was to pass again before even the more remote ape-like ancestors of man were to appear. East Norfolk, the present Broadland, did not yet quite emerge from the sea. But the sea-bed sediments had been raised relative to sea level and the seas flooding west Norfolk were now much shallower.

Fig. 2.4 The Chalk underlies much of Norfolk, but barely appears at the surface in Broadland. It is exposed, however, in the cliffs on the north Norfolk coast at Hunstanton, where it can be seen overlying the brown carstone, laid down in an earlier sea.

The Crag

The deeper the ocean, the less productive it is, because essential nutrients, lost to the bottom in carcasses and the faeces of small animals, cannot easily be returned from depths that the winds cannot mix. Wind mixes water down to 100 metres or so, but, on average, the ocean is over 3,000 metres deep. Tiny flagellates, such as coccolithophorids, with large surface areas compared with their volumes, do well in such waters, but are out-competed by bigger species such as diatoms and dinoflagellates in shallower, more fertile seas. The seas covering eastern Norfolk in the early Tertiary period (the Palaeocene and Eocene (Fig. 2.5)), the time that followed the chalk sea, were shallow and enriched. Into them came the nutrient-rich silts that were rapidly eroding from the Alps as they were pushed up by earth forces over several million years.

Rivers, tributaries of the Rhine, ran from the uplifted Chalk in the west and laid down clays, now called the London Clay, which bear the pollen of mangroves, Nipa palms and other warm temperate families, together with birch,

Fig. 2.5 A geological timescale. What is so striking is the recentness of all of Broadland's ecological history – a mere one five hundredth of one per cent of the time that has elapsed since the origin of Earth.

Time (millions of years ago)	Era	Division	Deposits in Broadland	Events happening
4500				Origin of Earth
3500	Precambrian	Archaean	Deep underlying rocks but not	Oxygen-free atmosphere
2500		Proterozoic	appearing at surface	Oxygen produced by photo-synthesis. Multicellular organisms
545-245	Palaeozoic	Cambrian- Permian	Most rocks from these periods eroded away in past. Others occur at depth but do not appear at the surface	Land vegetation develops Vertebrates evolve. Major extinction at end of Permian
245	Mesozoic	Triassic	No rocks in Norfolk	Arid conditions in Britain
208		Jurassic	West Walton Beds, Kimmeridge clay Kimmeridge clay	Norfolk a shallow, muddy sea
146		Cretaceous	Carstones in West Norfolk Hard lower chalk at first then soft upper chalk with flint nodules	Norfolk a shallow, clear sea Extinction of 'dinosaurs'
65	Tertiary	Palaeocene	No deposits - Norfolk above sea level	Mammals and birds diversify
56.5		Eocene	No deposits - Norfolk above sea level	
36.4		Oligocene	No deposits - Norfolk above sea level	
23.3		Miocene	No deposits - Norfolk above sea level	
5.2		Pliocene	London clay	Seas cover Norfolk/ Start of human evolution from apes
1.64	Quaternary	Pleistocene	Norwich crag, Cromer forest bed Many glacial deposits - till, boulder clay, loess. Norwich brickearth Lowestoft till	Climate cooling but still warm Human species evolve. Complex alternating periods of warmth (interglacials and interdtadials) and cold (glaciations)
0.01		Holocene	Freshwater peat and marine clay in Broadland valleys. Dunes on coast	End of glaciation, warming trend Colonization and settlement of valleys by people. Recorded history in the last thousand years (0.001 million yrs)

metasequoia and cedar. We may imagine large lagoons, rather than Samuel Woodward's lakes, but he was not far wrong. The climate became drier and the land continued to rise so that for the next 50 million years, Norfolk was land, for there are no sediments laid down over the London Clay in the Oligocene and Miocene periods. These were apparently arid times. Then, a very few million years ago, perhaps only five, the seas came back to east Norfolk and Suffolk and sands full of shells formed the sediments that now lie directly over the Chalk. They laid down 100 metres or so of sediment, now called the crag, in Woodward's 'great aestuary', full of the fossils of bryozoans, bivalves, gastropods and brachiopods, in confused deposits moved and reworked by the tides.

To the north of Norfolk, a large river, the former bed of the Thames, created a delta with huge freshwater marshes, whose remains are the exciting Cromer Forest Beds, full of fossils. Still the land was rising and the deposits from this delta now lie above the present sea level at Cromer and elsewhere along the present east coast. Deltas shift and move and this was no exception. Freshwater deposits interleave with estuarine ones, organic peats with clays, sands and gravels. Tree stumps were swept down the river; bones and teeth of elephant, rhinoceros, deer, hyena, sabre-toothed tiger, bear, beaver and hippopotamus were swept into muds occupied by cockles and other bivalves. The fruits of sedges and water buttercups jostle with those of the water chestnut and pondweeds. It was the prototype of the Broadland and the great fenlands of the Wash – a great wetland, a wilderness on the edge of the sea.

But its remains are scarce, for momentous events were happening. The climate was cooling then warming then cooling again. The last phase of the delta was a marine sediment of sand and chalk debris, typified by a bivalve shell, *Leda myalis*. And in these deposits are mineral grains transported by ice from far to the north. A glacial phase had already come and gone perhaps 500,000 years previously, its traces now largely removed by the bulldozers of later glaciers. The Cromer Forest Beds represent a warmer period prior to the subsequent Anglian glaciation, the next phase of intense cold.

The ice

Glaciations, when temperatures fall, on average, by only a few degrees, and when the polar icecaps and those on high mountains start to grow, have not been uncommon in the past. They seem to be a normal feature of history on Earth. We happen to live in the middle of one, though of course, we are not covered in ice at present! There are phases of warming (interglacials) then cooling, advance then retreat of the ice. During the retreats, sands, gravels and clays, eroded by the previous advance of the glacier, are washed out from under it to form chaotic deposits.

In the interglacial periods, swampy (wetland) vegetation, colonising hollows in the washout plain, may leave peat, with preserved pollen, to give clues as to what was then happening. The next glacial phase may then leave this evidence of the previous phases if the ice does not advance so far, or it may obliterate all previous evidence by clearing all the peats and deposits out of the way as it slowly, but unremittingly, moves forward. Sorting out the history of a period of glaciation is thus not easy. Indeed, a long tradition in geology rather disdained those who studied the Quaternary period, as that of the last set of glaciations is called, for they could not emerge with simple and clear-cut answers.

What causes glaciations? No-one knows for sure and the fleetingness of the evidence does not help. Anything that just slightly reduces the amount of the sun's radiation received per unit area of the Earth's surface, or causes the existing heat to be distributed a little more unevenly, can cause a temperature fall. Some people think there might be slight fluctuations in the heat output of the sun, others that as the solar system moves through space it might encounter dustier parts of the galaxy from time to time, so that less heat reaches the Earth. The orbit of the Earth around the sun changes slightly with a predictable long-term cycle taking it slightly further away from the Earth every 100,000 years or so.

Then the formation of mountain chains, the movements of continents, changes in the shape of the oceans and alteration of heat-carrying ocean currents might do the trick. So might release of dust into the atmosphere following periods of volcanic eruption, and changes in the carbon dioxide concentration. Carbon dioxide is one of several gases that trap heat radiation, previously received from the sun, before it escapes from the atmosphere out to space, so that the atmosphere forms a warm blanket. Presently we are increasing this effect by burning carbon previously stored as coal and oil. In the past, an increase in plant growth could have kept more carbon dioxide out of the atmosphere and precipitated a cooling phase.

We must distinguish a glacial age from a single glaciation. Glacial ages are periods, often very long, when conditions fluctuate between very cold and somewhat warmer. There seem to have been a relatively few of them, though we cannot be sure because the evidence quickly disappears. We are in one at the moment; the previous known one was 300 million years ago, long before the chalk sea. Glacial ages probably arise when the movements of the continents, or rather the plates of the Earth's crust that bear the continents like the superstructures of large ships, stop a free circulation of heat-bearing ocean water from the tropics to the poles. The poles then cool and the glaciers can start to grow. Within a glacial age there are frequent alternations of cold glaciations and warmer interglacials (Fig. 2.6). The clue to this often rather regular rhythm, may be in the changes that occur in the Earth's orbit around the sun.

The regularity of the phases of ice advance and retreat in the current glaciation can be dated by methods that ultimately depend on examination of deep sea sediment cores. In these there has often been a continuous history of sediment formation during the current glacial age. The sediments are magnetised in the direction of the Earth's magnetic field as they are laid down. The field itself changes direction frequently (north becomes south and vice versa), but the direction of magnetisation of minerals in the sediments retains strong elements of the direction acquired at first. This gives a basic chronology that can be correlated with parts of the history left in the washout deposits from the glaciers where sufficiently undisturbed sequences have been left.

Measurements of radiocarbon also give dates for interglacial peats and these can be combined to build up the picture. Radiocarbon dating depends on a relatively uniform rate of formation of radioactive carbon-14 in the upper atmosphere as particles from space bombard nitrogen. When it penetrates to the lower atmosphere this radiocarbon is taken up by plants, and thence animals, and then slowly decays in their organic remains (peat, wood or bone), with about half of it disappearing to non-radioactive elements every 5,700 years

Fig. 2.6 The glacial period has had a much more complex history of temperature change than was originally thought. The curve shows fluctuations in temperature indicated by changes in the ratio of oxygen isotopes in the tests of bottom-living foraminiferids. These lived on the sea bed and picked up different ratios of the isotopes dependent on the temperature at the time. Warmer periods are indicated by a lower value of the deviation of the ratio from a particular standard ratio (called the delta oxygen-18 value). These periods are conventionally given odd numbers, colder periods even numbers. There has been much more fluctuation than indicated by the previous belief in rather few glaciations and interglacials, as shown on the right, but the older terminology is useful in discussing major trends.

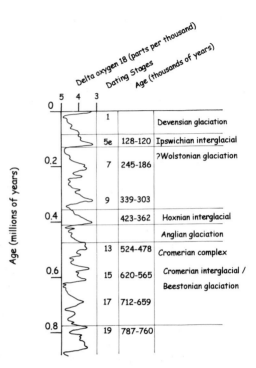

or so. From this 'half-life' and the ratio of radioactive to non-radioactive carbon in samples of organic matter, the age of the sample can be calculated.

Finally, studies on oxygen isotopes in cores of ice from the permanent ice-caps can give the temperature pattern. Ice ultimately takes its water from the atmosphere. Water gets into the atmosphere by evaporation from the ocean. Oxygen, which is, of course, a major component of water, exists in two forms or isotopes, both chemically much the same but one slightly heavier than the other. Water molecules with the lighter isotope, O^{16}, are more easily evaporated than those with the heavier one, O^{18}, and the differential is greater the higher the temperature. Thus a high O^{18} to O^{16} ratio in the ice cores suggests a lower temperature. In the water itself, organisms like foraminiferans also discriminate, taking more O^{18} up as the temperature falls. From analysis of their remains in sediment cores the pattern of temperature can again be deduced (Fig. 2.6).

When the results of the various methods are put together, a cycle of about 100,000 years, in practice 95,000–125,000, emerges for successive waves of ice advance in the current glacial age and this rather conveniently coincides with a change in the Earth's orbit that moves from roundness to a degree of ovalness on the same frequency. This is caused by the gravitational pull of the moon and other planets. At the extremity of the oval, the Earth is significantly further from the sun than during a near circular orbit. This difference alone does not seem to be large enough to bring about sufficient cooling. But the slight change in radiation received from the sun over time may cause a small shift in the pattern of the ocean currents that leads to a much larger redistribution of heat over the Earth's surface. These orbital changes, or Milankovitch cycles, were first described by a Yugoslavian, Milutin Milankovitch, in the 1920s.

The present glacial age has had interstadials as well as interglacials. During interstadials, there has been a lesser warming than in an interglacial before cooling has returned. These might be linked with other regular changes in the relationship of the Earth to the sun, including changes in the tilt of the Earth's axis towards and away from the sun on cycles of 23,000 years and changes in the time of the year when the Earth is closest to the sun (precession) which changes on a 41,000 year cycle.

In the last million years or so since the last of the crag deposits were laid down in the shallow sea that was covering what is now eastern Norfolk, including most of Broadland – the Pleistocene period (Fig. 2.5) – there were thought to be four very cold periods in the British Isles and four warmer ones intervening, of which we are now in the latest, the Flandrian (Fig. 2.6). Two of the cycles brought lots of debris to Norfolk which was deposited on the former sea bed and brought the bed level above the surface to form land at the same time as the sea level was being lowered by water being locked away in glacier ice. West Norfolk was probably dry land at the start of the glaciation; east Norfolk and the future Broadland contained in it was born of the glaciation.

One of the charms of ice age studies is that whole periods of major ice advance or melting back, momentous features of natural history, are given grand names after otherwise insignificant places, insignificant at least on a global scale (*pace* their present proud inhabitants). These are the locations where deposits from these periods were first recognised and described. Many of these places are in East Anglia, for the maximum extent of several of the ice advances was just to the north of the region, so washout deposits and inter-glacial peats have not been destroyed by subsequent glaciations.

Honesty compels me to say, and Fig. 2.6 makes it clear, that such a simple pattern of four warm and four cold periods, orderly and predictable as it sounds, is an oversimplification – even scientists like simple stories to order a complex world. The studies on oxygen isotopes from sea-bed Foraminifera show that the fluctuations in temperature were much more complicated, with lots of intervening short warmish periods especially in the Wolstonian glaciation (Fig. 2.6), and a sawtooth pattern of temperature in all periods. Still, we are unlikely to be able to correlate events on land with all the fine details of the marine temperature curve, so the comfortable pattern, simplified though it is, will suffice.

The first advance of the ice did not reach East Anglia. We know it, the Beestonian, from evidence of a cold climate at sites at Beeston on the Norfolk coast near Sheringham. There followed an interglacial, the Cromerian, preserved in the Cromer Forest Beds, when life was distinctly warm (Fig. 2.7).

The next glacial, the Anglian, was the big one for Norfolk. Ice from Scandinavia carried and pushed rocks, sands, gravel and clays from Norway, the North Sea Drift, and dropped them around the north-east coast of Norfolk. It left a few tens of metres of what is now called the Cromer Till and the Norwich Brickearth (Fig. 2.1), to bear currently heathy vegetation. Then waves of ice came down from the west with debris broken from the Chalk and

Fig. 2.7 Impressions of the landscape in Norfolk during the recent Devensian glacial, 20,000 years ago (top), and from the Cromerian interglacial, around 500,000 years ago (bottom). In the glacial phase, the ice front is some 50 miles to the north, with tundra-like conditions in southern Norfolk. In the interglacial, there is an open, deciduous wooded landscape. From paintings by N.J. Arber, published in a Norfolk Museums Service Information Sheet in 1984.

earlier rocks (Woodward's 'wreck of the [Jurassic] lias') to deposit the Lowestoft Till over much of southern and eastern Norfolk (Fig. 2.1). Where the lobes of ice met, south of Cromer, distorted deposits were pushed up to give a feature, the Cromer ridge, still very clear today, and the source of some of the Broadland rivers.

The ice then retreated, never to return to Norfolk in such force. This was probably 200,000 to 300,000 years ago. Hoxne, a small village in Suffolk, gives its name to the following interglacial. Then there was the Wolstonian glaciation, which reached the Midlands but stopped short of Norfolk, and the Ipswichian interglacial (hippopotami were back and also pond tortoises) beginning 128,000 years ago and ending 13,000 years later. The last glaciation, the Devensian, reached the north Norfolk coast and left glacial deposits, the Hunstanton Till, but merely cooled down the lands to the south. It was cold and dry in Norfolk and the winds blew the dust and piled deep, fine soils as loess in parts of Broadland, especially in the east, in the area later called Flegg, on the land between the valleys of the Bure and Yare and on the catchment to the north-east. These soils, deposited almost accidentally in the unpredictable chaos that accompanies ice, were to be seminal in determining the major courses of Broadland ecology and history.

The Devensian glaciation ended 10,000 years ago, leaving us in the Flandrian, having said goodbye to the polar bears, but awaiting the return of the hippopotamus! A paragraph thus covers 300,000 years, almost the whole history of modern man; a last sentence encompasses the ten millennia that were to see the immediate origin of Broadland, its development and near destruction in the last second of the hour of Earth history to date.

People and the ice

Human eyes were to see some of this. The earliest people moved into Europe, and probably into Britain, from Africa about 450,000 years ago, just before the first glaciation. There is no unequivocal evidence of them from Norfolk, but they had probably been there. They were more or less like us, though smaller, and we call them *Homo erectus*. Later there is more evidence, not bones, but mostly worked flints picked from the Chalk or the glacial rubble and chipped to give cutting edges.

Flint tools turn up serendipitously during building work or after flood erosion or sometimes during systematic scanning of ploughed fields (Fig. 2.8). The evidence from them is that people – ourselves, *Homo sapiens* – were present in the interglacials. These people sought the herds of game in an open tundra landscape at first and probably followed the game northwards as the ice retreated temporarily in the summers. When the climate warmed more and woodland grew, hunting became more difficult. Reindeer, bison and horses are easier to kill in the open than the red deer, roe deer and wild ox hidden in the forest.

The forests were dense, of oak and birch; their pollen rests in the interglacial peat. It was warm in the Hoxnian, warmer in the Ipswichian. The pickings must have been rich. But the Devensian ice brought back the cold, and sensible people moved back southwards. We know these people only from the shapes of the flint tools they made and sometimes from shaped and even decorated bone, but it is mostly from flint, which, unlike bone, does not dissolve in soils, which are often slightly acid.

This early human period is called the Palaeolithic, the old Stone Age, and it is concurrent with most of the last glacial age. Traditionally there has been the idea that the skills of flint tool working developed greater sophistication over the long period of the Palaeolithic and various 'industries' have been recognised, named, like the glacials and interglacials, from where they were first discovered. Unfortunately there are different systems of naming the glaciations and interglacials and the phases of tool-making and this can prove confusing. Many of the tool-making phases were named by French archaeologists, particularly the Abbé Breuil, from French localities, others were named from East Anglian discoveries. Thus we have the Clactonian, the Acheulian, the

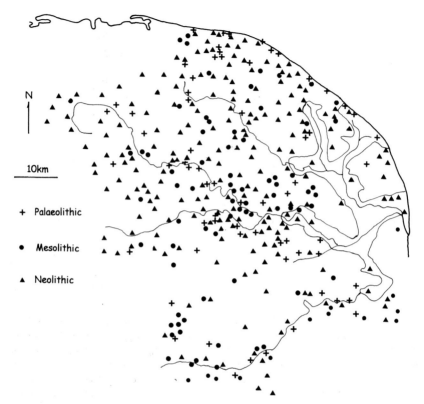

Fig. 2.8 Map of Palaeolithic, Mesolithic and Neolithic remains from the Broadland catchment. Most remains are finds of stone axes (mostly flint) and other tools, but there are very occasional burial barrows, enclosures and henges (circles) from the Neolithic. Based on Wade-Martins (1994) and Dymond & Martin (1999).

Levalloisian and the Mousterian industries, covering the nearly half a million years from 450,000 to 15,000 years ago in what is designated the Lower Palaeolithic.

Clactonian tools are known from chipped-off flakes and cores of flint and are associated with deposits around the Anglian glaciation. Acheulian tools are 'hand axes' – probably not axes at all in our sense, but sharp lumps for throwing, cutting or scraping flesh from skins. Levalloisian tools are associated with a particular group, the Neanderthals, and Mousterian tools have a distinctive flat butt. A few dozen tools of various kinds have been found in Broadland, though with no particular pattern. There are slightly denser numbers around Keswick in the valley of the River Tud, a tributary of the River Yare, and at Whittlingham on the Yare, but few in all (Fig. 2.8). We can only surmise the activities of these people from finds elsewhere – at Kents Cavern near Torquay, Paviland in Glamorgan, Caddington in Bedfordshire and Boxgrove in West Sussex.

The picture is no longer the caricature of rather unintelligent savages slowly developing some sort of culture and becoming very gradually more skilled

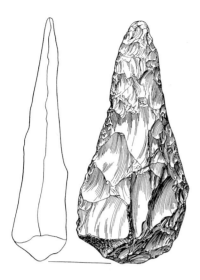

Fig. 2.9 A Palaeolithic hand axe, found in gravels in the River Yare at Keswick near Norwich and probably made 250,000 years ago.

at working the flint. It is rather one of intelligent people coping with difficult and varied conditions. The hand-axe cultures may simply be reflections of the quality of flint locally available, not a development in time. Elegant tools need fresh-dug flint, cruder ones are all that water-weathered flint can produce. Fine tools may have been made very early on. The idea that it took half a million years to learn how to shape flint to forms that delight our art experts is undoubtedly no less a libel on a people as clever as ourselves than would be a characterisation of our culture by Tupperware bowls rather than fine china. Traces of Palaeolithic culture anywhere have not, however, been well preserved. The bones exist, from Wales, of a young man covered in red ochre paint, and accompanied by ivory rods, a bracelet and the bones of mammoth, bear and rhinoceros perhaps hinting at funerary rituals, but a lifestyle dependent on following the game needs little baggage, and there is little to find.

The Upper Palaeolithic, the start of settlement

There were two slightly warmer interstadials during the last major ice advance in the Devensian. For a time a light forest cover replaced the bare terrain and patchy tundra that covered Norfolk when the Devensian was at its height 18,000 years ago. But for 100,000 years, the equivalent of 3,000 human generations, little happened in Norfolk. Two thousand metres of ice, over a mile thickness, covered Scotland and Scandinavia and its effects froze Norfolk into paralysis.

Then, as imperceptibly as it had come, the ice began to melt and the climate began to warm again in what may now be just the latest interglacial. Huge volumes, as much as 5 per cent perhaps, of the Earth's entire store of water, were locked up in ice, and the sea was much lower, 100–130 metres below where it is now. The English Channel became a forest, so also the North Sea. Less forested grasslands on the river floodplains of tributaries of the Rhine eventually led from what is now mainland Europe.

More evidence of humanity has turned up from the Upper Palaeolithic, the period from the height of the Devensian glaciation, 18,000 years ago, until the time around 10,000 years ago when the ice had finally retreated. The nomadic hunters continued to follow the game as the landscape became clothed with tundra, but as the forests began to grow again in the late Devensian, a more settled existence became possible. This was interrupted from time to time by the cold air following minor readvances of ice in the north, known from deposits in Lake Windermere and Loch Lomond. It was still very cold, and shelter was necessary – in the overhangs of cliffs or in shallow caves. From some 10,000 years ago we have the remains, in caves at Cresswell crags in Derbyshire, of groups of people who acquired possessions that they perhaps no longer carried around – bone tools, ornaments and bangles.

Norfolk has few caves – most rock that might bear them is covered with glacial drift. We thus have few remains from this period, but there is no reason to suppose that the future Broadland was not then being colonised in much the same way as elsewhere. The nomads left and the Mesolithic ('middle stone age') cultures who began to create their own shelters in Britain from 8500 BC to 3500 BC (10,500 to 5,500 years ago) moved in. It was not a forced migration of people, more an imperceptible drift over 5,000 years, probably barely noticeable over a life span. There was likely a continual occupation of the edges of the Broadland valleys. Shelters would have been built from fallen or cut branches, but the evidence has yet to be turned up. Archaeologists have tended to ignore Broadland so far.

The ice melts, a more familiar landscape emerges

Early every morning I am suddenly awoken by the tumult of our central heating system. There are great crashings as warmed and cold water jostle for position in the pipes. The end of a glaciation must be a bit like that. The meltwater roars and pours from under the ice sheet, and great bergs crack and roll off the edge to crash in a colossal heap among the sands and gravels washed out by the torrents onto the plain in front of the ice. From the dry windiness of intense cold, with dust storms blowing to the south of the ice edge, to the pervading wetness of the melt, the landscape wakes up.

The rivers, flowing eastwards across Norfolk, along the tilt of the underlying Chalk and Crag, but covered with up to 20 metres of glacial till from the Anglian glaciation, began to cut into the till and even the underlying Chalk. Because the sea levels were very low, the rivers flowed through the forests that occupied much of the southern North Sea onto the now European mainland. The river gradients were modestly steep, falling perhaps a metre every kilometre, creating V-shaped valleys. The Broadland was not then the present subdued flat expanse. That came a little later as the sea levels rose.

Our knowledge of these last 10,000 years in Broadland is really quite detailed. There are many deposits containing fossil evidence and there have been many interested people eager to understand them and to achieve a little fame with their peers for putting together a page or a chapter in the story. The key tools are simple – firstly, a borer or corer, a simple device that can be pushed or drilled into the deposits to bring back a sample from a known depth. Secondly, some surveying instruments so that the levels in one boring can be related to those in another and to the standard ordnance datum, a mark on the sea wall at Newlyn in Cornwall that was at sea level in the late nineteenth century.

Bore into the beds of the Norfolk rivers and you will eventually come to the gravel or sand base that represents the point to which the water had eroded in the early centuries after the ice finally disappeared from the north of East Anglia, about 10,000 years ago. Depending on where you are along the length of the river, that level will be up to 15 metres below the present sea level, perhaps sometimes 20 or more. When the rivers first started to flow, their beds must have been as many or more metres above the sea level.

The explanation is simple. The sea level rose as the meltwater from the glaciers poured back into it. By 7,500 years ago, when melting effectively ended, the sea level had risen by 120 metres, about 1.2 centimetres per year. For 2,000 or 3,000 years after the end of the Devensian, the most recent glaciation, the Norfolk rivers, however, remained well above the sea level and their lower reaches, as well as their interior courses, were distinctly fresh water.

The Mesolithic in Broadland

This period, 2,000 or 3,000 years after the ice started finally to melt back, is called the Mesolithic. In thickening woodland, it seems to have been the time when hafted axes became a key tool for people. You could cut trees with them, and make boats. There was a great plain sweeping from Ireland to Denmark of which the Broadland was somewhere in the middle, its rivers flowing out to meet the Thames and the Rhine somewhere under the present North Sea. It was not isolated. People moved over hundreds of miles and cultures mingled so that a general Maglemosian culture (named after a place in Denmark) can be identified. The Maglemosians made lots of spear points, bows and axes. Axes could be used to clear areas of forest to aid hunting, perhaps to encourage rich grazing for deer, tempted to expose themselves in the open. The Maglemosians re-sharpened worn axes by chipping at the edges and the remains of these can be found scattered in no particular pattern over Broadland (Fig. 2.8).

When people moved into Broadland to fish – the salmon, sea trout and eels were now running, and some coarse fish had returned from the main stem of the Rhine – or hunt, they left little trace. But the chances of finding a discarded axe or a lost spear point or the charcoal from a camp are low when these were likely to have been scattered in the first place. No doubt they were there though – small groups taking advantage also of game that encountered people so infrequently as to be easy to catch and kill.

There are two well-known sites in Britain where more coherent Mesolithic remains are found and both, Thatcham in Berkshire, dating to 9,800 years ago, and Star Carr in Yorkshire, 9,500 years ago, are waterside locations not unlike the edges of the rivers in Broadland at the time. The problem in Broadland is that the subsequent deposition of metres of more deposits has hidden any remains so that their discovery will be a matter of luck when an excavation for some other purpose chances to reveal them. Nonetheless, we can imagine something of the lifestyle from the Thatcham and Star Carr remains. Both were probably temporary camps, occupied in spring for hunting before the families moved to the uplands with the migrations of the game. At Thatcham, hearths are preserved and shallow pits with domestic refuse. Roe deer, red deer and wild pig were eaten; dogs were kept. Clothes were made and repaired

with bone needles, and spear points of antler and bone lie around. Star Carr
supported four or five families on a platform 200 metres square, made of
branches and brushwood. They hunted elk, roe deer and ox, wild pig and
water birds and kept dogs. Barbed small hooks suggest that they fished; brack-
et fungus was stored perhaps as tinder and rolls of birch bark for fire-lighting.

A paddle suggests that they had boats, and beads of amber, rock and deer
teeth were used for dressing up. Scrapers for cutting meat from skins are plentiful, and deer skulls were cleaned out and perforated to act as ceremonial
masks. They were clever beings, capable of prospering in difficult conditions,
and had feelings too. No graves are known in Britain, but the Maglemosians of
Vedbaek in Denmark buried a group of 22 bodies with due ceremony, the
women with their jewellery, the men with their tools of red deer antler, and a
young woman dead in childbirth with her baby lying on the wing of a swan.

The risen sea and the estuary

Seven thousand five hundred years ago, the weather was still cool, perhaps
rather windy; trees had returned to the drier uplands with pine and birch, but
the valleys were very wet, the water too deep for alder and willow to colonise
except in isolated shallow spots. Britain had become an island about 8,500
years ago. As the sea levels rose, and the coast crept further into Norfolk, the
rivers were discharging into a wide bay (Fig. 2.1) now occupied by the great
wedge of land that lies behind Great Yarmouth, the Halvergate triangle. The
valleys up to 20 kilometres or more from the edge of this bay became wide. The
landscape was flattish and water ponded on the floodplains, supporting
reedswamps that left their remains as a peat, now called the 'lower peat'.
Radiocarbon dating tells us that this was laid down between about 9,000 and
7,500 years ago. People settling around this area must have found the peaty
swamp difficult to negotiate.

The sea had risen so much by 7,500 years ago that in Broadland it came well
beyond the original bay and far up the river valleys. There was nothing to stop
it in the flat expanses of the lower peat swamps. It swept sand and silt into the
middle of the Halvergate triangle and as its waters quietened at the edges it
laid down the first of the great mass of clay deposits (Fig. 2.10) that were to
characterise the next 2–3,000 years of Broadland's history.

The nature of the water can be deduced from the fossils laid down in
the deposits, particularly of the calcareous protozoa, the Foraminifera. As I
counted diatoms from the later history of the area at the University of East
Anglia, my colleague, the late Brian Funnell and his student, Brian Coles, were
along the bench in the same laboratory, examining the foraminiferans from
this period. They had done their borings, using a mechanical corer to
penetrate the many metres of rather solid deposits on Halvergate, dried the
sediment and passed it through sieves to concentrate the Foraminifera, which
are a millimetre or so in size. It takes a small bag of sediment to obtain enough
to give a reliable picture of the time. They then picked out the animals using
a paint brush and mounted them on microscope slides covered with grid lines
on black paper pasted with glue. The dampened foraminiferans from each
sample were carefully arranged by species in the compartments, to be
identified and counted. I was quite charmed by it, a sort of scientific cottage
industry with a warmth about it somehow lacking in the analytical machines
along the corridor.

Coles and Funnell found many *Protelphidium anglicum, Elphidium magellanicum* and *Ammonia beccarii* in the marine sands that immediately covered the lower peat in the Halvergate triangle. These are estuarine foraminiferans, but they were mixed with completely marine species at first. This was a sheltered embayment, but it *was* the sea. Things changed, though (Fig. 2.10). The sands gave way to clays, even in the centre of the bay; the marine foraminiferans disappeared, the estuarine ones persisted and were joined by those now found mostly on salt marshes, *Jadammina macrescens* and *Miliammina fusca*. At the edges the common reed kept a hold (it can stand some salt) though in the middle we must imagine a great mud flat at low tide and shallow open water at high.

The estuary was becoming more sheltered. Sand creeps along the Norfolk coast forming spits or bars that block off the rivers and quieten the waters

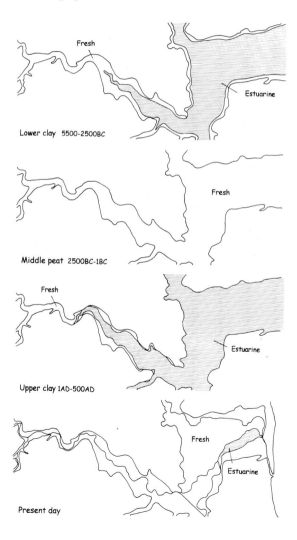

Fresh

Estuarine

Lower clay 5500-2500BC

Fresh

Middle peat 2500BC-1BC

Fresh

Estuarine

Upper clay 1AD-500AD

Fresh

Estuarine

Present day

Fig. 2.10 The changing environment of Broadland, reflected in successive landscapes of the River Yare between what is now Norwich and the North Sea. Based on maps in Coles & Funnell (1981).

Fig. 2.11 The upper clay is heavy, and boring through it to discover its history is hard work.

behind them. Great Yarmouth now stands on the spit that blocked the Broadland rivers. Behind it, as it formed and took the force of the waves, this spit created lagoon-like conditions and allowed the quiet sedimentation of metre upon metre of thick clay. Sometimes called the buttery clay, it is the sort of clay (Fig. 2.11) that you can make pots from, that squeezes through the fingers with smooth sensuality.

The lower clay, the land sinks

This deposit is called the lower clay (Fig. 2.10) and is thickest to seaward, and at the centres of the river valleys. It thins upriver and to the fringes of the valleys, giving a profile like wings or the blades of a leaf spreading outwards from the central midrib if you take a section across the valley at right angles to the river. In the valley of the River Yare, the wings disappear around Strumpshaw and the channel clay a little upstream, at Brundall. In the River Bure it disappears at Horning. Behind Great Yarmouth in the Halvergate triangle it is 11 metres deep, the relic of about 2,500 years of estuarine conditions. Its upper surface lies between 6 and 10.6 metres below the present sea level, yet it was laid down at sea level then and by the time it started to form, sea levels had reached the maximum of the rise they were to achieve by the melting of the glacial ice.

This sounds odd, but there is an explanation; the land was steadily sinking. Sea level changes are classed as eustatic and isostatic. Eustatic changes are those which directly change the amount of water in the oceans – freezing of it in glaciers, release of it on melting. They affect the sea level the world over. They were what caused the rise which brought the sea into Broadland from

18,000 until 7,500 years ago. Isostatic changes are local. They are not absolute changes in the amount of ocean water at all, but sinking or rising of the land locally relative to an absolute sea level. Both eustatic and isostatic changes can, of course, occur simultaneously.

Isostatic changes in Broadland, indeed in the entire lower half of the North Sea basin, have been due to adjustment of the land as the weight of ice has been removed. The ice sheets in Scotland at the height of the Devensian were heavy enough to depress the Earth's crust into the plastic layers below it by perhaps 800 metres – they exerted a pressure of 200 kilograms per square centimetre, or the equivalent of 200 extra atmospheres. When this ice melted the crust rebounded upwards – it is still doing so – and as Scotland rises there is a seesaw effect that causes East Anglia and the South East, including London, to sink a little. The fall is enough to be measurable as an apparent rise in average sea level of one or two millimetres each year. In the long run of time this process will stop, possibly even reverse, but the run is in millennia. The penetration of the sea into Broadland, as into the fenlands of the rivers draining into the Wash, was to reach an apparent maximum somewhere between 4,000 and 5,000 years ago, 2–3,000 BC: in reality the level is still rising, but the rise is masked by flood defences.

There would have been people living around the edges of the estuary, but, as is usual in Broadland, whatever possibly rich evidence might exist is deeply hidden by subsequent deposits. On the island of Oronsay and around Oban in Argyle, however, are archaeological sites that suggest the sort of small settlement that probably bordered the estuary of Broadland. The Scottish sites have middens full of limpet, whelk and oyster shells, the remains of gulls, gannets, cormorants and the now extinct great auk. Saithe, conger, bream, wrasse and haddock were eaten; seals and otters were hunted and whales, probably cast up on the beaches, were eaten. This diet was supplemented by nuts, for thousands of hazelnut shells are also present.

The people would not have perceived the gentle sinking of the land. A few millimetres per year reflected in a relative rise in sea level is nothing when the waves crash in at several feet and the tides make a difference of metres each day. Paradoxically, their later generations may have perceived the exact opposite. Though the land was still sinking and the sea was thus apparently rising, the sea began to retreat from the lower river valleys of Broadland and they became fresh water-dominated again as they had been a few thousand years earlier when the lower peat was laid down.

The sea was being kept out as the sand bar at the end of the estuary, presently bearing Great Yarmouth, became bigger and stronger, deflecting the river behind it, forcing it to take a longer path to the sea and constricting its channel. There were probably two or three outlets through the bar, where today there is one, for there has been much engineering of the rivers in recent centuries. A central outlet was probably the biggest, taking the Rivers Yare and Bure, then next largest a southerly one with the River Waveney emerging at the position of the present day Lowestoft. Finally a much smaller river, the original River Thurne with its tributary the Ant, flowed out to the north.

Sand was moving down the entire coast in the longshore currents and we can imagine the formerly wide outlets that allowed the sea to move far inland and lay down the lower clay, slowly becoming blocked. The sand was held by grasses that built the denes, a local name for sand dunes, higher and higher, resulting in a series of great dams that did not keep the sea out entirely, but occluded its passage on the high tide, limiting the amount of water that could enter the rivers before the tide turned. The mechanisms can still be seen. Groynes are set into the beaches up most of the coast to the north of Broadland to prevent further sand movement (Fig. 2.12); protection is given to properties not far from the cliffs that provide the sand, lest they be eroded away. The beaches to the south, now denied this source of sand, but still subject to further movement of sand southward, or out to sea, must be reinforced by sand dredged from offshore lest they disappear entirely, and the sand bar with them.

Neolithic and Bronze Age farming, the middle peat

Thus the balance of fresh to salt water changed. The Broadland valleys became fresh water again, except in their very lowest parts where estuarine conditions persisted. Mud flats and salt marshes gave way at first to reed and then to less salt-tolerant species as the water freshened further. The climate was warming more and the forests were turning from birch and pine to oak and elm, lime and alder. On the valley floors freshwater peat was again formed and the continued sinking of the land allowed a continuous build-up of deposits. At first the peat was from reed, then from alder and willow as the swamps succeeded to wet woodland in the warmer weather. In the lower parts, where the water was deeper, there were open lagoons in the sediments of which the pollen of bog-bean, water-crowfoot and sedges testify to shallow lakes.

It was a crucial period in human history, 3,000 years from around 2500 BC to just after the turn of the first millennium. It saw a warming in climate, a more settled farming existence and hence increased clearing of woodland from the uplands, but much less development in the valley swamps, treacherous to

Fig. 2.12 The processes that built the sand bar at the mouth of the Broadland estuary are still at work, but artificially impeded by groynes in the interests of minimising coastal erosion in north Norfolk.

cross, and easy to get lost in. Great alder trees grew from seedlings on the stools of the tussock sedge on the swamp floor and between these stools the peaty pools would swallow you to your waist were you to step into them. The water was rarely deep enough for a boat, never easy passage on foot and impassable on horseback. No wonder such wetlands have evil associations in folk memory.

Yet evidence from a similar terrain, Flag Fen, at the edge of the Wash Fens, close to Peterborough, reveals intricately laid out field systems at the drier edges. There was well-organised animal husbandry, with dry land fields occupied in winter and flocks grazed on the wet fens in summer, droveways and gates. Even the ruts left by wheeled carts may be found, and wheels from the carts themselves. It was the interface of the wetland and the dry land that allowed a sophisticated settled agriculture to develop. Wolves and bears still roamed the forests that remained uncleared, golden eagles flew the skies and the salmon and burbot moved up and down the rivers. If the evidence from the fens to the east is anything to go by, valley edge farming might have prospered in Broadland also for 2,000 or 3,000 years.

This period is referred to as the 'middle peat' (Fig. 2.10) in the sequence of deposits in the Broadland floodplains, and it marks also the start of the Bronze Age, the successor to the Neolithic cultures, which were the last to depend entirely on stone tools (Fig. 2.8). The weather was quite variable. Some of the peat layers are quite sloppy, others dry and very woody. Sometimes *Sphagnum*, or peat moss, was abundant, suggesting great wetness when the peat surface was kept acid by the rain, enabling this base-intolerant genus to grow and persist. At other times hypnoid moss and sedge remains, mud and calcareous marl (a light grey deposit of calcium carbonate precipitated from the water by photosynthesising plants) testify to dryer, more base-rich conditions. There was sometimes temporary formation of open water with the growth of charophytes on the bottom.

More change, the sea comes back, the upper clay

Then again there was change, perhaps this time much more quickly, for the reason seems to have been a catastrophic event not a gradual development. Around the turn of the millennium, 2,000 years ago, as iron tools were added to the repertoire of the local farmers, the sea came into the valleys again. The weather had been wetter for some time and colder. A well-studied fenland settlement at Fengate near Peterborough went into recession around 500 BC as the area became too wet for the system of summer pasturage in the fens to be maintained.

Birch was gaining ground on oak and elm in the forests and in Broadland, the rivers were flowing strongly, cutting their beds deeper into the middle peat that had been laid down in the outer parts of their channels and even into the underlying lower clay, laid down thousands of years before. The intervening 2,000 years of sinking of the land had raised the relative sea level by a metre or two. Perhaps the protective sand bars started to erode a little as a result, assaulted by the river on one side and the sea on the other.

Behind the bar, the Halvergate triangle had remained an estuary with quiet waters laying down fine clays whilst the middle peat had been forming just a little way upstream. Borings in the Halvergate triangle show, however, that around the turn of the millennium, the fine grey clays were replaced by a

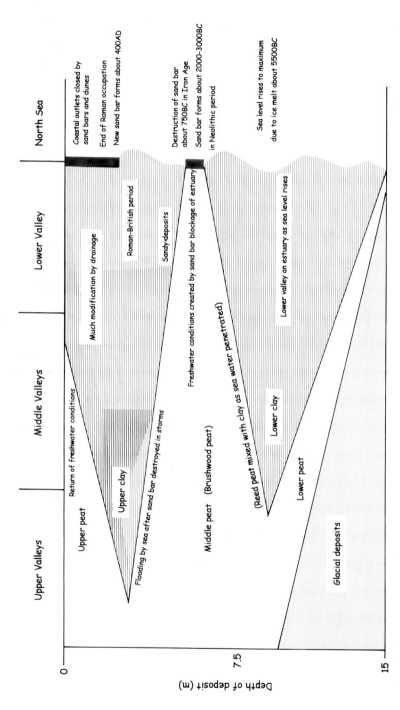

Fig. 2.13 A general summary of the deposits laid down in the Broadland valleys and their history. The diagram shows the general thickness of the deposits close to the rivers. To the edges of the upper and middle parts of the valleys, the clay is thinner and the peats thicker.

brownish clay at first, and then by coarse sands, with cockle shells. The sand bar had been breached, perhaps over a few years, most likely in a violent storm, for the transition to sand is abrupt. Perhaps overnight the Celtic farmers at the edge of the upland fled for their lives as the sea swept in, an event that was to be repeated on a lesser scale even in the twentieth century of Broadland history.

With the sea level now relatively higher than it had been in the previous sea flooding, saltwater conditions penetrated further up the valleys and wider out onto the floodplains, again leaving fine clay deposits (the upper clay) on top of the preceding peat, killing the alders and replacing them with mud flat and salt marsh. We cannot be sure enough of the exact date to know whether the Romans when they invaded in AD 43 saw the flood, or its aftermath, but for the bulk of the period before the armies were recalled to Rome in AD 410, the landscape in which they lived was dominated by a great estuary again.

Yet more or less as they left, Broadland was to return finally (for the present at least) to freshwater conditions. The closest date at which the deposits switch from the upper clay to a new freshwater layer, the upper peat (Fig. 2.13), is between 1,500 and 1,600 years ago, perhaps AD 350 to 450. The spit had apparently re-formed; fresher conditions may also have been helped by increased rainfall and, in the middle and upper parts of the valleys, reed and alder peat started to accumulate again. But no longer were the land- and waterscape to be dominated by processes in which people were minor players. Man was to become creator and destroyer. The modern period had begun.

Further reading

Samuel Woodward's 1833 book on the geology of Norfolk is not rare and there are copies in many libraries, whilst Huxley's essay about the Norfolk chalk has been republished in 1967 with comments and background material added. There is a standard regional guide to the geology published by the British Geological Survey (Chatwin 1961), though, like others in its series, it is not as user-friendly to most readers as it might have been. Good summaries of the solid and glacial geology are given in Wade-Martins (1994) and more technical accounts of the latter appear as Boulton et al. (1984) and West (1961). Jones & Keen (1993) is an up-to-date account of the last glaciation. I recommend highly the account of the glacial period and its associations with humans in Pitts & Roberts (1997), which describes excavations in south-eastern England, but gives a wider context in a very attractive piece of writing. It also has very good annotated lists of further reading. Though it covers evidence mostly from Wales, Green & Walker (1991), on ice-age hunting, is widely relevant. A series of interesting papers on archaeology in Norfolk appear in Margeson et al. (1996) and Chapters 1 and 2 of Ellis (1965) give clear accounts of the physiography of the Broadland valleys.

3

River and Catchment

The wildwood

The time is 5000 BC. Britain is an island and the sea forms a great estuary deep into Broadland. Soaring above the valleys, the sparrowhawks eye a near unbroken cover of forest. Trees, mostly lime and hazel with oak and elm, or alder and sallow, stretch from the uplands of the interior until the sea is almost reached. Only there does the forest stop and the open mud flats and salt marshes of the estuary lead to the offshore waters. Inland they merge with a narrow band of reedswamps, where the water at high tide is too salty for alder and willow, but too fresh for salt marsh. The upper stretches of the rivers, deep in the interior, are hidden by overhanging trees. Only when directly overhead can the birds see the open water of the rivers except where these widen in their lowest courses. At an angle they too disappear into a green uniformity as far as the eye can see.

At low tide, in the coastal shallows, there still remained the blackened remnants of submerged forest that had covered the whole basin of the North Sea only centuries earlier and which had linked the future island of Britain to mainland Eurasia. Through this now submerged forest, along the valleys of rivers that had formed the tributaries of the Thames then the Rhine, the animals of the forest had returned as the climate warmed. Through the rivers themselves had come the fish and some of the invertebrates. Through the air had come birds and insects, seeds and spores to recolonise the ice-devastated lands.

After some centuries of establishment (Fig. 3.1) the forest had reached a form of dynamic stability. There were still many changes of species as minor turns in the weather, and the longer-term temperature trends, favoured some over others and then reversed the change. Old trees fell, leaving small

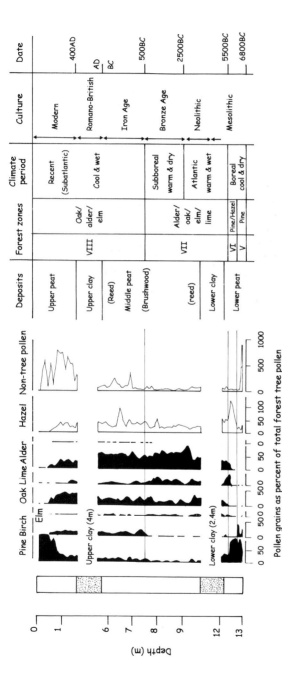

Fig. 3.1 The history of Broadland encapsulated in the pollen from a core through the 13 metres of deposits laid down between Ranworth Broad and the River Bure. Counting of pollen grains from samples of peat is a well-established method of assessing vegetation changes. Care is needed in interpretation because different trees produce greatly different amounts of pollen. Lime, for example, was a much more abundant tree than it seems from the core. Conventionally numbers are expressed as a percentage of the total forest tree pollen (hazel is not included in this group as it is a shrub). Time zones, numbered by Roman numerals, and later given names, are recognisable from the pattern of species predominance and have been dated by radiocarbon dating and linked with major archaeological periods. Marine clays do not preserve pollen well because the tides tend to wash the grains out to sea before they can be deposited and because grains that do become incorporated are often abraded in the sharp sediments. The tree pollen comes from quite a wide area, so reflects events within a region, not specifically at the immediate locality of the core. The recent rise in pine in this core probably reflects planting of pine forests in southern Norfolk in the twentieth century. The rise in non-forest (herb) pollen from Zone VIII onwards reflects the rise in agriculture, whilst that in Zone V probably indicates a more open woodland in cool, dry conditions. Pollen data from a core analysed by J.R. Jennings and originally published in Ellis (1965).

clearings that became grassy and were perhaps kept that way by the grazing of moose, red deer and wizent. Sometimes the crows and ravens flocked over a clearing where wolves had killed or where the smell of a brown bear dead of old age had attracted them to the carcass. Eagles hunted fawns and calves of the native deer and wild cattle and occasionally a group of men passed through, themselves part of the upper reaches of the forest food web.

There was much dead wood. Great tree trunks and branches crisscrossed on the forest floor, creating protected nurseries where grazers found it difficult to move without risking a leg, thus allowing tree seedlings to survive and the forest to continue its cycle of regeneration. The soils were no longer new. At first, raw with the fresh rock flour ground from distant lands by the ice, they had been rich in unweathered minerals. These, under the action of air and water, had at first yielded large supplies of plant nutrients – calcium, magnesium, phosphate and potassium. Soil bacteria capable of transforming the nitrogen gas of the air into usable nitrogen compounds had moved in. Rain had provided chloride, sulphate and sodium from the supply of sea spray swept into it from the breaking white horses during storms. Those airborne seeds flexible enough to cope with the rigorous microclimate of a bare land had multiplied, adding organic matter to the soil when they died.

But now things had settled. The first flush of soil nutrients had long passed down to the sea and was lost in the vast volume of the ocean and the great reaches of its bed sediments. The remaining nutrients were tightly held in the biomass of the trees, to be released on rotting of leaves and wood, but quickly recaptured by young roots and their associated mycorrhizal fungi. Some plant nutrients, nitrogen, for example, had always been scarce and conserved. Now almost everything was kept in a nearly complete cycle with only a little lost to the rivers and streams, more or less at the same rate as it was brought in from the atmosphere or by weathering deep in the soil profile. The streams dissolved very little in total amount, but contained a huge variety of different substances.

The chemistry of water

Water chemistry is an intensely interesting subject. It is not just water that flows out of the catchments and down the rivers, but a mixture of several thousand dissolved substances and perhaps as many in the form of suspended particles. Most of these substances are organic carbon compounds, the results of death and decay, and leaching of humus in the catchment soils. Some are rather resistant to further decay and may colour the water yellow or brown or become deposited in the river sediments. Others are very reactive and last for only a very short time before bacteria coating the sediments or stones of the river break them down further, eventually to carbon dioxide.

Then there are many inorganic substances, again some dissolved, others appearing as mineral particles eroded from the soils and contributing eventually to the river sediments. The dissolved inorganic substances tell us a great deal about the catchment and they largely determine the biological potential of the water. They can be divided into the major ions, minor ions and key nutrient ions. Major ions are major because they occur in the greatest concentrations, though these amount at most to only a few tens of milligrams per litre (parts per million) in fresh waters. They are ions because they exist in an electrically charged form, compared with the electrically neutral free-existing element. The minor ions occur at microgram per litre (parts per billion) or even lower concentrations, and the key nutrients at various concentration levels, but spanning the range up to only a few milligrams per litre. Unlike the former two groups, they are non-conservative – their concentrations vary considerably over short periods as they are biologically very reactive. There are also the gases dissolved from the air.

The major ions include sodium, potassium, calcium, magnesium, hydrogen, chloride, sulphate and bicarbonate. The minor ions include many of the trace elements such as copper, zinc, boron, iron and manganese – indeed if sufficiently sophisticated analytical equipment is available, it is probable that at least a little of almost every stable element could be detected in all natural waters. The key nutrients include compounds of phosphorus, phosphates and nitrogen, particularly ammonium and nitrate. Silicon may also be a key nutrient because one particular important group of algae, the diatoms, requires silicates for the formation of its cell walls. The important gases are nitrogen, oxygen and carbon dioxide.

In some waters the major ions are comparatively scarce because the catchments from which these waters come are floored by hard and resistant rocks, which weather slowly, and contribute little to the rainwater seeping through and over their thin soils. Such waters might have much lower than ten milligrams per litre of each of the metal ions, such as potassium and calcium, and the most abundant will be hydrogen ion. The pH values will thus be low, perhaps 5 or 6. pH is a measure of the amount of hydrogen ion expressed as a minus logarithm – the higher the hydrogen ion concentration, the lower is the pH and the more acid is the water. Calcium, bicarbonate and potassium, which come mainly from rock weathering, will be very scarce, and sodium and magnesium, chloride and sulphate, ultimately derived from the sea spray caught up in rain, the more abundant. Such waters, often called 'soft', are found in the uplands such as those of the English Lake District and the Scottish Highlands.

The waters of Broadland are rather different. They are 'hard' and come from the chalk and the finely divided minerals brought from under the glaciers as they ground their way over many different rock formations, including many soft sedimentary ones. From the beginning the Broadland waters would have been comparatively rich in major ions, with tens of milligrams of calcium, magnesium and bicarbonate, derived from the chalk. They would have had a higher pH, 7 or 8, because of neutralisation of the acidity by the carbonates, and high levels of sulphate and chloride, still from rain, but concentrated through evaporation of greater proportions of the rainwater in the warmer lowlands.

Although living organisms, be they bacterium, animal or plant, must have all of these elements, they need them in quite small quantities in relation to the supplies, even in soft waters. The concentrations of most substances in the water thus change relatively little in response to biological uptake. When they do change, it is mostly in response to factors such as evaporation and rainfall in the catchment. Heavy rain leads to more surface runoff and lower concentrations because less water percolates through the ground to pick up ions from the soils and rocks. Moderate rainfall leads to higher concentrations and low rainfall to the highest of all. The total load carried in a given time (say kilograms per day), as opposed to the concentration (milligrams per litre), generally increases, however, with the amount of runoff.

Major ions thus do not determine the productivity or fertility of natural fresh waters, but they may influence the nature of the biological communities (Fig. 3.2). Some groups of freshwater algae, in particular the desmids, a group of green algae, are abundant in soft, acid waters, and scarce in carbonate-rich ones. This is because most of their species cannot use bicarbonate for photosynthesis, but only free carbon dioxide. They are displaced by other algae when bicarbonate is abundant. Snails, and crustaceans such as the freshwater shrimp, are much more common in high calcium waters because of the need for lime for their shells and exoskeletons. Not surprisingly, Broadland waters have few desmids, but many snails and crustaceans.

The trace elements figure only a little in understanding the main features of the productivity of fresh waters. They are important, for organisms cannot manage without them, but, despite their very low concentrations, they are generally abundant in relation to organisms' meagre needs. Iron and manganese enter into reactions that affect the key nutrients and are important in this respect, but for the moment we can ignore them. What we cannot do is to ignore the key nutrients, for more than anything else dissolved in the water, their availability underlies the entire ecology of fresh waters in general and Broadland in particular. The key is that these nutrients, especially nitrogen and phosphorus, are relatively scarce and also, of course, crucial to life on land. Natural terrestrial communities have evolved mechanisms to retain them and so the natural supply allowed to run off into fresh waters is very low

Fig. 3.2 Desmids are green algae that are most common in low bicarbonate waters and hence very few species are found in the open waters of Broadland. Top, two species of *Micrasterias*, each over 100 micrometres in length. *Micrasterias* species, *Xanthidium* (the spiny cell) and *Pleurotaenium* (the long cell) at the bottom right cannot use bicarbonate and are very rare in Broadland, but *Cosmarium* (bottom left) can and is common in Broadland ditches.

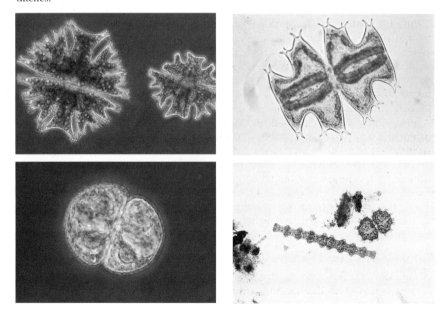

indeed. Often they are called the key limiting nutrients for this reason.

Phosphorus is very scarce in most natural fresh waters. Living organisms need its compounds to form some of the crucial biochemicals used in the cell for transferring energy and for making DNA, the material of the genes. They do not need much of it – only a fraction of one per cent of their weight, but it is a scarce element relative even to this need and its compounds, largely phosphates, are relatively insoluble in water. They can be tightly held in soils as minerals such as apatite (calcium phosphate) and attached to clays.

Rooted plants can winkle enough of this phosphorus from the soil minerals through the intimate contact of their finer rootlets and often the fungi or mycorrhiza that are associated with them. They also have the benefit of greater concentrations of the element, often grams per litre or kilogram (parts per thousand), even in the poorest soils. This advantage can apply also to the larger submerged plants, called aquatic macrophytes, rooted in mud that has been washed in from the land to freshwater habitats. The microscopic algae suspended in the water as plankton in lakes or growing as films over the rocks on the bottom of rivers do not have this advantage. For them the problem is of obtaining enough phosphorus from concentrations in the water that are usually only a few micrograms per litre, up to a million times lower than in soil.

Nitrogen is the second element that in short supply will limit aquatic growth. Supplies of nitrogen are greater than those of phosphorus, but so are needs. Nitrogen is needed in large quantities for the production of proteins by cells and about ten times as much as of phosphorus is required. There is plenty of nitrogen on Earth, but most of it is present as a gas in the atmosphere which, even when dissolved in water, is not readily available to living organisms. It must first be converted to amino compounds, a process called fixation, in which the nitrogen is combined with hydrogen. Apart from some chemical conversion by high-energy lightning sparks, which are minor contributors, this can be done naturally only by certain bacteria in soils and waters or associated with the roots of some plants, such as the legumes. Most of these bacteria, despite their immense importance as the main gateways for nitrogen to enter the biosphere, are nondescript organisms, but nitrogen fixers also include some of the blue-green algae or cyanophytes (Fig. 3.3), which are more spectacular to look at, but have a bacterial cell structure.

When nitrogen fixers die, or are eaten, their fixed nitrogen enters other parts of the food webs and is released, after decay, into the interstitial water of the soils as ammonium or nitrate, and washed out into the rivers. In contrast to phosphates, nitrates and ammonium compounds are very soluble and readily leached out. There is a problem, though, in terms of their later availability. Ammonium is readily converted by other bacteria, which derive energy from the reaction, to nitrate. Nitrate can then be used by yet more bacteria as an oxidising agent, under waterlogged conditions, when oxygen is scarce, to release energy from organic matter. This converts the nitrate back to nitrogen. All in all, events contrive therefore, under natural conditions, to keep most of the nitrogen as nitrogen gas and to make an otherwise abundant element relatively unavailable.

The early Broadland waters

As the rainwater fell onto the Broadland catchment in 5000 BC, it went through a series of processes that culminated in a small proportion of it – that quarter

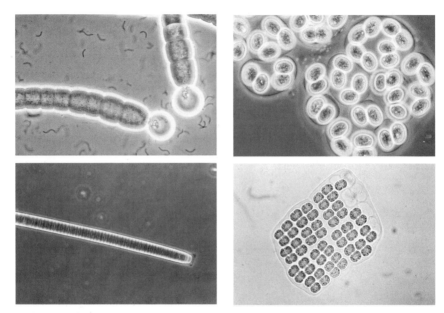

Fig. 3.3 Blue-green algae sometimes dominate the plankton communities of the Broads. Some can fix nitrogen, most cannot. Those that can usually have large, translucent cells (heterocysts) in which the particular conditions necessary for fixation (low oxygen concentrations) are maintained (e.g. *Gleotrichia* top left). The others are not fixers. *Chroococcus* (top right) occurs attached to surfaces, *Oscillatoria* (bottom left) may grow on sediments or be suspended in the water, as may *Merismopaedia* (bottom right).

or so which was not evaporated or transpired by the vegetation – pouring out into the streams as a much more complex chemical solution than had fallen on the forest. It was a dilute solution with perhaps a couple of hundred milligrams of dissolved solids in every litre. Half of these were organic, the humic compounds left over from the decomposition of wood and cellulose. About half was a complex of major ions, dominated by calcium and bicarbonate, at neutral or slightly alkaline pH (Table 3.1). Tiny fractions were made up of a few micrograms of phosphorus in the form of phosphates and a milligram or less in every litre of nitrogen as nitrate. Ammonium was vanishingly scarce; it is so reactive that bacteria quickly convert it, or plants take it up. A huge variety of other organic compounds and trace metals would have contributed a minuscule proportion of the total.

For most of the year this solution would have seeped gently from the forest floor as a very pale yellow fluid into channels only centimetres across, but which widened and joined to form streams metres wide and eventually rivers tens of metres from bank to bank. The Broadland rivers were never very large by world standards, not even falling into the upper echelons of a league of British rivers. Even the largest of these, the Severn, is a trickle compared with the Rhine, the Volga, Nile or Amazon.

But following heavy rain, a thunder shower in summer or steady winter downpours when the soils were saturated, the water draining the Broadland catchment would pick up debris from the forest floor. Where a tree had fallen and soil was temporarily exposed, some would erode; leaf litter would be washed in from the banks, twigs and sometimes, larger branches also. Sometimes banks might be undercut and whole trees collapse into the flow. As the spate passed, the finer particles would settle out behind obstacles such as stranded branches and tree trunks, and dead leaves would pack like piles of paper into crevices among the debris. The flux would leave a highly structured habitat, full of the architecture of woody debris, for the stream community.

Table 3.1 Major ion composition of Broadland rivers, compared with rivers elsewhere, rain and sea water. Values are typical ones – they vary a little with weather and river flow – and are given in milligrams per litre. nd: not determined.

	Ca	Mg	Na	K	HCO$_3$	Cl	SO$_4$
Amazon rain forest	0.04	0.06	0.2	0.16	2.2	1.1	nd
Western Cumbria	2.2	0.8	3.8	0.4	3.5	6.7	4.5
Southern Cumbria	8.3	3.5	4.7	0.9	18.3	7.6	9.9
River Yare (Colney)	143	5.9	37.1	4.3	336	48	nd
River Ant (Wayford)	128	11	46	9.4	238	77	nd
River Thurne (Potter Heigham)	234	306	856	31	165	544	nd
Rain (Norwich)	3.7	0.2	1.2	0.7	0.1	1	nd
Sea water	412	1409	10925	394	146	19667	2746

Amazon rain forest streams are very low in major ions because the underlying rocks and soils are so ancient that there is little new mineral left to weather and the throughput of rain is the only source. The rivers of West Cumbria drain igneous and metamorphic rocks which weather slowly and deliver waters with low levels of ions to the western English lakes. South Cumbria has more sedimentary rocks and this is reflected in the greater ion concentrations. Even so, they are low compared with those derived from the chalky catchments of Broadland (Rivers Yare and Ant). The River Thurne is influenced also by the percolation of sea water from the coast into it and hence has a composition that reflects a varying mixture of sea and soil water.

The soaring sparrowhawk looked down on a sheet of forest in which all but the lower reaches of the rivers would have been hidden by the tree canopy. Equally, for animals living in the upper reaches of the rivers, the sky would have been blocked by a dense network of overhanging branches, made nearly opaque by the summer leaves. The stream bottom was naturally a very dark, shaded place. Photosynthetic organisms had a hard time of it. There were, however, some algae on the larger of the flints washed out of the chalk and exotic stones brought in by the ice, which bottomed the main channel and on those few sections where the underlying chalk itself was exposed under water.

In spring, before the canopy leaves developed, a brown film of diatoms would have grown, to be grazed away in weeks by snails and mayfly nymphs and replaced by tougher green algae more entrenched in the surface crevices of the stones. Some water mosses and freshwater red algae may have colonised where the light was marginally improved by temporary breaks in the forest cover, but there would have been almost no higher plant growth until the widening rivers had almost reached the sea. Nonetheless, if the models with which we might compare this ancient ecosystem, in the uncleared hardwood forests of America and mainland Europe, are to be relied upon, there was a vigorous bottom community of invertebrate animals and of fish and other vertebrates.

The animal community of the early Broadland streams

Most of the food for this animal community did not come from green plants or algae in the stream, but from the organic silt, dead leaves and woody debris washed and falling into the streams. Much of this material was nutritionally poor. It was rich in carbohydrates such as cellulose and lignin, but these are difficult to digest for most animals, and low in nitrogen, for the trees move scarce nutrients back into their trunks before the husks of the leaves are allowed to abscise and fall to the ground.

But present in the streams was a specialist community of fungi, a group called the Hyphomycetes. These fungi are distributed by spores shaped like grapnels, anchors or hooks, which can catch onto organic debris even in swift flows, and then germinate, pushing their fine filaments, called hyphae, over the surface and deep into the dead leaves and wood. Such fungi absorb nitrate from the water and, with enzymes strong enough to digest cellulose and lignin, convert them into fungal material. This progressively softens the debris and enriches it with fungal protein. It is then far more palatable to invertebrate animals and is seized upon by insect larvae, crustaceans and others who shred it to gain access to the fungi. The leaves become skeletonised as the shredders bite out the softened parts between the harder veins.

The finer organic matter washed into the streams also becomes colonised by bacteria and fungi and a similar process goes on. Oligochaete worms and the larvae of flies burrow into banks of silt, swallowing the material and absorbing the digestible portions, largely the cells of bacteria and hyphae of fungi. The rest they defecate and the faeces become colonised by more microorganisms and eaten again. There are also animals that can filter fine particles from suspension using specially modified limbs, or by spinning nets. They capture material disturbed into suspension by wind, or spates, or watering mammals as they wade. The organic matter that entered from the forest, either as large lumps or fine particles, is progressively converted into carbon dioxide and invertebrate biomass.

We can add little reliable detail to this picture in terms of what particular invertebrate species were present in the pristine Broadland system 7,000 years ago. It has long been disturbed, not least by felling of the forest and human modifications of the water chemistry by farming and settlement. We can be sure it was a rich community, for insects colonise rapidly by air as flying adults and other invertebrates through floods that bring the headwaters of lowland river systems into contact. By 7,000 years ago, when the sea level had risen to around its modern position, there had been several thousand years of contact between the Broadland rivers and the Thames and the Rhine, for colonisation to occur. The headwaters of the River Waveney merge with those of the Ouse, which flows to the Wash, and there could easily have been transfer between them. Even in isolated experimental tanks stocked with water and a food supply, it takes only days for the first animals to arrive and only weeks to build up a community of several dozen species. There is still a considerable movement of insects between mainland Europe and Britain.

The modern community – a hint of the past?

In late 2000, the Environment Agency of the British Government announced that the state of English rivers was better than at any time since records began.

Alas, such statements are of limited significance, for the records are only a couple of decades old and, even with controls on recent modern pollution, the rivers are still far from the condition they were likely to have had some thousands of years ago. Upstream river communities, unlike those of floodplains and lakes where sediments are deposited, and with them some record of the past, leave no trace. They erode their beds and obliterate their history. All we can have for the Broadland rivers is the present and our judgement on its meaning. The channels are now much more open than they were. The source of the tree litter is gone and the greater light intensity encourages the growth of water plants, water-crowfoot, Canadian pondweed, watercress, brooklime, water moss, starwort, milfoil, bur-reed and water-parsnip. Much more nitrogen and phosphorus wash in from the land and encourage the growth of these and particularly that of filamentous algae such as the blanket weed. There is much more soil, eroded from the land, in suspension. Meanders have been straightened and former wet meadows at the bank side drained.

The animal communities of the river beds are thus likely to be poorer in species diversity, for nutrient enrichment encourages the competitive species that oust the more specialised. Alternatively they could be more diverse, for some litter still enters from trees along the banks and there are now the new habitats provided by the plants. They are likely to be poorer in the species that process litter, but richer in those that feed on fresh green matter, be it plants, or the algae that grows on them or on the larger stones and shingle. Current speeds will also have changed, not only because of natural fluctuations in rainfall, but because the runoff from agricultural land may be very different from that under forest. Agricultural land is often irrigated with water taken directly from the river or from the ground water, which also formerly fed it. Much of this water evaporates from the land and never returns to the river.

The invertebrate communities of the river beds (Fig. 3.4) are useful indicators of the quality of water and are widely used together with chemical analyses, to monitor it. In the past three decades, the former Freshwater Biological Association, now merged into the Centre for Ecology and Hydrology, a British Government research institute, has built up a high quality archive of data from over 600 reference sites, where the stream quality is believed not to be affected by gross organic or industrial pollution. Several sites in the upper reaches of the Yare, Wensum, Bure and Waveney were included and give a picture of the current community. The rivers were sampled by a standard and very simple technique, that of 'kick sampling', though what actually happens is often less active than the name suggests. The sampler stands upstream of a net held on a pole and disturbs the bottom with his or her feet, dislodging the animals into the net, and moving among the sub-habitats (gravel, silt, plants) of the location during a time of three minutes. This is done three times a year, in spring, summer and autumn, and a list of species compiled. The net is of fairly coarse mesh (half a millimetre) and designed to catch the macroinvertebrates, not the smaller animals such as Protozoa, nematodes, rotifers and copepods. These are likely to be at least as diverse as the macroinvertebrates, but their identification is much more difficult, which makes them less useful for practicable water quality surveys.

A total of 637 species, or species groups where further identification is not feasible (for example, with chironomid fly larvae) has been recorded, with about 200 of them in the Broadland rivers, though any given site will have

Fig. 3.4 Invertebrates tell much of the conditions in river water. This collection includes (top left to right) an oligochaete worm and a chironomid larva, which ingest sediment, and *Hydra*, which attaches itself to plants and captures smaller animals, only a fraction of a millimetre in size. In the middle are a shredder, *Asellus*, which feeds on leaf detritus and sometimes algal filaments, and a common snail, *Lymnaea pereger*, which scrapes algae and bacteria from surfaces. At the bottom are two predators, a water mite, *Hydracarina*, and a bug, *Corixa*. Both transfix their prey with sharp projections and suck out the contents.

between 50 and 90. The main groups of animals to be found (Table 3.2) include: flatworms, or triclads, each a few millimetres long and feeding on the damaged bodies or carcasses of bigger animals by sucking out the body fluids; the snails or gastropods and two-shelled bivalves among the molluscs; the oligochaetes, a group related to the earthworms, but much smaller in fresh waters; leeches (which feed mostly on invertebrates and are not usually bloodsucking); and various crustaceans, including the pond shrimp, *Gammarus*, perhaps the most ubiquitous of all the species, water hog-louse, *Asellus*, and crayfish. The snails feed by scraping the algae from stones or firm sediment

Table 3.2 General composition of the macroinvertebrate communities (as number of species or species groups in each location) in the upper reaches of the Rivers Wensum, Yare and Bure. Data were obtained by the Centre for Ecology and Hydrology as parts of contracts to the Department of the Environment and the Nature Conservancy Council (Wright et al. 1992).

Invertebrate group	Wens 1	Wens 2	Wens 3	Wens 4	Wens 5	Yare 1	Yare 2	Bure 1	Bure 2	Bure 3	Bure 4
Triclads	4	3	3	3	4	2	2	0	3	2	4
Gastropods	4	7	4	10	4	10	12	2	5	13	13
Bivalves	2	1	5	4	5	3	5	4	4	6	6
Oligochaetes	5	6	9	8	9	10	7	8	7	8	6
Leeches	2	5	3	4	3	5	5	3	4	6	5
Crustaceans	2	3	4	4	3	4	3	1	2	4	4
Mayflies	3	3	5	6	4	6	5	7	8	6	3
Stoneflies	5	5	0	0	0	0	0	2	2	0	0
Dragon/damselflies	0	0	0	0	0	0	1	0	0	0	1
Bugs	0	2	3	2	0	0	0	0	0	0	4
Beetles	3	3	3	3	4	3	4	2	1	1	1
Lacewings	0	0	0	0	1	0	1	0	0	0	0
Caddis flies	8	5	11	11	11	8	12	10	13	6	4
Dipterans	30	15	24	20	23	22	29	20	20	9	12

Locations, National Grid References and distances in km from the source are: Wensum 1 (South Raynham, TF885240, 5); Wensum 2 (Great Ryburgh TF964273, 20); Wensum 3 (Worthing TG005202, 30); Wensum 4 (north of Elsing, TG 052178, 38); Wensum 5 (Taverham TG161137, 56); Yare 1 (North of Barford, TG108084, 20); Yare 2 (Earlham, TG 190082, 30); Bure 1 (Corpusty, TG 105305, 8); Bure 2 (Whitehouse Farm Ford, TG164305, 16); Bure 3 (Buxton Mill, TG243231, 31); Bure 4 (Coltishall Bridge, TG 267198, 36).

surfaces, the bivalves by sifting sediments for bacteria and organic matter and the crustaceans on filamentous algae or by shredding leaf litter.

Then there are many insect groups, present as nymphs, juvenile stages that have the typical insect body pattern of head, thorax with six legs and abdomen, or as larvae, which look very different from the adults, or as all stages including the adult. The mayflies (Ephemeroptera), stoneflies (Plecoptera), dragonflies and damselflies (Odonata), lacewings and alder flies (Megaloptera and Neuroptera) and the very abundant caddis flies (Trichoptera) fall into the nymphal group, the even more abundant two-winged flies, the Diptera, into that which is represented by larvae, and the beetles (Coleoptera) and bugs (Hemiptera) are present also as adults.

Some of these insect groups, many of the beetles and bugs and the Odonata, for example, are predators on other invertebrates; others, including some Diptera, shred leaf litter and many, particularly the mayflies, stoneflies and caddis flies scrape algae and organic matter from surfaces. Some caddisflies, those lacking the cases characteristic of most of the group, spin nets to catch fine material as do dipterans such as *Simulium*, the blackflies, whilst other Diptera, including the abundant chironomids, feed on sediment organic matter with the oligochaetes and bivalves.

From the Britain-wide survey it is possible to calculate an average composition for stream communities, that shows Diptera to be the most frequent (28.9 per cent of the total list), then beetles (16.5 per cent), caddis flies (15.6 per cent), oligochaetes (8.1 per cent) and mayflies (5.9 per cent). All other groups constitute less than 5 per cent of the total. Among the upper Broadland rivers there are some interesting deviations from the average picture. Snails are much more frequent than the national average, as are triclads, leeches, crustaceans, bivalves and mayflies, whilst stoneflies, dragonflies, bugs and beetles are much less so. The abundance of snails and bivalves undoubtedly reflects the calcareousness of the waters, whilst stoneflies are generally much more associated with upland sites.

No very unusual species turned up in the Broadland river samples, with the exception of one somewhat rare beetle (*Haliplus laminatus*). The species found in all or almost all of the samples constitute a very characteristic list from lowland streams and small rivers: *Polycelis nigra*, *Dendrocoelum lacteum* (triclads), *Valvata piscinalis*, *Potamopyrgus jenkinsi* (gastropods), *Sphaerium corneum*, *Pisidium nitidum*, *Pisidium subtruncatum* (bivalves), *Lumbriculus* spp., *Stylodrilus heringianus*, *Limnodrilus hoffmeisteri*, *Psamorycitides barbatus*, *Aulodrilus pluriseta* (oligochaetes), *Glossiphonia complanata*, *Helobdella stagnalis*, *Erpobdella octoculata* (leeches), *Asellus aquaticus*, *Asellus meridianus*, *Gammarus pulex* (crustaceans), *Baetis scambus*, *Baetis vernus*, *Ephemerella ignita* (mayflies), *Elmis aenea* (beetle), *Hydroptila* spp., *Polycentropus flavomaculatus* (caddis flies) and *Simulium erythrocephalum*, *Simulium ornatum*, *Thienemannia* spp., *Cricotopus* spp., *Microtendipes* spp., *Polypedilum* spp., *Micropsectra* spp., *Paratanytarsus* spp. (Diptera, with the last six being chironomid species).

Current speed is a major factor in determining the existence of many of these species, and streams usually show a spectrum of speeds dependent on the effects of vegetation, bends and backwaters to complement the greatest speeds of the central channels. Some of the tributaries of the main rivers (for example, the Scarrow Beck and Broome Beck) can show speeds of more than 60 centimetres per second and have shingly bottoms. Parts of the Wensum and

Tas have gravels and speeds of at least 30 centimetres per second, whilst sandy, silt and muddy reaches can be found on all the rivers with speeds of 20 centimetres per second or lower. The nature of the bottom is important for what were probably formerly common fish, the sea trout and Atlantic salmon, which found their way up from the sea to spawn in the gravelly and shingly beds of these streams. Salmon are now absent for reasons of over-exploitation at sea as well as silting up of many of the former gravel beds, and the trout are widespread, but as their more resilient non-migratory race, the brown trout. Small, bottom-feeding fish, the three-spined stickleback, stone loach, dace, bullhead (also called miller's thumb) and minnow are widespread.

Down to the floodplain

All rivers lead to the sea. Well, not necessarily; there are many in the arid interiors of the continents that peter out in salt flats or saline lakes, but the Broadland rivers fit the biblical convention. As their catchments increase in size downstream, more water flows in rivers, more silt is carried to be deposited lower down the course, and the channel widens and deepens to accommodate the flow. It may need huge capacity to carry the winter floods and may have to spill out over a floodplain to do so. The area conventionally considered as 'Broadland' for administrative purposes starts as the rivers reach this floodplain stage and span a distance of a few tens of kilometres to the sea. This administrative convention is misleading and unhelpful, however, in considering and managing the area. The whole of the catchment needs to be looked at if events in the Broads are to be understood, but the floodplain is centre of the Broadland stage. Our sparrowhawk of seven millennia ago has moved over the swamps.

Further reading

There is an extensive literature on the changes in vegetation that followed the retreat of the ice and that developed in previous interglacials, detected through pollen analysis of peats and soils. Sparks & West (1972) is a standard work on it, whilst Godwin (1978) is a very approachable account of changes in the fens to the west of Broadland, written by the doyen of this field. Bennett (1983) and Peglar et al. (1989) illustrate some of the subtleties and complexities that arise from a study of individual sites in Norfolk, and which contribute to the larger picture. Familiarity hides the fact that water is a rather astounding substance and Ball (1999) gives a remarkable account of it. Still the best work on the natural history of stream animals is Hynes (1979) whilst Moss (1998) is a recent account of freshwater ecology in general with substantial attention to streams and rivers. Wright (1995) and Wright et al. (1996) give accounts of the methodology and results of the surveys of British river invertebrates that now form the bases of river monitoring in the UK.

4

Pristine Broadland – Floodplain and Estuary

'The great marsh lies on the Essex coast between the village of Chelmbury and the ancient Saxon oyster-fishing hamlet of Wickaeldroth. It is one of the last of the wild places of England, a low, far-reaching expanse of grass and reeds and half-submerged meadowlands ending in the great saltings and mud flats and tidal pools near the restless sea.'

Paul Gallico, *The Snow Goose* (1941)

Development of the swamps

Picture now what the sparrowhawks saw as they flew, 7,000 years ago, over the Broadland rivers where they widened towards the sea. As catchment areas steadily increase in size from the source to the mouth of a river, more water moves through the channel. If the surrounding rock is difficult to erode, it may constrain the size of the channel and the water must consequently move faster. If there is less resistance, the water widens its main channel and, in the flatter terrain of such areas, spills over a greater area, adjusting its current speed such that it moves rapidly in the middle, barely at all at the edges. There is always some geological resistance and with changes in the geology over quite short distances, the path of a river to the sea can become very varied as it continually adjusts to local conditions.

The Broadland rivers were no exception, though the thickness and softness of the glacial deposits that formed most of the catchments provided no gorges for fast flow, and a subdued topography further smoothed by the erosion of the water flowing off the land. The rivers cut into the Chalk quite deeply at times in the past when sea level was much lower and the gradient was consequently greater than it is now, but these channels are buried beneath the river alluvium that has been deposited since then. There are now very few places where the Broadland rivers still expose the Chalk. The present landscape is one of wide valleys and wooded valley slopes in the upper and middle reaches,. Meanders cut the glacial deposits and the alluvium, and there is a great flat plain where the rivers converge around the Halvergate triangle.

In wet winters natural rivers spread over the full width of their bed, occupying the floodplain to the edge of the uplands; in drier ones they submerge only part of it, but always a substantial area. With the increase in evaporation as summer approaches, they became confined to the main channel. There is an interesting issue of perception here. The river bed is the entire floodplain; what we now often call the river, merely a part of that bed, the summer channel. What has been seen in modern times as undesirable flooding over the valley is, in truth, the river only occupying the full extent of its natural bed, not invading what we have come to view, illogically, as 'land'.

Catchments are thought of as the 'upland' compared with the river valleys. The Broadland uplands are subdued, mostly around 60 metres above sea level, very rarely as much as 100 metres. As they moved down from the upland, the Broadland rivers brought with them particles of debris, both mineral and organic, especially after heavy rain. In the greatest flows they moved sand and gravel along their beds. The gradients were never steep enough nor the flows high enough to move boulders, even had there been boulders to move. As the channel widened into the floodplain, the gravels and sands were deposited first, on the main channel bed or as a bank parallel with it, called a levee. Smaller particles were carried a little further before the current slowed enough for them to fall to the bottom. Beyond that, the water spread sideways over the floodplain, devoid of much suspended matter. And as the rivers widened and meandered in their floodplain reaches a few tens of kilometres from the coast, their upstream heavily shaded ecosystem, dominated by litter falling in from the deciduous forests, steadily changed.

The main river bed remained scoured where flows were highest, but the reduced current at the edges of the channel allowed some submerged plants to colonise, at least until some high flow washed them away. But further from the middle of the channel, the deposited silt and shallower water allowed submerged plants to grow permanently. Silt particles are not inert; they may contain clays and minerals containing phosphorus, or organic debris rich in both phosphorus and nitrogen. They settle to form rich, wet soils for plant growth. The moving and widening channel kept overhanging trees at bay and forest trees such as oak, elm and lime, that had overhung the channel in the upper reaches, could not survive the seasonal flooding. They appeared only on isolated islands on the valley floor where some high flood had piled unusual amounts of debris and where the deposits had resisted the erosion of the moving channel as it meandered, century by century, across the plain.

At the edges of the main channel, where the water depth was a metre or two, water-lilies colonised with emergent reed-like plants where the water shallowed further. Our picture of what the characteristic plants of these reedswamps were, can be gleaned from nineteenth-century photographs (Fig. 4.1) and the observations of early twentieth-century ecologists, who were able to see the processes going on at the edges of the open water before modern impacts had obliterated much of this evidence. Though these pieces of information are really very recent, they probably give a reasonable clue to the dominant plants from much further back, especially when the evidence of recognisable plant remains in the peat laid down in the valleys is also used.

The bulrush (*Schoenoplectus lacustris*) joined the lilies in deeper water, for it tolerates greater water depths and more exposure from water movements than other reedswamp plants. It was backed by the lesser reedmace (*Typha angustifolia*) often also called bulrush, and then the common reed, now the most characteristic plant of Broadland, though that would not have been the case before human settlement of the area. There were other species too – clumps of iris or yellow flag, some of the larger sedges such as the pendulous and the saw sedge, and flote and reed canary grass.

Our picture of their detailed distribution is vague, but it must have reflected the different water depths, tidal ranges, exposures to scour, accidents of

Fig. 4.1 The edges of Broads in the late nineteenth century. P.H. Emerson's photographs show active colonisation of the open water by reed swamp plants, a situation that persisted well into the twentieth century. It is part of a natural succession as the water shallows under the burden of accumulated sediment.

destruction by high flood and of arrival to colonise, and perhaps also of grazing on young and tender shoots by water voles and coot. The reed is more tolerant of the richer nutrient conditions that were later to develop and has become dominant only recently as a result. The pristine Broadland will have seen big patches of it, but not the huge unbroken swards characteristic of the present day.

Reedswamp ecology

The productivity of some of these aquatic plants, rooted in sediment, submerged at their bases, but emerging into the air, is very high indeed. On a world scale, tropical reedswamp is by far the most productive of plant communities and the temperate swamps follow not far behind. Their habitat is an ideal one, though not devoid of difficulties with which natural selection has had to cope. Although water itself absorbs a lot of light and submerged plants have considerable problems as a result, emergent species have no such problem. They can store enough energy in their rhizomes (underground stems) at the end of one season to guarantee that their young shoots emerge above the water level in the next. Water is of course no problem for them; though water is the single most crucial limitant for plant growth on land, it is superabundant in a reedswamp.

Nor are nutrients a problem. The silts brought down by the river provide an annually renewed supply, at least for a long period until the catchments become thoroughly leached out over many hundreds of thousands of years. The perennial growth allows a great deal of storage of nutrients in the roots and rhizomes, and annual recycling to the shoots and back again. The problem for the reedswamp plants, however, is in getting enough oxygen to their rhizomes and roots for the roots to function, and in coping with some of the toxic substances produced in waterlogged soils. Plants that are not adapted to cope with these problems, such as crops grown on floodplains, do not survive flooding.

Waterlogged soils, unless they are almost lacking in organic matter and suffused by water currents, are anaerobic; they have no dissolved oxygen. The reasons are simple. Firstly, oxygen does not dissolve to any great extent in water. Oxygen and water are very different chemically and therefore tend to repel. Oxygen is non-polar, it is electrically neutral, whilst the electrons that are present in water, the oxide of hydrogen, tend to spend more time on the hydrogen atoms than on the oxygen, giving it a slight difference in electrical charge from one part to the other, a phenomenon called polarity. Water will readily dissolve strongly polar compounds, such as the major ions, phosphate, nitrate and ammonium, but has less affinity for the less polar, some organic acids, for example, and shuns the non-polar, such as oils and oxygen. Secondly, the small amount, a few parts per million (milligrams per litre) of oxygen that does dissolve, is rapidly used by bacteria decomposing organic matter in wet soil. The supply of organic matter is high because of the high production and the debris of plant growth tends to accumulate as peat, there being little oxygen available for bacteria to break it down.

Reedswamp plants cope with deoxygenation around their roots by tolerating the problem or avoiding it. Tolerance means that their root tissues can survive concentrations of the products of anaerobic activity, usually called fermentation, and akin to what happens to yeast in the brewing of beer. Ethyl alcohol (ethanol) is the main such product. The concentrations that build up are lethal to most plants if they are flooded, but reedswamp plants can survive them or convert the alcohol into something less damaging such as malic acid. Either way the root is handicapped and cannot be very active in absorption and energy transfer, so the plant must have a large root system, each element of which is operating rather slowly. Alternatively, atmospheric air can be pumped down to the roots through a series of air spaces, or lacunae, formed within the plant.

Water-lilies, for example, operate both strategies. Their rhizomes, when broken open, may smell of alcohol, giving the plant the local name of 'brandy bottle', but they also transfer air from the leaves at the water surface. In young leaves, especially in sunlight, the air pressure in the spaces between the cells increases as the leaf warms and this pressure is relieved by movement of air down through the air spaces of the leaf stalks (petioles) to the roots and rhizomes. This system cannot work unless there is ultimate relief of the pressure and this is achieved by escape upwards from the rhizomes and roots through the petioles of older and senescent leaves at the surface where insect-grazing has torn holes in the fabric through which air can readily escape.

The bacterial activity of waterlogged soils also creates chemical problems. The bacteria, once they have consumed all the dissolved oxygen, continue to mop up any further supplies that diffuse in from the overlying water, but this is not enough to support a booming population presented with enormous amounts of organic matter. The bacteria (there are many different forms each with specific chemical abilities) thus seek other oxidising agents in the soil water with which to release energy from the organic matter for their growth, or obtain energy from inorganic chemical reactions. They first attack any nitrate available, using its oxygen and releasing nitrogen (the process of deni-trification), then oxidised iron and manganese, present in soil minerals, to reduced (and often toxic) forms of these ions. Then they may reduce sulphate to sulphide, again using the contained oxygen. Waterlogged soils thus often smell of hydrogen sulphide and related compounds.

Some of the reduced iron reacts with the sulphides to form an intensely black precipitate of ferrous sulphide that gives some waterlogged soils their characteristic blackness, especially if sulphate was formerly abundant. Finally, organic matter may be reduced by the bacteria to methane or sometimes phos-phines, compounds of phosphorus and hydrogen. These may spontaneously ignite giving 'wills-o'-the-wisp' as they emerge as gases from the water surface. Hydrogen sulphide and reduced iron and manganese can be toxic to reedswamp plant roots. One solution has been to allow oxygen, pumped or dif-fusing down through the system of air spaces in the plant, to oxidise a thin zone around the plant roots and detoxify the immediate root surface. This can sometimes be seen, when the soil is dug up, as rusty red threads of re-oxidised iron in the grey or black matrix of the soil.

The switch from a river bottom, with sands, gravels, twigs and leaf debris, in the bubbling upper reaches, to this very different collection of fine silt deposits, vigorous plant growth and waterlogged soils, leads to major changes in the animal communities. In the silt, deposit feeders, such as the chironomid larvae and oligochaete worms, eat the mud, digesting bacteria from it and defecating the residue for recolonisation. Bivalve molluscs, the mussels, some big, such as swan mussels, others only the size of peas, suck in a stream of water and diluted silt and do likewise.

Like the rooted plants, they too may have problems obtaining enough oxy-gen, which some have solved by remaining close to the junction of sediment and water. Others produce haemoglobin, which colours some chironomids a bright cherry red and oligochaete worms a dull pink. Haemoglobin binds oxy-gen and gives a small store, which allows the animals to burrow for a longer time before having to replenish their supply at the sediment surface.

Above the sediment, among the plants, a much more diverse community grazes the softer parts of the submerged plants, though finds better pickings in a rich community of bacteria, algae and protozoa, the periphyton (Fig. 4.2). This coats the plant surfaces, including the stems and petioles of the reedswamp plants and the undersides of lily leaves. These animals include insects – mayflies, caddis flies, dipterans – snails and crustaceans, plus their invertebrate predators – leeches, dragonfly and damselfly nymphs, sucking bugs and beetles.

The reedswamp plants tolerate flooding, though they may grow even better when the water table is just below the soil surface, because of the soil deoxy-genation problems. In the main river channel, where there is always water, their prolific rhizomes may intertwine to form floating mats, dependent on the buoyancy given by their air spaces. In Broadland there is a traditional name for these, hover, or hove, and they must have been a feature of the earliest rivers, narrowing the open water and blocking the channel so that water flows were further encouraged to move out over the floodplain.

Fig. 4.2 The periphyton is a complex community that, given chance, coats any underwater surface. Upper left shows a lightly covered plant surface (the epidermal cells are still visible) along with a few oval diatoms (*Cocconeis placentula*), colonies of tiny bacteria and two protozoon amoebae with their extending pseudopodia, with which they engulf bacteria as food. Lower left shows a denser community with another diatom, *Achnanthes* (the coffin-shaped objects) as well as *Cocconeis*, complexes of bacteria and organic matter and, in the centre, a large protozoon, *Vorticella*. Filamentous green algae, as well as diatoms and a large amoeba, appear in the dense community shown at the right. Photographs and preparation by C.J. Veltkamp. Scale bars are 5 micrometres.

Peat and succession

The high productivity of the reedswamp plants and the inability of the system to decompose all the dead material at the end of the growing season, because of the shortage of oxygen, led to the laying down of peat in the Broadland valleys. Peat is partly decomposed aquatic plant debris, squashed into a deposit by the weight of successive years of accumulation. As the peat builds up it shallows the water and may eventually be eroded away in a high flood and washed out to sea. At the edge of the main channel this would have kept the river open, but over most of the Broadland floodplains very deep deposits were built up. This was true especially from about 5,000 years ago after the sand bar formed at the mouth of the estuary, and the floodplains were less and less affected by tidal erosion.

Throughout Broadland's history the land has been steadily subsiding and the sea, and therefore river levels, steadily rising. Peat accumulation more or less kept pace with the relative subsidence in the valley floors. Away from the main river channel, fringed by reedswamp, the peat grew and the water shallowed. The water table was soon above the surface only in winter and for most of the year the surface was dry though the soils were still waterlogged a little way below the surface. Plants less tolerant of permanent submergence of their bases were able to colonise. The bulrush and lilies at the river margin were succeeded by reedmace and bur-reed and then a complex of reed, sedges and other species (Fig. 4.3).

The tussock sedge, for example, moved in, a little way back from the channel edge, building up great mounds of old rhizome and leaf bases year on year, until the current year's growth was maybe a metre or more above the surface. Tussock sedge is a rather vulnerable plant, prone to keeling over if given too much of a push, but it was formerly very common, and many other plants colonised its tussocks, including alder, whose seedlings could establish in the dryer conditions above the reedswamp floor. The plants at first formed semi-floating rafts on the sloppy peat with water hemlock, great water dock, cypress sedge, hemp agrimony, and great hairy willowherb, mint and iris. There was meadowsweet, purple and yellow loosestrife, marsh parsley, bindweed and the now rare marsh pea. Smaller plants, horsetails, lesser water-parsnip, skullcap and even the tiny adder's-tongue fern also managed to find a niche.

The woody species, alder in particular, as they grew heavier on the tussocks, keeled them over, creating a swampy morass littered with dead wood and irregularly tangled trunks and branches. Such 'swamp carr' is perhaps the nearest to the popular concept of 'jungle' that western Europe can produce. But as time went on, the peat was building up and the trees were increasingly taking over. The dense summer canopy eliminated much of the ground flora leaving sallows, blackberries and currants, and broad buckler, royal and lady ferns on the damp, darkened floors and alder buckthorn, birch, ash and oak, garlanded with honeysuckle, with the predominant alder in the over-storey.

The great alder forest

Alder and sallow could establish easily on the drier ground beyond the influence of the river channel, where the floods were only temporary. Five thousand years ago, the floodplains of the Broadland valleys thus became a tangle of wet forest, spreading down river as the sand bar strengthened and the sea could not penetrate so far upstream. Where the water flow and tide were greatest, perhaps close to the estuary in the River Yare, the river, and the lagoons created at flood, bore floating mats of reed sweet-grass as their first colonists, perhaps with fringes of reed. This was an unstable habitat. The mats would easily break away under the tide so that few other species had time to colonise – woody nightshade, greater reedmace, kingcup, purple loosestrife, marsh woundwort, common meadow rue and stinging nettle. Eventually, however, the plants got a firm hold in the peat, and reed and reed canary grass established, followed by the alder and guelder rose, privet and forget-me-nots of a subtly different carr – but looking much the same to the sparrowhawk above!

Elsewhere conditions were different. At the heads of tributary valleys, where water flow was small and tidal influence absent, conditions were steadier and there was little impact of new nutrients brought in as silt or in the water from the main catchments. At the heads of the Rivers Ant and Thurne, where the top ends of Hickling Broad and Horsey Mere are now, succession to alder

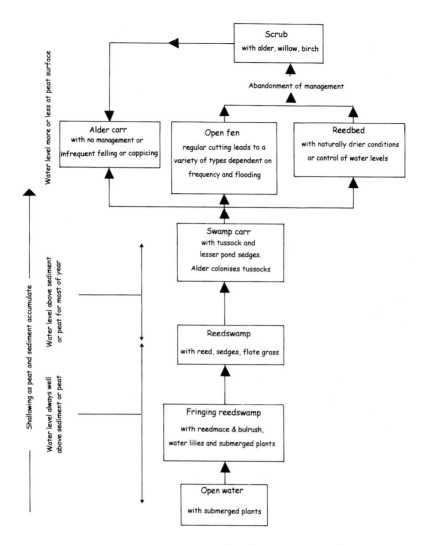

Fig. 4.3 The trends of vegetation succession in the Broadland floodplains. The natural sequence culminates in dense alder carr, but cutting arrests the succession, giving reed beds or open fens, which may regress, through scrub to carr, if management is abandoned.

forest involved neither the sweet-grass nor tussock sedge. Low water movement allowed the build-up of firmer peat, low water flow led to a shortage of bases and nutrients. Smaller sedges (*Carex nigra, C. lasiocarpa, C. rostrata, C. panicea*) survived with rushes, cotton-grass, black bog-rush, purple moor-grass, marsh bedstraw, greater bird's-foot trefoil, bogbean, common spotted- and southern marsh orchids, and narrow and crested buckler ferns. Where the water was at its most spartan, plants characteristic of acid bogs, *Sphagnum* mosses and even the occasional round-leaved sundew could grow. Reed and saw sedge were present, but not so prolific as elsewhere, for strong dominance initially needs a high nutrient supply. Alder carr developed eventually as trees established themselves, but it was a more open community than in the more nutrient-rich areas.

In various subtleties therefore the valley floors were covered by alder forest and it was this that laid down the thick layers of woody peat (brushwood peat) found in the middle sections of the valleys. Seven thousand years ago therefore, before any permanent settlement had occurred, the dense drier forests of the upland graded into equally dense wet forests of the floodplains. There was just a ribbon of open main river fringed by a few metres of reed and lilies to either side and alder forest beyond that, eventually merging with the forests of the upland. Alder swamp carr (Plate 7) is a truly difficult sort of vegetation to cross, for fallen timber on the forest floor alternates with peaty pools and tussocks of sedge. It was impenetrable by boat or on foot in the wet season, and little easier to cross in the summer when the water table had fallen.

Towards the valley margins, where water stood for only part of the winter, the ground was less treacherous, though the floor was, as in all pristine forests, liberally littered with dead wood and relatively dark. It was a productive forest, with trees growing up to 30 metres, not the stunted scrub that alder now forms as a result of repeated cutting, and its fertility was helped by the fact that alder bears nodules containing nitrogen-fixing bacteria on its roots. This was a great advantage in a habitat where nitrate in the soils was continually removed by denitrifying bacteria. As the valley edge was reached the alder forest became diversified with other tree species, oak and ash, lime and birch, until these species began to dominate as the upland was reached and alder became an occasional tree only found in ill-drained spots.

The larger animals of the river systems and floodplains

There is one more component to add to this reconstruction of the pristine Broadland river systems and that is the animal community. Many invertebrates, especially the insects, must have invaded quickly after the ice retreated. For others, such as the flatworms, which move only centimetres a day over the bottom, colonisation of the British Isles is even now not yet complete. Vertebrates also arrived sporadically.

Fish returned in two ways – from the sea and from refuges that had remained unfrozen in mainland Europe to the south of the ice sheet. Among the first to arrive in Broadland may have been those that have both marine and freshwater phases to their life history, such as the salmonids. These fish would have had long passages through the bigger rivers, of which the Broadland streams were mere tributary trickles, before they reached what would become Norfolk, but they swim strongly and can cover huge distances. The Atlantic salmon and the sewin, or sea trout, breed in fresh waters and would eventually have found suitable flinty gravel beds for spawning in the upstream sections of the rivers.

The eel, with the reverse sort of history, breeding, it is thought, in the Sargasso Sea, but living its adult life in fresh waters, would also have been early on the scene, for it can cross the marshy interminglings of watersheds on wet nights and eventually could have had access overland from the Atlantic coast. In the lower reaches the burbot and sturgeon, smelt, flounders, grey mullet and shads would have moved in from the coast somewhat later as the sea filled the North Sea basin and English Channel 8,500 years ago.

But the earliest fish to move in were probably the freshwater coarse fish that

Fig. 4.4 Perch, bream and roach are all characteristic fish of Broadland that would have moved in through the rivers from what is now mainland Europe before Britain was cut off by the rising sea about 8,500 years ago.

moved up the European rivers. By the time that the British islands were cut off by the sea, about 20 such species had moved in. The native fish fauna of Britain is tiny in number compared with comparable areas of the main continents and this reflects the comparatively short period, only 2,000 years or so, between melting and isolation. Through the early river systems came the typical fish of the more turbulent, gravel-bottomed upland rivers: the brown trout, dace, stone loach, miller's thumb, minnow and brook lamprey, and the fish of the floodplain reaches: the perch, ruffe, pike, tench, roach, rudd, silver and common bream and the river lamprey (Fig. 4.4). The upstream species need hard substrates for spawning – gravel beds or rocks embedded in the bottom, whilst the floodplain group attach their spawn to plant debris or live plants and can often tolerate much lower oxygen concentrations.

In winter they would spread over the floodplain as the waters rose, remaining there to spawn in the tangled debris of the alder forest floors or of shallow lagoons left by the random destruction of unusually high floods. The woody debris offered cover from predatory fish such as the pike and from birds and grass snakes, whilst also providing, as algal periphyton covering its surfaces, tiny items of food that the new young could swallow in spring. In late spring and early summer the fish, old and newborn, retreated back to the fringing reedswamps and main channel as the water levels fell and, as temperatures rose, the remaining pools in the swamp carr became severely deoxygenated.

Birds and mammals

For birds and mammals, the pristine Broadland offered a less varied habitat than it would some millennia later, when the structure of the floodplain vege-tation had been changed and varied by human activity, but it was nonetheless hugely attractive. The alder wood offered an extension to the upland forest, the estuary a huge roosting and feeding area for wildfowl and waders, though sheets of open fresh water were confined to the lower parts of the rivers and occasional small lagoons in the alder swamp.

Some species (Fig. 4.5), then present, have not survived the human distur-bance of the historic period, but were recorded as late as the sixteenth centu-ry or are known from other British wetlands as bones in sediments and peat deposits. Yet other birds, which exploit the consequences of human distur-bance, may have been very rare or lacking. Birds are much more mobile than fish, moving in and out of areas in response to quite subtle changes of habitat and climate and it is thus far more difficult to reconstruct their past commu-nities. The lower reaches of the rivers and the estuary may nonetheless have seen flocks of pelicans and spoonbills, avocet, ruff, black-tailed godwit and black tern, all species that have been present, but have now disappeared or visit only rarely. Many species characteristic of open grassland and extensive reedswamps must have been absent or far less common, but those of forest and carr very abundant.

Flocks of tits, the marsh, willow and long-tailed especially, moved through the trees gleaning seeds and insects from the branches and bark crevices; the

Fig. 4.5 Some Broadland birds common prior to the twentieth century, now rare.

great and lesser-spotted woodpeckers broke into dying trees for the beetles, demolishing them to furnish the forest floor with more debris for the freshwater community in winter; wren, tree creeper, chiffchaff, blackcap and redpoll likewise took insects and seeds, whilst in summer, the swifts and swallows overhead took advantage of the rich insect swarms emerging from the swamps and rivers.

Bats, the noctule, pipistrelle, Daubenton's, natterer's and long-eared caught insects among the trees at night. Tawny and long-eared owls nested in the carrs and hunted water voles, a small rodent sought also by stoat and pike; sparrowhawks, small birds and herons roosted in the tall trees, flying off to feed by the river or in the estuary by day. Kingfishers waited by the stream channels for fish moving to and from the river. Weasels hunted over the sedge tussocks, swimming through pools when they had to, nesting on the tussock sedge and in the lower crooks of trees. Otters abounded both in the wet carrs and in the fringing reedswamps, taking fish, frogs, the bigger molluscs and even the earthworms that grew juicy in the soft peaty debris. Magpies, carrion crows and rooks coped with the bodies of anything dead and large enough to provide a meal, and snipe sometimes nested on the wet floors. Some of the birds that have now adapted to wooded gardens – the redwing, blackbird, siskin, brambling and tree sparrow – found their natural habitats here.

There was a gradual change where the alder opened out into the fringing reedswamp. Here the moorhen and coot dabbled among the grasses and sedges with the water rail, whilst above them, perched on the stems, sedge and reed warblers and the reed bunting sought insects. Kingfishers fished with little and great-crested grebes. Black-headed gulls nested on reed debris where the surface had built up, and in winter the pochard, shoveler and tufted ducks migrated in to feed on the remaining submerged plants and invertebrates of the summer production. Perhaps the bittern and the bearded tit, now wellknown unusual birds of the reedswamps, had already established; perhaps they were very common; we can probably never know.

And landward, the large mammals, now gone, but behaving like those of the great pristine floodplain systems of America and Africa, kept to the dry upland in the winter when the carrs were impossible for long-legged species to cross. Then, in spring, they drifted through the tributary stream valleys towards the rivers, feeding on the lush vegetation of the drying floors, the young alder leaves and whatever animal prey they could find. We can imagine the aurochs and bison, the wolf, moose, red deer and the brown bear nosing in (Fig. 4.6). We can imagine badgers, characteristic of well-established undisturbed ecosystems, but few foxes, for these exploit the disturbed habitats created by man. And, in the summer movements of the ungulates (the bones of red deer found in the Broadland peat especially testifying to their abundance), we can see the precedent for the driving in of cattle a millennium or two later by the more settled herders. These were to replace the wandering Mesolithic hunter-gatherers who also followed their prey onto the summer floodplain in search of food and water.

The sea and the tides

Broadland is relatively flat and the gradient of the rivers was never very great in the middle sections and lessened as sea levels reached their highest. At most, the floodplains are only a few metres above mean sea level and at high tides,

Fig. 4.6 Prior to the clearance of the carrs and upland woodland by the Neolithic and Bronze Age farmers, the ubiquitous forest of the Broadland catchment housed animals that have long been extinct in Britain or are now unusual.

estuary water still penetrates far upstream. The highest tides bring salt water several kilometres inland, but most tides give a discernible change in water level (called a physical, as opposed to a chemical, tide) several kilometres upstream as the downstream freshwater flow is ponded back by the incoming sea.

Tidal effects are currently quite marked in the Broadland rivers, but present day physical tidal and saltwater penetration limits give us little clue as to the details of the river system 7,000 years ago. The rivers have now been embanked and thus the tidal water cannot move sideways over the estuary and floodplain in the lowest reaches as it would formerly have done. Freshwater flows may also be lower due to water abstraction and greater evaporation from disturbance of the natural vegetation in the catchments. Much of the fringing vegetation at the edge and within the main channels has disappeared, so there is less blockage to tidal flow. The outlet from the estuary through Great Yarmouth is much altered and there is now only one outlet compared with perhaps three or four in the remote past; and we have only vague clues as to detailed changes in rainfall and consequent flows.

In contrast, 7,000 years ago, much of the floodplain was estuarine. Five thousand years ago, following the closure of the sand bar, much more limited volumes of sea water could penetrate the narrowed mouth before the ebb. It is thus likely that tidal effects upstream in the rivers were then lesser than they are now, largely because the tidal water could spill out into a huge area of tidal mud flats and salt marshes behind the sand bar, which lined the estuary to sea-ward and graded into the freshwater vegetation upstream. Some tidal water must have moved upstream into the freshwater floodplains, but the chances are that this did not penetrate the 20 or more kilometres above the estuary that now regularly experience tidal rise, even if of only a few centimetres.

Salt marshes, mud flats and the estuary

The sparrowhawk had a better view of the ground when she flew down the river valleys and out over the estuary behind the growing sand bar. The reedswamps at the edges of the rivers widened, for alder and sallow are not tol-erant of the saltier water close to the coast. The forest was left behind and even-tually the reedswamps merged imperceptibly, at first with a greater proportion of the more salt-tolerant flote grass, into salt marshes, and then they too into the open mud flats uncovered at every low tide.

Once, in a Norwich second-hand bookshop, I bought an edition of *The Snow Goose* by Paul Gallico, illustrated in his early years by the painter and naturalist Peter Scott. It is a moving story and I read it in a single sitting, within the hour, perched on a low wall in the cloisters of the nearby Cathedral. What I remem-ber about it is the sense it conveys of the great salt marshes of East Anglia, a sense of what the marshes of the Broadland estuary would have been like in prehistoric through at least to Saxon times after the turn of the first millenni-um AD. It is something that cannot be seen today for the marsh has been fresh-ened and drained and remains only as pathetic remnants set at the edges of the larger but still emasculated mud flats of Breydon Water.

Salt marsh and mud flat are among the more productive yet structurally sim-plest of all ecosystems, subject to the immensely powerful control of the daily tides. At the lower tide levels, where the bottom is covered by water for most of the time and only exposed to the air for short periods at low tide, there are no flowering plants, with the exceptions of some of the sea grasses (*Zostera*). Prolonged immersion in muddy water, through which little light penetrates, and in a shifting medium for rooting, limits the possibilities.

Algae can grow well, however, and especially in spring the flats are covered by an olive-green or rich brown film of diatoms (Fig. 4.7). Their habitat is a dif-ficult one. There are plenty of nutrients available in the interstices of the mud, but there is also a constant risk of burial in the mud. The diatoms of these habi-tats are rather boat-shaped, and can move using a structure called the raphe running along their long axis. The raphe is a slit in the silica wall of the cells through which mucilage is extruded. On contacting water the mucilage expands and pushes against the mud particles thrusting the diatom forward. Because the cells respond to light they tend to move upwards at low tide, main-taining their position at the sediment surface.

There are other algae too – flagellates such as the euglenoids, which are green, the red or brown dinoflagellates and a host of tiny green algae, all of which move using fine, hair-like flagella. All grow well in spring and early sum-mer, but their populations fall in midsummer as grazing animals feed. Over the surfaces of the sediment, large numbers of small snails rasp away at the algal film, taking also bacteria, of which there are millions in every cubic mil-limetre, and organic debris washed into the estuary. The rivers, their catch-ments, the salt marshes, and the sea on the tide provide copious supplies. From what we presently know of the mud flats of Breydon Water we might

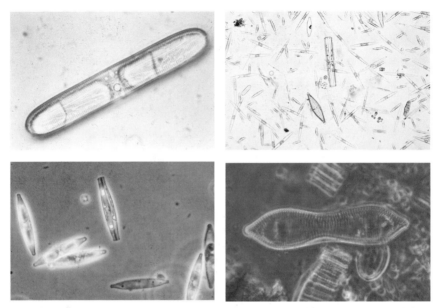

Fig. 4.7 Diatoms are important components of sediment and mudflat communities, staining these surfaces a chocolate-brown in spring. Shown are *Navicula* and *Nitzschia* species (top right), *Pinnularia* (top left), *Nitszchia* sp (bottom left) and the remaining walls of *Cymatopleura* (bottom right).

guess that the tiny snails *Hydrobia ulvae* and *Potamopyrgus jenkinsii* and the famil-iar winkle *Littorina littorea* were present. And feeding on these surface snails in winter were resident and migratory flocks of duck – shoveler and shelduck, goldeneye, scaup and tufted. Pochard, mallard, pintail and wigeon joined them to feed on sea grasses and vegetation debris.

Deeper in the mud were huge populations of a few tolerant species of bur-rowing invertebrates. Estuaries pose problems for animals because the salinity of the water varies a great deal and this causes difficulties for maintenance of the salt balance within their bodies. Nonetheless, small crustaceans (*Corophium volutator, Neomysis integer, Leptocheirus pilosus, Idotea linearis, I. viridis, Palaemon squilla, Gammarus duebeni, G. zaddachi, Jaera marina*), polychaete worms (*Nereis diversicolor*) and bivalve molluscs (*Mytilus edulis, Ceratostoderma edule, Tellina baltica, Scrobicularia plana, Mya arenaria*) were almost certainly present, dividing the apparently uniform muddy habitat among themselves so as to minimise competition (Fig. 4.8). They do this partly by feeding at different depths in the sediment or by living deep and extending siphons or feeding tubes to the sur-face. Different species favour slightly different mud textures, some more sandy, others finer and more likely to deoxygenate.

Waders flocked on the mud flats – grey plover, curlew sandpiper, dunlin, redshank, black- and bar-tailed godwits, curlew, whimbrel, spoonbill and avo-cet – gulls fed on debris and carcasses of fish and molluscs, terns on fish at high water. The division of the spoils among these birds is more readily understood than that among their invertebrate prey. Waders have differing lengths of beak with which to probe the sediment, and exploit invertebrates at different levels

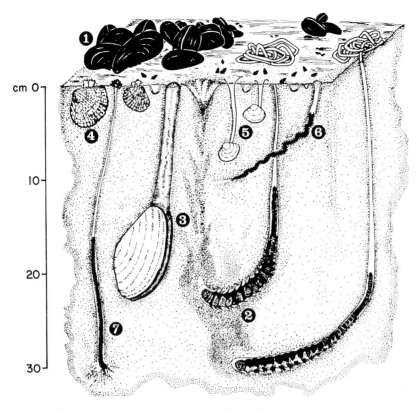

Fig. 4.8 Mudflats support a very large number of invertebrate animals, though of relatively few species that can tolerate the changes in salinity, exposure and disturbance of the habitat. Some common species from Breydon Water are shown here: 1. Common mussel (*Mytilus edulis*), 2. Lugworm (*Arenicola marina*), 3. *Mya arenaria*, 4. Common cockle (*Cerastoderma edule*), 5. Baltic tellin (*Macoma balthica*), 6. Ragworm (*Nereis diversicolor*), 7. *Heteromastus filiformis*. Small snails, *Hydrobia ulvae,* can also be seen on the surface and there are very shallow burrows of a crustacean, *Corophium* sp. Based on a figure in the 1985 Report of the Netherlands Institute for Sea Research.

and of different sizes. It is one of nature's great lessons that evolution has tended to minimise competition between species by development of increasing specialisation of food or habitat among different species. Competition is a wasteful business, though prominent among the individuals of any one species in maintaining maximum fitness for the conditions to which it has become specialised.

Salt marshes grow only at the upper tide levels where the bottom is under water only at the highest tides. Salt-marsh plants suffer the same problems of root deoxygenation as reedswamp plants. Estuarine muds are often intensely black below the surface because there is so much sulphate in sea water that huge amounts of sulphide can be formed. They also have problems of obtaining sufficient water when the source is so much saltier than the sap of their cells. The water must be pumped in against a salt gradient and this requires

energy – so much that salt-marsh plants often have the waxy or scaly cover associated with plants of arid environments. Waxy scales give a mealy or rather grey
appearance to the plant surfaces, but minimise water loss from the leaves.
Other salt-marsh plants are glossy with thick cuticles for the same reason and
may even be succulent, such as the samphire or glasswort, apparent refugees
from the desert among a plethora of sea water.

The plants also have a problem in resisting the effects of waves and currents
and at the lowest tidal levels at which they can survive it tends to be the annual glassworts that are the first colonists. The succulent glassworts give a pop-
ping sound when stepped on, hence their common name. Their growth tends
to encourage sedimentation and a slight raising of the mud-flat level. They may
then be succeeded by other species that can only tolerate less frequent tidal
immersion. The sea-purslane is particularly characteristic of the east coast
marshes and occupies the lower part of the marsh and the banks of the creeks
that drain the water from it as the tide ebbs.

Then at higher levels, which the tide covers less frequently, is a mixture of
just a few species – scurvy-grass, sea aster, thrift, sea plantain, sea-lavender,
annual seablite, greater sea spurge, sea arrowgrass and the common salt marsh
grass. These may form great swards below where the salt marsh merges with
freshwater swamps of reed and sweet-grass. The marsh surface is firmer than
on the mud flats and will take the feet of large grazing animals; it supports also
flocks of swans and geese. The ancient estuary of Broadland would have seen
huge flocks of white-fronted, pink-footed and perhaps Brent, bean and barna-
cle geese as well as whooper, Bewick's and mute swans, all grazing over the lush
pastures from which, on the high tide, quantities of debris were washed out to
enrich the mud flats and even the coastal waters. On the tide, young fish
moved in – flounder, goby, smelt, eelpout, whiting, pogge, sprat and sole, for
the invertebrate food bounty from this rich system was great indeed.

Settled man

The Broadland was a complex system of catchment, river, floodplain and estuary in its pristine state. We can reconstruct only the gross features of what must
have been the same sort of subtly patterned patchwork that can be discovered
in the few remaining intact wetlands on Earth. There is a satisfaction to be had
in contemplation of this system: the steady, parsimonious movement of water,
nutrients and organic matter from the catchment to the river; the ways that the
river communities processed these materials; the rise and fall of the seasonal
floods and their consequences for fish, birds and mammals; the solution of
problems of adapting to habitats that were short of oxygen; and the steady laying down of sediments, recording their own history, as peat was deposited in
valleys whose water levels also rose with that of the sea. These are the key features of the pristine Broadland, a great forest stitched together by river threads
that coarsened towards the coast, where a border of grass and mud fronted the
North Sea.

It was not a static system; it responded continually to changes in weather and
sea level, but it was clearly a system of connections in which events in one part
had consequences for another; in which there were no boundaries, but continual merging as conditions gradually altered from place to place. Modern
ecologists would reject any notion of a balance of nature; the system had no
grand design beyond a mutual adjustment, through natural selection, to an

environment always changing in some minor or major way. Loss of a component, a particular species, would have had little consequence. The resources it had used would have been taken over by some other invader or resident; the 'services' it might have provided for others would have been gleaned elsewhere; nothing was ultimately indispensable.

Investigation of any natural system always reveals a myriad of connections and consequences and ultimate adjustment of the survivors. Ecosystems have a built in capacity for this, almost by definition. Sometimes they must cope with glaciation or vulcanism or drought. Since about 6,000 years ago in Britain, they have had to cope with the equally powerful influence of what was to become one of their major parts, that of settled man. The Broadland was no exception. The generations of soaring sparrowhawks, having given us a view of their terrain during the 2,000 years or so from 5000 BC to 3000 BC, when the sand bar formed and the pristine alder forest dominated the freshwater floodplain, were about to start a rougher ride.

Further reading

Hydrology is a well-established area of environmental science, with a considerable specialist literature, but a very readable account of river dynamics, meander and floodplain formation and the like can be found in Leopold (1974). The chapter by Lambert in Ellis (1965) gives an excellent summary of vegetation in Broadland, much influenced by the earlier work of Marietta Pallis (1911) who was one of the earlier British ecologists, working when the vegetation of Britain was being systematically described by Arthur Tansley and his students. Lambert (1951) and Lambert & Jennings (1951) add much detail to the general picture of vegetation in Broadland in earlier periods. Wetlands are now very prominent in discussions on environmental issues and several well-illustrated books, for example, Dugan (1993), give accounts of their interest, beauty and importance. The more fundamental literature on their functioning can be approached through Etherington (1983) and Moss (1998). The specifically Broadland literature is thoroughly covered in George (1992). Ranwell (1972) and Long & Mason (1983) give good coverage of salt marshes, but Teal & Teal (1969) has the advantage of having been written with passion.

5

Invasion and Settlement

'History is the propaganda of the victors.'

Anonymous, probably apocryphal and likely true.

Maps of archaeological remains and ancient monuments show a disappointing sparsity in the Broadland floodplains. The views of former scholars were that this was due to Broadland's remoteness and impenetrability in the prehistoric period. It was isolated from much colonisation by dense forests on the heavy boulder clays laid down by the Anglian glaciation over the middle of Norfolk. There was, in contrast, much human activity in the west of Norfolk where the higher ground and thin soils of the chalk ridge allowed freer passage. Yet similar areas of river and wetland around the Wash are rich in archaeological remains and the Broadland is not totally deficient. Perhaps the scarcity is just apparent. The remains of one period would have been quickly buried by the accumulating peats and clays in an area where the land was sinking so rapidly and thus little trace was left at the surface. The Broadland was not inaccessible in later periods. There is plenty of evidence of successive waves of immigrants, the last of whom, the Vikings, were to start the digging out of the Broads themselves.

A common view of history portrays these immigrations as conquests, the victors subduing and enslaving the former population. The truth is more prosaic and more interesting. Certainly there were raids from the sea, short skirmishes and local violence, but mostly there was a steady influx of people from elsewhere, probably in quite small numbers to join existing populations and to introduce different, sometimes new ways of doing things. There was also a working out of new technologies by the existing population. The Bronze Age farmers (around 1700 BC to 500 BC) had a well-organised society in the centuries prior to the Christian era. The societies that became familiar with the use of iron, however, seemed to have become more fragmented, perhaps at odds with one another in a wetter climate that was temporarily worsening and replacing the open woodlands of the northern plateaux of the English hills with blanket bog. Iron, however, produced harder, sharper tools and ploughs than bronze, and allowed the further clearance of more intractable heavy lowland soils in Britain from about 650 BC.

The Iron Age and the Romans

Iron rusts; it is not as easily preserved as bronze and flint, but scattered remains, coins and pots tell of a continued presence of Iron Age peoples in Broadland (Fig. 5.1). The characteristic hillforts and homesteads of the period are found only in the west and north of Norfolk, however, away from Broadland. There is nonetheless a late Iron Age field system close to Loddon,

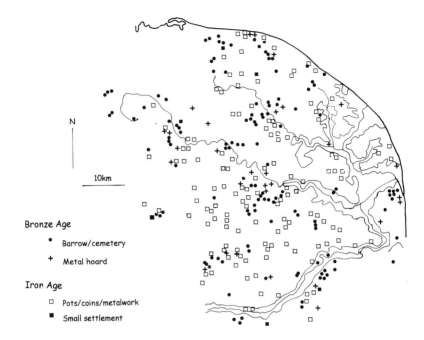

Fig. 5.1 Map of Bronze and Iron Age remains in Broadland. Based on Wade-Martins (1994) and Dymond & Martin (1999).

on the River Chet, a tributary of the River Yare, and a small settlement on the upland between the Bure and the Yare in the vicinity of Acle. The artefacts found in and around Iron Age sites tell of a tribal society, building round-houses, keeping cattle, sheep and pigs and cultivating a range of cereals, the chaff of which was hard on the teeth, but excellent for the bowels. They also kept horses and ponies and used two-wheeled carts and chariots.

The first written evidence of history comes from this period, following raids by Julius Caesar in 55–54 BC and some later documentation by Roman authors. East Anglia was occupied at the time by the tribe of Cenimagni, or Great Iceni, whose King, Prasutagus, treated with the Romans when, in AD 43, they decided to annex Britain as part of their Empire (the powerful have always been presumptuous). At first the Iceni formed a client kingdom, paying tribute and taxes to the Romans, but with considerable self-rule. Following Prasutagus' death, however, a revolt by his wife, Boudicca (Boadicea) in AD 60, which failed, led to direct control of the area by the Romans. They established a centre of government in Broadland, at Venta Icenorum, or what is now known as Caistor St Edmunds, on the River Tas, a tributary of the River Yare, and a smaller industrial town, with many potteries, on the River Bure at Brampton.

Broadland consequently has many Roman remains (Fig. 5.2), including a road network and two coastal 'forts'. These are at Caister on Sea and Burgh Castle, on the outer edges of the great estuary that had been re-formed by the breaking of the sand bar and the return of the sea far into the Broadland valleys (Chapter 2). There was possibly also a settlement at Reedham, which

Fig. 5.2 Roman remains, including roads and remains of probable roads in the Broadland catchment. Based on Wade-Martins (1994) and Dymond & Martin (1999).

would have occupied a prominent position where two arms of the estuary came together, and which in the nineteenth century was reported to have had a Roman pharos or lighthouse. There is a great deal of recycled ancient tile and quartz arenite, a sandstone from some distant source, used in the local parish church, which may have been gleaned from this structure.

The three centuries of Roman occupation, from AD 43 to 410, appear to have been peaceful ones in Norfolk, with a largely rural population, a number of large estates with villas, and evidence of sea trading. Scatters of remains suggest concentrations of Roman settlements between the Rivers Chet and Waveney, in the Hales, Loddon and Heckingham areas, with an extensive hamlet of several farms at Loddon. At Witton, near North Walsham, there were eight farmsteads.

The two forts on the coast (Plate 8) are both called Gariannonum (from which the name Yare derives) in the literature of the day, including the *Notitia Dignitatum*, a handbook of civilian and military posts, that gives some detail to supplement various excavations that have been carried out. There is little evidence that they had a major military function, however, as suggested by the common description of them as castles in position to defend the estuary from invasion.

The structure at Caister on Sea was built in the third century AD, probably in 211–217. It would have commanded a view out to sea, but had only a small garrison and apparently no naval units. It was not well sited to move troops into the hinterland to pursue raiding parties, being on an island in the estuary, the area now called Flegg. Numerous animal bones, hairpins, beads, bracelets and infant remains suggest a much more domestic function, perhaps as a centre for sea trade and export and for monitoring of trade routes. Burgh Castle, equally, despite its impressive walls, has no major ramparts or defensive ditches and no view out to sea. There is little evidence, beyond the size of the walls, of military might, much more of domesticity with extensive field systems to the north and north-east. It was perhaps a port and dockyard, commanding shallow but very sheltered waters just inside the mouth of the estuary.

Roman writings tell of raids on the Broadland coastline, nonetheless, and of instability in the third century AD, marked by a tendency for the people to bury hoards of metal valuables in the countryside. Rome itself was under pressure from peoples to its north and the army was withdrawn from Britain in AD 410, though leaving numerous settlers of Roman origin. As this cultural change was in progress, so also were changes in the coastline as the sand bar, breached since around the turn of the millennium and perhaps also a casualty of the worsened weather, re-formed and the fresh waters began to push the sea again from most of Broadland. This established the main geography of the present river and floodplain network and sets the natural stage for the digging out of the Broads five or six centuries thence.

Saxons

Into this renewed system of floodplain, rivers, salt marshes and mud flats, sailing their boats from the glaciated plains of what is now northern Germany and Holland, came the Angles, the Jutes and the Saxons. It was probably not an organised military invasion as had brought the Romans and was to bring the Danes, but more a set of prospective raids from the third century onwards, followed by a steady settlement over a century or so after the Romans left. It was a steady infiltration that rapidly replaced Romano-British customs. This is reflected in the nature of burials, as in the Saxon cemeteries at Caistor St Edmunds, the former Roman headquarters, and Burgh Castle, the former shore fort. Grave goods, pots and jewellery were left with the bodies. This had not been the Romano-British practice.

Perhaps a relative lack of organisation, perhaps chance or climate change was responsible, but the Saxons left less imprint than the Romans. The names of tribal groups remain, as in Happing (Haeppingas) and Loddon (Lodningas), but the 15 Roman farms of the fifth century in the Chet area were replaced by only four Saxon farms in the sixth and the eight at Witton were reduced to four. Place name evidence suggests a more wooded upland around Broadland – Acle is *ac leah*, an oak wood, Fishley is the wood of a fisherman and Ruston means a settlement among brushwood. There is evidence of a greater emphasis on grazing rather than cultivation. Horsey means Horse island, Woodbastwick is a grazing farm or ranch and Winterton and Somerton suggest movement of animals between winter and summer pasturage. Saxon pottery of the period was poorly fired and made without a wheel. The suggestion is of a decline in prosperity compared with the Roman period and of a population retreating further inland away from any threat of further sea raids. The estuary and rivers provided a quiet and sheltered route for stealthy robberies on isolated villages and farms.

There were peaceable visits too. Irish and Roman missionaries moved in during the seventh century AD and the pagan population was converted to a form of Christianity that adopted a compromise between old and new religious practices. There were monasteries founded, one of which, called Cnobheresburh, was either at Burgh Castle or Caister on Sea and the seat of an Irish cleric and later saint, called Forsey. There was probably also a Saxon monastery on the site of the present St Benet's Abbey by the River Bure. Meanwhile, the valley edge farming, using summer pasturage in the drying wetlands established in the Bronze Age, must have continued in much the same way as it had for 2,000 years. Then there appeared an ominous cloud on the horizon.

The Vikings

In AD 793, far to the north, there had been a brutal raid on the monastery housed on the island of Lindisfarne by a band of Danes, the Vikings, capable of efficient military and civic organisation. Their empire had spread from North America to Russia and the Middle East. The islands of Britain promised rich pickings for their longboat crews as they moved around almost all the coastline, taking in the Irish as well as North Seas. Armies were landed and advanced westward, eventually to be stopped by Alfred, the Saxon king, who treated with the Dane, Guthrun, at Wedmore in Somerset.

England was divided along a line running from London to Chester, with land to the north and east coming under Danish control, the Danelaw. *The Anglo-Saxon Chronicle*, a book written shortly afterwards by a monk, the Venerable Bede, records how East Anglia was shared among Guthrun and his followers. A period of some terror was replaced by integration and compromise as the existing ways and the new were yet again melded. The Vikings adopted Christianity, even issued coinage to commemorate Edmund, the Saxon King and Saint whom they had murdered 30 years before; like all invaders they had to be politically astute to persist.

Persist they did. Plentiful remains of Viking metalwork have turned up in Norfolk as people armed with metal detectors have plodded their way across the fields. These are not the relics, swords and shields, of military might but of domesticity – brooches and dress fastenings. They are moulded with designs of trefoils, Thor's hammer and cat-like animal heads, that turn up over all the Viking world. They are not the artefacts of the rich, but relatively cheap every-day ware, the cast-offs and lost property of peasant farmers and their families (Fig. 5.3). The demobbed artisans of the army had married the local girls or brought their women with them and settled to something of harder work but lesser risk than war. It was much the same sort of immigration as that of the Romans. Following settlement in the late ninth and early tenth centuries there was still some mayhem. Svein Forkbeard, in an alliance with the Norwegian, Harald Bluetooth, finding their mainland empire less profitable than it had been, reinvaded in 1004. They burned Norwich and eventually left Cnut, Forkbeard's son, to rule much of England in a relatively peaceable way and to leave the imprint of Viking settlement from East Anglia to the Scottish islands, Dublin and west Wales.

Broadland contains a particular concentration of Viking place names (Fig. 5.3). The suffix -by has long been associated with such names, and on and around the region of Flegg (a Norse word meaning reeds) are Ashby, Billockby, Clippesby, Filby, Hemsby, Herringby, Mautby, Oby, Ormesby, Rollesby, Scratby, Stokesby and Thrigby. It was the custom to combine -by with

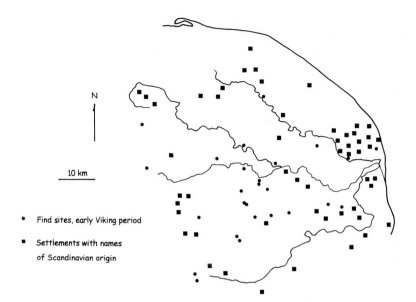

Fig. 5.3 Remains of the Vikings in Broadland are reflected in a legacy of place names, especially the dense group of village names ending in -by on the former island of Flegg, and in chance finds of metalwork. Based on Margeson (1997) and Dymond & Martin (1999).

the name of the landowner and the sharing out of land by Guthrun is reflected in a much greater proportion of such combinations in England than in Denmark itself. The word dyke, common in Broadland for channels in the waterway, is the Danish *dik*, a ditch. The Vikings also founded (and later sacked) Norwich, or Northwic, some of whose streets, Fishergate, Pottergate and Finkelgate, still bear their original Viking names. But the most fascinating evidence of the Viking settlement lies in the nature of the basins of the Broads, set in the valley fens, which had long been exploited for their natural products, but which were probably first exploited for their peat by the Danes. Chapter 6 gives some account of these natural communities and Chapter 7 continues the story of their exploitation.

Further reading

There are several extremely useful recent books covering, among other topics, the period of Broadland history from the Neolithic, around 3000 BC, through the Bronze and Iron Ages to the invasions by Romans, Saxons and finally the Danes in the ninth century AD. Margeson et al. (1996) is a collection of short articles by specialists on each period. Wade-Martins (1994) is a historical atlas with much information condensed onto a series of maps. Williamson (1997) specifically examines the early history of Broadland, and cannot be recommended too highly; and Margeson (1997) is a beautifully illustrated account of the Vikings in Norfolk. Place names contain a wealth of interest, if authoritatively interpreted. The standard work is Ekwall (1960). Rye (1991) has extracted information for Norfolk from this.

Part II

Cutter, Digger, Toiler, Reeve

6

Medieval Broadland and Modern Fens

Pristine Broadland began to disappear as soon as the Neolithic settlers first set their stock to graze, began to cut trees for houses and stockades and burnt the brash to clear spaces for grazing – around 5,000 years ago. By the time of the Viking immigration, the great alder forests of the pristine floodplain were looking decidedly patchy, the upland forests also much dissected into blocks surrounded by fields. The smoke of cooking fires hung over a landscape already shaped for three millennia by human hands.

Much of the floodplain forest of alder and sallow had been converted to open grass- and sedge-rich fens by grazing and cutting. The fens and the salt marshes of medieval Broadland were rich and interesting habitats for wild nature. They were also the bases for the local farming system, which determined the character of the fens whilst playing second fiddle to the sea for the salt marshes. We have some detail of farming and industry in Broadland in late Saxon times, under the Danelaw, and for the few centuries that spanned the Viking settlement of the ninth century until a new wave of the land-greedy moved in in the eleventh, this time from Normandy and beyond. Broadland under the influence of the Saxons was not a landscape of run-down hovels, as is usually portrayed following the loss of firm Roman Government; it was one of prosperous farming, especially on the fertile loess soils that had been the gift of the dry Devensian winds.

For the most part it was a system of individual farming rather than of communal manorial enterprises. The division of land under the Danelaw had led to a higher proportion in Broadland of untied landowners, more able to innovate than in conservative large manors. Fodder crops were grown on the uplands bordering the Broadland floodplains; elsewhere, communal fields were left as bare fallow, and around Broadland, manuring was regular. Villages began as groupings around churches, whose number and density reflected a prosperous individualist community, buying its hoped-for salvation in flint towers (Plate 9). Many of the characteristic round-towered churches of Broadland date from this period, or a little later, particularly 1050 to 1150. Their design perhaps reflects the difficulty of building towers in irregular flints, the only building stone conveniently and cheaply available, but more likely it was simple fashion. Round towers were popular across the North Sea in North Germany and southern Sweden at the time.

A textile industry developed, based on the abundance of sheep, along the Waveney valley and at Aylsham and North Walsham. The churches there reflect, in their glory and expensively shaped square flint blocks (Plate 9), the even greater prosperity of the manufacturing middleman. Close to the fens and middle course of the Bure, the great churches at Ranworth and Woodbastwick, Acle and Ludham particularly reflect a confident and prosperous rural society. During the medieval period, the imposing cathedral at Norwich was raised substantially in its present form – an achievement no less remarkable for its time than putting men on the moon in ours.

The intensity of farming reflects the natural resources available. The sea had begun to retreat around the fourth century AD, late in the Roman period, as the sand bar across the estuary steadily rebuilt following the storms that had breached it 1,500 years before. There would not have been a precipitous change, more a slow freshening of the middle sections of the valleys leaving a huge area of intertidal mud flats and salt marshes in the Halvergate triangle behind the slowly re-forming sand bar. The sinuous channels of the original great estuary can still be seen, in maps and especially from the air, in the present drainage system of the Halvergate triangle. In time, several centuries, this area built up its marginal silt and peat deposits to beyond the highest tide level. They succeeded to freshwater or brackish fens, but over the bulk of what was to become the grazing marshes, salt marsh and mud flat prevailed until built embankments, developed in the post-medieval period, started to confine the tide to the main channels.

The pattern of the main rivers (Fig. 6.1) was not as it appears today. There were then at least two outlets through the bar and the courses of the middle sections of the rivers were probably different from those presently seen. The Thurne and Ant now join the Bure, and the Bure, Yare and Waveney merge into the single estuary of Breydon Water to discharge through a single outlet at Yarmouth. In late Saxon Broadland the Thurne discharged in the north, flowing in the opposite direction to that which it now takes. It had the Ant as its tributary, the original course being that of the Hundred stream just to the north of the River Bure. There are several streams called 'Hundred' streams because they were used as parts of the boundaries of local government units called Hundreds in the early medieval period.

A suspiciously straight stretch of the Bure just below the present confluence of the Thurne and Bure, and the odd angle at which the Bure and Thurne merge, suggests that the middle and upper courses of the present Bure were then a tributary of the Thurne. The Thurne discharged as quite a large river through the sand bar, though it appears to have been easily prone to blockage as sand moved down the coast from the north. Sometimes it might have flooded overland, discharging its waters into the Bure, but then regained its original outlet as the sand shifted in the winter storms. Clay deposits around Horsey Mere and Heigham Sound, and the present diminutive Hundred stream (a different Hundred stream from that which bore the Bure), the former outlet, testify to the estuary of the Thurne. Later, after the Bure had been realigned (if it was), it did not enter Breydon Water in the way that it presently does, but had an outlet to the north of Yarmouth, isolating Yarmouth on an island section of the coastal sand bar as late as the sixteenth century AD. This outlet was probably deliberately closed and the Bure diverted into the eastern end of Breydon Water in the eighteenth century.

In the south, the Waveney almost reached the coast near the present position of Lowestoft, but was blocked by the dunes and turned inland again to join the Yare near Burgh Castle. The land where Lowestoft now lies was drained by short streams, along the line of the present Oulton Broad and Lake Lothing, that might sometimes have connected with the Waveney wetlands. The block of land ringed by the main estuary to the north, the Waveney and its floodplain to the west, the coast to the east and the fens of the short Lothing stream to the south, was essentially an island which became known as Lothingland. It was

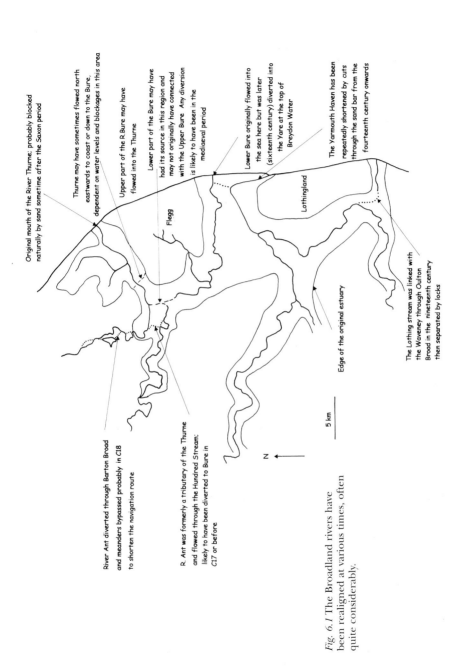

Fig. 6.1 The Broadland rivers have been realigned at various times, often quite considerably.

matched by the island of Flegg, isolated by the Thurne estuary to the north, the Bure to the west and the main estuary and sea to the south and east.

Medieval farming

The salt marshes of the estuaries were used by the Saxons. The mud flats would have attracted great flocks of wildfowl and waders, and the marshes, of geese, and these were joined by the Saxon flocks of sheep. There were medieval farms at the edge of the saltings, for example, at Ash Tree and Six Mile House, where remains of pottery, ashes, slags and bones indicate husbandry and salt production; there are old English and Scandinavian names in the area that suggest flocks – Skeetholme, or dung-island, for example – and the very act of naming might indicate orderly use. Along the estuary, detached portions of parishes whose main areas were elsewhere (Fig. 6.2), existed by AD 1100 to 1150. These suggest that the salt marshes were used for grazing by parishioners whose farms were at the freshwater fen edge, but who moved flocks in summer onto the saltings. These detached portions were discontinued only in 1935 when parish boundaries were rationalised. The Domesday Book, a survey of

Fig. 6.2 Parishes fringing the lower part of the estuary inevitably included parts of its saltings, mud flats and eventually grazing marsh. More distant parishes also 'owned' parts, usually in the more distal reaches. Here the detached portions of some distant parishes are shown. Based on Williamson (1997).

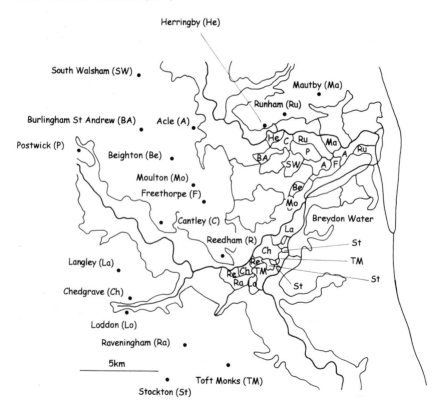

potentially taxable assets compiled in the late eleventh century, lists 1,500 sheep attributable alone to the large Abbey of St Benet's, which had grown up at the head of the saltings of the River Bure.

Back in the village, the fields on the nearby upland and the pastures at the fen edge created by cutting and burning of the alder and other trees, continued to be used in a tradition dating back to the Bronze Age farmers. The wetlands, when the river level fell in summer, could be used to graze cattle, and hay could be cut and stored towards winter needs. Native crops could be taken too. The wetlands would naturally succeed to alder and willow carrs if left (Chapter 4), but if cut, experience taught that a vegetation of reed, or of gladden (iris), or of sedge or rushes could be maintained. All of these plants were potentially useful and if the remaining alders were cut at the base (coppiced) they would shoot up over a few years into straight poles that could be used for building or fencing. Building stone was very scarce and import expensive. Flint could be used for walls but not for roofs, and poles and clay were much cheaper anyway.

The common reed that grew in the wetter parts of the fens was hard stuff. Full of silica absorbed from the water and rich in lignin, it did not rot very quickly. Scythed and bundled, it could form a watertight roof that provided insulation as well. Cutting was easiest in early winter, when the leaves had blown off, leaving just the tough stems, and removal then did not damage the new shoots, or colts, which would sprout from the peat in February. Scything every year or two would also keep down other plants, though the very competitiveness of reed brooked little competition anyway. A few hundred bundles laid overlapping would provide a very effective cottage roof, a few thousand that for a church or barn.

But the very hardness of reed stopped it being bent over the ridge of the roof. It splintered and water could penetrate to drip on the family below. The fen provided a solution. Saw sedge, sometimes called great fen-sedge, cut green in summer, would bend without breaking, even when dry. You had to be careful; it had sharp edges, not for nothing was it called saw sedge; but it too was competitive and if not cut too often would grow up in nearly pure stands. Hazel, cut from the remaining scrubby woodlands of the uplands, could be used to fix the reed and sedge in place, even to create decoration and the thatcher's trademark, along the ridge and around the doors and windows (Plate 10). Alder poles and reed fixed on frames provided fencing around the property.

Where the fen was more varied, perhaps because of reduced competition following grazing, the cut litter still had uses. It could be spread on the floor as absorbent, cheap and disposable carpeting or the animals could be bedded on it. If it had the sweet flag in it, it would even smell pleasant as feet crushed it. Rushes, peeled of all but a thin strip of their outer skin to hold them together, but leaving the internal pith, could be dried and bundled and eventually sold to be made into wicks for candles of tallow fat. Tussock sedge, which grew year by year on its previous bases, formed tall mounds among the alders, and the tussocks, cut or sliced to size, could be seats or (hard!) pillows or even church hassocks. Iris and reedmace, both called gladden, could be fashioned into mats or horse collars, bulrush into mats, willow shoots into baskets. There were plants too that would cure ills or flavour otherwise insipid stews of cereals or salted meat.

The consequences of these activities, multiplied through to the present day, give us the superficially uniform, but in fact quite varied, pattern of vegetation in the present-day fens in Broadland. The teasing out of the relationships between the environmental effects of water chemistry and patterns of local flooding, together with past management and current use and the nature of the biological community, has been a fascinating business. It is worth looking at some aspects of vegetation science to see what has been achieved.

Plant communities – sources of dispute

Plants, big or microscopic, are the bases of almost all ecosystems – the exceptions are some vents in the deep ocean where the biological community is supported by bacteria that oxidise hydrogen sulphide from deep in the Earth's crust. Collectively plants form vegetation. Vegetation is what we see, and its appearance from place to place is what we use to order the complexity of the ecological landscape. Sometimes, especially in Britain, we see obvious patterns – blocks of woodland on a valley side, swamp in the valley bottom, moorland on the hilltop above. The pioneer British ecologists of the early twentieth century, led by Arthur Tansley, seized upon this to classify vegetation into woodlands, moorlands, swamps, heaths, salt marshes, bogs and grasslands. They had a sense of boundaries, of blocks or compartments separate from one another, reflecting the local soils and climate and, sometimes, human management.

They also had a sense of change in time. They could see that bare rock, newly accumulated blown sand and deposited marine mud became colonised and the pioneer vegetation progressively developed greater complexity, a process they called succession. Sometimes this process could be perceived as a zonation on the ground as when sand dunes were forming and older and newer ones could be compared. Indeed, the transition from open water through to fringing reedswamp then alder swamp carr and drier alder carr described in Chapter 4 was one of the earliest examples they described, and called the hydrosere.

This concept of succession had been adopted from an American, Frederick Clements, who had the idea that, in a given spot, vegetation succeeded to a climax community that was more or less fixed, if human influence did not intervene, and determined by climate. The British ecologists were working in a landscape that had been divided into compartments by field boundaries and moorland walls for centuries; they nonetheless saw a certain stability and had no intellectual problem in classifying the different successions and the stages of them as a series of ecosystems. Clements, in contrast, saw the turn-of-the-nineteenth-century American landscape with vast tracts of forest and prairie, seeming uniform for miles and clearly related to the greatly contrasted climates of a huge continent. He too had no problem with classification and created a system of biomes, just big ecosystems. As knowledge grew, however, all these ideas were modified and modern understanding is much more complex and more in tune with a time when all things seem to be in a state of flux and nothing is fixed. Perhaps like those of Tansley and Clements, our view is still determined by our environment and our times.

The modern view is a compromise! Firstly it acknowledges that pristine plant communities exist as continua – there is an almost infinite number of combinations of species grading into one another as the environment steadily changes from place to place. The variety to some extent also reflects accidents of plant distribution and local extinction. One community, in which, say, alder is prevalent, will never be exactly the same as another still with alder prevalence. Secondly, despite this continuous variation, it is possible to group nearly similar units or stands so that some means of description and classification is possible.

Formerly this sort of grouping was based on the most obvious, the 'dominant' species, but dominants are dominant because they are highly competitive and have wide ranges of tolerance for different conditions. They are thus less useful as indicators of the subtler patterns – of the detail. Modern groupings use species that are consistently present, but may not necessarily be among the more abundant or voluminous, to characterise stands of vegetation. The idea of discrete types of vegetation is largely a function of the compartmentalisation of the British landscape, but nonetheless can be useful in a common-sense way.

Characterisation of different stands into detailed classification systems, using the indicator species of subtle variation, needs computer programs that can compare lists of dozens of species in hundreds of stands and recognise degrees of similarity or difference. There is a National Vegetation Classification that lists some hundreds of classes in an orderly, numbered system and that uses both the concepts of dominance and of subtle indicator species. Thus it recognises several communities characterised by reed, among them, for example, S24 *Phragmites australis–Peucedanum palustre* tall herb fen, with seven sub-communities, characterised by *Carex paniculata, Glyceria maxima, Symphytum officinale, Cicuta virosa, Carex lasiocarpa, Schoenus nigricans* or *Myrica gale*; S25, *Phragmites autralis–Eupatorium cannabinum* tall herb fen, with two sub-communities; and S26 *Phragmites australis–Urtica dioica* tall herb fen, with four sub-communities.

This sort of approach – at least 13 different sorts of what casual observers would simply call reedswamp – allows recognition of the subtleties present in the present-day vegetation of the Broadland floodplains. It aids an understanding of how variations in the environment, coupled with past and present human use and management, have come to give the complex tapestry still present, but which was probably even richer during the medieval and later period when the floodplain was very actively farmed. Abandonment of many of these practices in the last century has removed some of the former detail, but sufficient traces are still left for us to explain some of the features still remaining.

The Broadland fens

We can start by listing the sorts of factors that might determine the vegetation at a particular spot in the floodplain. These include the amount of water movement, the water level at different times of year, the concentrations of different major ions, the availability of nitrogen and phosphorus, the salinity and the sort of management. All but the latter are features that determined subtleties in the former alder forest discussed in Chapter 4. In addition, on a wider scale, the balance of evaporation and rainfall is important.

In wetter, cooler regions, as, for example, the western side of Great Britain and Ireland, where the rocks tend often to be poorly weathered and give acid soils, the early ecologists recognised that floodplain and other wet vegetation had species such as the mosses of the genus *Sphagnum*. There were also cotton-grass, heather (ling) and heaths, cranberry and crowberry and insectivorous plants such as the sundews as well as numerous small sedges. They called this vegetation 'bog'. It lays down peat prolifically, for decomposition is even slower under acid conditions than under the more alkaline waterlogged conditions found in Broadland.

There are small patches of this acid-loving community in the Broadland floodplain, usually associated with seeps of more acid water at the valley edges. This water comes from patches of glacial drift with sand rather than calcareous loam. *Sphagnum* can also develop in the alder and willow carrs, where mounds of wet litter build up and where rain leaches the major mineral ions (bases) from the surface, creating raised spots of acidity that allow *Sphagnum* to colonise. Under the shaded conditions of the former extensive carrs, *Sphagnum* may have been quite common, but when the carr is cut to create more open vegetation, evaporation and the creep upwards of base-rich ground water make it much more difficult for *Sphagnum* to grow.

The open herbaceous and grassy communities on waterlogged soils in base-rich areas, particularly in the east of England where rocks and drifts are more mineral-rich and where evaporation is high, were called 'fen' by the early ecologists. Fens, too, laid down peat, but decomposition was greater than under acid conditions so the rate of accumulation was somewhat lower. It is thus fen that dominates the Broadland floodplains, having been maintained in its open state by removal of the alder and willow from large areas. The modern synthesis tends not to use the words bog and fen, but rightly treats all such waterlogged vegetation as 'floodplain mires', with recognition of a continuous series of changes from base-poor mires at the acid end to base-rich mires at the other. Three general areas along this continuum are used in day-to-day parlance – the old term *bog* for the really acid mires, *poor fen* for those in the middle and *rich fen* for the most calcareous and base-rich. Again it is a question of finding common-sense compromises to be able to handle lots of information whilst also recognising the far more complex reality of the situation. Most of the Broadland fen types are rich fens and their subtleties are then determined by how they have been managed.

As documented earlier, the Broadland floodplains were used probably from the Bronze Age for grazing and for provision of products such as hay and reed. Settlements by the edge of the former alder carrs perhaps began by cutting wood for fuel and building, and in summer their cattle, goats and sheep would graze on the herbaceous vegetation that sprang up in the cuttings in the better light. Some of the stock might wander a little further in, perhaps down a tributary stream valley, and small alder seedlings developing on the forest floor would be nipped and killed. Grasses and sedges survive grazing by growing from their bases. Tree seedlings have their growing points high on the shoot – so do most broad-leaved plants, but many non-trees can survive grazing better by having rhizome systems or propagating annually by seed. Tree regeneration is therefore held back by grazing and once they had realised this, the graziers no doubt took advantage of the knowledge. Getting the cattle and sheep to create their own pastures was a great deal less work than cutting trees by hand with axes. There were thousands of years in which a steady encroachment on the valley carrs could take place before the almost completely open state of the fens had been established in the post-medieval period. It was a very slow but inexorable process.

There are very few places in Broadland where possible, but not certain, rem-

nants of the original carrs of Chapter 4 remain (Plate 7). Most areas now dominated by alder and willow have been open in the past, but have recolonised
with trees when cutting and grazing have ceased in the recent period. One
genuine remnant may be just south of Hoveton Great Broad, between the
Broad and the River Bure, at a place called Larkbush. It is richer in woody
species; hawthorn, alder buckthorn, purging buckthorn and holly as well as
alder and sallow, and contains the magnificent royal fern. The computer programs distinguish several other woody communities, some of them developed
on formerly cleared areas, with a greater dominance of sallow and bog-myrtle,
others with birch or alder. Table 6.1 lists the main types currently recognised
and the nature of their origin.

Water level is a particular determinant of the type of open fen vegetation.
The deeper areas in winter and spring (in summer the water table may
descend below the peat surface almost anywhere) bear communities similar to
those of the riverside reedswamps. Such deeper areas arise where the former
peat surface has been cut for fuel. The Broads themselves were cut in this way,
as will be related in the next chapter, but to much greater depths, and still
retain open water. But after the period when the Broads were dug and then
flooded in the thirteenth century, shallow peat-digging continued and in these
areas, called turf ponds, reedswamps occur, dominated by common reed, and
sometimes with bulrush or saw sedge (Fig. 6.3). Cutting of them in winter led
to reed dominance, in summer to saw sedge dominance. A reedswamp, characterised by cowbane, gives variety also to the edges of the dykes that were cut
through the fens so that the products could be brought out by boat.

Combinations of cutting and grazing in the drier areas, away from the river
or where the peat had not been excavated, resulted in conversion of the alder
carrs to a large variety of communities. These occupied the bulk of the floodplain area until very recent times and about 11 distinctive types, called associations, eight of them grouped as large-sedge/grass communities, can be
revealed by detailed work (Table 6.1). Some are in wetter spots and characterised by tussock sedge or another large sedge, the tufted sedge, on the edges
of old turf ponds and dykes and represent remnants of the successional
sequence that spanned riverside reedswamp and alder carr in the pristine system.

The remainder reflect the availability of nutrients and the past management.
Nutrient availability is the consequence of a balance between the supply and
the processes that remove nutrients from a locality. The fens are supplied by
water from springs and surface runoff at the valley edges, or from the main
rivers as they flood out in winter, or some combination of these. The valley
edges of the floodplains, apart from those of the Waveney and the southern
banks of the Yare, which have heavy boulder clays, have fertile loams that
might be expected to be rich in nutrients. Indeed they are, but the nutrients
can be held tightly in the soils and in the scrubby woodland that clothes many
of the immediate valley slopes.

Fens at the valley and river edges

The water that percolates at the edges may thus be fertile, but equally may be
much less so such that the valley edge fens can be quite poor in major ions and
nutrients and mildly acid. Such fens occur in the Ant valley and west of
Hickling Broad. They have rushes and purple moor-grass, thistles or, in more

Table 6.1 Classification of fen and carr vegetation in Broadland. The grouping follows work done by Wheeler (1980a,b,c), which took the same approach as the National Vegetation Classification, but incorporates more of the subtleties found in Broadland. Wheeler recognises eight major groupings or Alliances (in bold type) with sub-groups of these called Associations and, in the group which characterises the central parts of the Broadland fens, seven sub-associations. Only the more common or distinctive ones are listed here. Each group is named after its characteristic species and is given a Latin name based usually on this.

Alliance/Association	Notes
Phragmition	Very wet communities, often part of the unmanaged natural succession
Bulrush–reed	Natural unmanaged swamp vegetation
Saw sedge	Favoured by summer cutting
Cowbane–reed	Transitional between swamp and fen in the succession
Magnocaricion	Very wet swamp communities with large species of sedge
Tufted sedge	Edges of turf ponds and fen dykes
Tussock sedge	Tussock fen, very wet, transitional to swamp carr
Cinquefoil–bottle sedge	Low base, low nutrient fen ('poor fen') at valley edges receiving acid water from the Norwich Brickearth. Contains bog species
Angelica–reed	On abandoned, previously mown or grazed fens. Coarse, nutrient-demanding species, often flooded with nutrient-rich river water. Common in the Yare valley
Milkwort–reed	The characteristic vegetation of the Broadland fens, with several sub-associations. Well developed in the Ant valley *Typical.* Species-poor, widespread in former mowing fens *Sweet gale.* Bushes (sweet gale, willow) prominent. On solid uncut peat often on neglected saw sedge beds *False oat-grass.* Drying-out fens, river banks *Sweet-grass.* Nutrient-enriched, abandoned marshland. Common in the Yare valley *Cowbane.* Shallow, low nutrient water, restricted flow. Turf ponds in the Ant valley *Black bog-rush.* Mown fens, low nutrient conditions. Tolerant of wide range of salinity and low summer water levels. Contains several rare species. Mostly in the Ant valley, sometimes in commercial saw-sedge beds.
Reed	Reed fens, species poor, cut regularly for thatching reed in winter

Table 6.1 cont.

Alliance	Association	Notes
Saw sedge	Commercial beds, cut in summer. Species-poor but sometimes with milk parsley (and swallowtail butterflies) and the rare marsh sow-thistle	
Sweet-grass	Species-poor, tolerant of variable salinity and tidal change. Yare valley	
Caricion davallianae	Acid communities of upstream valleys	
Bulrush–blunt-flowered rush	High species diversity. Smallburgh fen is the sole example in Broadland	
Junco (subuliflori) Molinion (rush–purple moor grass)	Rush, coarse grass communities Fen margins with low base status	
Calthion palustris	Fen meadows with marsh marigold, mown for hay or used as rough pasture. (Typical of Burgh Common)	
Filipendulion	Nutrient-demanding, species-poor, coarse communities with meadowsweet. Develops when water table is lowered in enriched, abandoned grazing and mowing fens	
Willowherb–meadowsweet		
Reed–nettle		
Salicion cinerariae	Scrub and woodland fen with sallow	
Sweet gale	Successional stage	
Birch–crested buckler fern	Low nutrient, developed over shallow peat cuttings. Acid-loving successional stage following reed or reed-mace colonisation. Common in the Thurne catchment	
Birch–sweet gale	Successional to previous. More woody, more acid. Common around Upton Broad	
Sallow carr	Develops eventually on abandoned mowing fens. Low-growing, bushy thickets	
Alnion glutinosae	Swamp and fen carrs, with alder prominent in woodland vegetation. Extensive in the Bure valley	
Royal fern–alder	Mostly previously cut and coppiced but includes also terminal natural communities of floodplain succession. Management almost entirely now abandoned	

extreme cases, even some plants associated with bogs such as bogbean, cotton-grass, marsh cinquefoil, marsh St John's wort, soft rush and *Sphagnum*. These sites, fed with water from the Norwich Brickearth (see Chapter 2) are, however, comparatively unusual.

Where the water comes from very fertile soils in narrow valleys, such as that of the Muck Fleet on Burgh Common, the community is dominated by what are called fen meadows, with marsh-marigold and rushes. They were formerly mown for hay and bear shallower peats than elsewhere, perhaps because decomposition was hastened by the fertile water. In consequence, the Romano-British clay, resulting from the sea flooding 2,000 or so years ago, is close to the surface and its minerals are accessible to the plant roots.

The fens close to the main rivers receive more nutrients, especially nowadays when the rivers carry the leachates of intensive agriculture and the effluents of urban areas. Here tall, competitive species grow quickly with this rich water and a few species come to dominate, such as common reed and angelica, with willowherb, nettles and other vigorous weeds.

Fens in the middle of the floodplains

Sandwiched between the influences of the valley-edge waters and those of the main rivers is the central mass of the fens where nutrients are relatively scarcer. New supplies come in only at very high water and centuries of cutting and removal of reed, sedge or hay have depleted the stock. The general rule is that the lower the fertility, the greater the plant diversity (and the consequent diversity of invertebrates) except perhaps on the very poorest peats (not found in Broadland) where the stresses of extreme acidity may limit the range of what is able to survive. Deep in the Broadland fens, away from the rivers, communities may have as many as 50 or 60 species per hectare, including some unusual and even very rare species such as the crested buckler fern and fen orchid.

Here also *Sphagnum* may develop on tussocks of sedge or birch and it is these communities, characterised by milk parsley and reed in the computer programs, which are the most extensive of the open fens and which can be subdivided according to subtleties of location and management. Less species-rich are sedge-grass fens that are heavily managed, often by lowering of the water tables in winter or frequent cutting, or both, and which may form near monocultures of reed or saw sedge. Where these have been abandoned recently, or are only infrequently cut, they may become characterised by meadowsweet, nettles and willowherb that join the persistent reed, and eventually they become bushed over by bog-myrtle, birch, sallow and alder.

The effects of management of this central fen block in the past are being obliterated by abandonment of practices carried out over thousands of years, but modern experimentation, together with documentary accounts from the historic period, give clues as to how the vegetation was altered by it. Thus summer mowing favours sweet-grass, blunt-flowered rush, black bog-rush and purple moor-grass, but discourages big *Carex* sedges and reed, for they need to build up reserves in the leaves to supply the rhizomes from which a new start is made in the spring. Winter mowing kills saw sedge, which has long-lived perennial leaves, necessary to start the new growth in the following spring. Winter mowing favours common and purple small-reeds, for their aerial shoots are then dead and removal of what would become a dense litter allows the spring shoots an easier passage to the light. Tussock sedge was often a nuisance to mowing by scythes and was removed.

Burning in autumn removes woody plants and those with winter-green leaves, but favours plants with deep rhizomes in wet peat. Cattle grazing can promote the growth of coarse rushes and sedges over grasses and cattle tram-

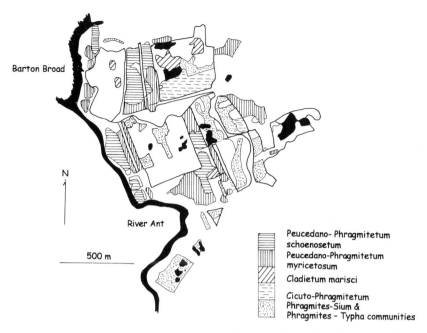

Barton Broad

N

River Ant

500 m

Peucedano- Phragmitetum schoenosetum

Peucedano-Phragmitetum myricetosum

Cladietum marisci

Cicuto-Phragmitetum Phragmites-Sium & Phragmites - Typha communities

Fig. 6.3 The open fenland is a mosaic of communities dependent on local water conditions and past and present management. Some of the pattern of communities is shown here in a section of the Catfield and Irstead fens close to Barton Broad. The heavier lines indicate the extent of shallow peat cuttings made in the eighteenth and nineteenth centuries. These wetter spots often contain the more species-rich communities. The various communities are described using a formal latinised system that uses both dominant and characteristic species. Based on Giller & Wheeler (1986).

ple out low-growing brittle plants. The mosaic of fen communities, at a casual glance a spread of mostly reed with occasional bushes, turns out to be a palimpsest – a pattern created by the physical and chemical conditions of water availability, nutrients and bases on which is superimposed the consequences first of clearance by early farmers, then of different uses and practices in different places.

Animal communities

Several features combined to make the fens a naturalist's paradise. They included the mosaic of plant communities and the diversity of plant species brought about by a management that essentially kept nutrient levels low by removing crops, year after year, without any return fertilisation. Then there were the highly specific relationships of invertebrates, particularly insects, with particular plants. Sometimes tens or more of different species may be specifically associated with a particular plant, and these are also wide-ranging.

Some groups – the butterflies and moths, the beetles and the dragonflies and damselflies – have received more attention than others, such as the spiders and dipterans, and most of the information is in the form of lists and records of occurrence. The lists are still being extended, for there continues to be a coterie of gifted, largely amateur, entomologists collecting and identifying.

Some 440 of the 860 larger moths and butterflies known from Broadland fens have been recorded for the first time since 1960 and include unusual species such as the silver barred, the rush wainscot, marbled clover, dotted and small dotted footman. There are also about 20 species of small moths of restricted distribution in the UK. Perhaps the best known butterfly, however, is the swallowtail, of a specific British race, whose caterpillars usually depend on milk parsley, a characteristic species of the open fens and saw sedge beds. The eggs are laid on the flowering stems of the milk parsley, where they are visible to the females above the general level of the vegetation. Cutting of the fens thus favoured this species.

Beetles are also very numerous: at least 200 terrestrial species were found in one well-collected area of only a few hundred hectares. One third of the British list of water beetles is associated with the fen dykes, many of them becoming quite rare elsewhere through simple loss of their habitat. The dipteran fauna also is very rich and the dragonflies and damselflies include the Norfolk aeshna, a species that does not occur elsewhere in the UK. The pond spider, which builds a 'diving bell' of silk containing an air bubble, in which it sits and waits for prey, is present in the fen dykes.

Birds of the fens are also diverse and to some extent associated with particular types. The best known have been the bearded tit, the sedge warbler and the greatly valued bittern, associated with the reed beds, and the marsh harrier. Snipe, redshank and mallard nest in the wetter mown fens and Savi's warbler is associated with areas of isolated bushes. Otters were common, indeed once controlled because of their alleged destruction of too many fish. But again, mostly we have lists and records from the past and rather little insight into how any of these animals linked into the complex ecology of the habitat.

Back to the medieval period

Our understanding, through documents, peat profiles and modern vegetation ecology shows that the valley wetlands were very valuable in the medieval period and for long before and afterwards. They were the builders' yards, chandlers and furniture stores of the medieval economy. Many of the crops were bulky, but the invention of flat-bottomed wide boats and the digging of a network of shallow dykes in the fen provided a way of getting them out. The fen produce was so valuable that by the thirteenth century, fen reeves, essentially local magistrates, had to be appointed to sort out disputes where there was disagreement over rights, or uses. Peat cutting by some people, for instance, would preclude hay or reed harvesting by others. But peat digging was clearly an important part of the domestic and industrial economy of the area. The present day Broads are the evidence of that.

Further reading

Williamson (1997) is the best reference for medieval agriculture in Broadland and Ellis (1965) and George (1992) give much information on past uses of marsh products. The considerable controversies about how to classify and describe vegetation have a large literature and it is interesting to follow the development of ideas. The two classic works are Tansley (1939), which can still be read with profit for anyone travelling around Britain who is interested in vegetation and landscape, and Clements (1928) which gives the early American view of climax vegetation. Development of the idea of continua in

Europe can be approached through Poore (1955) and in America through McIntosh (1967) and Whittaker (1967). Some of it is heavy going! The National Vegetation Classification is edited by John Rodwell and the volume relevant to this chapter is Rodwell (1995). The standard works on the Broadland fens are Wheeler (1978, 1980 a,b,c), Wheeler & Giller (1982) and Giller & Wheeler (1986). A wealth of information on the common reed is contained in Haslam (1972).

7

The Origin and Limnology of the Early Broads

To most naturalists the word 'water' will bring to mind images of fish or water birds or perhaps reeds and pondweeds. We are mesmerised by the macroscopic, but in the functioning of these, indeed of any, ecosystems it is the invisible and countless microorganisms – bacteria, fungi and algae – which are far more important. The biosphere, the embracing ecosystem of the Earth, is able to function only because half of the carbon is cycled through the algal phytoplankton of the oceans. Crucially, the cycling of nitrogen, its conversion from nitrogen gas in the atmosphere, its movement between larger organisms through decay, and its return to the atmosphere through denitrification, is almost entirely the province of bacteria.

Larger organisms may have the apparent beauty, microorganisms do most of the work! Not that microorganisms are not beautiful – the algae, in particular, are intricate and fascinating and the bacteria (Fig. 7.1) have their attractions in the versatility of their activities. Chemically they can collectively function in a far greater range of habitats, including some very extreme ones at high temperature and acidity, that defy any larger organism. To cap it all, current understanding of how the cells of all larger organisms arose is that they are collections – symbioses – of bacteria. The symbioses came together as co-operative units in response to some rather dire circumstances: the first production of a rather toxic gas, oxygen, in the atmosphere over two billion years ago.

The keys to microorganism importance are their small size, which gives a large surface area in relation to their volume and hence an ability to take up and release substances that is very efficient, and their phenomenal birth and death rates. Sometimes life is measured in only minutes, allowing a fast response to changing circumstances. By contrast, macroscopic organisms are slow and lumbering. The upshot of this preamble is that to understand the Broads themselves, both in the past and at the present, the microscope is of rather greater importance than the binoculars and the fishing net – though these too have their place.

Lakes and limnology

Freshwater lakes were once thought of as self-contained microcosms – like the vegetation, further intellectual casualties of a world view that saw boundaries. They are not at all self-contained, however, for they receive materials from their catchments and deliver others to the streams that drain them. They process carbon and nitrogen and all the other substances required for living organisms as part of a grander scheme and it is the microorganisms that are key to this. Nor are lakes uniform bodies of water like newly run cold baths. There is a structure to them, and the study of this structure and the functions that go on in it is the province of limnologists, a term derived from *limnos*, the Greek word for lake.

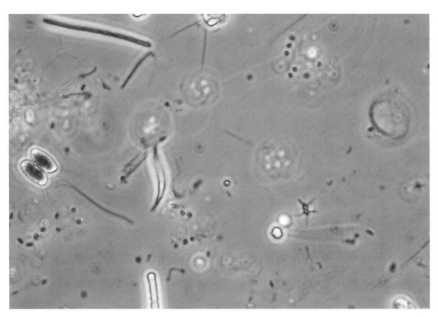

Fig. 7.1 The water of Hickling Broad has a huge variety of algae and bacteria. The paired cells with spines, and the curved large cell to the left and centre left, are algae. The remainder are bacteria, including the colonies of *Aphanothece*, a blue-green bacterium (also called blue-green algae), with tiny spherical cells, and the blue-green filament at the edge of the picture at bottom left. Bacteria that decompose organic matter include the tiny isolated spherical cells and fine rod-shaped cells and the small spined cell at centre right.

In a body of water, the amount of light dwindles rapidly as you go downwards. Only a few decimetres below the surface of even a very clear lake, the environment is one of shade. Water itself, and all the substances dissolved and suspended in it, absorb light, and moreover absorb it selectively. Of the conventional spectrum of daylight, violet and blue light, which have the shortest wavelengths and the greatest energies, penetrate furthest through pure water. Were one to descend through a lake of pure water or containing just mineral ions, the surrounding light climate would become bluer with depth as the less energetic bands of colour were filtered out. Real lake water, however, usually has dissolved yellow and brown humic substances, washed in from the soils of the catchment and produced by the decomposition of plants within the lake. These absorb the blue and violet light as effectively as the water itself absorbs the least energetic red. A descent into a real lake is thus a voyage into a gloomier and gloomier green and yellow medium (Fig. 7.2).

The flux that enters from the sun also includes very long-wave radiation, the infra-red, which is absorbed by the water very quickly and heats up the surface layers. As winter gives way to summer and the sun's angle increases, the surface lake water in north-west Europe rises in temperature from near zero to perhaps 20 to 25°C. In a shallow lake, say up to two or three metres depth, the wind is sufficient to mix this heated water downwards and the water column is said to be isothermal, but in deeper waters or very sheltered sites, the warmer water, which becomes less dense the warmer it gets above about 4°C, floats on

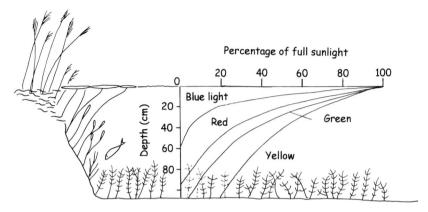

Fig. 7.2 Light is rapidly absorbed by even apparently clear lake waters, because of the coloured organic substances dissolved and the particles suspended in them. The absorption is logarithmic (exponential), with a constant percentage absorbed with every increment of depth. After a metre or so only a few percent of the surface light is left.

the colder deeper water, giving a condition called thermal stratification. The bottom water is then isolated for several months from the surface water and the atmosphere, and may become remarkably different in its chemical composition.

This deep water may become rich in substances released from bacterial decomposition in the bottom sediment and devoid of oxygen, which is used up by bacteria and cannot be replaced from the air. Even in a shallow exposed lake, hot, calm weather in summer can lead to stratified conditions that may persist for a day or two. If a lot of aquatic plants are present they can hinder mixing by wind and give a stratification that is more persistent, with oxygen-deficient conditions at the bottom of the plant beds (Fig. 7.3).

Water enters lakes from the catchment through streams, or seeps in from ground water. Former river water, described in Chapter 3, this has dissolved and suspended material in it, whose composition is determined by the nature of the catchment area. Once in a lake, it changes a little. The turbulence of the flow ceases and although the dissolved material is unchanged, the suspended matter, be it leaf litter or fine particles, falls out, usually in the delta of an inflowing stream or river. If the inflow is through ground water, filtration through the subsoils takes out any suspended matter even more efficiently.

In the more complexly structured lake environment, the biological communities are more complicated than those of rivers. There are communities of aquatic plants, behaving similarly to those already discussed in the rivers and swamps of the floodplains, and communities of microorganisms and invertebrates, processing the sediments, again much like those of the larger rivers and swamps. But in addition there is an overlying community of the plankton (Fig. 7.4), dependent very much on the amount of available nutrient in the water and on the penetration of light for its production. It has a key role, for, in an ecosystem that depends on photosynthesis and hence on light entering through the surface, it has the first bite of the cherry. The phytoplankton, the photosynthetic part of this open water community, and in particular the

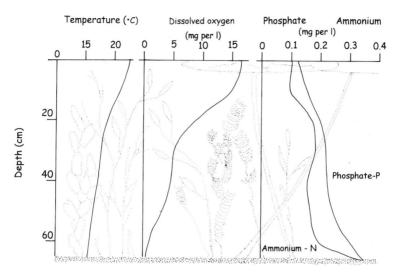

Fig. 7.3 The change with depth of temperature, dissolved oxygen, ammonium and phosphate in a shallow, plant-dominated lake. The plants inhibit wind mixing, whilst their shading of the bottom results in deoxygenated conditions and the release of ammonium and phosphate from the sediments. Based on data from Alderfen Broad in August 1983, given in Moss et al. (1986).

amount of it as well as its nature, turns out to be the central player in determining the natural history of the Broads, both soon after they were formed and subsequently. But before we discuss their role, how were the Broads formed?

The digging of the Broads

There was originally a mystery about where the Broads, over 50 of them, came from. They are not recorded in Roman writings. None of the place names in Broadland suggest large lakes, nor do the Broads appear on maps until the fifteenth century. Nonetheless, there was much speculation about a natural origin for them until the 1960s, when a spectacular coup of interdisciplinary scholarship produced a much more convincing explanation for their origin.

Earlier writers had believed the basins to be formed from streams dammed by the Romano-British marine clay (Chapter 2), or relics of the estuary isolated as lagoons on its edge by the overgrowth of vegetation. However, some peculiarities, consistent with a man-made origin had been noted by the geologist Samuel Woodward even in the nineteenth century. To anyone used to looking at natural lakes, the Broads have some strange features. They are flat bottomed, presently containing about a metre or so of water, and they lack sloping shores; sometimes they have long parallel promontories running out into them, or chains of small islands following such lines, though these have often now been destroyed by wind, wave and boat erosion. Flat bottoms and straight lines are very odd features for any natural lake.

In the 1950s and 1960s, Dr Joyce Lambert, then of the University of Cambridge, made a series of borings with a peat borer, often quite close set.

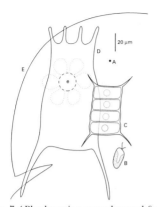

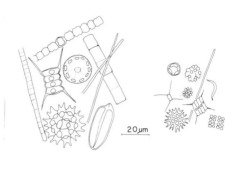

Fig. 7.4 Plankton is a complex and fascinating community. Top left shows the
huge range of size present, even in the
microscopic domain. A is a bacterium,
only 1–2 micrometres in size.
Phytoplankters (B and C) are bigger, up
to perhaps 1,00 micrometres. Some
examples are given at the top from
Wroxham Broad (left) and Hickling
Broad (right). The zooplankton includes
the rotifers (D), up to a quarter of a millimetre long and the much bigger crustaceans, of which E is the head (and e
the eye) of a water flea. The lower panel
shows three typical water fleas from
Broadland: *Daphnia hyalina* (right)
Simocephalus exspinosus (top left)and
Bosmina longirostris (bottom left). In all
but *Bosmina*, just the bases of the long
antennae that extend to either side from
just below the head, and with which the

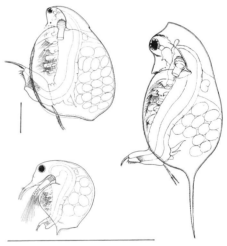

animal swims, are shown, so as not to obscure the body. The scale bars are 1 millimetre.
Top left from Moss (1998), top right from Moss (1977) and bottom from Lilljeborg (1982).

They were made through the valley deposits on transect lines from the rivers
through many of the Broads. Though the overhanging vegetation often
obscured it, the Broads had vertical or stepped edges. They were always set in
areas with little or none of the upper clay, but with thick deposits of the middle peat, in the middle sections of the valleys. Their promontories and islands
turned out to have a layering of deposits repeating that of the mainland edge
of the basin (Fig. 7.5), and sometimes the promontory deposits were compressed at the surface and covered by a layer of gravel.

It seemed clear that the basins had been cut through later surface deposits
of the upper peat and Romano-British clay, into their deeper middle peat.
Barriers, or balks, were left, as the promontories or their island remains, to separate the holdings of different people or villages or to facilitate bailing out of
the hole as water seeped in during cutting. The middle peat is often rich in the
woody remains of alder (brushwood peat) and when dried would have burned
well in domestic fires. Gravel was used to strengthen the surfaces of balks so

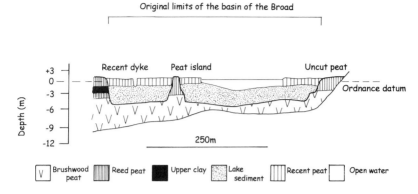

Fig. 7.5 A section across Hoveton Great Broad, on the River Bure, shows many of the features of the Broads' basins. The river is to the left, the upland to the right. Based on Lambert & Smith (1960).

that wheeled carts could be used to barrow out the peat blocks once they had been air dried.

The deposits in the basins themselves, the lake sediments, turned out to be quite unrelated to the underlying or adjacent peat and clay layers and were much more recent. The Broads must have been dug long after the Roman retreat, for the diggers cut through both the upper peat and the Romano-British clay where the clay was thin enough at its edge to present little impediment. Calculations based on the rate at which peat can be cut by hand, and the original volumes of the basins, suggest that the 900 million cubic feet (nearly 26 million cubic metres) would have taken at least 300 or 400 years to be removed, probably from the tenth to the thirteenth centuries. But who was to have performed this rather prodigious feat and why? And how has the timing been deduced?

The fertile soils of Broadland, particularly the glacial loess soils of the Flegg area between the present Rivers Thurne and Bure, supported a large population in the post-Roman Saxon period. Norwich was becoming the second largest city in England and timber for fuel was becoming increasingly scarce, as the forests were cleared, but needs for energy were increasing. Into the area, following the Viking raids, came Danish settlers, experienced and familiar with the practices of peat cutting developed over many previous centuries in their native homeland. The purported origin of the basins coincides nicely with the Viking settlement among the wood-starved Saxons.

There were a number of problems, however, with this interpretation. Firstly, was there direct evidence of peat cutting in the area and when, and could such large basins really have been cut out by hand? Secondly, how could they have been cut, to depths of often three metres or so, in a wetland? Surely there would have been severe risks of flooding? And thirdly, when were they abandoned and finally completely flooded (for there is no question that they could be worked for peat under their present lake regime)? And why were they abandoned?

Supporting evidence for peat cutting comes from documents. These are common from the later medieval period and there is much reference to turbaries, an old name for peat exploitation. They include parish records, particularly when peat was contributed as tithes, or tenths-of-the-income offerings required by the Church, and manorial accounts, where large establishments kept domestic records of their income and expenditure. In the late thirteenth century, one manor at South Walsham sold 200,000 peat turves, each about a quarter of a cubic foot in volume, each year, and tithe figures suggest similar rates of cutting at Martham and Hemsby. Norwich Cathedral Priory, supporting several hundred hungry young monks, used 400,000 turves a year in its kitchens in the early fourteenth century.

The eleventh-century Domesday Book lists many saltpans along the Broadland coasts and in the valley of the Muck Fleet where the Ormesby, Rollesby and Filby group of Broads lies. Quantities of salt were needed to preserve meat and fish over the winter when there was not enough fodder to support all the beasts reared in summer. Salt evaporation from sea water needed much fuel. There is a reference to Alderfen pyttes, now Alderfen Broad, in 1209 and the later tithe maps of some parishes show the peat fens were subdivided along lines that parallel the promontories that reached out into the Broads (Fig. 7.6).

Peat is still cut in Ireland and elsewhere using a spade or becket, which has a flange that shapes the block and cuts it on two sides, so observations can be made on how fast it can be done. There are also accounts of continued digging in the fens of Broadland even into the nineteenth century. These suggest that an acre (0.4 hectares) of fen could have been dug to about three metres, by a family for domestic purposes, in eight to 16 years depending on the wetness of the peat and access. Estimates from the Domesday Book suggest that there were at least 1,400 families around the Broadland floodplains and not even allowing for export and industrial use, calculations suggest that only about 350 years would have been needed for excavation of the basins now forming the Broads.

Fig. 7.6 Long-standing divisions of land reflect the allocation of the wetlands for peat digging and fen management centuries earlier. The tithe apportionment map of 1839 shows strips of land worked by individuals across what is now Surlingham Broad on the River Yare. Promontories extending into the Broad parallel the strips and were bunds separating workings and allowing peat to be transported out. Based on Lambert & Smith (1960).

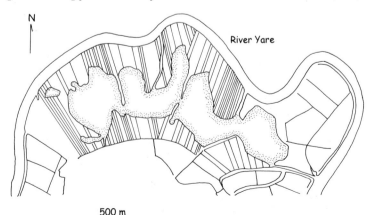

Flooding of the pits, whilst they were being worked, was less of a problem than might be thought. Our perception is determined by the fact that they are now sheets of water, connected with the rivers. At the time of their digging, however, they were isolated from the rivers and the climate may have been somewhat drier than now. Part of the evidence comes from the upper peat, formed just before and during the period when it is thought the Broads were dug. It is less structured, more humified, than the middle peat. Peat decomposes and loses its structure more if it dries out in summer, allowing more air to penetrate and bacteria to break down the remains of the plants into a more amorphous material. This suggests warmer, drier weather at the time.

At the time of their being dug, the basins were separated from the rivers and streams, often by hundreds of metres, sometimes by banks of uncut peat only a few metres wide. They were not the wide expanses suggested by the present sheets of water, but adjoining small compartments, each worked by an individual or family. The compartments were separated by banks of uncut peat and easily baled by hand or by scoops swung on poles to lift water over the banks and into the river or a nearby tributary stream. Sea level was about a metre and a half lower, in relation to the land, than it is now, and water seeps through highly compressed peat quite slowly. In winter the pits doubtless flooded from seepage and rain, perhaps to a foot or two. However, it would have been the labour of only a few days in spring to bale them out for the summer cutting before the new cut blocks were piled on the balks to be dried before being transported to the village or sold elsewhere.

There was excavation for other materials also. The beds of Martham Broad, Horsey Mere, Heigham Sound and the eastern side of Hickling Broad are set in clay. At the time this area was, of course, estuarine, and it is unlikely that the inhabitants of the local parishes would have excavated so extensively into the clay, even in a search for high-calorie brushwood peat, when a few small test pits would have established that here there was none. More likely the clay was excavated for a local pottery industry, though little evidence has yet been found of this bar the naming of the local village of Potter Heigham.

Late medieval changes

In landscape and in natural systems, little stays the same for long, at least in detail, though general traditions can last for millennia. After only a few centuries of modest development, the pictures of medieval farming described in Chapter 6, and the peat industry, were to start changing in a major way. The use of the fens and the grazing of the saltings were to continue right up to the twentieth century, but documentary records indicate that, although it too was still cut until very recently, peat began to become more expensive in the thirteenth century and the scale of the industry became greatly reduced. The population declined following the great epidemics of the Black Death around 1349, possibly caused by bubonic plague, and with it the market for peat. And the climate was changing to wetter.

These happenings are associated with the abandonment and subsequent flooding of the peat pits to form the lakes of the Broads. Documents start to mention dredging rather than digging of peat in Broadland from the fourteenth century, and 'fisheries' replace 'turbary' in the listings of local manorial wealth. The cathedral priory at Norwich was having to buy in wood, and land once described as turbary became described as fen and waterground or water and marsh. The word Broad enters documents in the sixteenth century.

When the weather worsened in the thirteenth century, there were serious floods, particularly in 1250 and 1287, documented by John of Oxnead, a monk at St Benet's Abbey. These led to the drowning of many people – 108 in Hickling alone. The pits were becoming deeper, and although there were still extensive deposits of very good, combustible peat below the floors at the time of abandonment, it may have become harder to keep them baled out. It was not possible to extend them sideways, for the fens were used for a variety of valuable products that could not be produced in peat workings because the vegetation surface was destroyed. Furthermore, following the Black Death the labour force was smaller, and peat excavation by hand was certainly labour intensive.

The worsening weather would also have made communication by trackway across and along the valleys more difficult as water tables rose. Somewhere, a peat pit spanning a valley edge village and the main river became abandoned to the extent that it filled with water to the fen surface. Perhaps in winter there was a continuous sheet of water so that a boat could be sailed across to the river. Channels had already been cut in the fens so that heavy crops of reed, gladden, sedge and hay could be brought out to the village or taken down river to sell. Someone noted that cutting of a couple of short new channels would connect village and river and give access to developing fisheries in the flooded pits. Ideas born out of necessity spread rapidly. Whatever the future weather, the Broads, now connected with the rivers, would remain permanent lakes.

New lakes, new features

Look at the current Ordnance Survey map. The distribution of Broads is much the same as in the earlier, reasonably detailed maps of William Faden, geographer to King George III, who had Norfolk surveyed and published his map in 1797, and of Andrew Bryant, whose map was published in 1824, a few years after the Ordnance Survey had begun work. Some water bodies, present on these maps, have now disappeared, but these have generally been small, very shallow pits that must have fairly rapidly filled with lilies and reeds and succeeded to fens, much like the many more recent shallow turf ponds.

The main Broads have persisted since their formation about 700 years ago. One somewhat pointless exercise is to argue about how many there are. It depends on whether different interconnected basins are counted separately or not, but Table 7.1 gives a common-sense view. In the past, what is now one sheet of water may have been subdivided and this has led to different names for different basins, as, for example, Turkey Broad, now the southernmost bay of Barton Broad. Two things stand out from the modern, more detailed, maps. Firstly, all the Broads lie in the middle, floodplain sections of the rivers and secondly some lie at the sides of the rivers, others along the lines of tributary streams (Plates 11 and 12). Barton Broad is an apparent exception, lying along the line of a main river.

The placing of the Broads in the floodplains coincides for the most part with the location of substantial deposits of the middle peat close to the surface. There are few Broads, Oulton and the group around Hickling being the exceptions, close to the sea, for there the peat is usually overlain by thick deposits of marine clay. Horsey Mere, Martham Broad and part of Hickling Broad may-have been excavated partly for clay and partly for peat at their distal ends.

Table 7.1 The present-day Broads

Name	Area (ha)	Depth (m)	Hydrology
River Ant			
Alderfen	5.1	1.0	Landlocked following isolation
Barton	77.3	1.5	On main river
(including Turkey)			
Catfield	1.2	0.5	Landlocked
Crome's	4.3	0.8	Landlocked
Sutton		1.5	Channels only
River Bure			
Belaugh	1.9	0.5	Dyke to main river
Bridge	2.8	1.3	Dyke to main river
Burntfen	4.6	1.0	Dyke to main river
			Stream from upland
Cockshoot	5.3	1.0	Stream fed, blocked to main river
Decoy	10.0	1.5	Dyke to main river
Hoveton Great	24.9	1.0	Dyke to main river
Hoveton Little	19.9	1.2	Dyke to main river
(also called Blackhorse)			
Hudsons bay	4.5	0.8	Dyke to main river
Malthouse	11.1	1.5	Dyke to main river
Mautby Decoy	2.5	1.0	Stream fed
Norton's	0.7	0.8	Dyke to main river
Ranworth	28.9	1.2	Dyke to main river
Salhouse (Great)	12.2	1.5	Linked with main river
Salhouse Little	0.5	1.0	Linked with main river
Snape's water	2.5	0.5	Dyke to main river
Sotshole	1.3	0.5	Dyke to S. Walsham Broad
South Walsham	20.8	1.3	Dyke to main river
Upton Broad	6.9	0.8	Landlocked
Muck Fleet			
Filby	41.9	2.0	Connected with other Broads
			Blocked from river
Little	1.3	0.8	Linked with stream
			Blocked from main river
Mautby Decoy	2.5	1.0	Stream fed
Ormesby N. Broad	56.4	2.5	Stream fed. Blocked from main river
Ormesby Little	49	2.5	Linked with Filby and Rollesby
			Broads
			Blocked to main river
Rollesby	26	1.3	Linked with Rollesby
			Blocked to main river
Lily	13	1.0	Stream fed. Linked to Rollesby
River Thurne			
Blackfleet	1.6	0.5	Isolated in fens
Calthorpe	1.2	0.5	Landlocked
Heigham Sound	34.4	1.3	Dyke to river
Hickling	141	1.3	Dyke to Heigham Sound
Horsey Mere	32.8	1.5	Linked to Heigham Sound
Martham (N and S)	16.0	1.0	Linked with main river
Womack Water	1.3	1.5	Dyke to main river

Table 7.1 cont. The present-day Broads

Name	Area (ha)	Depth (m)	Hydrology
River Waveney			
Barnby	2.5	0.5	Landlocked
Flixton Decoy	7.0	0.5	Landlocked, outflow to river
Fritton Decoy	60.7	2.5	Landlocked
Oulton Broad	35.6	1.3	Dyke to main river
			Locks to sea
River Yare			
Brundall Inner/Outer	1.8	1.2	Outer open to river
			Inner semi-isolated
Buckenham/			
Hassingham	4.6	2.0/0.5	Dyke to river blocked
Rockland	20.8	1.0	Dyke to river
Strumpshaw	1.0	1.5	Dyke to river now blocked
Surlingham/	14.4	0.5	Dyke to river
Bargate			
Wheatfen	4.0	0.5	Linked with Rockland

There are some small Broads at the upper end of the floodplain reach, but none as the valleys narrow upstream, and swifter flowing gravel-bottomed rivers gave no opportunity for peat accumulation. There are notably fewer Broads along the Rivers Yare and Waveney. This is understandable because the Romano-British clay deposits are thick well up these rivers and the opportunities for peat excavation only lay at the upper ends of the floodplains, where the peat is close to the surface. The Yare has probably always been the most tidal of the rivers and only far upstream would the erosive power of rising tides least threaten any riverside peat balks.

Within the middle floodplain reaches, locations close to the river would have provided the deeper layers of peat, compared with places at the valley edges, but would have stood more risk of breaching and flooding from the river. Nonetheless the risks were apparently worth it, for Broads such as Wroxham, Hoveton Great, Hoveton Little, Salhouse and Decoy in the Bure valley lie close to the main channel. Salhouse Broad and parts of Wroxham Broad, at the upper end of the reach, abut onto the mineral soils of the valley edge. These Broads are separated from the river by narrow bunds in places and where these have been breached in recent times, the Broad has become almost a widening of the river. This is somewhat ironic for one former idea was that the origin of the Broads was as natural widenings or broadenings of the river channel.

Lower down the Bure floodplain, the Broads are placed further from the main channel and are connected with it by quite long dykes. This too reflects the depth of usable peat below the surface. Below Horning, where Broads such as Ranworth, Malthouse and South Walsham lie, the clay is thick close to the river and only thins sufficiently for there to be access to the underlying peat half a kilometre or more inland. At the time of their formation all of these Broads would have been much more isolated from the river than at present. The wide dykes now connecting them with the rivers are old features, but probably at least 200 years younger than the flooded basins themselves. They would have been connected by more modest channels or not at all in the early stages.

The model for the early Broads would be more like the isolated Upton Broad in the Bure valley or the very small Broads, such as Barnby Broad, close to the River Waveney and linked with it by thin channels. The anomaly of Barton Broad is easy to explain. It could not have been excavated with the River Ant running through it and indeed it was not; the river at the time took a winding course to the east of the Broad, bypassing it in the same way as the Bure bypasses its Broads. The river was diverted through the Broad much later.

The side-valley Broads such as the Ormesby, Rollesby and Filby group, Burntfen Broad, Fritton Decoy and Flixton Decoy are really not fundamentally different from the bypassed Broads. Their pits would originally have closely flanked both sides of small tributary streams that never offered too much of a flood risk and that simply merged with the Broad as water levels rose. Hickling Broad, Horsey Mere and Martham Broad rather defy classification for they were constructed alongside a small separate river system that was realigned some centuries later. Probably they were made alongside the former River Thurne, which then flowed in the opposite direction to the present, and had an estuary on the nearby coast, near Martham Broad. It would have been a small stream, though it is also possible that it took the River Bure water before realignment of the latter and was not insubstantial. Hickling Broad and Horsey Mere were probably side-valley Broads on very small tributaries, but Martham was bypassed by the main channel flow. The estuary close to them must also have been partly blocked by sand in the medieval period for it would not have been possible to excavate the clay unless it was above low tide level and the balks could withstand high tides.

Early limnology of the Broads

The early Broads were thus much more isolated than they are now, some with small channels to the river, others in contact perhaps only during the winter floods. They were surrounded by open fens, cleared for the most part of the ancient alder carrs, windswept, fringed by reedswamp and lilies, and, like the rivers, very low in nutrients, but rich in calcium and bicarbonate. They had very clear water allowing their bottoms, two to four metres deep and covered with low-growing plants, in particular the charophytes, to be visible from a boat (Plate 13). But just how do we know this? The chroniclers of the time were much more preoccupied with documenting the flow of cash and inheritance to have bothered with the minutiae of flooded peat pits.

The answer is several-fold. Firstly, the sediments, laid down year by year in lakes, preserve in their chemistry and the remains of former organisms, many clues to the history of a lake. There is a well-developed science of palaeolimnology, which examines and interprets this evidence. Secondly, we can draw parallels from lakes in similar situations elsewhere that have not been changed so much in recent years as have the Broads. Lastly, because we now have a reasonable understanding of how ecosystems work and a great deal of experience, it is possible to make deductions and inferences that would not have been possible until recently.

Coring the sediment

It is not difficult to take from the Broads, cores of sediment that extend down through the lake deposits into the basal peat and contain a complete historical record to the present day. All that is needed is a section, about three to four metres long, of plastic water pipe, about 8 to 10 centimetres in diameter, sliced longitudinally in half and then firmly taped back together with waterproof tape. It helps if the bottom end is sharpened for easy penetration, for you stand in a very well-anchored boat, eventually on the thwarts of it, and push the tube as far into the deposits as it will go (Plate 14). A change in firmness can be sensed as the peat is reached, for the peat is less watery than the lake sediment.

The pipe must then be pulled up, a somewhat tricky technique when standing on the thwarts of a small boat. The sediment will start to slip out unless there is a firm plug of peat, at least five centimetres long, at the bottom and as the bottom of the tube comes close to the water surface a rubber bung must be rammed in before the peat plug is pushed out by the weight of a metre or two of sediment and one or more of water in the tube.

You must then carefully pour out the overlying water without disturbing the sediment. Such manoeuvres can be hazardous but I should say that I have survived a large number of these operations, with dry humour if sodden clothes.

The next stage is always fascinating. You take a sharp knife or razor – the old cut-throat ones are best – and carefully slice along the tape holding the tube together on one side. Then you open the core along the hinge of the tape on the other side like opening a lid from a box, and displayed before you will be several centuries of ecological history (Plate 15). Sometimes it will appear as several shades of amorphous dark brown and you will have to wait for more detailed analysis to learn very much. More usually in the Broads you will be presented with a sequence of different coloured layers like a block of Neapolitan ice cream.

At the bottom will be peat, coarse in texture with fibrous remains, and soft bits of old alder twigs. The peat will be dark brown in colour, lighter if there is a lot of alder in it. This is the brushwood peat sought for drying and burning by the peat diggers. On top of the peat will be a beige-brown layer, only a centimetre or two deep. This is where thirteenth-century burrowing invertebrates have mixed the top layer of peat with the first of the lake sediments. Then there is often a whitish-grey layer, often occupying half of the remaining core, full of tiny tubes, each a couple of millimetres long and less than a millimetre thick (Fig. 7.7). There may be snail shells, and the material will have a satisfying crunchy texture when you slice it, with a palette knife, into sections for analysis. This is the evidence of what the Broads were first like; the remaining, more recent sediment is brown, black and amorphous and I will deal with it in Chapter 12.

Analysing the sediment

A lot of information can be gleaned from very simple analysis of the sediment. The core slices, usually taken every centimetre, are carefully stored in plastic bags at just above freezing point and small parts are removed for various analyses. Subtle changes can be seen just from changes in water content by drying in a 100°C oven and re-weighing a few grams of wet sediment. The more rapidly sediment is laid down, the less it is consolidated and the wetter it is. Burning the dried sediment at 400°C removes organic matter and leaves just mineral ash. This can tell stories of inorganic river silt moving in and of the deposition of lime, usually called marl, which is mostly laid down through the activities of plants and algae in the water. Finally, heating the sediment at 900°C can drive

Fig. 7.7 Profiles of the lake sediments in Broadland. The locations of the cores used to construct the profiles are shown to the right. Based on Osborne & Moss (1977) and Moss (1980, 1988).

off carbon dioxide from carbonates and give a reasonable calculation of the amount of marl as opposed to siliceous grains and iron oxides derived from the catchment soils. In the earliest sediments of most of the Broads, especially those fed ultimately by the Rivers Bure and Yare, which rise on the chalk in the west of Norfolk, it is marl that dominates.

Marl formation

Marl is mostly calcium carbonate with substantial amounts of magnesium, iron and other carbonates as well. It can be formed in fresh waters simply through chemical equilibria, but mostly through biological reactions in calcium-rich water. As rain penetrates chalk rock or chalky glacial drift, it is charged with large amounts of carbon dioxide dissolved from the soil, where it has been produced by the respiration of soil bacteria. Dissolved carbon dioxide forms a weak acid that dissolves the chalk as calcium bicarbonate, $CaHCO_3$, which is much more soluble than calcium carbonate, $CaCO_3$:

$$CaCO_3 + H_2O + CO_2 \longrightarrow Ca\,(HCO_3)_2 \text{ or strictly } Ca^{++} \text{ ions and}$$
HCO_3^- (bicarbonate) ions.

The amount of carbon dioxide dissolved in the soil water, however, is much greater than that which can indefinitely stay in the water in contact with the atmosphere. The atmosphere has a low concentration and surplus in the water, even loosely combined as excess bicarbonate, must eventually return to the atmosphere to maintain a simple physical gas equilibrium. As the calcium bicarbonate-rich water emerges from the ground water into the river and flows downstream, this return to equilibrium takes place. Very fine particles of marl are formed in the water, by a reversal of the equation above, sometimes giving the water a pearly or slightly milky appearance. Eventually the marl particles settle out as a very fine floc.

The process can be hastened, and even overshot, however, by the action of plants and algae. Some can absorb and use only carbon dioxide for photosynthesis; others can use bicarbonate ions as well. There is an interesting evolutionary story behind this. Algae evolved in water and most can take advantage of bicarbonate, which is generally much more abundant than free dissolved carbon dioxide. Natural selection will have favoured those able to use bicarbonate, except in those very acid waters of the igneous uplands and sandy plains, where there is little or no dissolved bicarbonate in the water.

The flowering plants evolved and diversified on land, where only atmospheric carbon dioxide was available for photosynthesis, and the colonisation of fresh waters by flowering plants has been a relatively recent event of the last 50 million years or so. Many aquatic flowering plants have not yet developed the ability to use bicarbonate or have it to only a limited extent, but some, especially those in calcareous waters and the periphyton algae that cover them, have the ability to a high extent. The evidence is in the roughness of their leaves or even visible grey deposits of marl covering their surfaces. The charophytes, a group of large algae that evolved much earlier from the same microalgal ancestors as flowering plants, often deposit so much marl as to gain them their alternative common name of stoneworts.

Marl formation by plants and algae

What happens is that the bicarbonate-using plants and algae more than reverse the process described above that took place in the soils and ground waters of the catchment. Carbon dioxide is split from the bicarbonate that is otherwise able to exist in equilibrium with the atmosphere by enzymes (the protein catalysts of all reactions in cells) to release carbon dioxide at the cell surface for use in photosynthesis:

$$Ca^{++} + 2\ HCO_3^- \longrightarrow CO_2 + H_2O + CaCO_3$$

Calcium carbonate is rather insoluble in water and precipitates out as more marl. But then the proportions of carbon dioxide and bicarbonate readjust to form more bicarbonate. The chemistry of carbon dioxide, bicarbonate and dissolved carbonate ions and the hydrogen ions that are produced from water is quite complex and interlinked:

$$CO_2 + H_2O <\longrightarrow> H_2CO_3 <\longrightarrow> HCO_3^- + H^+ <\longrightarrow> CO_3^{--} + 2\ H^+$$

The arrows pointing in both directions indicate that the reactions can move in either direction until a chemical equilibrium is established.

The proportions of carbon dioxide, bicarbonate and carbonate that can exist together in the water in such an equilibrium are governed by the acidity of the water, measured as the amount of hydrogen ions (H^+) and expressed as pH. The more H^+ (low pH) the less carbonate, the less H^+ the more carbonate. At pH values below 4.5, carbonate is not stable and there is virtually no bicarbonate. The carbon is mostly in the form of free carbon dioxide or bicarbonic acid (H_2CO_3), in a loose combination with water; at above pH 8.4, there is an increasing proportion of carbonate and virtually no free carbon dioxide. Between pH 4.5 and pH 8.4, bicarbonate dominates, with no carbonate and decreasing proportions of free carbon dioxide as the pH increases.

As plants and algae first remove carbon dioxide, then start on the bicarbonate, they cause changes in the chemical equilibria. The different forms of carbon immediately begin to reinstate the equilibrium and some carbonate starts to change into bicarbonate and some bicarbonate reacts to form carbon dioxide. But in doing this the amounts of hydrogen ion also change and H^+ is reduced in amount. The pH thus rises and favours more of the remaining carbon being present as bicarbonate and carbonate. The outcome is that carbon disappears from the water in absolute terms as it is taken up into the plants and algae, and of the carbon that is left, more is in the form of carbonate, with pH values that can rise to 9 or more. Such a situation is, however, unstable, for carbonate cannot remain dissolved in water that has more than a minimal amount of calcium, magnesium and iron in it. The metals and the carbonate combine and precipitate the poorly soluble carbonates – hence the often heavy marl deposits on the plants.

Charophytes

The tiny tubes in the early sediments of the Broads are largely the casts of marl that formed around the stems of the stoneworts that dominated the bottoms of the Broads in their first few centuries. We know they were charophytes because no other group of plants forms such regular tubes – the marl deposited on others tends to crumble on death of the plant – and because we also find

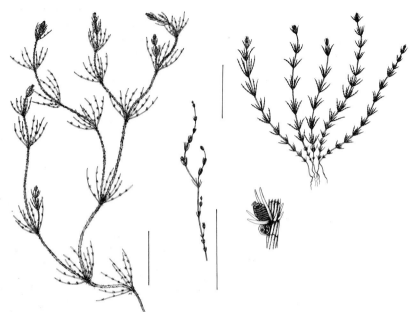

Fig. 7.8 Charophytes have a characteristic structure in which long, thin, single cells, centimetres long, form the main axis, punctuated at intervals by plates of smaller cells, the
nodes, from which similarly structured branches arise in whorls. *Chara hispida* var. *major*
(left) is a large species reaching up to 90 centimetres. As with most of the species it produces characteristic oospores (bottom right) in the axils of the branches. These are originally eggs, fertilised by spermatozoids that are released into the water from adjacent rounded structures (also shown in the drawing). The oospores are often preserved, with a coating
of marl in sediments, together with tubes of marl that originally coated the stems. Smaller
species include *Chara vulgaris* var. *crassicaulis* (centre), which is a rare variety of the much
commoner *Chara vulgaris* var. *vulgaris* and *Chara aspera* (top right), which covered much of
Hickling Broad in the late nineteenth century. The scale bars are 5 centimetres. Drawings
by Margaret Tebbs from Moore (1986).

the preserved oospores of charophytes in the sediments. So what exactly are
charophytes (Fig. 7.8) and do they have some particular significance?

Charophytes are large algae, sometimes up to a metre high, often only a
decimetre or two. They have colourless threads of cells called rhizoids that
anchor them in sediment and may, like roots, absorb nutrients, though the
green portion above the sediment can also absorb nutrients. They have long
'stems', at intervals along which are whorls of branches, that may themselves
have similar whorls. The stems are long single cells, several centimetres in
length and up to a millimetre or so wide, and are among the largest cells of all
organisms. At the points where the whorls of branches emerge there is a plate
of smaller cells called a node, and from these cells the branches, which have a
similar basic structure of long single cells interrupted by nodes, emerge. In
some species, cells emerge from the nodes and appear to creep up the main
axial cell like vines around a tree and the nature and presence of these cells is
one of the features distinguishing the different species.

From time to time, structures are produced from the nodes which are
egg-shaped and contain either spermatozoids (male sex cells or gametes) or

oogonia (eggs, female gametes). These structures are often rich in orange carotenoid pigments and are very obvious. Some species are annuals; sperma-tozoids are released and fertilise the oogonia, which are then called oospores and acquire a thick coating of marl and fall into the sediment to germinate into a new plant in the next year. Other species are perennial and persist as green plants in winter, reproducing sexually, but building up a bank of oospores in the sediment that germinate when a suitable space is created by damage to older plants.

The charophytes are classified as algae because the cells that produce the gametes are not surrounded by a sheath of non-reproducing cells; they are said to be naked, whilst other plants do have such a sheath – the wall of the ovary or anther in flowering plants, for example. The charophytes, nonetheless, have many features similar to the mosses and liverworts and their spermatozoids are very similar to those both of these and of ferns. It was from within the same group of green algae that both the charophytes and the ancestors of all the green plants were drawn.

There are only a few genera of charophytes, *Chara*, *Nitella*, *Nitellopsis* and *Tolypella*, and all were probably present in the early Broads, with at least ten dif-ferent *Chara* species. The Broads were one of the main centres of occurrence of this group in Britain. In general the charophytes require very clear water, for reasons that are not obvious, and such clear water is only achievable if the supply of nutrients from the catchment is low. Low nutrient supplies mean that the suspended phytoplankton algae are strongly limited in their growth and therefore scarce, though always present to some extent, whilst the periphyton – the algal community that coats surfaces underwater, including those of plants – is also thin for similar reasons.

The importance of nutrient limitation

The early Broads would have been low in the key nutrients, nitrogen and phos-phorus. The catchments, although cultivated in parts, still had much woodland and semi-natural grassland and were not heavily fertilised. The only fertiliser was that from the stock grazed on them, which essentially recycled the limited amount available. The Broads were connected to the rivers, which brought such nutrients as were leached from the land, mostly by small dykes that allowed only limited interchange of water. They were surrounded by fens full of nutrient- especially nitrogen-hungry plants that mopped up most of any incoming supply.

Microalgae in the phytoplankton and periphyton had a hard time of it. In the early Broads' sediments we find the siliceous spores of a group of algae called the chrysophytes, which, as their name suggests (Greek *chrysos*, yellow, as in *Chrysanthemum*) have abundant yellow carotenoid pigments, giving them an olive-green or brownish colour. They are most diverse in nutrient-poor waters. Chemical analysis of the sediments reveals only small amounts of phos-phorus compounds and of organic matter. The charophytes can absorb nutri-ents from the sediments and therefore had an edge over the phytoplankton and periphyton.

Comparison with lakes that are currently still very clear and dominated by charophytes, for example Malham Tarn in Yorkshire and the Bosherston Lily Ponds in Pembrokeshire, as well as Upton Broad and Martham Broad, suggests that the concentrations of phosphorus in the water, in all forms – dissolved, suspended, organic and inorganic – was much less than 50 micrograms per litre and probably less than 25 micrograms per litre. These values might mean more if compared with an average soil that has more than a million times as much. Concentrations of nitrogen compounds were equally low. We could expect a maximum of perhaps 250 micrograms of nitrogen per litre in winter and undetectable amounts in summer when the plants were growing and removing ammonium and nitrate from the water.

The sediment in a freshwater lake is a sort of soil, of course, and accumulates much greater amounts of nutrients, especially phosphorus, than are present in the overlying water. Some of the supply comes in from suspended silt, other as animal faeces – from the zooplankton animals, as they graze the phytoplankton and produce a continuous rain to the bottom. There are also fish and bird droppings. Some comes as phytoplankton cells simply sinking out and as periphyton disturbed in their feeding by snails and other invertebrates; and in calcium-rich lakes phosphorus may easily be precipitated out as calcium phosphate, the rather insoluble stuff of bones and teeth. Not much nitrogen stays in the sediment, for the same bacteria that eventually convert nitrogen compounds to nitrogen in wetland floodplain soils do much the same in lake sediments, but phosphorus can accumulate.

In the sediments, phosphorus is available to rooted plants and those with rhizoids such as the charophytes, but not to the free-living algae suspended in the water. Phosphorus readily combines with iron, calcium and manganese to form poorly soluble salts under oxygenated conditions and at the sediment surface a brownish oxidised crust of these salts forms, called the oxidised microzone. This forms a barrier to diffusion of phosphates back into the overlying water. The brown colour, essentially rust, comes particularly from oxidised ferric iron. Below the top few millimetres of the sediment, however, bacterial action removes oxygen and creates anaerobic conditions because new oxygen simply cannot diffuse back into the sediments nearly as fast as the bacteria use it up. In anaerobic conditions, the oxidised iron and other compounds of phosphorus are converted to much more soluble reduced ones and there is plenty of free phosphate in the interstitial water between the sediment particles. It is accessible to the plant roots and rhizoids, but cannot easily diffuse through the oxidised microzone into the overlying water (Fig. 7.9).

In spring, therefore, in a charophyte-dominated lake, the scarcity of phosphorus in the water limits algal growth in the plankton or as periphyton, whilst the rooted plants and charophytes can draw on supplies in the sediment. They are thus able to exploit the available nitrogen in the water and achieve substantial growth, whilst at the same time making conditions even more stringent for the free-living algae. Little phytoplankton can grow and the water remains clear.

In such lakes nitrogen becomes undetectable in summer. Some ammonium is released by excretion of the animals, but it is immediately snapped up by the plants. Supplies from the catchment are negligible as river flows decrease and it is not until the winter floods that the nitrogen supply is renewed for the following spring. In late summer, as the beds of plants reach their densest and plant material at the base of the beds starts to die and slough off, the water just above the sediment may become oxygen-deficient and the oxidised microzone may break down, allowing some phosphorus to diffuse into the water. But by then it is too late for the phytoplankton to take advantage of it, for nitrogen is

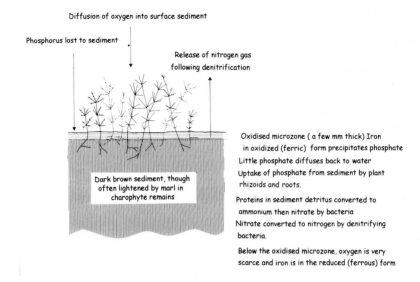

Very clear water. Nutrient shortage limits phytoplankton growth.
Plant community of charophytes and other slow-growing species.
Charophytes may secrete algal inhibitory substances. Plants
obtain phosphorus from the sediment, nitrogen from the water,
but as supplies are low, production is limited

Diffusion of oxygen into surface sediment

Phosphorus lost to sediment

Release of nitrogen gas
following denitrification

Dark brown sediment, though
often lightened by marl in
charophyte remains

Oxidised microzone (a few mm thick) Iron
in oxidized (ferric) form precipitates phosphate
Little phosphate diffuses back to water
Uptake of phosphate from sediment by plant
rhizoids and roots.
Proteins in sediment detritus converted to
ammonium then nitrate by bacteria
Nitrate converted to nitrogen by denitrifying
bacteria.

Below the oxidised microzone, oxygen is very
scarce and iron is in the reduced (ferrous) form

Fig. 7.9 Exchanges between sediment and water in the Broads early in their history. The sediment was of marl, the plant community a diverse one of charophytes and the water low in nutrients. The oxidised microzone prevented much release of phosphate to the water, and the phosphate in the sediment was quite tightly held in both iron and calcium compounds. Plant production was low because nitrogen supplies were also limited.

now strongly limiting, and without supplies of both nitrogen and phosphorus, growth is not possible. Moreover, the season for growth is ending as the days shorten and temperatures fall.

The phytoplankton and periphyton may also have had their growth suppressed by a process called allelopathy, Greek for 'damage to others'. At least in laboratory experiments, aquatic plants including the charophytes secrete organic substances, whose nature is largely unknown, that inhibit microalgal growth – they are natural algicides. Charophyte-dominated lakes are often exceptionally clear and it may be the extra help of these inhibitors, on top of the mechanisms preventing the microalgae from getting much nitrogen and phosphorus, that promotes this.

The early Broads, a summary

The early Broads, as deduced from the evidence of their sediments and comparisons with lakes still dominated by charophytes, were thus extremely clear, and nutrient-poor, with phytoplankton limited by supplies of phosphorus in spring and nitrogen in summer. The bottom-growing charophytes and the vascular plants present, were limited largely by nitrogen supplies. The plants were largely clean of periphyton growth, for although these algae can sometimes take advantage of small supplies of nutrients leaking from plants damaged by grazing invertebrates and birds, they too were generally starved of nutrients. The waters were deeper than now because sediment has steadily accumulated and would have been two or three metres deep, with precipitous edges where the peat cutters had left vertical or stepped faces. This would have inhibited invasion of reedswamp plants, though floating hovers could have formed. To a large extent, however, these would have depended on dissolved nutrients in the water for their growth and they could not have been vigorous.

From the ground, most of the Broads were hidden behind the fen vegetation, accessible only to birds, fish and fishermen poling their boats through the narrow channels. A descendent of our Mesolithic sparrowhawk would have seen lakes often still internally subdivided by old peat balks, and when the sun shone in winter the bottoms of the Broads would have been a patchwork of the winter-green charophytes and the grey whiteness of bare marl sediments. In wet winters the lakes would have increased greatly in size as the floodplain filled and the fish would have moved out, eventually to feed and spawn in the decaying litter of the fens and reedswamps. Then, in late spring, as the water levels fell to isolate the lakes and rivers again, they would have been forced to retreat to the deeper waters of the main river channels and the Broads.

There, in the early summer, mayhem would have reigned as enormous numbers of young pike began to feed on the young of other fish and on each other until, after a few weeks, the stocks had been reduced to the limited carrying capacity of the remaining water space. It was a system that can still be seen in the remaining great floodplains of the world. The Florida Everglades dry out in summer and fish, snakes and birds congregate in the deep sloughs kept open by alligators to await the spreading waters of the winter rains. In the Pongolo valley of KwaZulu-Natal, South Africa, the Tembe Tongan tribesmen take advantage of the movements of the fish on the rising and falling floods to reap a harvest essential for their survival. But in the Broads it was a system that would soon be constrained and then lost. Historic ignorance took more and more of its resources, leaving a legacy in the black, amorphous sediments that were to take over from the grey marls in the sediment cores after only a few centuries.

Further reading

The classic work on the origin of the Broads is Lambert et al. (1960). It contains much detail of peat borings and historical evidence. It is very much the epitome of the value of an interdisciplinary approach. Shorter, very accessible versions are in the chapter by Lambert in Ellis (1965) and in a *New Scientist* article by Lambert & Smith (1960). I particularly cherish the latter, for I still have a yellowing copy culled from the magazine when I was in the sixth form. At the time I had no idea I would ever have any further connection with the Broads, but the clarity of its writing and the sheer magic of the study were immediately appealing. The early maps of Norfolk of Faden and Bryant are reproduced in Barringer (1989 and 1998). Moss (1998) will give an introduction to the extensive literature of limnology, and the fruits of many wet and muddy days discovering the early history of the Broads through sediment cores are to be found in Moss (1978, 1979, 1980, 1988), Osborne & Moss (1977) and Moss et al. (1979).

8

Broadland from the Normans to Victoria

1066 and all that

The digging of the peat pits that were to become the Broads was steadily progressing. A tentative date for the start of digging can be calculated as the ninth century. This comes from surveys of their fullest extent, the rate at which peat could be removed by the local population in the medieval period, and the records of the floods of the thirteenth century. The Danes thus saw the start, indeed probably made the start, and the Normans saw the end. The year 1066 is (or used to be for older generations) more or less engraved on every British memory as that of the Battle of Hastings, when William of Normandy defeated the Saxon army and went on to annex England. What did this mean for Broadland?

In England as a whole it meant the imposition of a harsh new regime in which a former rich culture was ruthlessly suppressed. A contemporary observer, Odericus Vitalis, wrote that: 'the native inhabitants were crushed, imprisoned, disinherited, banished and scattered beyond the limits of their own country'. Through a new power group of Normans, French and Flemings, William controlled the land with 5,000 knights and their castles. He began a period in which England would be taxed and exploited and its wealth expended in acquisition through war, then defence and sustenance, of a mainland European kingdom, not finally lost until 1558.

There are advantages in such times to being tucked away in the nether reaches of the land. The rural lifestyle of Flegg and Lothingland, the estuary saltings and the river valleys of Broadland went on relatively undisturbed. Eventually William's surveyors came around, doubtless meeting suspicion by asking questions about ownership, assets and activities whose answers were to comprise the Domesday Book of potentially taxable property in 1086. In Norwich the newly twinned forces of Church and State were displaying their powers in the form of cathedral expansion and castle-building late in the eleventh century. Word got around that there were new rulers, the coinage had a new head, but the agrarian regime was less affected than that in areas closer to the centres of power. This latest bunch of invaders established a new feudal system with lords, freemen, smallholders, cottagers and slave-like serfs and gained their glory retrospectively, in the usual propaganda of the victors.

Expansion of the monasteries

There was nonetheless a tangible influence, not least in the large numbers of churches built in Broadland, and in the establishment or expansion of many religious houses (Fig. 8.1), with their acquisition of lands. They were not necessarily original. The monastery of St Benet's, in the valley of the River Bure,

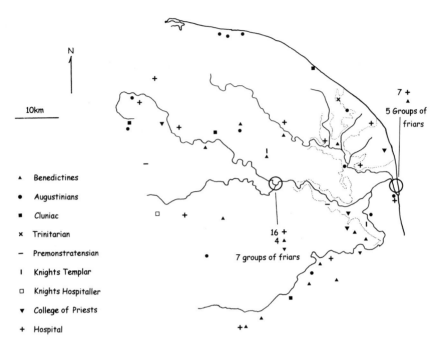

Fig. 8.1 Monasteries and other religious foundations proliferated in Norfolk, as elsewhere, in the medieval period. Based on Wade-Martins (1994) and Dymond & Martin (1999).

was founded for the Benedictines in 1019 by the last Danish king, Cnut, nearly half a century before the Norman invasion. Almost every new religious building was based on a previous church.

The Broadland expansion has its wetland parallels at Ramsey and Ely in the Wash fenlands and Glastonbury in the Somerset levels. Between 1066 and 1154, the number of religious houses in England increased sixfold to over 300 and the Church then owned a quarter of the land. Monastic houses had gone into decline in the late Saxon period, but were revived by the Norman barons, doubtless fearful for their souls, following the gains of land they had acquired by not entirely laudable means. The isolation of the wetlands allowed communities to be minimally distracted by the secular influences of the town and gave strong defensive positions for communities that accumulated much wealth.

The religious houses were hand in glove with the Norman power base and chose locations with profitable lands to annex nearby; farming wealth was necessary to support communities of several hundreds of people. Broadland houses were founded in the Yare valley at Langley by the strictly vegetarian Praemonstratensians in the late twelfth century, and at St Olaves and Acle in the thirteenth, and persisted until Henry VIII dissolved almost all of them nearly half a millennium hence in the sixteenth century. There were foundations also: at Ingham in 1355 by the Trinitarians; at Haddiscoe by the Knights Templars; at three places by the Augustinians and at seven, including Horsham St Faiths, by the Benedictines.

Little or nothing remains of most of these houses, but where it does, it is

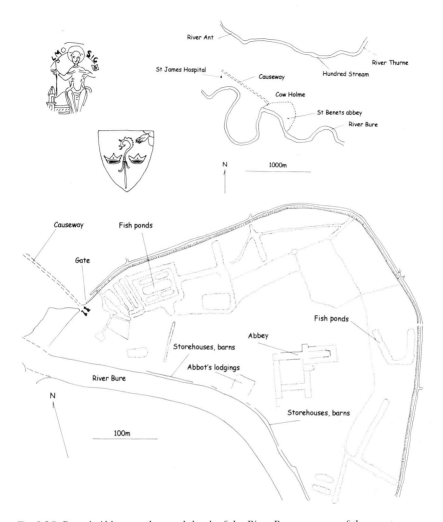

Fig. 8.2 St Benet's Abbey, on the north bank of the River Bure, was one of the great medieval monastic foundations, developed on an island, Cow Holm, in the wetlands between the Bure and the Ant/Thurne. These were connected at the time by what is now the Hundred stream (upper right). The foundation was not dissolved by Henry VIII and the Bishop of Norwich also still holds the title of Abbot of St Benet's, but the monks left soon after the reformation and the buildings began to deteriorate. Only a small amount of masonry still stands (lower diagram). There are extensive fishponds, where carp and swans would have been kept to provide fresh animal protein in winter. The Abbot's seal (extreme top left) still exists (in the British Museum). The Arms of the Abbey (top left) represent a pastoral staff between the Crowns of England and Denmark (Cnut financed the original foundation in 1020) and the guiding hand of providence. Based on Snelling (1971).

impressive. St Benet's (Figs 1.4, 8.2), by the side of the River Bure, had a huge church with cloisters, gardens, stores, refectories, kitchens, dormitories and chapter house, farms and fish ponds. By one means or another, these institutions appropriated the livings of many local parish churches, placing their monks as incumbents and taking the tithes of the parish into the monastery coffers. These were the agri-businesses of the day. Perhaps in revulsion to values that were perceived as no more spiritual than those of the avaricious Norman barons who had paid for their beginnings, orders of friars arose, groups of preachers assuming a life of poverty, especially in Norwich and Yarmouth, in the thirteenth century (Fig. 8.1).

There was a Norman influence too in that an authoritarian government created conditions for commercial prosperity. Norfolk in general, and Broadland in particular, remained a wealthy and densely populated region, because of the fertility of its soils and the large proportion of independent small freeman landowners. Broadland retained its innovative approach at the ground level.

Farming prosperity

By 1300, a document called the *Inquisitones post mortem*, a follow-up to the Domesday survey of 1086, but concentrating on manors and lay lords, suggests that land was at a premium in Norfolk. The county was predominantly arable, with arable lands valued at four times those of pasture, and only vestiges of forest remained. Arable values were especially high for Broadland, and maximal, on a national basis, for Flegg. The farming pattern in the Broadland uplands was one of barley, legumes, wheat, cattle, pigs and sheep, with continued innovation in the use of legumes, crop rotations and the use of horses, which work harder than oxen, especially on light soils.

Labour was plentiful and freedom from communal controls helped, together with the urban markets in Norwich and Yarmouth. The *Nomina Villarum*, a directory of land holdings of 1316, shows land ownership in small units, usually less than 75 acres (30 hectares), compared with a national average of more than 300, except in the Waveney valley, and often with joint owners. A lot of land was at least partly ecclesiastically owned, which tended to increase the proportion of arable.

The county was organised into units called Hundreds, each of variable size dependent on the fertility of the land and the taxable income that could be derived from it by the State. Hundreds had been established by the Saxons as the subunits of the counties or shires, and their land was owned by individuals, the King, institutions such as the Church, or cities. They were presided over by a High Constable and a Court and used as the basis for tax collection and military recruitment. The Hundreds of Broadland were small, with boundaries sometimes following the rivers or their tributaries (Fig. 8.3), in stretches that often became known as 'Hundred streams' and which allow us to trace some of the former river courses (Fig. 6.1) where they have been subsequently altered.

Broadland villages tended to expand away from a nucleus around the church as owners settled close to their holdings at the edge of the floodplain commons, to hold on to them, if necessary, as populations increased. Norwich and Yarmouth expanded and Norwich (Fig. 8.4) was the second most important city in England. By the thirteenth century it was an important market, industrial and administrative centre with 20,000 people, more than 60 churches and 30 monastic institutions within its walls. Yarmouth depended on a fishery for herrings in the North Sea and on export of woollen cloth (worsted) made locally from the large flocks of sheep.

By 1396, Yarmouth had burgeoned from a fishing settlement to a walled

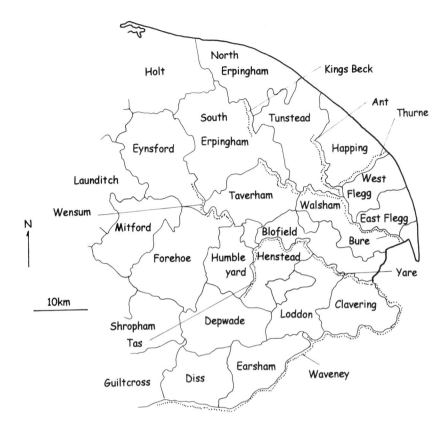

Fig. 8.3 Divisions of the land from the Saxon period were based on 'Hundreds' and persisted as administrative units until 1834. The names may often perpetuate the territories of ancient tribal groups. The Hundreds often took streams or rivers as their boundaries, as show here by the dotted lines. There has also been a persistence of the name 'Hundred stream' for channels near Martham Broad at the top end of the River Thurne and between the Rivers Ant and Thurne, now abandoned because of diversion of the rivers. (Based on Wade-Martins 1994.

town with 16 gates and ten towers, and had some problems. The harbour, behind the shifting sand bar, tended to silt up and there was a passage of several miles parallel to the bar before the outlet to the North Sea was finally reached. Several attempts were made to shorten this passage, which was treacherous and shallow, but these all failed until 1559. A cut was made that year through the bar at the modern location and strongly piled with timber to discourage the river from re-establishing its natural course. There was much trade up and down river and the navigation reached higher than at present. In 1670 the town of Bungay obtained powers to re-dredge the Waveney between it and Beccles, further downstream, to allow boats to pass; and there were legal obligations for Yarmouth and Norwich to clear encroaching reedswamp in the rivers and to cut weeds to maintain the navigation in the River Yare.

Fig. 8.4 Norwich was very wealthy in the medieval period. The Guildhall, built in 1407, was the seat of local government until 1938, though it was almost demolished in 1908. It was used to confine Robert Kett before his execution and is a prime example of the use of public buildings to demonstrate the power and authority of the State.

There were many Broadland villages, often with charters to hold markets granted between 1198 and 1345 and sold by the Crown. This reflects a steady prosperity over two centuries following the Norman Conquest, but matters were to change again.

Floods and the Black Death

The weather was worsening in the late thirteenth century and the Black Death, bubonic plague, was to cause epidemics of such proportions in 1349 that something of a decline set in. There was an increase in the incidence of gales from the north and north-west. Such gales tend to pile water up in the southern North Sea, causing surges of water up the rivers which, if they coincide with a high spring tide, can mean very high water levels in the Broadland valleys. Some Broadland settlements, for example, at Heckingham and Loddon, moved to higher ground. The higher water tables led to the flooding and progressive abandonment of the peat pits that became the Broads, though the peat trade may have declined anyway as coal was brought in through the ports of Lynn and Yarmouth to meet urban needs.

Fewer markets were chartered following the Black Death, possibly because of population decline, but also because transport had improved. In 1381 there was an uprising of the poor peasants. This Peasant's Revolt was speedily put down for it threatened the good order necessary for those in power to retain their privileges. But it was the first major skirmish in a trend that was to become one of the most prominent threads of history: change in the balance of power within the population. In Norfolk, a substantial proportion of the dissenters came from among the independent thinkers of Flegg.

The Norman dynasty had, by then, been replaced by the Plantagenets. Kings were often absent in their French domains, with the result that the keeping of financial and other records on parchment rolls began in the King's chancery and in the courts. This laid yet another foundation for the study of modern Broadland, for it is in the wealth of recorded information that history must be read. There was still great misery. The heavy rains of the late thirteenth and early fourteenth centuries, which led to the abandonment of the Broadland peat pits, also led to failure of harvests, especially in 1315, and famine. The national population of four or five million was not well served by the agriculture of the day, and the bubonic plagues of 1349, 1361, 1369 and 1375 devastated a population already inured to high infant mortality and death by the age of 40. It was also the start of an erosion of the power of the Church, for many of the clergy, faced with a stricken flock, chose to save themselves. Such things are long remembered.

It would, however, be wrong to impute total disaster. Broadland, as it had done following the imposition of the Romans, Saxons, Danes and Normans, adjusted and modified and continued its day-to-day existence on its fertile loams and on the bounty of its wetlands. It had now the additional resources of fisheries in the Broads, and perhaps greater wildfowl populations to exploit as more open water attracted migrant birds in winter. Some hint of the value of these resources comes in a charter granted to the City of Norwich by Edward IV in 1461 that allowed the City to 'have search in the river of Wensum [now the Yare] by all the length of the same river ... from a certain place on the north part of the City of Norwich, called the sheepwash, unto the cross called Hardele Cross near Bredyng, to survey, and search all the nets weirs and other engines for taking fish being found in the same water ... and to take, carry away, retain and ... burn all and singular the things ... placed or erected there against the destruction of young fish called Fry ...'.

The post-medieval period

The Plantagenet kings were at the beginning of a progressive transfer of power to a wider group. They needed funds to pay their armies in the defence of their French and English kingdoms. War protected trade, but as it became more costly, the raising of taxes became more difficult without a transfer of power from the king to the Council and eventually to Parliament.

The Wars of the Roses in the fifteenth century, though appositely named, were merely the minor power struggles among rival families to be king. They had little impact on most of the populace, but the accession of the Tudors with Henry VII in 1485 was a much more significant event. It coincided with the use of printing presses for the first time in England by William Caxton in 1486, thus greatly expanding opportunities for the recording and dissemination of information, but also brought in a new phase of relationships between the monarchy, the people and the Church.

The Tudors, by and large, avoided wars; they established an efficient civil service, through chancellors of repute. They replaced a system of power and influence dependent on private armies by one of patronage and influence in the King's Council and at court. London flourished; Norwich declined a little, but remained important, but the court, especially by the time of Elizabeth I in the mid- to late-sixteenth century, was moving around the new large houses of the great – and sometimes good. Status was reflected in prominent mansions of brick and oak, with plenty of glass and chimneys, demonstrating the wealth of the family. Gardens were ornate and geometric, reflecting a need for order, both in the face of recent political turmoil, but also in face of what was perceived as a threatening wild nature beyond the boundaries.

East Anglia in general, and Broadland in particular, were still well away from the main routes of communication across country and settled into a backwater existence. The problems of plague and depopulation in the fourteenth century had lead to some increase in the sizes of estates, as farms were cheaply bought by ambitious landowners, but the number of huge estates centred on large country houses was few in Norfolk and fewer in Broadland. That at Blickling (Plate 16) was founded in the early sixteenth century and Langley Hall, Somerleyton Hall and Woodbastwick Hall soon followed, but all are small compared with the eighteenth-century manifestations of power and wealth at Holkham (1734–1761), Wolterton (1726–1739) and Houghton (1721–1735), elsewhere in the county.

Tudor Norfolk was for the most part a county of prosperous yeomen. They built timber-framed houses, often with distinctive rounded gables, thatched at first with the local reed, but by the seventeenth century roofed by new status symbols, pantiles imported from the Low Countries. Huge barns were built in Broadland to store the harvest, with that at Waxham being built in 1581; bullocks became more important than sheep and were fattened in yards on turnips during the winter. The land remained largely unenclosed and attracted high rents, though enclosure of some common land in the late sixteenth century led to riots in Norfolk, led by John Kett. Like the peasants' revolt over a century earlier, they were swiftly put down. The increasing group of landed rich, now embracing merchants, lawyers and officials as well as the aristocracy, was not about to have its gains threatened. In Tudor times, as ever, the poor were persecuted.

Perhaps the most significant legacy of the Tudor period, however, was the changed relationship between Church and State. Henry VIII, somewhat insecure concerning his right to the throne, like all the Tudors, and needing a strong, male heir, had set in train events that led to the separation of the English Church from Rome. The Roman Church was not popular for, particularly through its monasteries, it had taken a huge share of the country's wealth and was not a benevolent landowner over the one third of the country it then owned. There was little opposition to the dissolution of the 800 or so monasteries in 1535 and the seizure of their lands and wealth. The abbeys of Broadland, built up since the eleventh century, had had their day by the sixteenth.

The Broadland churches, like all the rest, were stripped of their painted walls and ornate decorations (Fig. 8.5). Whitewashed walls, simpler ceremonies, the Royal Coat of Arms, the Authorised Version of the Bible and the Book of Common Prayer epitomised the new Church of England. The changes were not entirely driven by Henry, for a wave of Protestantism was arising in mainland Europe as well. Nonetheless, they were to have immense impacts through religious strife in parts of the United Kingdom until the present day and represent a major watershed of English history.

When Elizabeth I, the last of the Tudors, died in 1603, she left a society that

Fig. 8.5 Following the Reformation, the interiors of English churches became much simpler. St Helens at Ranworth epitomises this, but managed to retain a fourteenth-century painted rood screen. It also has a tower from which a fine view of Ranworth and Malthouse Broads and the Bure valley can be obtained.

stressed rank, order, degree and obedience, and in which the way to the top was via influence at the court, ability and office, rather than through the church, as previously it had been. More people, about ten per cent of the population, lived in cities. Elizabeth kept her 60 nobles in check by obliging them to spend money entertaining her in fine houses rather than by spending it on private armies. There was a burgeoning of the gentry. The squire and the parson were the leaders of the parish communities. Land and education had become important; craftsmen prospered. But for most of the population, including that of the Broadland catchment, much was unchanged. It was still largely a populace of subsistence farmers beholden to large landowners, growing oats for fodder, barley for brewing and keeping stock for meat, milk and fertiliser. The landscape was one of woods and greenery, coppices, common and ploughland, some hedged pastures, meadows and parkland, plus the fens and reedswamps of the valleys.

Tudor fisheries

Fisheries remained important to the ordinary people. John Kett, prior to his suppressed rebellion and subsequent hanging, presented a petition to Edward VI in 1549 that suggests that attempts were being made to appropriate what had been common rights: 'We pray that the Ryvers may be ffree and common to all men for ffyshyng and passage   ... We pray that the pore mariners or ffyshermen may have the hole profightes of their ffysshynges ...'. There were sensible conservation measures too. The Norwich Assembly Book for 1556 lists regulations for freshwater fishermen in the River Yare: 'No one to bete in the night time for Perches or any other fish; No fisherman shall put any long netts into the river to take fish there in spawning time, that is to say three weeks before Chrowchmas (May 3) and three weeks after Chrowchmas'. Otters were common, for the same regulations required every man 'shall be bound to keep a dog to hunt the otter and to make a general hunt twice or thrice in the year or more at time or times convenient upon pain to forfeit ten shillings'.

Yarmouth too, valued its local freshwater fisheries. There exists a 1619 manuscript by Manship that lists eel setts. Setts were nets placed across the river that could be raised or lowered to accommodate passing boats. In 1576, Elizabeth I had written to the town asking that some 35 setts be leased to John Everest, the town water bailiff. The town failed to do this, largely because its clerk was ill, and a local powerful family, the Pastons, attempted to seize the setts for their tenants. The issue became one of the 'poor fishermen' versus the rich burgesses of Yarmouth, the relative rights of which are not clear. The Pastons would doubtless have taken a portion of the profits from their tenants. The case was eventually settled, by a commission, in favour of the town. There were restrictions on salmon fishing also, listed in the Norwich Court of Mayoralty Book of 1667, though salmon may not have been common. Sir Thomas Browne, a Norwich physician and naturalist wrote that 'among the fishes of our Norwich river, we scarce reckon salmon, yet some are yearly taken'.

Sir Thomas Browne and the rise of scientific enquiry

Sir Thomas Browne (1605–1682) (Fig. 8.6), whose statue stands in the centre of Norwich, close to the market, was a sage of considerable distinction and author of a major discourse on his religious faith and its relationship to his profession of medicine, *Religio Medici*. His importance to Broadland lies in the records of natural history that he made at a time when scientific classification was only just being rescued from the mythologies of Aristotle. This was the work of Browne's acquaintance and contemporary, John Ray, somewhat before the revolutionary approaches of Linnaeus in the eighteenth century.

Browne lists cranes (eaten at a dinner given by the Duke of Norfolk to the Mayor) and pelican (shot upon Horsey Fen in May 1663, though he is critical enough to say it might have been one escaped from the King's collection at St James's in London). He records the bittern as common. Indeed, he kept one in his yard for two years and was able to counter the then popular belief that the characteristic booming was made by putting their bills in to hollow reeds. He noted ruffs as abundant in marshland between Norwich and Yarmouth. Among fish he describes salmon in the Bure, the Yare and the Waveney, pike 'of very large size', bream, tench, roach, rudd, dace, perch, minnows, trout, ruffe (in great plenty in Norwich rivers), lampreys, burbot, gudgeon, miller's thumb, loach, two species of stickleback, eel and carp.

Browne was one of the group of scientists, though they would not have referred to themselves as such, who, nominally led by Isaac Newton, were to begin the revolution that has led to the understanding of natural phenomena that we enjoy today. But understanding was still very unsophisticated. He was a man of the seventeenth century, when the Stuart kings succeeded the Tudors, bringing with them renewed debate about religion, a further transfer of power

Fig. 8.6 Sir Thomas Browne was the first of the Broadland scientists. His portrait, painted in 1641, when he was 36, may be seen in the National Portrait Gallery in London and his statue stands close to the marketplace and Hay Hill in Norwich.

to a wider constituency and the horrors of civil war. Births, marriages and deaths were now recorded, the population was more literate; documents had become increasingly complex. But the Stuarts, James I and Charles I and II held to the divine right of kings, did not suppress corruption at court and continued to favour the privileged over the poor.

The countryside began to change as the influences of building styles, based on classical Roman and Greek themes, penetrated from the continent and were espoused by the Royal surveyor, Inigo Jones. Britain had begun to establish an empire with colonies in America, where the poor and religiously persecuted had fled the hegemonies of alternate Catholic and Protestant dominance in the previous century. Great houses, built in geometric classic styles, replaced the more rambling Tudor mansions, reflecting the uncertainties of a king, Charles II, obsessed with order and discipline. But there were no such mansions in Broadland, which clung to its medieval traditions belatedly tempered by the influence of the Tudors.

There was a trend in the building of duck decoys in which duck were lured by small dogs into long netting pipes set at the edges of lakes. The Broad at Flixton was modified for this in 1652 and decoys were built at Acle in 1620, Buckenham in 1636 and Fritton in 1670. By the eighteenth century Broadland had 15 decoys, the earliest to be built in England, and among the greatest concentrations in Europe. But their use declined in the late nineteenth century owing to foreign imports, dietary changes and greater disturbance of the area by new influences such as shooting and tourism.

Civil war

Parliament was dissolved for a time; the country drifted into civil war on the basis of a religious divide among extreme and moderate versions of Protestantism, but with Parliament hitched to the former, the king and his nobles to the latter. The eventual parliamentarian leader, Oliver Cromwell, came from East Anglia, near Huntingdon, and Parliament held East Anglia. Broadland cannot have been unaffected – by 1643, ten per cent of the male population had been inveigled into one army or another, but the traces are now few. What was good was that censorship of publications ceased with the breakdown of government and new political ideas circulated like wildfire.

In 1659 the army was disbanded (for one thing it was a hotbed of radical ideas) and, in 1660, Parliament was recalled. Little had apparently been gained; the civil war had begun partly over religious tolerance, partly over demands for taxes by the King, but taxation to support armies was even greater. The gentry had found that the underclasses were a greater threat than the King, whom they now saw as a stabiliser to the threat of revolution. But much of more subversive importance had been achieved. There was a rich legacy of new ideas and realisation by the less privileged that there were alternative ways of thinking to the feudalism that still persisted – in mind and in practice. Everyone might eventually have a stake in governance and power.

When Charles II came to power in 1660, royal patronage returned, but there was also a commercial revolution. Navigation Acts were passed to limit the trading activities of foreign ships, a large merchant fleet developed, the slave trade expanded, together with merchant companies in East India and the Levant, and there was an emergence of the professions in a clearer form, including the Universities. New manufacturing techniques had been introduced by Protestant refugees from the Continent, agricultural methods improved, the coal industry expanded and living standards generally rose. Politics became polarised between the conservative, royalist Tory party and the more radical Whigs who put more of their trust in the people. Both terms originally were ones of abuse for minor factions. The civil service began to develop considerable professionalism and the vote was extended to property and office holders. There was commercial dominance, but the lower classes were better off and the Industrial Revolution had begun.

Norwich, for long the second city of the kingdom, began its decline into comfortable semi-rural complaisance, whilst influence shifted to the industrialising towns of the midlands and north. Broadland remained sidelined, continuing its systems and traditions much as before, but the stage was being set for events that would bring to it its current significance.

Isaac Newton (1642–1727) was fomenting the scientific revolution that would replace interpretation of the planet and the universe through opinion and dogma to one based on observation and experiment. God the magician was being replaced by God the great engineer. John Boyle was making sense of gases, Thomas Harvey of the functioning of the human body and John Ray of the relationships between living organisms. The modern understanding of Broadland has its roots in all of these, but apart from the writings of Thomas Browne, little was actually to be recorded of it for more than 100 years.

Conspicuous consumption and the Georgians

The turn of the eighteenth century saw the start of a line of Hanoverian kings. They were helped by the establishment of powerful chief ministers: wheelers, dealers and fixers, epitomised by Robert Walpole, a Norfolk squire, large in body and brusque in manner. For 20 years, from 1721, he managed, through a cabinet of ministers, a network of the elite that gave the gentry peace and prosperity. Trusted by the city financiers, he exerted an economic, social and military dominance that still excluded many Englishmen, and almost all of the Scots and Irish, from any political rights. Money was flowing in from the colonies, which bought nearly half of English domestic products. These interests were defended by military might, in the West Indies, India, Canada and America. The wealth funded development of new tools, new ways of land management and the construction of great houses, hidden in walled parks, yet demonstrating wealth and power in a society that was still hierarchical, male-dominated and dependent on deference.

Land and property bestowed status and the 400 biggest landowners, half of them peers of the realm, controlled the elections to Parliament, supported by a gentry of 15,000 or 20,000, who provided the backbone of parish administration. In Norfolk, whilst the huge pile of Holkham Hall was built on the north coast by Walpole's family as one of these Georgian monuments to conspicuous consumption, Broadland yet again seems to have missed the tide. Its many small landowners continued a system that must have benefited from developments like crop rotation, and from the profits of investment in the distant industries, but which remained conservative in approach, trusting the known, and now spurning the wildly innovative.

The poor, half of society, remained wretched, and were viewed as an illiterate rabble of labourers, servants and soldiers. Occasionally mob riots erupted against unpopular groups such as Jews, dissenters and Catholics, but most people remained largely deferential to authority, sturdily Protestant, and conservative in their own way. Only later were the news of the French Revolution, and the loss of confidence among the rulers that followed the rebellion of the American colonies, to bring the next step in emancipation. Meanwhile, radicalism in the form of religious movements such as that preached by John Wesley divided the populace. There were those comfortable with the orderliness of the surpliced parson, the whitewashed church, the Royal Coat of Arms, regularity and seemliness, a heaven already on Earth. And there were those seeking change through zeal, self-denial, opportunity, even for women, and work.

For the nobility, the gentry and the middle classes, England was the richest country in the world by the mid-eighteenth century. The wealth was spent on towns and parks, furniture and silver, paintings, concerts and the theatre. Life was centred in the country where the great estates, designed for field sports as well as agricultural production, saw the demolition of labourers' cottages inconveniently sited for the view from the House. It saw also the enclosure of more land, convenient for the management of new breeds of cattle as well as jumps for the hunts. The Georgians effectively created the present countryside of England, a great landscape garden, sometimes with deliberately built elegant ruins aping the genuine articles of Greece and Rome. There were views across parkland to wilder country: the remaining common land, in the distance, and the farmland disguised behind avenues of trees, copses, and even deliberately built banks. Artificial lakes were popular, crafted to appear as of infinite size. Like Inigo Jones with his late seventeenth-century buildings, Lancelot (Capability) Brown designed an ordered countryside that hid the problems of the poor in a new art form.

The Bill of Rights

The idea of revolution was nevertheless not lost. In 1791 Thomas Paine, following the overthrow of a contemptuous ruling class in France in 1789, published his *Rights of Man*, a denouncement of a society founded on inherited privilege. The wars that erupted on a huge scale with the French in the late eighteenth and early nineteenth centuries became a great watershed that anticipated the great changes that resulted from the Second World War in the twentieth and which were to be the defining influence on modern Broadland. These wars with Napoleon Bonaparte were costly. Taxes had increased to pay for them and at their end in 1815, with the Treaty of Vienna, huge numbers of soldiers were released back to the job market. There was mass unemployment, made worse by a depression in trade and poor harvests.

Revolution came very close with the decadence of the reign of George IV; political unions arose, demanding universal male suffrage, lower taxation and poverty relief. Uprisings were put down with violence, even massacre. A ruling few still dominated the many and Parliament did not reflect either the distribution or the nature of the population. The chief minister of William IV, Earl Grey (of the tea) was astute enough to realise that the rule of the elite could only be prolonged by major concessions. The Reform Bill of 1831 did not give a universal vote; it applied only to those with a vested interest in the state because they owned property; but it redistributed the seats in Parliament more equably. Together with other liberal Bills, on catholic emancipation, abolition of slavery, the regulation of factories and the commutation of the tithes that had been payable to the Church, it paved the way for a general calm during the reign of Victoria. In that period, Broadland was to emerge in greater prominence from its bit part of the previous seven centuries.

Further reading

Choice of history books can be a matter of taste! There is a huge variety available covering the periods skated over in this chapter. I found Strong (1998) and Lacey & Danziger (1999) extremely readable. Wade-Martins' *Atlas of Norfolk* (1994) and Williamson (1997) provide the local historical detail to illuminate the events of the grander national scale. The Proceedings of the Norfolk and Norwich Naturalists Society offer interesting antiquarian insights, largely from the interests of one of its editors, Thomas Southwell (1904) in fisheries, and its secretary, W. A. Nicholson (1889) in Sir Thomas Browne. Dutt (1906) also brings together information on former fishery regulations in Broadland.

Part III

Gunner, Yachtsman, Wherryman, Naturalist

9

The Development of the Grazing Marshes

Five hundred AD, the lower reaches of Broadland; in the huge waterscape behind the fishing village of Yarmouth, the Halvergate triangle, where the three main Broadland rivers merged, the wilderness of salt marshes and mud flats began to change. Sea water penetrated less as the sand bar closed again after its breach as the Iron Age arrived in Britain. A new freshwater regime developed, with a laying down of the upper peat over the Romano-British clay at the edges of the estuary. It was still a tidal regime, with the sea water pushing into a bigger Breydon Water than its present tiny extent and forcing a back-up and rise of the fresh waters piling in from the rivers.

This rise and fall, at the edges of the triangle, led to only a slow accumulation of the upper peat, which started to oxidise when it was left dry. It led also to a fertile regime, as river silts flooded over the land close to the channels at high water, especially in winter. The coarser fractions of this silt, falling out close to the channel, left low embankments or levees parallel to it. The new regime, a sheltered, huge vista of open water, mud flat, salt marsh and fringing freshwater reedswamp, behind the low bar of sand dune at the coast, became the stage for a very distinctive grazing economy. Begun by the Saxons, it developed in the medieval period and persisted into the twentieth century. This chapter describes the development of the area and the farming practices.

Flooding was a problem. The wetter climate of the thirteenth and fourteenth centuries was coupled with a steadily rising sea level as the land sank at a millimetre or so each year and water tables and levels were thus increasing in the triangle. But occupation continued and prospered. Land continued to be leased and the leases mention permanent sheepcotes; there are some early seventeenth-century farm buildings, at Raven Hall and Seven Mile House, which are built on much earlier settlement sites. Water levels were a problem, however. The earlier buildings had all been built on natural low mounds, but there are references in manorial account rolls in the thirteenth and fourteenth centuries to embankments and to the clearing out of ditches so that drainage could be freer.

These artificial embankments were heaped on what had been the natural levees and enclosed an area, channel-wards, that acted as a reservoir after heavy rain and at high tides. Ditching and embankment works began at least as early as the thirteenth century, perhaps as much to claim salt marsh for pasture improvement as to combat rising sea levels. Leases from the fifteenth century stipulate maintenance of the drainage works, which by then included not only the floodbanks but flap sluices, opening on the ebb, closing on the flood tide, where the rivers intersected the increasing network of drainage dykes.

Progressively, the wilderness was tamed, the mud flats and salt marshes became confined within the walls that now hem in Breydon Water, and lost to

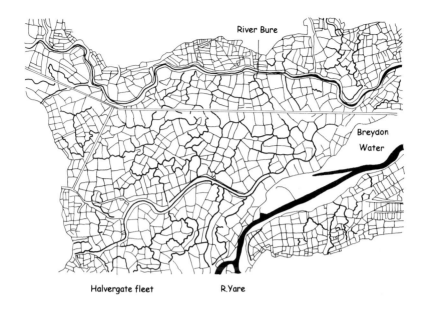

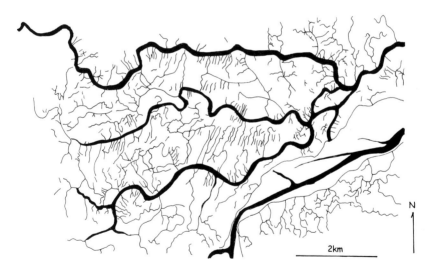

Fig. 9.1 The former courses of the salt marsh creeks (lower) are still reflected in the more sinuous drainage dykes of the present day drainage system (upper). The straight dykes are those which have been dug since the medieval period and particularly since the eighteenth century. Based on Coles & Funnell (1981) and Williamson (1997).

grazing pastures, to the landward of walls that confined the lower parts of the rivers as they passed through the former estuary (Fig. 9.1). Thus maintained, this grazing marsh land retained high value such that it could command twice the average arable rent payable in the uplands and could be mortgaged to raise very high sums. At the same time, inheritance among the several sons of families led to further division into smaller parcels of ownership, especially in the middle of the area, towards the main channels where the grazing was best on the clay soils.

The economy and management of the grazing marshes changed little from the thirteenth century until quite late in the twentieth. Sheep predominated in the thirteenth century, together with some horses and bullocks, but by the sixteenth century cattle were much more important. This perhaps reflected a national taste for beef over mutton, but possibly also a greater susceptibility of sheep to liver fluke disease as the previously salt pastures were made fresh by embankment. From the early seventeenth century young cattle, usually of stocky resistant hill breeds, were brought in by drovers to the market at Norwich and to local fairs, from northern England and Scotland and even from Ireland.

The buyers were often local arable farmers who fattened the cattle on turnips in yards in winter and put them to the marsh in summer, before selling them on in Norwich or London 12 or 18 months later. Grazing leases contained stipulations, which would have conserved the quality of the land, usually by limiting grazing from 1 May until 24 October. This, and restriction of numbers per acre, avoided poaching, the creation of bare muddy patches. Hay cutting was generally forbidden, except in the ronds, the areas within the floodbanks, where hay or reeds might be cut. Ploughing was unusual and landlords tried to prevent it, even when grain prices, and therefore temptation, were high during the Napoleonic Wars of 1793–1815.

The landscape throughout this long period was a huge grassland, tapestried with different greens reflecting minor variations in level and wetness and plant communities. It was dotted with black cattle, its atmosphere often misty as the wet air cooled overnight and it was relieved only by the gates with their characteristic sloping sides across bridges over the dykes and eventually by the tall bodies of drainage mills.

It was remote and access was difficult. Owners did not personally tend their cattle, but left them in the care of marshmen, who lived in cottages on the marsh, each looking after a section, or level, of perhaps 1,000 acres (400 hectares). Marshmen counted the cattle each day, tended ailments and wounds, repaired gates and fences, cleared dykes of colonising plants and repaired the river walls. In the spring, using the wooden boards of the sluices, they adjusted the water levels in the dykes to about half a metre below the land surface to give access to drinking water for the stock yet to maintain the dykes as adequate boundaries discouraging cattle from crossing between levels.

In November, they dropped the level to a metre below the bank to leave room for the winter rain. They kept some cattle of their own in the ronds, and shot wildfowl and fished for sale or the pot. This lifestyle persisted into the mid-twentieth century from its origins 1,500 years previously, responsibility for the levels often being passed from generation to generation within the same family. It was not necessarily, however, the idyllic life that it might sound. If accounts from similar areas in the Wash fens and the Kent marshes are anything to go by, malaria (ague) was rife and infant mortality was high. Clerics in the seventeenth century declined to accept livings in the Kent marshes for fear of their health.

More intense drainage

Through the centuries, the water tables continued to rise and often the thin line of dunes between Happisburgh and Winterton was breached and the sea flooded in. Mechanical help became possible and the first of the characteristic drainage mills, set by the river at the ends of long curving dykes, was built in the eighteenth century. This was to be the start of a quickening of the impacts of man. The more the land was drained, the more it shrank, or even oxidised away if it was peat, and the greater was the difference between the height of the land surface and the level of the rivers held between the floodbanks.

It was the start also of institutionalisation of the marsh, for mills drained the holdings of many individuals and charges had to be levied. The first institutions were the Sea Breach Commissions, responsible for repair of the sea defences. They were temporary bodies, set up first in 1608 in response to an immediate need to close the breaches in the dunes, then again in 1791, following several eighteenth-century floods, and in 1802, 1822, 1832, 1844 and 1855. In 1861 the Commission was made permanent, later continuing its responsibilities under frequently changing names. The map drawn up by John Faden in 1793 shows the extent of the coastal breach that opened up in 1791, with nine breaks totalling over 440 metres in the line of sand dunes stretching between Horsey and Waxham (Fig. 9.2). The sudden flood of sea water had led to house damage in the village of Hickling and to fish deaths in Hickling Broad. The Sea Breach Commissions initially comprised a number of Justices of the Peace from Norwich and Yarmouth, chaired by the Bishop of Norwich. They had considerable problems in collecting the rates to which they were entitled for repairing the coastline, despite the availability of an important Statute of Sewers passed in 1531, which established the principle that property could be taxed to pay for services made available to it.

The drainage pumps

The drainage mills, or rather the derelict remains of them, are one of Broadland's best-known features (Plate 17). They were built, from 1753 onwards, to drain the clay soils of the Halvergate triangle and the lower parts of the river floodplains. A few were also built, in attempts that failed, to drain the freshwater fens higher up the valleys. A few of the pumps have been restored and appear as the windmills of scores of paintings of Broadland.

Most now lack their sails and even their upper brickwork, but they add a characteristic quality to the appearance of the grazing marshes as stanchions in a wide, flat land. They vary in size from the six metres of that at Swim Coots, near Catfield, to the towering 22 metres of the restored Berney Arms mill by the River Yare, and they form the greatest concentration of such structures in England. Perhaps this reflects a tendency in Broadland to hang on to old technology longer than in areas such as the Cambridgeshire fens where the mills were supplanted and demolished.

Those mills built in the eighteenth century are mostly in the Halvergate triangle. Many were much modified and heightened in the nineteenth century as new devices became available or as the existing towers suffered subsidence and the brickwork cracked. Most had wooden sails, covered by canvas and mounted on a moveable wooden cap. The direction in which the sails pointed had to be adjusted (a process called reeving) as the wind direction changed

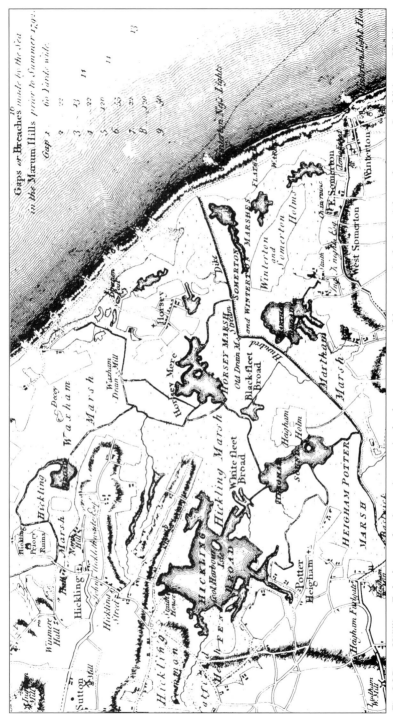

Fig. 9.2 Part of William Faden's map showing major gaps in the dune system created by storms in the late eighteenth century. In addition to Hickling Broad, Horsey Mere, Martham Broad and Heigham Sound, eight small Broads, none of which now exists, are also shown. They were drained and filled following the Enclosure Acts of the early nineteenth century.

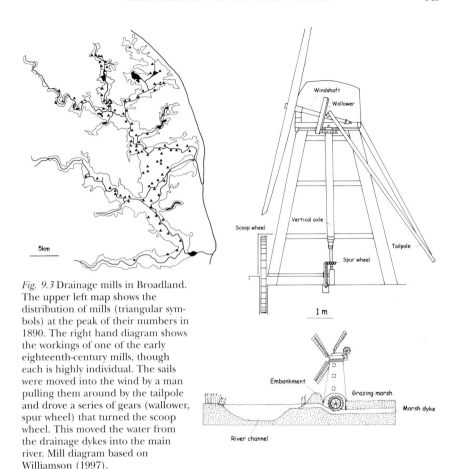

Fig. 9.3 Drainage mills in Broadland. The upper left map shows the distribution of mills (triangular symbols) at the peak of their numbers in 1890. The right hand diagram shows the workings of one of the early eighteenth-century mills, though each is highly individual. The sails were moved into the wind by a man pulling them around by the tailpole and drove a series of gears (wallower, spur wheel) that turned the scoop wheel. This moved the water from the drainage dykes into the main river. Mill diagram based on Williamson (1997).

and this was done with a winch and a long tail pole that stretched from the cap to a track built around the mill at its base. The leverage needed for this limited the size of the mill and therefore the length of the sails and the power they could generate. The movement of the sails was transmitted through a set of gears to drive a wheel, with scoops in it, that lifted water from dykes dug into the marshes, over the river embankments and into the river (Fig. 9.3). The shrinking of the drained soils rapidly led to a lift of two or three metres being required.

There is some mystery as to the stimulus for building the mills and pumps in the first place, for the earliest were in long-embanked areas. There the gravity drainage system, with one way flaps, built at the junctions of dykes and rivers, operated satisfactorily for the grazing regime of the day. All the early mills were on private land, not on commons, and there may have been an element of acquisition of status in their building – the complements of the impressive Georgian houses or the flashier status symbols, such as expensive cars, of the present day. There was a general, if manufactured, belief in their need at the time. Sea level rise may have led to the flap sluices working less well.

There may also have been more tidal flow, due to dredging of the rivers to improve navigation, discussed in Chapter 10, and there may have been more water coming down river as wetlands higher up the valleys, particularly in the Thurne, were embanked and drained. (If so, this presages the new realisation that the more the flood control higher up a valley, the greater becomes the same problem lower down. Once drainage and flood control are embarked upon they become a self-feeding problem.) It may also be just that the landowners wished marginally to improve the pastures by getting the water more quickly off their land at the end of winter.

There was a period of proliferation of mill building at the turn of the eighteenth century, when numbers may have doubled. The maps drawn up by Faden and by Bryant in 1824 show an increase from 47 to 73. This increase coincides with the Acts of Enclosure, discussed below, that often stipulated that a mill should be built, and made arrangements for Drainage Commissioners to build it and maintain its function. The styles of the new mills at first resembled those of the old. Improvements invented much earlier elsewhere were not adopted until well into the nineteenth century. These included the fantail built onto the cap, which allowed the wind direction to change the orientation of the sails automatically, and new styles of shuttering on the sails that maximised the power generated.

Perhaps this was reluctance to embrace new technology (in current parlance) or because knowledge spread slowly, but there was also a mild recession following the boom years of the Napoleonic Wars, and anyway, the old styles were cheaper. After 1825, however, agriculture became more profitable and more innovations arrived. Scoop wheels were replaced by more efficient turbine pumps, and a variety of designs was used in response to local conditions. Where small areas were to be drained, hollow post and trestle mills (Fig. 9.4) were adequate. These worked on the same principles as the brick-towered mills, but had an open structure of timber to support the sails and machinery and were much smaller. Extensive levels (the name given to the area drained by a particular mill), on the other hand, demanded tall mills with fantails and turbines.

By the late nineteenth century there were fewer mills. Drainage areas had been amalgamated and one big mill often replaced several small ones. On the other hand, the Victorians were to embark on the 'improvement' of more marginal land and erected mills in the peat fens, coupled with embankments. Most were cheap trestle mills and the attempt was not unduly successful. They did not have the advantage of tidal drainage, which had helped the development of drainage in the grazing marshes, and the peat soils shrank very quickly. Possibly the mills were intended mostly to keep dry the shallow turf ponds, where peat cutting continued, but none were very successful, so that we still have remaining the extensive undrained fens.

In the lower reaches, mills were versatile structures. In winter they pumped; in summer when water levels were low they were often used for other purposes – grinding oil seed or corn, or even cement clinker, or to drive saw benches. Indeed, some of the mills were still used in Broadland up to the outbreak of the Second World War, in 1939, supplementing new forms of power. Wind power, however, was being supplanted. The first steam pump was installed at Buckenham in 1844 and there were up to 46 steam pumps by 1930, sometimes used to supplement wind by driving scoop wheels in calm periods.

Fig. 9.4 The simplest mills were based on skeletal timber structures (trestles), most of which have now decayed. Hobbs drainage mill, intended to drain some of the fens in the middle part of the Bure, near Cockshoot Broad, still stands.

Steam pumps were replaced by diesel engines in the early twentieth century, but this was late compared with changes in other drained wetlands in Britain. In the Cambridgeshire fens, steam had completely replaced wind by the end of the nineteenth century, but there the dominant agriculture was arable, requiring much lower water tables than did the pastures used in Broadland. Eventually the national grid for electricity displaced wind, steam and diesel pumps with very powerful electrical ones, the consequences of which were to be very great indeed, but that is material for Chapter 14.

Enclosure

As the threats of rising water from the sea were met in the lower reaches, there were different pressures upstream. People like boundaries; they are a territorial imperative. Boundaries that are not marked can be infiltrated and land that has common rights over it restricts an owner from doing as he or she wishes. Land can represent independence; it can also be a millstone around the neck if it carries common responsibilities. Better then to enclose the land with fences, restrict the rights of the peasantry and exploit it at will.

In 1797, one sixth of Norfolk was common land – marshland, heath, sheepwalks and warrens. Much of the Broadland river valleys was wet common from which reed, hay, grazing, animal bedding, fish, eels and wild birds had been taken for a millennium. In the sixteenth and seventeenth centuries there was some enclosure of the upland and stealthy appropriation of the wetland commons in the valleys of the Yare, Waveney and Chet. Sometimes it was by 'assent', the commoners giving up their rights by what could only have been threat from the strong, for there was nothing in it for them. Sometimes there was outright protest. But Enclosure through Acts of Parliament, a body heavily representing land ownership at the time, legalised a process that had redistributed the land in the first place among the Danes and the Normans, and been perpetrated as the opportunity arose ever since. The first Parliamentary Enclosure was at Stokesby in 1720, followed by that at Acle in 1797, then there was a deluge between 1800 and 1815. The time was right; grain prices were high because of the demands of the Napoleonic Wars, landowners were thus willing to invest, and also keen to control the rural population and make it more dependent on the wages they could pay and less on the free exploitation of the commons.

The greatest effect in Broadland was on the common grazing of the fens and the edges of the grazing marshes in the Lower Bure and Thurne. More dykes were dug to act as boundaries in the freshwater fens and drainage mills were built, fed from major new dykes called the Commissioners Drains. The Enclosure Acts established bodies of drainage commissioners to be responsible for drainage and to levy rates. Seventeen such bodies were set up between 1800 and 1820. One of them even proposed to drain the whole of Hickling Broad, but gave up the idea following a general finding that draining the peat fens was not so easy as draining the silts and clays of the grazing marshes. Nonetheless, it managed to extinguish at least four small Broads in its area – Wigg's, Gage's, Hare Park and Chapmans as well as three Broads that are unnamed, but appear on Faden's map between Horsey and Somerton. There were, however, too many streams and springs in the Hickling area and the peat shrank very quickly, making drainage progressively difficult. After about 1870, many of these areas were abandoned, often after a major flood, and the land was again used traditionally, though now under the control of the estate owner rather than the community.

Protest over Enclosure was rife, sometimes to the extent of near riots. The response was a sweetener in the form of the Poor Allotments (Fig. 9.5), smaller areas of land that the peasants could use traditionally, but regulated by committees of landowners, clergy and the gentry of the area. It was control in just another form. The Enclosure Acts manifested themselves in a much more ruthless use of the land. There was a renewed phase of peat digging, not in deep pits, which left most of the fen available for other uses, but in shallow trenches, 50 to 80 centimetres deep, which had formerly been discouraged. Shallow digging was cheaper, peat was saleable as a fuel, demands for energy were increasing. The 1880 Ordnance Survey maps of the Catfield and Irstead fens in the valley of the River Ant show half of the area as peat cuttings (Fig. 6.3). The cuttings were sporadically continued into the twentieth century, but rapidly filled in with water to form turf ponds and became recolonised by vegetation, often characteristically different in species composition even now from that of uncut peat surfaces (Chapter 6).

The large landowners were less interested in subsistence products such as

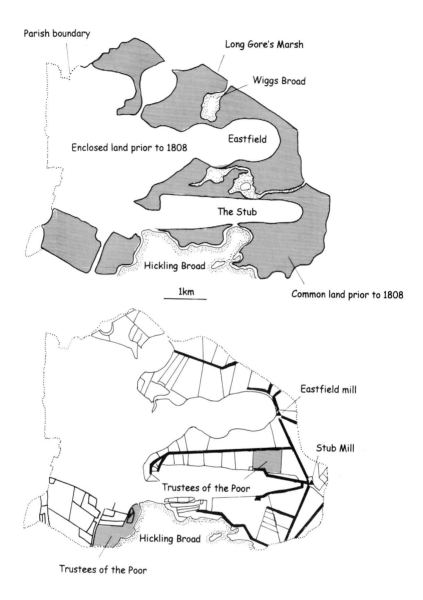

Fig. 9.5 'The fault is great in man or woman, who steals a goose from off a common; But what can plead that man's excuse, who steals a common from a goose?' (Anon, *The Tickler Magazine*,1 February 1821). The shaded areas in the upper map of the Parish of Hickling show the Parish common land before 1808, when the Enclosure Act for Hickling was passed. The lower map shows the effects of enclosure, with a new series of dykes installed for drainage, together with Eastfield and Stub Mills. Wiggs Broad and another, unnamed one north of the Stub, have been drained, and part of Hickling Broad has been converted to marsh. Only two small areas where the products of the former commons could be harvested remain remain as poors' allotments, administered by the Trustees of the Poor. Based on Williamson (1997).

marsh hay, for they were exploiting the uplands with more intensive systems of fattening cattle on turnips and grazing them on the richer pastures of the grazing marshes. The poor had neither many beasts to graze on the fens, or control over their management. The landless poor were thus worked hard and were prey to all sorts of exploitation. It was the common theme of human history repeated yet again.

Further reading

Both Williamson (1997), who takes a particular interest also in the engineering of drainage mills, and George (1992) are strong and detailed on aspects of the history of the grazing marshes and drainage in the region. Insights into the life of marshmen, drawn from the Kent marshes, are given in Dobson (1980) and in the classic work on the Wash fens of Darby (1983).

10

The Rise of Profits, the Start of Decline?

The nineteenth and early twentieth centuries were key times for Broadland. It was still a backwater, but a flood of national events began to swirl and engulf it. The first inklings had come with the Enclosure Acts beginning in the eighteenth century and with the impetus given to drainage of the grazing marshes by the introduction of mill technology. Over the next 150 years, there was new industry, improved transport, the movement of an increasing population to the towns, water pollution, mechanising agriculture and increasing leisure. These were to be mixed with social changes that gave greater democracy and literacy and development of more governmental responsibility that led to increased legislation and more governmental control of almost everything. Some ingredients of this new mixture were to undermine the natural history interest of the area and, more importantly, to impede attempts to recover it made possible by others.

The Broads – what the sediments tell us

Sediment cores taken from some of the main Broads of the Bure, Ant and Yare show a major change in the freshwater ecosystems in the nineteenth century. The crunchy beige or white sediment, rich in charophyte remains and shells, disappears from around 1860 in the Bure Broads, to be replaced by amorphous dark brown, even black, sediment, still with snail remains, but with a greatly increased organic content (Fig. 7.7). The annual rate of sedimentation began to increase a lot and there was a rise in the numbers laid down each year of a particular group of diatoms, called epiphytes, part of the periphyton community.

We know when these things happened because we can date the sediment using naturally occurring radioactive isotopes. The best-known way of dating the remains in lake sediments and peats is by using carbon-14. This works very well for the underlying peats in Broadland and is how the dates of the various peat layers are known. The method should theoretically be easily usable to date the sediment of the very recent period as well, except that one of the major changes of that period prevents it. The burning of coal and then oil during the Industrial Revolution of the nineteenth century and afterwards released carbon dioxide that came from very ancient deposits with scant levels of carbon-14 in them. This upset the natural initial carbon-14 to carbon-12 ratio in a rather random way, so that the initial carbon-14 to carbon-12 ratio in the sediments was no longer constant and this prevents reliable calculations.

Fortunately there are other dating methods that use radioisotopes which can be used for the recent period. Radioactive uranium-235 occurs widely, though in tiny amounts, in many rocks and soils, and very slowly decays to radioactive radium-226. In turn the radium undergoes a series of changes that rapidly

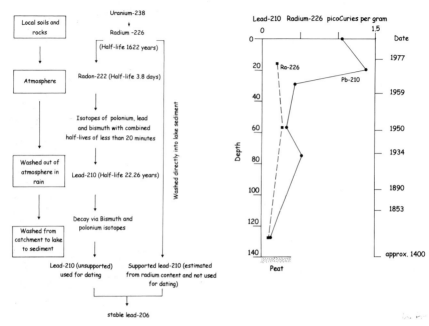

Fig. 10.1 Dating lake sediment cores using lead-210. On the left are shown details of the origin of the lead-210. Some of it in the sediments comes from direct wash-in of radium-226 and this cannot be used for dating as the amounts may vary greatly from time to time. The amount of this is called the supported lead-210 for it is present in conjunction with the radium-226 that gave rise to it and a correction can be made. The unsupported lead-210 is that which came in via the atmosphere and the amounts delivered to the sediment each year are much more uniform. On the right is a graph of the amounts in the sediments of core HGB 1 taken from Hoveton Great Broad in 1980. The dates are calculated from the concentrations and also from the density of the sediment to allow for changes in the nature of the sediment and hence dilution of the lead-210 reaching it. Data from Moss (1988).

convert it to radioactive radon, a gas, which enters the atmosphere and decays, also very quickly, to a radioactive isotope of lead, lead-210. This is removed from the atmosphere by rain and washes into the lakes, ending up in the surface sediment and steadily decaying to a stable form of lead, this time with a short half-life of about 22 years. By measuring the concentration of lead-210 in the surface sediment at successive depth levels, and fitting the concentrations into an equation that describes the course of radioactive decay, it is possible to date sediment back to about 1850 or a little before (Fig. 10.1). After about seven or eight half-lives there is usually not enough lead-210 left in the sediment for present instruments to detect.

    Analysis of diatom remains in the sediment is then used for determining the ecological history of the lake. Diatoms (Fig. 10.2) are exceptionally useful, firstly because they are photosynthetic algae that are very widespread and important components of the algal communities of lakes and rivers. Secondly, they have walls of silicate, like glass, which do not decompose, though they may dissolve chemically under certain, usually highly alkaline conditions. Thirdly, these walls have patterns of holes and slits, which, together with the overall

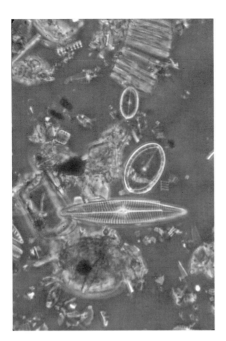

Fig. 10.2 Diatoms from a core taken from Strumpshaw Broad before it was dredged out in the 1980s. Whole diatoms, fragments of walls and inorganic debris remain following heating of the sediment in nitric acid to remove organic matter. Left comes from deep sediment and the diatoms are those of a well-developed plant community (see Figure 10.3). They include the oval *Cocconeis placentula*, the boat-shaped *Navicula radiosa* and the chain of *Fragilaria* cells at the top. Right is from mid-twentieth-century sediment when the Broad had lost its plants and was dominated by circular planktonic diatoms such as *Cyclotella meneghiniana* (see Chapter 12).

shape of the cell, characterise particular species. And lastly, the attention given to diatom ecology over the past century means that particular species and groups can be used as indicators of ecological conditions and particular habitats. Thus quite a lot can be said about ecological events in the Broads during the last 200 years.

The number of diatoms is quite low in the early parts of the Broadland cores, when charophytes were predominant (Fig. 10.3). Nutrients were scarce in the water and the number of diatoms is an indication of the overall productivity. It is possible that numbers are also low because of dissolution of the silica, but the remains in the cores do not show the blurred edges of dissolving walls. Then, as the charophyte sediments give way to the dark amorphous sediments of the nineteenth century, the numbers of epiphytic diatoms rise, whilst there is no increase, or very little, of the diatoms of the planktonic communities that are found suspended in the water.

Epiphytic diatoms are part of the periphyton, They attach themselves, by stalks or mucilage pads, to the surfaces of plants, where space can become a limiting factor. More diatoms mean more diatom production, and thus an increase in their living space – the surfaces of water plants. The deduction is thus that the crop of submerged plants in the water was also increasing and the

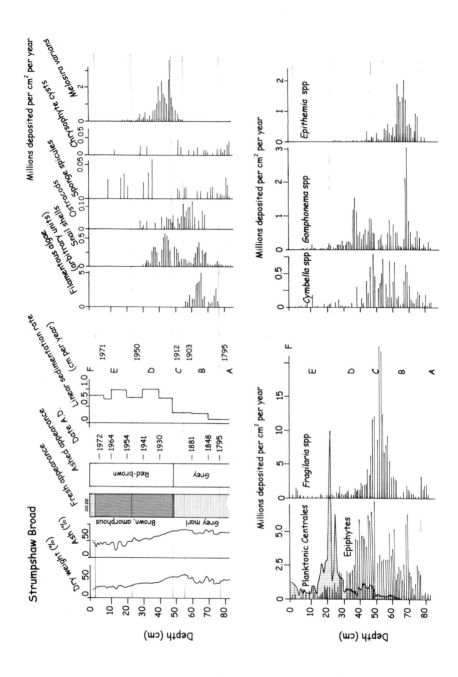

loss of the charophyte remains suggests that the plant community had changed in composition. The paucity of planktonic diatoms is consistent with the water remaining clear. There is also an increase in another group of diatoms in the cores at the same time or shortly after the rise of the epiphytes. These are particularly of one genus, *Fragilaria*, most of whose species live in ribbons on the sediment or among other filamentous algae, such as the green algae *Cladophora*, *Ulothrix* or *Spirogyra*, which form green, cotton wool-like clouds in the water. These too suggest an increase in algal production and thus an increase in the amounts of nutrients – nitrogen and phosphorus compounds – entering the rivers and Broads.

The changes and the consequences

New changes in the catchments were being reflected in changes in the fresh-water communities, and the changes in the catchments were the results of changes in human society, now documented more thoroughly than ever before. Sir Thomas Browne, his bittern booming in the yard, had begun a process – that of writing down his observations – which added much more information to the story of Broadland. To the records of the sediment cores come the comments, the diaries, the learned discourses eventually given to the Norfolk and Norwich Naturalists Society, of a handful of worthy men, each reflecting his own time as well as what he saw. And what was being seen was staggering.

Industry

The rise of industry in Britain was the fundamental change, from which much else followed. It had had its roots in the enterprise of Tudor England, but with more steam and water power in the eighteenth century, the pace quickened. The demands of more organised production, refined skills, timekeeping and consistency of workmanship, led in turn to an ethos of hard work, sobriety and self-improvement in the workforce. There was the confidence given by victory

Fig. 10.3 (facing page) Data from a core taken from Strumpshaw Broad in 1976. The variety of information that can be gleaned from such a core is very great. The letters indicate zones of the core where major ecological changes were taking place. During A, the Broad was a clearwater lake depositing marl, and with a plant population, including charophytes, of modest biomass. In the mid-nineteenth century (B), increasing nutrients coming from the disposal of Norwich sewage led to a growth of filamentous algae, greater plant growth (indicated by the epiphytic diatom total and the genera shown at the bottom right), snails and ostracods, which are animals associated with plant beds. In the early twentieth century (C) this process resulted in a continued development of taller plants and a greater growth of unattached diatoms such as *Fragilaria* and *Melosira varians* which drape themselves over the plant surfaces or bare sediments. The plant growth was reaching its zenith as the city expanded. In D, the early to middle twentieth century, planktonic diatoms of a group called the Centrales, which has spherical cells, were increasing rapidly and the nature of the sediment changed, with more iron-rich sediment moving in from the catchment as the channels were opened up and the tidal water brought material more easily into the Broad. The sedimentation rate also was increasing and the Broad was filling in. The plankton reached its zenith in about 1950, following a complete loss of the plant communities a few years earlier, shown by the decline in the epiphyte graph. After that (E) the water was too shallow and replaced by the tide too frequently for the plankton to be easily deposited. There are reed fragments in the sediments in this period. By 1974 (F) the Broad was a bare mud flat at low tide and was dredged out to re-establish open water again. From Moss (1979).

over Napoleon in 1815, a brisk trade with a widening Empire and the promotion of Queen Victoria and Prince Albert and the Royal Family as the epitome
of domestic virtue. Albert's encouragement of a fabric of royal pageantry and
splendour, grafted onto an otherwise grey industrial world, led to an enthusiastic cadre of entrepreneurs anxious to make their pile and join the established, landowning classes.

Broadland offered no raw materials such as coal and iron that would bring it
to the forefront of the Industrial Revolution, but it served the many small
industries needed to employ and provide for an increasing population. The
fruits of production had led to warmer, securer housing, a more predictable
food supply and these in turn to earlier marriage, more children and greater
life expectancy. Chalk and lime, bricks and cement, malt and flour were
Broadland's contribution to the populations increasingly gathering in the
towns and in Norwich.

Chalk had been dug out, crushed and spread on the fields since the medieval
period, but there was greater need as increased crop production was expected
in the seventeenth and eighteenth centuries. In east Norfolk, chalk is deeply
buried below the glacial and crag deposits, but reaches the surface, where the
rivers have cut into it, between Norwich and Brundall in the Yare valley, and
Aylsham and Coltishall in the Bure. Here a large industry arose, with the product, usually quicklime, transported elsewhere by boat. Quicklime is produced
by burning chalk, has equivalent neutralising power for soil acids, but is less
than half as bulky as the parent material. It can also be used for making mortar and plaster and as a whitewash for walls, which chalk cannot. A lime kiln
has been restored at Coltishall on the Bure, and at Horstead, a little way
upstream, a confused area of terrain ('Little Switzerland') is the remnant of
the docks, pits and heaps of the chalk industry (Fig. 10.4). This industry
declined as improved transport meant that lime and cement could be produced more cheaply elsewhere.

Estuarine clay and the sandy clays of the soils of the Flegg district were used
for brick making. There are nineteenth-century brick pits at Martham, drawing on both sources, which were mixed before firing. Estuarine clay is abundant, but bricks made entirely from it flake and weather badly, whilst the
glacial clay is harder to come by and is farther from the river, for transport, but
makes better bricks. There were brick works also at Rockland and Surlingham
on the River Yare and at Burgh Castle and Somerleyton on the River Waveney,
which closed as late as 1939. The Burgh Castle works was built in 1859 and also
produced cement by firing chalk with clay, using coal brought in by river as the
fuel. Even the Berney Arms Mill on the Yare, responsible for drainage, was
used to grind chalk with river clay and mud to be fired as cement.

Watermills also had a role in grinding the grain needed for food. They could
not be built in the lower parts of the rivers, for gradients were too shallow to
generate enough power, and mill sluices would have interfered with navigation. In the upper reaches, however, they were common, and substantial
remains can be seen at Horstead, Burlingham, Chedgrave, Ellingham,
Hainford and Ebridge Mill near Honing. In a prime barley-growing area, malt-
ings also were prominent. Barley is malted by soaking and germinating it on
extensive floors then heating it slowly to kill it and preserve the sugars produced from starch during the germination. This malt was then sent to brew-
eries for beer making – again using the rivers for transport. Malthouse Broad

Fig. 10.4 In the nineteenth century, Broadland supplied itself with a range of essential industrial commodities, transported by water. The photographs are of the Burgh Castle Portland Cement Company (upper), from Malster (1993) and from a local brickyard, taken by P.H. Emerson.

takes its name from the industry and malt houses remain, though unused now, at Coltishall, Womack, Wayford and, huge buildings, at Oulton Broad and Ditchingham.

Transport

One key to industrialisation in the country as a whole, as well as in Broadland, was the development of transport. Since the Romans, road building had been in abeyance. Efficient armies need roads as much as industrialists, but though the seventeenth-century Puritan army had been well organised, civil war does not lend itself to civil works. In the eighteenth century, new roads, the turn-pikes, had been established, but not without strife, for the poor populace had

Fig. 10.5 Wherries proved to be a very serviceable design for commercial boats in the eighteenth and nineteenth centuries and some were converted for holiday hire around the turn of the nineteenth century. They epitomise the apparently slow, steady rhythm of traditional life on the Broads, but the work of moving cargoes of coal, grain, bricks and reed must often have been hard and unpleasant. Photograph by G. Christopher Davies.

to pay to use them. In Broadland, the better solution was to use the more than 100 miles of river and fen-dike that would take shallow-bottomed sailing boats.

Wherries – solid, clinker-built boats (Fig. 10.5) of oak planks, with a big, black, rhomboidal, tarred sail – were the innovation of the seventeenth century and became the quintessential features of many paintings of Broadland in the eighteenth and nineteenth. There were other classes of boat also. Keels, the predecessors of wherries, were smaller, with square sails and drawing more water, but were ousted by the capacious wherries in the carriage of coal, tar, grain, bricks, tar, iron, lime and malt. In the upper rivers, cargoes, especially the harvests of the fens, were taken by smaller boats and transferred to wherries at the many small quays or staithes, where sometimes small warehouses were built. At Stalham, on the River Ant, quite a large complex still stands.

With increased river traffic, and money to be made, issues of navigation and its maintenance became pressing. The Enclosure Acts had supported and often guaranteed existing rights of navigation, but there had previously been only minor recognition of them. There was a Norfolk and Norwich Commission of Sewers, which in 1679 instructed local dwellers to clear weeds by April 1 from the River Bure above Woodbastwick, where it was becoming blocked in summer. By 1722, when the Yarmouth Pier and Haven Act was passed, the Commission could levy tolls on cargoes to pay for keeping the rivers and haven open. In 1860, separate commissions were set up for the Yare, Bure and Waveney, so important had commercial navigation become.

There were also schemes to extend the natural navigation (Fig. 10.6) so that water-borne trade could penetrate further into the upper reaches of the valleys where the larger boats would otherwise ground. They began with the estab-

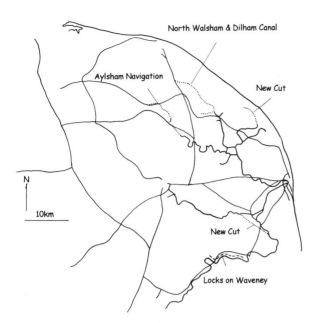

Fig. 10.6 In the nineteenth century, transport and communications in Norfolk were greatly increased. At first it was the river network that was extended (dotted lines) by canals and cuts, but as these were being brought into use, the railways (thin lines) were already veining the land in all directions. Sadly they too met their demise with the rise in road traffic from the 1920s onwards and in the mid-1960s the system throughout Britain was decimated by economic rationalisation. Now few of these lines remain.

lishment of locks in the 1670s on the Waveney at Geldeston, Ellingham and Wainford, in an attempt, ultimately abandoned, to connect the navigations of the Waveney and the Little Ouse and hence provide an inland route between Yarmouth and Kings Lynn on the Wash. The most successful schemes were at the top end of the River Bure, where in 1779 a canal with locks was built near Aylsham, paralleling the shallow river, and the North Walsham and Dilham Canal that in 1826 extended the navigation on the River Ant by eight miles.

The Bure scheme was instigated by the Parish in 1708, when the churchwardens paid out a sizeable sum for 'viewing and measuring the river'. At that time there was little in the way of local government spanning Parliament and the Parish, which, at an annual Vestry meeting, appointed officers and kept accounts and records. It was not until 1773, however, that an Act of Parliament was passed 'for making and extending the navigation' of the River Bure (commonly called the North River) by and from Coltishall and Aylsham bridge. On its completion, which led to some financial problems for the contractor, cargoes could be sent direct to Yarmouth and 26 wherries traded from the town. The locks were damaged in a severe flood in 1912 and it was too expensive to repair them, but remnants of the canal, now overgrown, may still be seen.

Probably around this time or a little before, the River Ant was diverted from its natural, meandering course through the fens to the east of Barton Broad through the Broad itself, thus saving perhaps half a day by a shorter route and a fairer wind. Time has always been of the essence! The Waxham New Cut was a canal extending parallel to the coast from Horsey Mere and built partly for drainage, partly to give access to the brick works at Lound Bridge, where estuarine clay was abundant.

The most prominent new waterway resulted from disputes over tolls between Norwich and Yarmouth, two towns that have almost always had rivalries. In the early nineteenth century, Yarmouth was charging ships, travelling to and from

Norwich, high tolls to use its haven. Moreover, cargoes from sea-going ships had to be transferred to smaller boats to navigate the estuary and the lower parts of the Yare, where the channel shifted and could not be permanently deepened. The proposed new scheme was to give Norwich direct access to the North Sea through Lowestoft, then an insignificant village, but a safe harbour.

Firstly, a 1,400-feet long channel was constructed between a small lake, Lake Lothing, ponded by dunes from the sea behind Lowestoft, to Oulton Broad, a little further inland, and then a longer channel, Oulton Dyke, was dug from Oulton Broad to the River Waveney. Finally, the New Cut, a straight channel, two-and-a-half miles long, was dug from St Olaves, lower down the Waveney, to Reedham on the Yare, and the Yare was dredged to nearly 12 feet up to Norwich. There were problems with tides because the Oulton Dyke stretch received two tides, the first from Lowestoft, the second, 90 minutes later, from Breydon Water, so locks were constructed close to the sea at Mutford lock and ships passed through them when water levels were about equal on both sides.

By 1833 this gave a 30-mile length improved for navigation, which bypassed Yarmouth and caused inevitable protest, not only from Yarmouth, but from the owners of the canals at the top ends of the Bure and Ant, whose trade could also be diminished by a greater importance of Norwich. In the end the New Cut scheme was not a success, and Norwich has never really prospered as a port. The New Cut soon became too narrow as ocean-going ships became bigger and the costs of maintenance were greater than the tolls that could be raised. The company that built it was bankrupt in 1847 after only 14 years. There remains to this day a rather ugly, dead straight channel connecting the rivers, an early indicator that the consequences of civil engineering need to be thought through on long timescales.

Commercial water transport in general, though still used on the Yare until the 1970s to supply a sugar beet factory at Cantley, declined in the nineteenth century and died out by the 1930s on the other rivers. Railways and roads were its demise, for they offered faster penetration into the hinterland. The first railway in Britain, from Stockton to Darlington, was built in 1825. By 1850 there were 6,000 miles of track, by 1870, 13,000. Broadland was not left out. The track from Norwich to Yarmouth was laid by 1844, from Reedham to Haddiscoe by 1847 and Norwich to Cromer by 1874. Eventually railways criss-crossed the county (Fig. 10.6), opening Broadland to much greater contact with the rest of the country than ever before and paving the way for the eventual tourist industry of the late nineteenth and twentieth centuries. Remarkably, none of the industrialisation, per se, had much effect on the wildlife of Broadland. It was to be the secondary effects that had the consequences.

Population and urbanisation

The end of the Napoleonic Wars, in 1815, released many men back to the labour market and caused widespread unemployment. The problem was solved by rising industry, which in turn supported further absolute increases in the population, with a major drift to the towns, where jobs were more readily available. Labour requirements on the land were decreasing as more machines were introduced to cultivate, seed, fertilise, harvest and thresh. The population in Britain rose by 73 per cent, two million per decade, during the first half of the nineteenth century. In 1825, only 25 per cent of it was in the towns, but by 1881 this had risen to 80 per cent.

Norfolk was no exception to the trend. Norwich and Yarmouth, and even small towns such as Aylsham, grew, and with them the stresses of public health that resulted from cheap, cramped housing built to exploit as well as to accommodate. In Aylsham, for example, though the water supply was ostensibly from wells, there were still ten or so typhoid cases per year in the parish as late as 1905. Brick-lined sewers had been built to drain the streets since the early nineteenth century, but a report of 1851 found the system very unsatisfactory, with uncovered cess pools, open drains and dung heaps, onto which the contents of domestic lavatory buckets were emptied and eventually washed into the sewers. Unauthorised connections of houses had also been made to the street drains. Effectively the raw sewage of a town that had expanded from about 1,000 people at the start of the nineteenth century to 2,700 by 1851, was discharged to the river. It was not until 1938 that a piped water supply was provided and 1953 that a sewage treatment works was built.

Indeed, sewage, throughout Britain, was commonly discharged raw to the rivers, from which drinking water was also taken. Epidemics of typhoid and cholera were common and greatly feared. The churchyards still show the evidence of whole families obliterated within days. In 1842, the Edwin Chadwick Society produced a report linking illness and premature death with such environmental conditions, but nothing much was done about it for another 30 years.

Sewage and the Broads

The consequences were not only for public health. Sewage, treated or untreated, is rich in plant nutrients. The rise in population and the gathering into towns exacerbated the situation. When the population was small and largely rural, the sewage, one way or another, was spread across the landscape and incorporated by earthworms and other soil organisms into the soil. Some of the phosphorus was held there, some taken up into the food webs and a little leached out to the streams. Likewise, the nitrogen compounds were taken up by plants, denitrified and circulated with again only a little running off into the streams. Most food was locally grown so there was little import of food (and therefore nutrients) and so the stock of nutrients in a given area was held relatively constant.

Urbanisation changed that. Town populations must import food from a larger area, but discharge the concentrated wastes to a much smaller one and that directly to the river with little benefit of soil filtration. The sewage decomposed foully in the rivers below the towns, usually completely deoxygenating a stretch of river completely for a kilometre or two and causing low oxygen concentrations for a much longer distance until decomposition into inorganic compounds – carbon dioxide, phosphates, ammonia, nitrate and others – was complete.

Raw sewage, which includes not only faeces and urine, but cooking and bathing water, would contain as much as 100 milligrams per litre of phosphorus and 300 milligrams of nitrogen per litre. In contrast, the water draining the nineteenth-century agricultural landscape might have had 25–50 micrograms of phosphorus and 0.5 milligrams per litre of nitrogen. Allowing for a hundred-fold dilution in the river, the sewage might thus have increased phosphorus concentrations by 20 to 40 times and nitrogen by six to ten times. Not surprisingly, the main rivers of Broadland became richer in nutrients from the mid-nineteenth century onwards.

Rural lifestyles

On the land, there was no rural idyll, despite the romanticised accounts of the middle-class writers and pictures of the many artists of the time. The Enclosures, though they had increased production by encouraging landowners to invest in new methods and machinery and to drain wet land, at first brought work to the glut market of labourers at the end of the wars, but then reduced them to servitude. Common rights – gleaning of the fields, common pasture on the fens, free fuel and fish – disappeared. Poaching became a way of survival and was severely put down by the Game Laws. It became a capital offence in 1803. One famous case of alleged poaching of eels on Hickling Broad turned on whether the Broad was tidal or not. It certainly is now and certainly was then, but the magistrates, drawn from the gentry, conveniently found that it was not and convicted.

For the first half of the century, the Corn Laws kept high the price of home-grown grain and kept out cheaper imports, favouring the landowners again and depriving the poor, who had little influence over anything. There was a great and patronised gulf between them and the ruling elite. The Reverend Richard Lubbock, a well-connected Norfolk parson, born in 1798, saw the poor through rose-coloured spectacles as he went about a leisured existence that gave him time to write an early classic on *British Birds* in 1837 and a *Fauna of Norfolk* in 1845. Riding about his Broadland parishes of Rockland and Bramerton, he became acquainted with those living among the fens:

'When I first visited the broads, I found here and there an occupant, squatted down, as the Americans would call it, on the verge of a pool, who relied almost entirely on shooting and fishing for the support of himself and family, and lived in a truly primitive manner. I particularly remember one hero of this description. "Our broad," as he always called the extensive pool by which his cottage stood, was his microcosm-his world; the islands in it were his gardens of the Esperides-its opposite extremity his *ultima Thule*. Wherever his thoughts wandered, they could not get beyond the circle of his beloved lake; indeed, I never knew them aberrant but once, when he informed me, with a doubting air that he had sent his wife and his two eldest children to a fair at a country village two miles off, that their ideas might expand by travel; as he sagely observed, they had never been away from "Our broad". I went into his house at the dinner hour and found the whole party going to fall to most thankfully upon a roasted Herring Gull, killed of course on "Our broad". His life presented no vicissitudes but an alternation of marsh employment. In winter, after his day's reed-cutting, he might be regularly found posted at nightfall, waiting for the flight of fowl, or paddling after them on the open water. With the first warm days of February, he launched his fleet of trimmers, pike finding a ready sale at his home door to those who bought them to sell again in the Norwich market. As soon as the pike had spawned and were out of season, the eels began to occupy his attention, lapwing's eggs to be diligently sought for. In the end of April, the island

in his watery domain was frequently visited for the sake of shooting
the Ruffs which resorted thither, on their first arrival. As the days grew
longer and hotter, he might be found searching, in some smaller
pools near his house for the shoals of tench as they commenced
spawning. Yet a little longer, and he began marsh mowing-his gun
always laid ready on his coat, in case flappers should be met with.
By the middle of August, teal came to a wet corner near his cottage,
snipe began to arrive, and he was often called upon to exercise his
vocal powers on the curlews that passed to and fro. By the end of
September, good snipe shooting was generally to be met with in his
neighbourhood; and his accurate knowledge of the marshes, his unas-
suming good humour and zeal in providing sport for those who
employed him made him very much sought after as a sporting guide,
by snipe shots and fishermen; and his knowledge of the habits of different birds enabled him to give useful information to those who collected them. These hardy fen-men, inured to toil and privation, were
the great supporters of an old Norfolk pastime, as they doubtless
thought it – "Camping". It required muscle and endurance of pain
beyond common limits, and somewhat resembled the *pancratium* of
the ancients, but was rather more severe.'

Lubbock was a keen naturalist and aware of changes. He feared for the
extinction of the great-crested grebe (shot for its plumes), which was eventually averted by the Bird Protection Act, and noted the filling in of Surlingham
Broad, with silt and vegetation, over a span from 1819 until 1875. A few
decades later, P.H. Emerson continued the theme of rural romanticism in his
photographs (Fig. 10.7), and in 1906, William Dutt continued both that and
regretted a decline in the local wildlife. He tells of life on a remnant of fenland
at the edge of the Waveney valley, where springs from the upland have prevented 'the old fen' from being drained like the adjacent grazing marshes. It
is possible that this area is the landward edge of the Carlton marshes, close to
Oulton Broad. Dutt describes the lifestyle of an 'old grey bearded marshman
... a man of many occupations – the River Commissioners' marshman and mill-
man, a farmer's cattle tender and dike-drawer, a reed cutter, an eel catcher,
and a flight-shooter.'
He had cut peat in the fen and in his early years there had been an annual
race among the villagers to establish who would cut where. Starting in the village, each armed with a shovel, the first to reach the fen would have his choice
of where to cut for the season. Flocks of starlings were a problem for the reed
cutting for they flattened the reed by their roosting, but the fen harvest was:

' ... nothing now compared with what it once was, and almost every
year the stack made of the reed sheaves seems smaller than that of the
previous year. For, in spite of what the marshmen say, the old fen is
becoming gradually less fen-like, and the time will come when it will
be a fen only in name. It has seen the extinction of some of its wild
flowers; others which still bloom there are numbered among those
the botanists consider doomed to extinction; and, like the reeds, the
bogbeans, sundews, and some of the orchids are less plentiful than
they were a few years ago. But unlike the fenmen of the Seventeenth

Fig. 10.7 P.H. Emerson has left us with a picture of traditional activities in the Broads at the end of the nineteenth century. Though carefully posed and conveying more an idyllic view than what was probably a realistic one, they are nonetheless highly informative.

century, the marshmen of today make no complaint when they see the swampy lowlands slowly changing into profitable pasture land. They know that the days when a good livelihood could be obtained by wild-fowling, egg collecting, and other fen pursuits are gone never to return, so they behold unmoved the disappearance of the few – the very few – remaining tracts of sodden marsh which remind them of what has been. Indeed they realise that the changes which have taken place and are still proceeding, are to their benefit rather than other-wise, for where the wildernesses of reed and rush provided intermit-tent occupation for the wild-fowler, egg-collector, and reed cutter, the reclaimed lands must be kept well drained and protected by marsh and river walls, or they cannot be preserved although they are won: and this banking and draining means frequent labour for many hands. So we must admit that the gain is greater than the loss, and that however much we may lament the loss of the wild life and primi-tive charm of the fen, others will be better for the changes we deplore.'

The changes can, to some extent be indicated by the list of animals and plants Dutt casually mentions on the fen in this chapter of his book (Table 10.1).

Table 10.1 Species listed by W. Dutt in a description of a favourite fen in 1906. Species with asterisks are now locally extinct or very unusual

(a) *Butterflies and moths*: swallowtail*, meadow brown, five-spotted burnet, convolvulus hawkmoth

(b) *Fish*: eel, roach, bream

(c) *Reptiles and amphibians*: viper, frog, crested newt*, natterjack toad*

(d) *Birds*: reed warbler, water rail*, peewit, bittern*, black-winged stilt*, bearded tit*, grasshopper warbler, pheasant, corncrake*, heron, marsh harrier*, Montague's harrier*, redshank, reeve*, tern, willow wren, yellow wagtail, snipe, lapwing, lark, meadow pipit, cuckoo, sedge warbler, great reed warbler, ruff*, kestrel, water hen*, swift, swallow, owl, nightjar*, titlark, reed bunting, linnet, starling, goldfinch, fieldfare, redwing, redpoll, green woodpecker

(e) *Mammals*: otter*, water vole, hare, stoat, weasel, field vole, pipistrelle, great noctule bat

(f) *Plants*: bog moss, reed, sedge, rush, greater spearwort, marsh sow-thistle*, fen ragwort, tufted sedge, meadowsweet, marsh orchid, bur-reed, lady's smock, angelica, jointed rush, marsh stitchwort, dwarf reed, marsh thistle, marsh vetchling, bogbean, bog-myrtle, duckweed, alder, sallow, marsh marigold, flowering-rush*, bog pimpernel, grass of Parnassus, marsh fern, sundew*, spotted-orchid, green-winged orchid*, tway-blade*, marsh cinquefoil, marsh St John's wort, meadow thistle, yellow iris, cat valerian, red rattle, sorrel, oak, water-plantain, water-lily, meadow rue, valerian, dock, bur marigold, water mint, fen parsley and hawthorn.

What is remarkable about this list is the number of species, indicated by asterisks, that would now be regarded as extremely unusual or very rare.

Fig. 10.8 Eels were an important product of the waterway in the nineteenth and early twentieth centuries. Sometimes they were speared, as in this painting from Dutt's book; they were more effectively caught in setts, nets laid across the river and tended against the potential damage of boat traffic by fishermen living in ark-like houseboats (photograph by J. Payne-Jennings 1891).

Angling and fisheries

The fishing was, on the other hand, in a good state. This is not surprising. The ingress of nutrients from sewage was increasing the production of plants on the beds of the rivers and Broads, away from the grossly polluted stretches below the sewage outfalls near the towns and larger villages. More weed meant greater habitat for spawning, more invertebrates for feeding. Dutt describes a night spent with an eel catcher on the River Waveney. At the time, eel catchers worked setts, which were walls of netting placed across the river, weighted at the bottom and with floats at the top. They were fitted with long pouches or

pokes trailing downstream, into which the eels found their way as they attempted to swim down river. Because of the wherry and other boat traffic, the catcher had to stand by the net to pull on ropes to lower it to the river bed when a
boat came by. The best fishing was at night when the eels could not see the net,
especially on nights after rain had quickened the river flow.

Catches could be several stones, sometimes 50 or more (311 kilograms) in a
night and a succession of catches was stored live in submerged perforated
wooden boxes (eel trunks) until there were sufficient to take to market or send
to London. Though the supply was supposed to be declining for a number of
reasons, including the 'growing up' (encroachment of vegetation) of the
Broads and the increase in river traffic, eels were still abundant enough to
make spearing a feasible catching method also. Flat-tined forks were plunged
into the bottom and the eels speared (Fig. 10.8). Eels were also caught on baited lines and other fish, particularly pike, were also accidentally caught. This
led to restrictions on commercial fishing with the passing of the Norfolk and
Suffolk Fisheries Act in 1877.

There is a lot of anecdotal evidence of heavy fishing in Broadland during the
nineteenth century. There had probably been substantial exploitation long
before this, as evidenced by pieces of fisheries protection legislation as far back
as the thirteenth century, but with the rise in population and urbanisation it
may have intensified. It was, at least, documented in the eighteenth century to
a much greater extent. As well as the various methods of eel fishing, pike were
caught on lines baited with roach and held in mid-water by floating rolls of
reed (liggers or trimmers), around which the line was wrapped. Tubular bow

Fig. 10.9 Fishing in general was important in the nineteenth century, both commercially
and for sport, when large catches were often made in waters fertilised by sewage. These four
photographs by Emerson and Payne-Jennings illustrate different aspects.

nets, held open by hoops, were set in the gaps between the weed beds for tench (Fig. 10.9). Loops of wire were used manually to snare large pike in the clear waters, when the loop could be manoeuvred over the fish's head and behind the gills. There are descriptions of barrowloads of small fish taken with drag-nets being used as manure, and though this can only have been on a small scale it certainly caught the attention of the anglers.

There was, nonetheless, no shortage of prodigious angling catches. Two anglers on Wroxham Broad in July 1875 took more than 16 stone (99.5 kilograms) of bream in a single day, so it is difficult to know exactly what the state of the freshwater fish stocks was. The drag netting was said to have been the work of a rather few individuals on the River Yare, using nets 100 yards (91 metres) long and 16 feet (5 metres) deep and often in spring just as spawning was starting, but it was probably more widespread. The anglers were mostly gentry and influential, the commercial fishermen mostly poor and feeding the poor. In 1857 the anglers began to note that netting was extensive and through it rationalised their perceived declining catches. *The Field* of July 1858 published an article on bream- and roach-fishing in Norfolk. Daily catches were said to have fallen from 20 stone (124 kilograms) or more to ten, eight, even five stones (31 kilograms)!

An Angling Society was convened in Norwich in 1857 and plans were laid to buy out the fishermen on some of the Yare Broads. There were, however, still some common rights of fishing that undermined these plans. The Society berated the Mayor of Norwich for the City not upholding its duties under the charter to conserve the fish granted by Edward VI in 1461 and an Act of George III prohibiting the taking of 'unsizable' fish. Eventually, in 1877, an Act was passed under which bylaws were made. The bylaws were very detailed and specific to different sorts of fish. They prohibited drag netting with pokes, any net with less than a seven inch (18 centimetre) mesh (knot to knot), bow nets in the rivers and liggers or snares, except for taking eels. Smelt fishing was confined mostly to March–May in certain locations, but eel fishing (a fish in which anglers were not interested) was largely unrestricted.

Social changes and government influence

Perhaps as much as industrialisation, population increase and movement of people to the towns, the political changes of the nineteenth century were important in determining what was ultimately to happen to the natural history of Broadland. The trends were towards a shift in power from the aristocracy and gentry towards the ordinary people, and the recognition by governments that the impacts of the Industrial Revolution had to be regulated in the interests of health, and ultimately that of the environment.

Throughout the nineteenth century, the aristocracy and gentry had held grimly onto the influence they had acquired since the Norman Conquest, manipulating their funds to take advantage of the opportunities of industry whilst hanging on to the bulk of the land and continuing to dominate the ministries of government. In 1873, 80 per cent of the land was still owned by only 7,000 out of a population of 32 million and, in 1914, one per cent owned two-thirds of it. One third of the population still lived in severe poverty, but the elite were accepted because there was also a sense among them of public duty and philanthropy. It was a religious age of missionary zeal and Christian ethos. It was as the Lord had ordained.

The Crimean War led to a challenge to that and the First World War consolidated it. The invention of mass printing, the sending out of war reporters, the spread of newspapers, all started to reveal some long-concealed truths. The land-owning leadership, though sometimes highly competent, was often useless at maintaining anything but its own interests. Reforms such as the establishment of competitive civil service examinations in the 1870s helped to bring in an ethos of merit over birth and wealth; and the ideas of Charles Darwin, dangerous and revolutionary, brought in concepts of competition and fitness.

The excesses of industry were being felt. Broadland took the consequences of urbanisation, but largely escaped the atmospheric and river pollution and the scarring of the countryside of the north and midlands. The Government evaded the problems. Governments had previously held to a passive role in all but the maintenance of foreign policy and trade protection. Their stance was the utilitarianism of Jeremy Bentham – in which the State should intervene only to prevent chaos and ensure that enterprise and initiative could flourish. This was all very much to the advantage of its ministers' and members' freedom to exploit the nation's natural resources. In the end, though, environmental and public health conditions became so scandalous that the Government was forced to act and regulate.

Royal Commissions of Enquiry were set up, registers of births, marriages and deaths were established and entry made compulsory in 1874. Statistics were collected and local government organisations were established to manage what could not be overseen centrally. Borough Councils emerged in 1835, County Councils in 1888 and Urban and Rural Councils in 1894, replacing the influence of the Lord Lieutenants and Justices of the Peace, hitherto the agents of the Crown in the provinces. Acts were passed concerning labour, factory conditions, the Church, the railways, the Bank of England, postal services, education and the poor.

Revolution was always distant in the nineteenth century – the masses accepted their lot as inevitable and occasional riots were quickly put down, but one attempt to maintain the status quo was to backfire. Education, originally considered dangerous for the lower orders, for it might give them ideas above their station, gradually became more widespread for it was seen as a means of averting any revolutionary potential. With it, though, came not the intended indoctrination, but a release to question, which was gradually to bring about sweeping changes in society.

The well off maintained the public schools and the previously aristocratic clientele folded into them the newly rich, and inculcated the attitudes of gentlemen, thus preserving the insularity and conservatism that had been the watchwords of the ruling classes for some time. The poor were taught in church-maintained schools at first, but in 1870 it was decided that the State should provide education for all children in its newly founded Board Schools and the State paid for it all by 1891.

Arthur Patterson and Breydon Water

One of the initial problems of introduction of universal education was in persuading the populace it needed it! Arthur Patterson (Fig. 10.10), born in 1857 in the Yarmouth Rows, a district of tightly built slum housing within the medieval walls, had an early career as elementary school teacher, an assurance agent, postman, tea peddler, showman, menagerie keeper and warehouseman.

Fig. 10.10 Arthur Patterson is justly revered as an observer and recorder of the natural history of Victorian and Edwardian Broadland. He made a few cruises upriver in various boats, including the 'Yarwhelp' but was particularly wedded to the life of Breydon Water, with its smelt fishermen (upper right) and punt gunners (lower right).

Eventually, in 1892, he was appointed school attendance officer, chasing truants to school. This he did in the light of strong Victorian Methodist convictions for 34 years. But it is in his role as 'John Knowlittle' that he is best known. Knowlittle was a pseudonym he adopted in 1896 to write articles and books on natural history for local papers. He used his own name for more formal publications in journals of natural history and, without benefit of any formal qualifications, was eventually elected an Associate of the Linnean Society of London.

From his early teens, Patterson hung around the group of people that made their living from Breydon Water. They lived on ramshackle houseboats like Noah's Arks, a hardy, grim, observant, self-centred and illiterate set of toilers, sometimes far the worse for drink, but carrying on many of the activities documented by Richard Lubbock 50 years earlier (p.162). Patterson recorded them without the filter of romanticism of Lubbock and Dutt. In winter they shot wigeon, mallard, pochard and waders, in spring godwit and knot and in summer spoonbills, sandpipers and almost anything else that flew and could be sold to gentlemen collectors for stuffing and display.

They used large guns (Fig. 10.10) charged with powder and handfuls of shrapnel and shot, from low-lying punts that allowed them to get within shooting distance. The discharge of these ancient and malfunctioning guns sometimes did more damage to themselves than to the flocks of birds. They fished for eels, flounder, then called butts, and mullet in the estuary and sold the lot locally or shipped it to Norwich, Bath or London to be served at the tables of the fashionable and omnivorous.

Patterson recorded what he learned from them and from his own observations on trips in various punts and houseboats that he bought and modified. He collected eggs and went shooting himself at first, but eventually ceased these, though he accepted their role in the local economy and did not disapprove. He corresponded with Eliza Phillips, the founder of the Fur, Fin and Feather Society which was eventually to become the Royal Society for the Protection of Birds and may have been influential through this in the drawing up the contents of the eventual Bird Protection Acts. He was also a keen observer of change in the Broadland system during the latter half of the nineteenth century.

In 1902 he was documenting the decline of the punt gunners of Breydon as the bird populations fell. This he attributed to the progressive drainage of the lowlands around Halvergate, a silting up of the remnant Breydon estuary, the expansion of weed (probably eelgrass or wigeon grass) on the mud flats, and the disturbance by commercial traffic passing through. The establishment of a close season by the Bird Protection Acts was the final straw for the punt gunners. The Acts were passed in 1872, 1876 and 1880 by an ethically more conscious late Victorian Society attuned to the ills of industrial expansion – but also careful to preserve the sporting shoots of the gentry.

The poulterers' stalls, once groaning with duck, dunlin, ringed plover, knot, turnstone, terns and small waders, and even gulls, were no longer so full and the fishing was said to be declining too. Of all the various ills that the system was apparently suffering, it may well have been the very shooting that was most responsible at the time. Another writer, John Gurney, in 1904, noted the very low numbers of coot on Hickling Broad in the early 1880s and a remarkable increase in 1895 following the legal protection of their nests, from which eggs had previously been collected.

Patterson and the Broads

Patterson only rarely ventured upriver from Breydon, but when he did he remained an acute observer. His notes tie in very well with the deductions that can be made from sediment cores taken from the Broads, and from the effects of urbanisation on sewage disposal. In 1919, he took his boat first up the Waveney, then the Yare and the Bure and its tributaries, contributing accounts of this tour to the local newspaper, the *Eastern Daily Press*. He found the River Yare particularly weedbound: 'Weeds! I sailed through acres of floating weeds: once went through what seemed to be "The Lake of the Thousand Islands". Twice I ran on patches and got clear only with difficulty; the oars were like Venetian masts, with streamers.'

It took him six hours of hard rowing to reach Brundall from Reedham, a distance of about 13 miles (21 kilometres). He returns to this issue repeatedly:

'I must just once more revert to the floating and subaqueous vegetation … The plethora of them has set a motor boatman complaining to me of how often he had to clear his screw: the ferrymen at Buckenham and at Coldham Hall seem to bring them up as a trawl net around the chains and have to stop cranking to rid the links of their fearful gleanings; and my host's fifteen anglers' boats lie idle today "folks come but once and not again" he told me.'

Patterson notes in particular the density of weed on the Yare and this may be linked with the greatest discharge of sewage to that river from Norwich, by far the largest town in the area. He talks of the placid, translucent Bure, and the crystal flood above Horning that suggests the water was not turbid, even if very weedy. He knew about the sewers too. In Yarmouth he noted that the water for once was relatively clean: '... yesterday it was black, the day before green, red, brown, and so on, exudations from a proximitous sewer opening'. Upstream on the Ant, he was glad of the weed, or at least the water-lilies, for, in what was a very hot summer, he relieved his touch of sunstroke by placing two fresh lily leaves under a towel over his head. Later though:

> '... the Barton weeds; they cloyed my oar blades, they caught in the bows – dead lily leaves, sedges and what not, a queer place for fishermen to cast angle, as some did, only to have their baits held up. It was just then a seemingly hopeless wilderness of vegetable abominations. But my opinions became reversed in the morning when the wind or some more mysterious forces of nature had driven the weeds to the sides, and to my surprise lusty marshmen were hauling it out, and piling it on the shore with long handled, four-pronged forks.'

Birds and people were Patterson's main interests; he deigns to identify the weed, but the fact that it drifted around in floating masses suggests that it might have been the hornwort, but probably not charophytes, which are always firmly fixed to the bottom. This is consistent with the evidence of the sediment cores, in which *Chara* disappears, or at least is no longer predominant, in the Broads of the Yare and Bure after the middle of the nineteenth century. Charophytes may have persisted longer in the remoter Ant, as they did in the Thurne system.

They are associated with low phosphorus concentrations, not necessarily because phosphorus is toxic to them, but because many are low-growing for the most part and soon disadvantaged if other, faster growing plants and filamentous algae or epiphytes grow over them in response to higher nutrient supplies. Several experiments (Fig. 10.11) have shown this to occur with low-growing aquatic plants, including hollyweed, a vascular plant found in Broadland, which has many of the same vulnerabilities as charophytes. Many of the taller vascular plants can also take up nutrients from the water as well as the sediment and as the supply from sewage increased, these would have been advantaged.

Hickling Broad

Charophytes did not relinquish the entire Broadland waterway, however. At Hickling Broad, *Chara aspera* was recorded by the Reverend Arthur Bennett in 1883 as profuse to the exclusion of almost all other aquatic vegetation and was present with *Chara polycantha* and *Chara stelligera* in Somerton (now Martham) Broad. His description has the charm of a leisured middle-class society in the new railway age:

> 'So on July 20th 1883, my daughter and I, with Mr A.G. More of Dublin, went to Liverpool Street Station, had tea together, and Mr More saw us off by the mail train to Yarmouth ... Finding our way to the Draining Mill below Heigham Bridge, we engaged the lad there

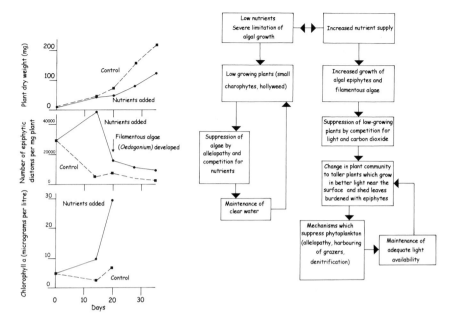

Fig. 10.11 The first effects of increasing nutrient levels on submerged plants are seen in changes in the periphyton (or more precisely, epiphyte) community that covers their surfaces. On the left are shown the results of an experiment in which seedlings of hollyweed (*Naias marina*), a short-growing annual plant were germinated and grown in low nutrient (control) conditions and with added phosphate and nitrate. The epiphytic diatoms and, a little later clouds of filamentous algae, like green cotton wool, grew in response to the nutrients, and the plant growth was reduced. (Based on Eminson & Phillips 1978). Experiments such as this and observations that epiphytes developed early in response to discharge of sewage to the Broadland waterway (Fig. 10.3) led to development of an earlier form of the hypothesis shown on the right. The low-growing charophytes are replaced by taller-growing plants as a result of the epiphyte development. The original version proposed that an eventual total loss of plants resulted from epiphyte smothering, but such loss is now seen to come from other mechanisms (based on Phillips, Eminson & Moss 1978).

and his boat to take us up to Hickling. After passing through Kendal [Candle] Dike into the Sounds, we here and there "dragged" for plants, found many Charas,&c. '

They also found charophytes abundant in Filby Broad, on the Muck Fleet. The charophytes were still abundant in these places and in the Thurne Broads in general, in 1899. All of these locations are at the distal ends of the river system, unaffected by towns or villages of any size. In almost all of them (the exceptions are Martham Broad and the isolated Upton Broad) charophytes were eventually to diminish or disappear in the twentieth century. Nutrient inputs increased from sources other than sewage (a gull roost at Hickling Broad, probably agricultural sources in Filby Broad), but the survival of charophytes to later dates in these locations is notably linked with the absence of sewage.

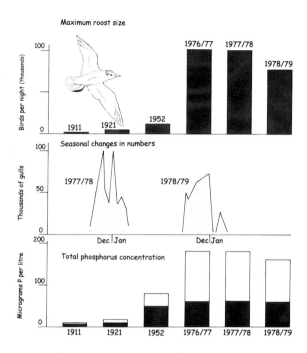

Fig. 10.12 Hickling Broad was one of the last Broads to show effects of nutrient enrichment and this was owing to an increase in its roost of migratory black-headed gulls. Progressively they came to dominate the sources of phosphorus in the Broad (bottom, shaded areas), with the catchment (unshaded areas) contributing less than half of the total. In the 1980s and 1990s, the gulls, which had been attracted by a close-by waste tip to feed, dispersed, and the Broad has undergone further changes (Chapters 12 and 13).

Hickling Broad and its gulls

A black-headed gull roost at Hickling Broad expanded rapidly in the early twentieth century and the stimulus appears also to have been due to increasing human influence. The gulls were winter migrants, nesting around the Baltic, where their eggs had been collected until protective legislation was passed in the early twentieth century. This was one stimulus to increase, but others were at work. As sea fishing became more intensive, stocks declined and fish were processed on land rather than at sea. Previously the offal was thrown overboard and the gulls followed the boats for it. Lacking fish and fish offal, gulls progressively changed their behaviour and fed much more on land – in ploughed fields and open municipal rubbish tips. Coupled with the other influences, a tip near Martham appears to have resulted in gull roosts at Hickling Broad rising from only a thousand birds each night in 1911 to more than 100,000 by the 1970s (Fig. 10.12). These provided rich sources of nutrients, which progressively increased the biomass of plants in Hickling Broad for two-thirds of the twentieth century, as human sewage had in the rest of the system in the nineteenth.

A last influence – the rise of tourism

Late in the nineteenth century, legislation was passed to provide paid holidays and a working week limited to five and a half days, with statutory holidays (Bank Holidays) on four other days. The railway companies, with cheap excursions, encouraged the idea of the residential holiday and in the 1870s and 1880s the seaside came into vogue. The scene was being set for Broadland's most important modern industry, surpassing even agriculture: that of tourism

Fig. 10.13 Christopher Davies (1849–1922), an affable solicitor who became clerk to the Norfolk County Council, was the first to publicise widely the attractions of the Broads for fishing and boating, in his writings and photographs. Campbell & Middleton (1999) provide an interesting biography.

– both hedonistic and ecological.

The Broads were well known locally and used for popular 'water frolics', an early form of regatta, even in the eighteenth century, and the wealthy kept boats for recreations such as sailing and fishing. Doubtless there was a network of awareness through this, but the Broads were not widely known outside Norfolk until the last two decades of the nineteenth century. The wealthier sections of society were adventurous and keen to exploit new opportunities offered by the railways to get about. Fortuitously, Christopher Davies (Fig. 10.13), a Norwich solicitor who eventually became clerk to the Norfolk County Council, not only had become acquainted with the system, but also enjoyed communicating what he was discovering.

He wrote a short book, published in 1876, called *The Swan and her Crew – the adventures of three young naturalists and sportsmen on the Broads and Rivers of Norfolk*, which was well received. Then, in answer to many requests that he began to receive for travel information, he wrote a guidebook, *The Handbook to the Rivers and Broads of Norfolk and Suffolk* in 1882. This book ran to 50 editions over 40 years until his death in 1922. He also wrote a more thoughtful and

Fig. 10.14 John Loynes, perhaps the first commercial boat hirer on the Broads, advertised in Christopher Davies' guidebook, as did the railways essential for bringing his clientele to Wroxham.

detailed book in 1883, *Norfolk Broads and Rivers or the Water-ways, lagoons and decoys of East Anglia,* which ran to 11 editions by 1888. His books were popularising the Broads, listing boat yards where yachts might be hired, and fuelling the abilities of the Great Eastern and other railways to bring people from London to Norwich in less than four hours.

Others were also copying Davies' example with their own guide books and over 30 were produced between 1880 and 1900, though all of them very repetitious of each other and romantic in their view – just like most modern guide books! The Broads were being well and truly marketed by a bunch of enthusiastic amateurs, no less effectively than by the hugely paid consultants of the present.

Some cracks were appearing, though, in the idyll of restful waterscapes, abundant fishing and manly sailing. Davies berates some bad behaviour – the bottle shooters, coot potters, noisy revellers, swans' egg robbers and grebe destroyers – and castigates those young men who failed to confine their nude bathing to before eight o'clock in the morning. But boating on the Broads was a very minor influence compared with what it was to become. In the first edition of Davies' handbook, only a single boat hirer, John Loynes (Fig. 10.14), advertised, but the numbers were to build up with successive editions.

The boat hire industry

Loynes, formerly a footman at Brooke Hall in south Norfolk, learned to sail on the estate lake, then became apprenticed and eventually a master carpenter in Norwich, and began to design and build boats for his own use. Friends prevailed on him to hire them out from about 1878. By 1882 the business had grown, with a good selection available, some based at Norwich, some at the growing village of Wroxham. 'Wroxham' is actually a pair of villages, Wroxham and Hoveton, on either side of the River Bure, north of Norwich, and was to develop as the centre of the boat hire trade. By 1888 the previously open boats had collapsible cabins fitted and the industry was poised to provide greater and greater comfort.

A firm of millers, Press Bros of North Walsham on the River Ant, fitted out five of their wherries, then becoming redundant, as rail replaced water as the major means of transport of goods. They put cabins in the holds, and installed toilets and pianos, at first for the summer only, then permanently. They were hired out, complete with skipper and steward, but affordable only by the upper classes. Eventually wherries, called pleasure wherries, were built specifically for the hire trade and made sleek with smart white sails, to replace the black tarred sails that had characterised the workhorse wherries with their mundane cargoes of grain and coal. By 1891 there were 37 boat-hirers and the centres at Thorpe and Brundall near Norwich, Wroxham and Horning on the River Bure and Potter Heigham on the Thurne were becoming well recognised.

The business was largely in the upper, apparently more picturesque reaches of the rivers, where the Broads were mostly situated. The flat landscapes of the grazing marshes were spurned, except at Oulton Broad, close to the bathing beaches of Lowestoft. Yarmouth stayed rather aloof, or perhaps was spurned by the trade, because it lay beyond the dreary marshes. Advertising expanded and Ernest Suffling, one of the many nineteenth-century guidebook authors, organised the first agency to co-ordinate bookings. Eventually the two main agencies of Blakes and Hoseasons created an efficient structure that not only

Fig. 10.15 The boats formerly hired on the Broads were mostly sailing yachts. The trend, as the industry has developed, has been towards motorised craft, culminating in the fibreglass hulls of the current fleet.

Fig. 10.16 Development of riverside properties, especially along the Bure between Wroxham and Horning, was at first deprecated, but is now seen as part of the cultural landscape of an area that has seen the influence of human activity for 4,000 years.

managed the business, but acted as its advocate as well.

Comfort continued to be sought and steam yachts became fashionable, much to the chagrin of the sailing devotees, but even these were rapidly to be superseded by motor cruisers (Fig. 10.15). As the hiring season lengthened from an initial six weeks to an eventual six months, the number of boats increased from less than 50 in 1890, all of them sailing yachts, to 105 in 1920, of which four were motorised. In 1949 there were 547, with 301 of them petrol or diesel-driven, and in 1979, 2,257, of which only 107 were sailing boats.

With the increase in the hire trade came a development of land-based facilities. Provision shops, notably Roys of Wroxham, opened in the main centres and would completely equip a hire boat for the week. Especially after the First World War there was a ribbon development of holiday homes (Fig. 10.16) along the banks of the Bure around Horning and at Potter Heigham. These houses were built of light materials on piles or concrete rafts on the waterside peat, and often thatched and timbered in a Tudoresque style. They obscured the view of the marshes and fens from the river, and replaced the reedy fringes with timber or metal protection for their moorings. For many years they were regarded as eyesores, but, their spread having been checked, they are now looked upon more affectionately as yet more symbols of the past relationships between people and the Broads. They also stand as the portals for an intensifying relationship later on in the twentieth century.

Further reading

The continued history of the Broads reflected in their sediments is documented in the references given for Chapter 7 (p.124). More details of dating techniques are to be found in Moss (1998). Stevenson (1879) gives a flowery account of the life of Richard Lubbock, whilst Middleton (1978) and Turner & Wood (1974) tell of the photographers who were using Broadland as a subject in the late nineteenth century and thereby documenting its environment, albeit in a deliberately picturesque way. Tooley (1985) is a biography of Arthur Patterson and the quotations about weeds in the rivers and Broads come from his book of 1920. His account of punt gunning (1902) is typical of his style. Gurney (1904) also begins to document declines in Broadland wildlife late in the nineteenth century, whilst Sapwell (1960) gives a valuable picture of developments in a Broadland town, with particular detail on the sewage disposal. Bennett (1884, 1910) describes the charophytes in Hickling Broad and the development of the gull roost there is documented in Leah et al. (1978) and Moss & Leah (1982). Early guide books to the Broads include Davies (1883) and Davies (1912), which also includes detail on the fishery controversies of the time. Suffling (1892), Goodey (1978), George (1992) and Malster (1993) describe the development of the boat hire industry and Williamson (1997), as ever, is particularly interesting on industrial developments in Broadland. Campbell & Middleton (1999) give a biography of G. Christopher Davies, with reproductions of some of his photographs.

11

War and its Consequences

If the Wars of the Roses had been minor dalliances of ambitious families, the wars of the twentieth century most certainly were not. The years between them continued and accelerated the social changes that had been taking place during the second half of the nineteenth century and the early part of the twentieth. The tenor was of increasing humanity. The upper classes remained very wealthy, but the spread of technology such as electricity, central heating, plumbing, telephones and typewriters was making the need for servants redundant and with it the passing of the attitudes of a class of servitude and deference. The wealthy had lost political and social dominance, but held on to cultural influence and subtly imposed it on the new leaders through the public schools, whose values were not the Victorian ones of hard work and zeal, but those of gentlemen of style and leisure – of the country house, not the urban masses. Caution and conservatism and a devotion to the past and its preservation were the watchwords, with consequences for the rest of the twentieth century.

In 1890, Victoria had reigned over 400 million people and a fifth of the globe. The Empire was seen with patriotic pride, compared with previous times when the colonies had been seen as a burden, necessary for trade, but a nuisance to defend. In the early twentieth century, however, Britain the great power was being overtaken by America and Germany, whilst turning its face strongly to links with the Empire and Commonwealth. Britain was a success, stable and rich, and complacent about its position. It lived in splendid isolation, remaining remote from events in Europe. Its policies simply opposed any European hegemony, following the failed attempt at superiority of the Spaniards with their Armada and the putting down of Napoleon by Marlborough, Nelson and Wellington.

This isolation encouraged the development of German aspirations to expand Germany's empire and inevitably drew Britain into war in 1914, when the German economy had created a battle fleet clearly superior to what had been until then the prime naval power. The Germans gambled that Britain would wish to stay out of further European involvement, but when Germany invaded Belgium and failed to answer a British ultimatum to withdraw, Britain was dragged into a long and monotonous war. It traumatised a generation and perhaps forever undermined confidence in the leadership of the elite. Millions were killed on all sides; new weapons such as poison gas brought horrors that removed any glory from warfare, and any return to the comfortable, well-ordered society of before 1914 was impossible.

After the War, there was widespread depression. Both agriculture and industry fell into decline. Only 4.2 per cent of the people worked on the land, the rest in towns and cities and unemployment there increased. There was a general strike in May 1926, when unemployment had reached 23 per cent. The heavy industries of the nineteenth century were undermined as other countries joined the competition and the response was not the innovation of the previous century, but a resistance to change, coupled with tariffs on imported goods set by the Government to protect trade. New industries arose in the South East in electrical goods, cars and plastics, many of them needing a better-informed workforce, and the role of the State in controlling the economy and most other aspects of society reached an apotheosis.

New ideas were abroad though. The Fabian Society, a group of theoreticians rather than activists, modified the ideas of Marx. They called for the emancipation of land and industrial capital for the general community, the replacement of profit-mongering capitalism with collective ownership and co-operative management of the means of production and distribution. Keir Hardie, in 1893, had proposed reforms along these lines including Clause 4 of a document that advocated collective ownership. The Liberal Party, the latest development of the Whigs of the eighteenth century, failed to respond and was eclipsed by the Labour Party. The Conservatives, the new Tories, held on to their support in the business and industrial middle-class vote, with no particular ideology other than to support king, Church, State and respectability.

There was a shift in land ownership after the First World War, for land was no longer the basis of political power and was subject to high taxes on inheritance. Nearly a third of the population by 1939 became homeowners, compared with 10 per cent in 1914.Consumerism and car ownership were increasing and the working week had decreased from 56 to 48 hours. At least 11 million people were entitled to at least a week of paid annual holiday. Britain had a very advanced unemployment welfare system; the State played a major role in most of the activities of the population, from the economy to education.

But the tide had turned from the attributes that had held together Victorian society in a time of comparable upheaval following the Napoleonic Wars. Improvement, enterprise, hard work and position were all still present, but there was less confidence in the stability of the future. There were the first signs of emphasis on individual gratification and of indifference to the rest of society. As the masses had gained power, some of the values of previous elites had rubbed off.

The Broads between the Wars

In the Broadland waterway, the changes that had resulted largely from urbanisation were complete. The waters, especially the Broads, were choked with weed, if looked at from the point of view of a sailor or fishermen, rich expanses of submerged plants if you were a naturalist. Patterson's place as the doyen of the local naturalists had been taken by Ted Ellis, who had typed notes for him as a teenager. Ellis surveyed Wheatfen Broad, close to Rockland and Surlingham Broads on the River Yare in 1941 and gives a full list of species. The hornwort was predominant with plenty of yellow water-lily, fan-leaved water-crowfoot, mare's tail, spiked water-milfoil and common water-starwort. There were the water soldier, Canadian pondweed, shining, curled and grasswrack pondweeds and great beds of fennel pondweed, together with four species of duckweeds, common, fat, ivy-leaved and greater, and frogbit.

It was not only a long list of plants with a high biomass, it was very much a list of those plants thriving at high nutrient concentrations. For although raw sewage was no longer being discharged from Norwich, the sewage works upstream at Whitlingham was releasing an effluent almost as rich in nutrients

as raw sewage. Conventional sewage treatment for most of the twentieth century removed the organic matter and therefore the deoxygenating capacity
and obnoxiousness of the sewage, but released the inorganic products of this
decomposition as a nutrient-rich effluent.

On the Bure, where the towns of Aylsham, Wroxham and Hoveton had
expanded, the water plants were still abundant, but there are also some
records of the algal plankton suspended in the water. Benjamin Millard
Griffiths, a lecturer at Durham University, had taken advantage of a base provided by the Gurney brothers, Eustace and Robert. This was the first freshwater biological laboratory to have been founded in Britain, in 1901, at Sutton
Broad on the River Ant (Plate 18). Griffiths had taken plankton samples with
a net in 1924. He gave no indication of the size of the algal population or
whether it was sufficient to make the water turbid from time to time. However,
he described the water in Wroxham Broad as brown at the time of sampling,
and the list of species he gives is one of nutrient-rich conditions.

The same species occurred in Rockland Broad, where Griffiths describes
large beds of plants – pondweeds, water-lilies, mare's tail and arrowhead. In
Ormesby Broad, there was a surface bloom of blue-green algae, which Griffiths
established by local enquiry not to be unusual, but he makes no mention of
plants. The Broad was described as lily-covered, however, in 1897 by the photographer Payne Jennings who published a set of tourist photographs, *Sun
Pictures of the Norfolk Broads*, that year.

The relationship between plants and plankton is a complex one in which the
plants are at a great disadvantage. Eventually, as discussed later, the plants were
to disappear completely from much of Broadland, to be replaced by dense
growths of plankton from February or March until November. This had not
happened by the Second World War, but in the early and late season before the
plants had fully developed, and as they were senescing for the year, the planktonic algae were demonstrating the greater potential for growth offered by the
increased nutrient supplies.

Charophytes persisted until the early twentieth century in Hickling Broad,
but were progressively replaced by vascular species with increasing amounts of
filamentous algae, *Cladophora sauteri*, which began to interfere with boating
activities and had to be cut. The most common vegetation of the inter-war
years seems to have been of vascular plants, pondweeds and lilies, hornwort
and lemnids, water soldier and frogbit. They formed a dense tangle in summer
and accompanied increasing diatom growths in spring, and green and blue-
green algae in the late summer and autumn.

Serious freshwater biology!

Yet another change that affected Broadland was the establishment between the
Wars of freshwater biology as a science. The Gurney brothers were members of
a family wealthy enough, from the profits of Gurneys Bank, later Barclays, in
Norwich, to be able to lead the existence of gentlemen-naturalists. Eustace
built the house at Sutton Broad in 1901 (Plate 18), which was to become a laboratory from 1903 to 1907, mainly to house the work of the brothers, especially Robert, but others were encouraged to use the facilities.

The brothers were somewhat critical, perhaps, of the abilities of some of
their visitors (including Griffiths) and so the place did not become very popular and Robert retreated to work at his home, Ingham Hall, near Sea Palling

and Hickling, for many years before finally moving to Oxford. He was shy, self-critical and diffident, but produced major works on crustaceans, especially the copepods and decapods, that made him a world authority. He also kept detailed diaries and notebooks of his collections in Broadland, especially from Calthorpe Broad, which he owned. His work was essentially taxonomic and evolutionary, but very valuable in establishing the nature of the crustacean communities in Broadland during the first half of the twentieth century.

What is particularly interesting, however, is that in 1929, Robert Gurney was invited to be a member of a committee, seeking to establish a freshwater biological station in Britain. This committee included the main freshwater worthies of the day – Frederick Fritsch, Benjamin Millard Griffiths, H.S. Holden, William Pearsall, Edward Russell, J.T. Saunders and Frank Balfour-Browne (who had briefly directed the Sutton Broad laboratory in 1903). After a discussion at the British Association for the Advancement of Science Meeting in Glasgow, the committee agreed a circular making the case for a station and association. Their grounds were those of a need to establish fundamental information on freshwater bodies, which were becoming polluted, and to advise Government on freshwater problems, such as fisheries and water supply. Gurney was at first unwilling to put his name to the document, which was to lead to the founding of a famous laboratory at Windermere in the English Lake District.

His reasons were that it seemed that the laboratory would do applied work, in, for example, the regulation of fisheries, as opposed to the pure science that he found most amenable. He rationalised his gentlemanly objection by saying that that he thought the document promised firm solutions to problems and he felt these could not be delivered, in the light of current knowledge. He was, in the end, persuaded at least to be a signatory, but not before he had been accused by Balfour-Browne that his view was 'because you have lived in such isolation in Norfolk that you have not advanced with the times'. His feelings towards applied science, however, were much more widespread and the same imbalance of esteem still persists. The irony is that the Broads in 1929 were developing just such problems as the Freshwater Biological Association was amply equipped to investigate. A man less retiring than Gurney could easily have influenced the committee to locate the Association in Broadland rather than Cumbria, where the freshwater problems, though also developing, were nowhere near as severe as they were to become in the lowlands.

The Second World War

The Second World War revived a sense of community. Britain had emerged triumphant from the First, the Great War. France and Germany had suffered devastation. Future war was considered unlikely and Britain disarmed. The recession in Germany, however, brought renewed promises of glory by the Nazi party in 1933 and an invasion of Austria in 1938. Britain was drawn in, again by movements of hostile forces into Belgium and now also Holland in 1939. The bigger Broads were closed off to boats from 1940 to 1943 and the hire cruisers were moored in the open water to prevent the landing of German seaplanes. There followed a major air war, the Battle of Britain, in 1940, which the Germans were forced to abandon, then a sea war, when food supplies from America and the Commonwealth were jeopardised by submarines. This alone was to have major effects on agriculture in general and Broadland in

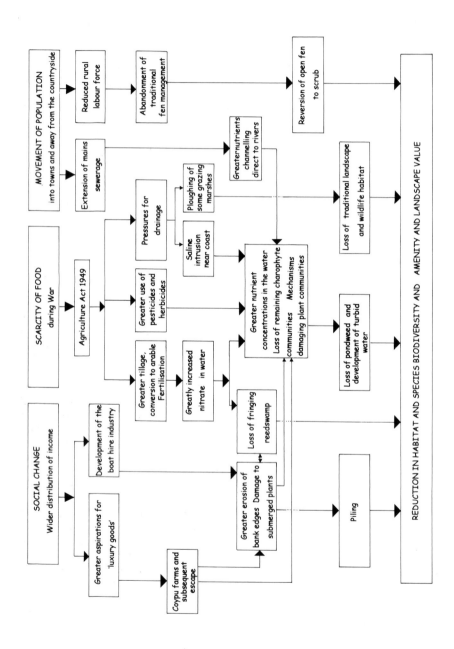

particular in the post-war period. Eventually Germany and its allies were defeated in 1945.

The Second World War affected everyone. Fewer were killed than in the First, but society had changed remarkably. The war effort had created a near totalitarian, regimented state for six years. There were identity cards, rationing of food, clothes and enforced conscription into the army. Huge taxation levelled out a society of few comforts and considerable hardships, but a renewed sense of unity and nostalgia. Economically, Britain once again attempted to remain insular, whilst America and Russia left its influence far behind. But, especially with the revelation of the horrors of the German concentration camps after the War, there was a moral dimension of good triumphing over evil. The British of 1945 were led to believe that a new and enlightened age was about to emerge, especially with the accession of a young Queen in 1953, fortuitously with the name Elizabeth, who, it was hoped, might have the influence that Elizabeth I had had.

In Broadland, it was impossible to foresee exactly what would happen over the next 50 years. For many, the omens appeared good – agriculture was to be well supported, a better distribution of wealth gave a greater market for the boat hire industry, the waterways were rich in plants and fish and the bird communities continued to display the recovery that had followed the Bird Protection Acts. Increased legislation was passed to protect natural areas. Better housing, better water supplies, improved sewerage and sewage treatment all bade well.

But Broadland had traditionally been managed in a labour-intensive way and the post-war population rightly demanded a status and payment that was not affordable by the owners of large Broadland estates. Moreover, the quality of the waters was to change as post-war technology introduced domestic and agricultural chemicals that the natural systems had not met before and with which they could not easily cope. And the sea was continuing to rise, as it had for centuries, whilst the established ways of controlling its tendency to invade Broadland were coming under increasing pressure. Broadland, in the last half of the twentieth century, was to suffer almost all of the ills to which freshwater systems are prone under severe human pressure (Fig. 11.1). It is this situation and the possible future that will be explored in the remainder of this book.

Further reading

The survey made by Ellis of Wheatfen Broad is in Ellis (1935), whilst the subsequent history of the plant populations in the Yare Broads is documented in Moss (1979) and Jackson (1978). Comprehensive references to the changes in plant populations are given also in Moss (1983) and a summary of the impending changes caused by the First World War in Moss (1987). The Sutton Broad Laboratory is described by Gurney & Gurney (1908); Griffiths' work on phytoplankton is in Griffiths (1927). Examples of Robert Gurney's work in Broadland are Gurney (1904, 1911). His diaries are kept in the Castle Museum, Norwich and his role in the foundation of the Freshwater Biological Association is documented in Moss (1991). Hardy (1950) wrote a detailed obituary of him.

Fig. 11.1 (opposite) The implications of the World Wars of the twentieth century – a chart of some of the impacts on the Broadland system.

12

Developments in the Broads and Rivers

After the Second World War, the change in the Broads was spectacular. Sometime in the 1950s or 1960s, over most of Broadland, the submerged aquatic plants that had filled the waterways with a rich jungly growth, disappeared. Their going was abrupt and generally realised some time after the event. One year they were there, a couple of years later they had completely gone. A few patches of lilies hung on, but the fringes of bulrush and reedmace at the edges of the Broads had been lost and the offshore water no longer had pondweeds and the floating mats of water soldier. Instead there was turbid water. Studies of sediment cores pick up this change as the epiphytes, the diatoms and other algae attached to plant surfaces, disappear and the planktonic diatoms become predominant (Fig. 10.2). The sediment also changed from an amorphous black, with snail shells, to a dark even more amorphous brown, but with no snail shells at all (Fig. 7.7).

This change caused alarm among organisations concerned with nature conservation in Broadland. The first fingers of blame were pointed at the boats, stirring up sediment and destroying the plants, then others at the sewage effluent, either for its nutrient content or perhaps other substances, such as the new detergents that were to be found in it, and at the nutrients coming in from agriculture. None of these things was entirely responsible; all, and yet others, may have been subtly involved together; the story is still being unravelled and it is far more involved than was thought at first.

Unravelling it is important, for the Broadland waterway had become and remains far less attractive, far less diverse in almost every group of animal and plant than it was before the Second World War, and subject to a number of other problems that arise from the loss of the plants. These include greater susceptibility of the banks to unsightly erosion and to eventual breaching where they protect low-lying grazing marsh, less rewarding angling, and reduced bird populations due mostly to loss of their food, but also to diseases such as botulism. To be able to restore something of the former interest of the waterway demands a knowledge of what has destroyed it. But firstly, what might the waterway be expected to have looked like by now if the prewar trends had continued uninfluenced by the post-war impacts?

The ecological development of shallow lakes and rivers

There would have been far less open water. Inspection of the Ordnance Survey maps since the nineteenth century shows a progressive loss of open water as vegetation, laying down peat and trapping sediment brought in from the catchment by the rivers, encroached from the sides (Fig. 12.1). Eventually, apart from the channels kept open by frequent boat passage, the Broads and the river edges would have succeeded to floating hovers of reed and then to alder carr as described in Chapter 4. This process, called terrestrialisation, can be very fast once it begins, especially when much inorganic sediment is washed

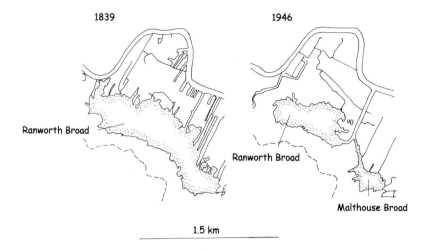

Fig. 12.1 Lakes naturally fill in with sediment from the catchment, and with peat and litter from swamp plants growing at the margins and encroaching steadily on the open water. Successive maps show the dwindling of the open water area of Ranworth Broad. The process has now greatly slowed owing to boat and wave erosion, especially as the protection given by submerged plants against wave erosion has been lost. The Broads may now be slightly larger than they were in 1946 as a result. Based on Ellis (1965).

in from the catchments. Some of the Broads undoubtedly were obliterated, or nearly so, in this way in past centuries. It is possible that the process was arrested by cutting of the edges and dykes for maintenance of commercial navigation until the later decades of the nineteenth century. The expected rate of terrestrialisation may then have only resumed in a period from then until the Second World War, when boat traffic was comparatively light compared with the periods before and after.

Even with creeping terrestrialisation, there would still, however, have been substantial areas of open water for submerged plants. If the wind can travel without obstruction over large sheets of water then this can prevent vegetation encroachment by reeds through wave disturbance, especially in storms. The post-war years should thus have supported much the same sort of communities that Patterson had found troublesome and Ellis had described in the 1940s. The earlier change from low-growing charophytes to taller charophytes and vascular plants had reflected the increased nutrient loading from sewage, then sewage effluent. However, the human population had stabilised by the middle of the twentieth century and there was no abrupt increase in sewage nutrients in the immediate post-war decades to explain the dramatic loss of plants.

There was, however, an increase in the amounts of nutrients coming in from agriculture. Algal growths, giving turbid water, were associated in other areas of Britain and abroad with such ingress of nutrients in a problem called eutrophication. Experience elsewhere showed that an initial symptom of this was an increase in submerged plants, then sometimes a complete loss as algal growth was stimulated and the algae apparently shaded out the plants.

The answer to the problem of why the fringing emergent plants, such as bulrush and reedmace and sometimes reed too, had disappeared, also seemed obvious. Boats had damaged them. The increase in commercial boat traffic in the nineteenth century and tourist traffic in the twentieth had not only kept the Broads open, but reversed some of the filling-in that had previously occurred. The rooted plants at the edge were clearly most vulnerable to this disturbance. They are comparatively brittle. The sheer physical damage, as boats brushed through them, or moored in the reed beds, or simply created an undermining wash as they passed, would easily cut away floating hover and gouge out more firmly rooted patches.

Old photographs show substantial edge vegetation even in the busier rivers during the period of active commercial traffic. The twentieth-century hire boats, however, could move much faster and were more prone to moor almost anywhere compared with the previous commercial traffic, which confined itself to the staithes for loading and unloading. In the early 1970s it seemed that with sewage effluent and intensifying agriculture, the problem of explaining submerged plant loss had been solved, and with increasing motor boat traffic so had that of the loss of fringing reedswamp. However, it turned out that the problem was far from well understood. This chapter will look at the loss of the submerged plants. The next will examine the loss of the fringing communities.

Breaking down the problem – eutrophication

There were some inconsistencies in the idea that eutrophication had led to the loss of the submerged plants, and these stimulated further inquiry. There was also a widely held view in the 1960s and 1970s that boat activity was to be blamed for the loss of submerged as well as reedswamp plants.

Let us start with the eutrophication issue. Large planktonic algal populations in the water, making it turbid and colouring it a prominent green or brown, do usually signify high nutrient addition (called loading), especially if they are prolonged throughout the spring and summer. Such populations (loosely, though incorrectly, referred to as algal blooms) had been appearing in the large deep lakes, on which limnologists had concentrated, since the 1940s. The American Great Lakes, Lake Washington, Lakes Geneva, Maggiore and others near the Alps, Lake Windermere, and many others, all had shown evidence of increased algal turbidity as populations crowded into the towns and cities on their banks. Sometimes the algal growths were accompanied by filamentous algae developing on the rocks at their edges or in free-floating blankets and by weed clogging the harbours of the steamers that plied up and down them. The whole ethos of limnology at the time was geared to the idea that the key process in lakes was the control that nutrients, particularly phosphorus, with nitrogen a distant second, exerted on the whole of the lake system.

As the plant and then algal crops grew there were consequences for other organisms. Snails and their predators, the flatworms and leeches, became more abundant at the edges, in preference to mayflies, stoneflies and other insects. Chironomids and oligochaetes came to dominate the deeper sediments as hypolimnia (the deeper layers of water in a lake that is deep enough to stratify in summer) became partly, or even completely, deoxygenated. White fish and salmonid fish declined, for the oxygen-rich cold water in the hypolimnia that they had depended on in summer was now less oxygen rich. The whole concept was one now called 'bottom-up control'. The nature of the lake ecosystem was ultimately determined by the nutrients, at the bottom end of the food webs, having consequences on all the rest. Had the biological research stations of the world developed on shallow wetlands rather than big, deep stratified lakes, this intellectual hegemony may not have developed. As a general concept it is still valid for the deeper lakes, and in the early 1970s it naturally pervaded the thinking about Broadland.

One of my graduate students, Paddy Osborne, came to Broadland with a Commonwealth Scholarship, fresh from working on a lake in Zimbabwe (then Southern Rhodesia) heavily polluted by the sewage effluent from the city of Harare (then Salisbury) and intent to continue work on heavily eutrophicated lakes. Barton Broad presented a similar situation. He constructed a phosphorus budget for the lake (Fig. 12.2), which showed that effluent from two sewage treatment works dominated the input, that from the surrounding agricultural land being only a small contributor. There was also a considerable recycling of phosphorus from the sediment, but we argued that this originally came from the input and was simply being recycled and was thus ultimately part of the catchment input.

Later we constructed a budget for the entire River Bure (Fig. 12.3) and again phosphorus from sewage effluents dominated it; and then a budget for Hickling Broad showed a case of guanotrophication, eutrophication by bird sewage (Chapter 10, Fig. 10.12). Throughout mainland Europe and North America, the problem of eutrophication was being tackled by the diversion of sewage effluents or by treating them to precipitate the phosphorus and this was proving spectacularly successful where the phosphorus removal was considerable. The omens appeared very good for a similar approach in Broadland. We gradually developed a three-pronged argument. The loss of plants was associated with increased nutrient, specifically phosphorus loading; most of this

Fig. 12.2 The sources of phosphorus entering Barton Broad, largely through the River Ant, in 1975. The sediment load entering from the river was originally derived also partly from the discharge of phosphate in sewage effluent. Phosphate is released in summer in a soluble form into the water from this source. Some of it is re-precipitated in winter and some is washed downstream with the outflow river water. Based on Osborne & Moss (1977).

Phosphorus budget for Barton Broad (1975)

Input   Unaccounted

| Sewage effluent | Sediment moving in on river bottom | Catchment | |

Output

| Stored in sediment | Lost through outflow |

5 tonnes P per year

10 grams per square metre of lake per year

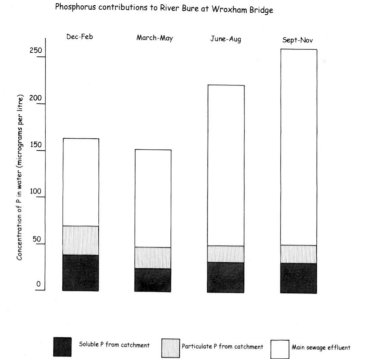

Phosphorus contributions to River Bure at Wroxham Bridge

Fig. 12.3 Changes in the concentration of total phosphorus in the River Bure at Wroxham Bridge in the 1980s and the component sources of the total. Values increased in summer because the sewage effluent was much less diluted. Based on Moss et al. (1988 (b)).

phosphorus came from effluents; thus removal of the effluent phosphorus should be the first, perhaps the only, necessary step in restoring clear water and the plant communities to the Broads.

Meanwhile we were also developing ideas about the mechanisms by which the plants were replaced by phytoplankton and it was again a 'bottom-up' mechanism. The evidence of the sediment cores showed that epiphytic diatoms started to increase long before the phytoplankton (Fig. 10.2). Epiphytes formed a dense blanket over the plant surfaces that not only shaded them, but could compete for nutrients and carbon dioxide. Some plants had been shown to secrete allelopathic organic substances into the water, which suppressed growth of some algae. Epiphytic algae normally associated with plant surfaces would be those that had evolved resistance to such substances. Thus as nutrients increased, the epiphytes would increase first whilst the phytoplankton remained suppressed. But as the epiphytes weakened the plants' ability to grow and therefore produce such substances, the phytoplankton would increase, make life even more difficult for the plants, and eventually suppress them altogether.

The information was all nicely coming together into a coherent story, but there was local resistance to the idea, some of it well founded, other of it to delay expenditure by the newly established Water Authority. The latter could see that phosphorus control might be expensive and would also create precedents for such control elsewhere in the UK, which lagged far behind other countries in the sophistication of its sewage treatment.

The red herring of boats and sediment

Boats had frequently been blamed for Broadland's problems and a whole official report, the *Broadland Study and Plan,* published in 1971, had been largely directed at control of the hire boats and boating, largely on this assumption. As they motored along, often in excess of the speed limits, they stirred up sediment, made a noise, and damaged banks when inexpertly moored. They also created wash that disturbed and undermined banks, including those of the now expensive waterside dwellings built especially on the River Bure between the Wars, and set the hulls of moored private boats crashing against one another. Boats also discharged raw sewage, which not surprisingly was found objectionable in a small waterway.

All of these things created a scapegoat of the hire boats, particularly the smaller day boats, which were even described as ploughing up the bottom. The more numerous boats of the local residents were not blamed; they were less used and the residents considered themselves more skilled at boat handling than the hire clientele.

Were boats causing enough turbidity by stirring up sediment to cause the loss of the submerged plants? There were logical inconsistencies in the idea. Broads such as Hoveton Great Broad, which was totally closed to boats, had lost plants, except for a few clumps of water-lilies, and just across the River Bure, Wroxham Broad, frequently used by boats, had lost them too. But the tiny Salhouse Little Broad, just upriver, and accessible to boats, retained a good stand of lilies. Filby Broad, in the group of Trinity Broads on the Muck Fleet had lost its plants and so had the connected Lily Broad, but Ormesby Broad, also connected with them, still had a reasonable crop. Boats were excluded from all of these Broads.

Hickling Broad and Horsey Mere had extensive crops of plants in the 1960s (they lost most of them a little later, in the 1970s) and had free boat access, as did (and still does) the northern part of Martham Broad, also in the River Thurne catchment. The isolated Alderfen Broad lost its plants during the 1960s without influence of any boats at all, as had the dykes that permeated the Woodbastwick marshes on the River Bure.

Ideas once sown are hard to shift, and many people, especially yachtsmen, so disliked the motor cruisers, the dominant craft, that all sorts of arguments were put forward to pin blame upon them. Barton Broad, for example, had had abundant plants during the Second World War, especially, it was alleged, when it had been closed to boats from 1940 to 1943. But the evidence that boats were causing the turbidity was simply not there. Cruises around the system in 1975, when I took many water samples and related their contents to a survey of boat movements, showed no relationship between turbidity and boat activity, nor did detailed studies in Barton Broad.

Eventually, I waited by the River Bure close to the entrance to Malthouse Broad for several days in summer, counted boats going up and down river and into the Broad, and measured turbidity. I showed that although boats did stir up sediment in the rivers sufficient to be measurable during the afternoon, it was temporary and in the heavily used Malthouse Broad, it was not measurable

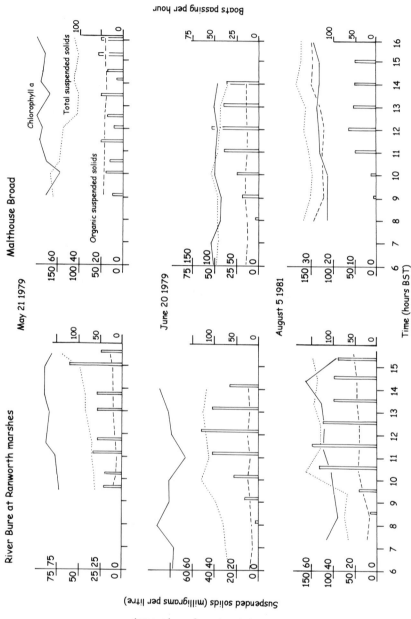

Plate 1. Large-scale experiments contributed much to understanding changes in the Broads in the twentieth century. Here in Hoveton Great Broad, the effects of removal of the fish population are being investigated in the large enclosure, whilst subsidiary experiments on the survival of plants are being carried out in the smaller structures.

Plate 2. The rivers upstream of the main Broadland floodplain have been greatly modified in the interests of protecting agricultural land, but often retain some charm. Stretches of the Wensum, a tributary of the Yare above Norwich, are attractive to both naturalists and fishermen.

Plate 3. The swallowtail butterfly epitomises the traditional natural history interest of Broadland.

Plate 4. The undrained wetlands in the upper parts of the Broadland floodplain are very varied and contain much of interest for botanists and birdwatchers. Those that are or have been managed for crops like common reed give a characteristic landscape.

Plate 5. The grazing marshes dominate the area of Broadland. They constitute the largest single block of permanent grazing in England.

Plate 6. The sea is as important to Broadland as the land. The Norfolk beaches, with their thin fringe of sand dunes, have a welcome simplicity.

Plate 7. Alder carrs have their own 'feel' – dense, treacherous to walk into, difficult to penetrate. Large, old trees are uncommon owing to coppicing in the past. Pools support tussock sedges and irises.

Plate 8. Burgh Castle overlooks a sheltered part of the estuary now but would have commanded more open waters when it was built. In the distance is the tower of the Berney Arms mill on the north bank of the Yare.

Plate 9. Broadland has the greatest concentration of round-towered churches – a mediaeval fashion – in Britain. The walls are often of rough flint cobbles gleaned from the glacial drift or river deposits and bound with mortar (right). Churches in richer parishes, often those with a profitable local industry, have sections built with flints expensively knapped into cubes (below).

Plate 10. Reed thatch, once the roofing material of everyone, is now costly. The ridge top is bound with saw sedge and hazel twigs are used to decorate and strengthen the ridge and the curves around the windows.

One way of classifying the Broads includes those in small side valleys (*Plate 11.* above, Cockshoot Broad) and those closely bypassed by the main river (*Plate 12.* below, Belaugh Broad). The distinction has little modern meaning, however. All the Broads were excavated at the edges of the floodplain; the edge was close to the river in the upstream sections, giving apparently bypassed Broads. With distance downstream, the edge was further from the river and the Broad was eventually connected with the river by a longer dyke, giving the impression of a tributary valley.

Plate 13. The Broads were originally very clear lakes with low-growing charophytes on their beds. Such 'marl lakes' have high calcium and bicarbonate concentrations and a strong tendency for the plants to precipitate marl (mostly calcium carbonate) on their surfaces.

Plate 14. The sediments of the Broads can be easily sampled with a length of water pipe, cut longitudinally in half and re-taped together. The tube is pushed into the sediments from a boat and the core is later exposed by cutting the tapes.

Plate 15. A layering of sediments is often seen in cores taken from the Broads. The earliest sediments of Cockshoot Broad show a dark underlying peat deposit then grey sediment with white speckles including snail shells and the remains of marl tubes which coated the stems of charophytes.

Plate 16. The Tudor period was marked by the building of more ornate, less fortified great houses than hitherto. Broadland has comparatively few but Blickling Hall, by the River Bure, is a beautiful example.

Plate 17. Drainage windmills, mostly now derilict, are among the best known features of Broadland. That at Horsey has been restored.

Plate 18. The first freshwater biology laboratory in Britain was founded at this house at Longmoor Point, close to Sutton Broad on the River Ant.

Plate 19. Suction dredging is often seen as a key need in lake restoration. Dredging is often necessary to maintain water depth for navigation but may not be the panacea for restoration of conservation value that it is often believed.

Plate 20. Ponds created by wooden boards in dykes in the Woodbastwick Marshes were instrumental in helping to develop the current understanding of alternative states in shallow lakes.

Plate 21. White Slea Lodge, built in the Edwardian period as a shooting lodge, nestles in the centre of the Hickling Broad National Nature Reserve.

Plate 22. Coypu escaped from fur farms in the 1930s and 1940s to establish large feral populations that damaged reedbeds and sugar beet crops. They have now been eliminated.

Plate 23. Steam lasted only a short time in powering the drainage pumps. The few remains of steam pumps include this desolate chimney at Seven Mile House along the River Yare, flanked by the brick housing of the modern electric pump.

Plate 24. Away from the river edges where leakage of poor quality, often saline water may limit the diversity, the dykes of the grazing marshes may contain rich collections of plants and invertebrates, including the bladderwort, water violet and the water soldier.

Plate 25. Biomanipulation involves the temporary removal and then exclusion of fish. This can be problematic, especially where boats must pass and designs of fish-proof but boat-passable barriers are being tested.

Plate 26. Grazing by cattle and Konic ponies is being used to reinstate the farming management that traditionally maintained the open fens. The ponies are very hardy but can sometimes be difficult to manage.

Plate 27. Fen cutting is necessary to maintain characteristic vegetation, but is expensive in labour. The Fen Harvester cuts a wide swaithe cheaply and exerts little pressure on the soft fen surface. The cuttings are then blown down a pipeline to a waiting lorry.

Plate 28. The future of Broadland – the epoch of belief.

Plate 29. The future of Broadland II – the spring of hope.

at all (Fig. 12.4). The turbidity was much more closely linked with algae and longer term studies in the Broads of the Bure showed that it was no less in Broads free of boats than it was in those heavily used by them (Fig. 12.5).

Raw sewage discharge from the boats was dealt with on public health grounds, following two reports, commissioned in the first instance by the boat hire industry in 1964 and later by the local Medical Officer of Health. The first found that there was no problem, the second that there was a definite risk of enteric disease! It took a further eight years or so for bylaws to be passed requiring the boats to have sealed tanks and to discharge into the shore-based sewerage system. Although it had been suggested, there was never any major contribution of nutrients from the boat sewage. Compared with a resident population of over 250,000 discharging for 52 weeks into the Broadland rivers, a holiday population of 100,000 person-weeks accounted for less than one per cent of the total.

Problems with release of phosphorus from the sediment

The other objection to trying to restore the prewar condition of the Broads by controlling the phosphorus supply came from the fact that there was so much phosphorus contained in the sediments. Any attempt to reduce the inputs would be frustrated by the huge amounts already stored, and likely to leak out from the sediments. This was a very interesting issue for the only ways that such release can be dealt with are by chemical sealing or by removal and disposal of the sediment (Plate 19). Both are expensive and, worse, often ineffective in permanently stopping phosphorus release. Chemical sealing involves injecting oxidised iron compounds or nitrate into the sediment using special equipment. The iron is supposed to react with the phosphates in the interstitial water of the sediment and fix them as insoluble compounds as described in Chapter 7. Nitrate is supposed to create the oxidising conditions necessary for iron naturally present to do the same thing.

Theoretically either might work in physically stable sediment on a very small scale. But bare sediment, unstabilised by plants, shifts easily, mixing the compounds downwards or allowing them to be re-suspended and washed downstream in the water. The costs of the chemicals are high, as is that of their application. Both are only temporary remedies anyway, unless the external sources of phosphorus are removed, even if they were to work perfectly. The alternative, dredging, either by scoops or suction, has a strong following among civil engineering contractors, for it is a lucrative business. It may be necessary to create deeper water for navigation and in Broadland there has been substantial shallowing of the initially shallow waters in recent decades.

However, sediment removal is unlikely to result in much reduction of phosphorus release from the sediments, unless they are removed entirely. This is extremely costly, mostly because of the expense of disposing of the material,

Fig. 12.4 (opposite) Changes in the chlorophyll *a* concentration (which measures the phytoplankton crop) and in the organic and total suspended solids concentration throughout three summer days in the River Bure and in the adjacent Malthouse Broad. The suspended solid concentrations increase a little by day in the river coincident with the rising boat traffic (shown as vertical base), but there is no such relationship in the Broad, despite great changes in boat activity. The material stirred up resettles overnight to give low values by dawn. Unpublished data of Brian Moss.

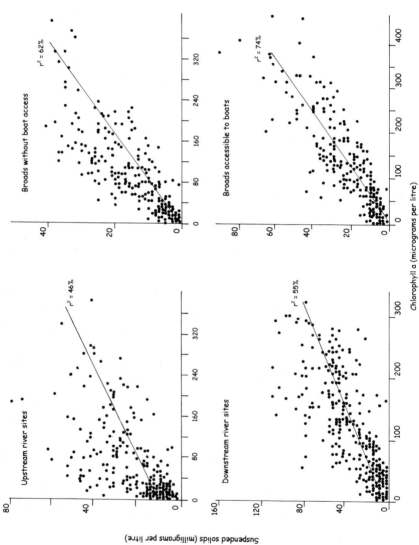

Fig. 12.5 (opposite) More evidence that boats had a negligible effect in creating turbidity in the waters of the Broads. Values of total suspended solids are plotted against chlorophyll *a* concentrations for a large number of dates and locations along the River Bure. The data are grouped into upstream river stations (between Swan Bend and Belaugh), downstream river stations (Swan Bend to the confluence with the Thurne), Broads accessible to boats (Wroxham, Salhouse, Hoveton Little, Malthouse) and Broads barred to boat access (Hoveton Great, Decoy, Burntfen, Ranworth, Cockshoot). The values of r^2 (a statistic that describes the closeness of the relationship between the two entities) suggest that chlorophyll *a* (or rather the algae that contain it) explains most of the suspended solids in the water. Indeed it explains more in the Broads with boats than those without. It explains a little less in the river sites, but algae still dominate the relationship. The statistic gives a measure of the proportion of the suspended solids attributable to algae. The remainder arises not only from boat disturbance but from disturbance by wind and tidal currents. The allegation that boats were causing the high turbidity in the water, which was rife in the 1960s and 1970s, was simply wrong. Unpublished data of Brian Moss.

which is bulky. The problem is that even if the sediments are dredged down to layers that were laid down even when external phosphorus loading was low, there is, after a pause of a few months, renewed release. This is because deep in the mass of almost any sediment, there are anaerobic conditions. At the sediment surface, where there is contact with oxygenated water, the phosphate is incorporated into oxidised compounds in the oxidised microzone. Soluble phosphorus then diffuses upwards from the deeper layers towards the surface, along the gradient of decreasing soluble phosphorus concentrations. Much higher concentrations are then re-established close to the surface to provide ample release whenever the oxidised microzone is destroyed or disturbed by burrowing invertebrates.

A particularly good example of this occurred in Cockshoot Broad, where sediment was removed down to the ancient charophyte layers, but release resumed after a couple of years. Phosphorus seems to be released at times from all sediments and in shallow lakes, where the dilution with the water is lower than in deep lakes, the concentrations can build up to high levels. Where plants are present, the release can be considerable, because the plants provide a large amount of organic matter that falls to the bottom, creates low oxygen conditions and destroys the oxidised microzone. Deoxygenation can be so severe that sulphate in the interstitial water is reduced by bacteria to sulphide, which reacts with any available iron to form a very insoluble black precipitate of iron sulphide and further impedes the sediment's ability to retain phosphorus (Fig. 12.6).

It is this sulphide that gives the intense blackness to sediments laid down in the Broads when the plant communities were very dense in the nineteenth and early twentieth centuries. It seems there has always been substantial phosphorus release from the Broads' sediments and hence phosphorus is unlikely to have been the nutrient driving eutrophication in these and other shallow lakes. This is a reappraisal of the problem diagnosed in the 1970s.

Phosphorus control in the 1970s

Nonetheless, at the time, the arguments for phosphorus control seemed very substantial. In the late 1970s, the Anglian Water Authority, which was then responsible for water quality, was persuaded to reduce the inputs of phosphate into the River Ant. This it did first by diverting the effluent from the North Walsham sewage treatment works to the sea. The works was old and

Charophytes and other short species

Oxygen
Nitrogen

Oxidised microzone (a few mm thick) Iron in
oxidised (ferric) form precipitates phosphate
Little phosphate diffuses to water
Uptake of phosphate by roots Proteins in
sediment converted to ammonium then nitrate
by bacteria Nitrate converted to nitrogen
by bacteria In deeper sediments, oxygen very
scarce, iron in reduced (ferrous) form

Dark-brown sediment

Taller, more competitive rooted plants

Oxygen

phosphate
Ammonium

Nitrogen

Oxidised microzone destroyed at night,
reforms by day More release of phosphate
Some diffusion of ammonium to water
Root systems less well developed in more
hostile deoxygenated sediment

Plants not dependent on root systems

Oxygen

In anaerobic sediment, sulphate is reduced
to sulphide Sulphide combines with ferrous
iron to form very insoluble black precipitate
Phosphate loss to water is unimpeded because
there is no iron available to precipitate it

Ammonium Methane Nitrogen phosphate

Oxidised microzone cannot form in summer
because bacterial activity is too great
Root systems rudimentary in extremely toxic
sediment with high concentrations of sulphide
and reduced iron

Black Anaerobic sediment

Increasing nitrogen supply and increased plant production
Decreasing plant diversity with increasing nitrogen
Increasing amounts of organic debris fall to sediment from plant beds

Fig. 12.6 The relationships between nutrients and aquatic plant communities are interestingly complex. As nutrients increase (phosphorus particularly from release from the sediments, nitrogen from the catchment), the communities change and become reduced in diversity.

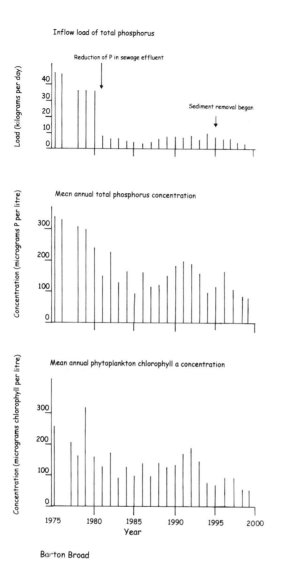

Fig. 12.7
Changes in the annual phosphorus loads to Barton Broad and concentrations of phosphorus and phytoplankton chlorophyll *a* in the Broad from 1975 to 1999. Data from Osborne (1980, 1981) and Phillips et al. (1999) and Environment Agency registers (see Chapter 16).

replacement was more expensive than diversion. Then the effluent from the Stalham sewage treatment works was treated with iron ammonium sulphate to precipitate the phosphate, a process called phosphorus stripping. A third source, from a canning factory discharging to the river, was also partly treated. In the early 1980s, when all these works had been completed, we waited for Barton Broad to recover, but (Fig. 12.7) in vain. There was some effect on the nature of the algal communities and an apparent drop in the chlorophyll *a* concentration, a convenient way of measuring the algal population overall. But the water did not clear and the plants did not return.

Nitrogen control

In hindsight, it might have been better to have attempted to control nitrogen. This would have been very difficult, for most of the nitrogen entering the system comes not from the sewage treatment works, but from many thousands of small agricultural sources – streams and small pipes draining agricultural land. Nitrate is the main form in which nitrogen enters and nitrates are very soluble, unlike phosphates, which are readily incorporated into chemical precipitates. To control nitrogen is thus difficult because its sources are many and diffuse and there are no cheap methods of chemically destroying it.

The best way is to use natural processes. Densely plant-dominated shallow lakes and reedswamps and fens are very good at removing nitrate simply because their waterlogged soils become anaerobic and denitrifying bacteria use the nitrate as an oxidising agent (Fig. 12.6). The waters of such lakes and swamps have barely detectable available nitrogen concentrations in summer, for the plants also readily absorb it. Ammonium is produced in the sediments and by animal excretion, but the amounts are small and ammonium is so reactive that it is readily taken up by plants, algae and bacteria, and eventually converted back to nitrate and nitrogen gas, which escapes to the atmosphere.

The immediate way of controlling nitrogen inputs is thus to create extensive wetlands through which water has to pass before it reaches the river and then lakes, but this requires large areas of land and appropriate diversion of the water. The better way is to put less nitrogen on the land in the first place and

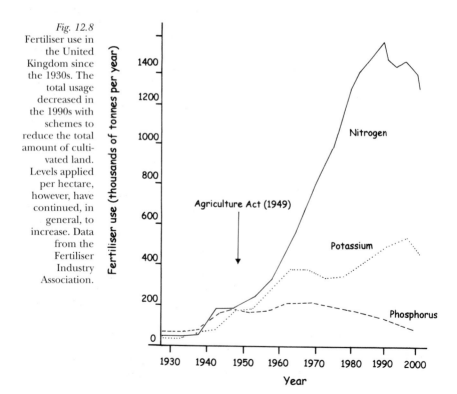

Fig. 12.8 Fertiliser use in the United Kingdom since the 1930s. The total usage decreased in the 1990s with schemes to reduce the total amount of cultivated land. Levels applied per hectare, however, have continued, in general, to increase. Data from the Fertiliser Industry Association.

this is a difficult issue, to be discussed in Chapter 16. If eutrophication is key to the loss of plants from the Broads (and there is no suggestion that it is not a major part of the explanation, as we shall see), it is likely that nitrogen has been the driving nutrient in the twentieth century, steadily increasing in the post-war years as agriculture became more and more intensive.

One of the consequences of the threat to food supplies in the Second World War had been a major intensification of agriculture after the passing of the Agriculture Act in 1949. Essentially this Act gave immense support to agriculture through subsidies and grants, in a highly successful attempt to increase production. Fertilisation of arable crops and temporary grass leys was about ten kilograms per hectare of nitrogen in the 1940s, but increased more than 20-fold by the 1970s and even more since then (Fig. 12.8). Our 1970s view was too simple in its emphasis on phosphorus. Nonetheless, and despite the lack of change in Barton Broad, phosphorus stripping was installed at a number of works on the River Bure in the 1980s.

Arguments for nutrient control

However, all of this understanding has come in hindsight. In the 1970s, the idea that nutrient control, specifically phosphorus, was the single major solution was the state-of-the-art understanding, supported by three pieces of evidence that seemed to show that it could be effective.

Cockshoot Broad (Fig. 12.9) was the first. It was supplied with water from the effluent-rich River Bure and at the time it seemed unlikely that phosphorus stripping would be soon introduced on the river. It was connected to the river by a wide dyke at its north end, and received water from a tiny stream draining a small catchment of woodland and swamp at its south. From the east came water from Ranworth Broad through a narrow dyke, Old Hall Dyke. Furthermore it had become very shallow (as little as ten centimetres of water over much of it in dry summers) as sediment had washed into it from the river on the high tides. A single remaining bed of lilies and reed had blocked the connection between the dyke and river to the extent that boats had not been able to enter for many years. There was thus no objection from boating interests to eventual damming of the dyke so that river water, bearing a heavy load of nutrients, could not enter.

Old Hall Dyke was fitted with a one-way sluice so that water entering by the southern stream, or through percolation, could leave. Firstly, though, about one metre of accumulated sediment was sucked out and deposited in a lagoon created in the nearby alder carr by construction of peat embankments. The water in the Broad became clear almost immediately after all these works were completed and this suggested that nutrient control was working. Plants were slow to recolonise, however, and after a year or two, the phytoplankton populations increased again and very high concentrations of phosphorus were re-established in the water (Fig. 12.9). The significance of the facts that in the initial clear phase there had been an abundance of grazing zooplankters, and that there was a whole new dimension to the problem, were not fully appreciated for some time and are discussed in Chapter 16.

Additional apparent evidence of the effectiveness of nutrient control came from Alderfen Broad. Here, the Broad was not dredged (this was to come later, with no effect), but a small stream that had brought effluent-rich water into the Broad was diverted into a dyke that skirted the Broad and discharged into its

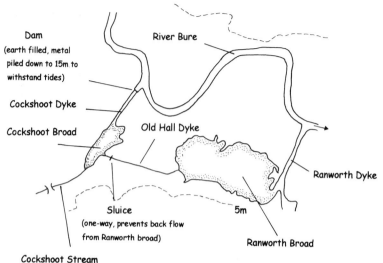

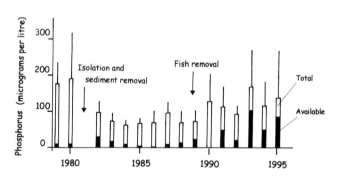

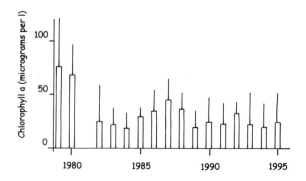

Fig. 12.9
Cockshoot Broad was one of the first Broads used for experimental restoration. It was dammed from the River Bure and much of its sediment was removed. This gave an apparent immediate improvement, though this was short-lived (see Chapter 16). Eventually clear water was restored by manipulation of the fish community, but a stable community of aquatic plants has yet to be achieved. Based on Moss et al. (1986, 1996) and Phillips et al. (2000).

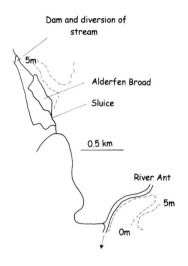

Fig. 12.10 Alderfen Broad was isolated from its inflow stream, which was nutrient rich, in 1980. Since then the Broad has shown cycles in its phosphorus chemistry, phytoplankton and aquatic plant crops. In 1995 the sediment was removed, but there has been no further improvement. Based on Moss et al. (1986), Moss et al. (1990) and Perrow et al. (1994).

Alderfen Broad

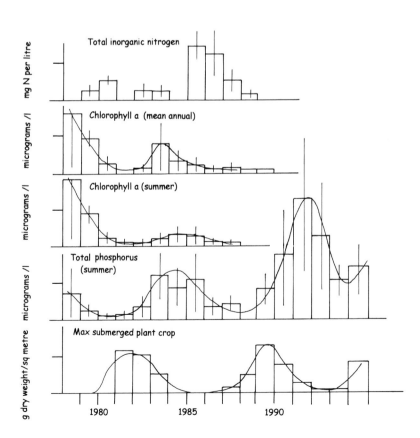

outflow. Again there was an initial apparent improvement and some plants, albeit a fairly sparse population only of hornwort, reappeared, but then disappeared with a resumption of growths of blue-green algae. There followed an oscillation of years with clearer water and years with phytoplankton turbidity (Fig. 12.10) and again it was not until later that possible biological reasons for this became clearer.

The third instance was the case of the dykes at Woodbastwick marshes, part of the Bure Marshes National Nature Reserve. These too had become silted up and lacked many plants and a decision was taken to clear them of silt, using a pump mounted on a boat, that squirted the sloppy sediment over a swathe of fen to either side of the dykes. This would open them up to a vigorous flushing from the tidal river. Removing the sediment was a continuation of a centuries' old practice of 'dydling and bottomifying' the dykes to keep them open, and is known to promote water-plant growth in dykes by removing competing reeds. Opening the system up to the river was a courageous decision by Martin George, the regional officer of the Nature Conservancy, which managed the reserve.

At the time it was not realised that nutrient-rich water might be part of the problem and intuitively a good flushing out seemed a sensible thing to do. As the potential role of nutrients was realised, Martin George had dams constructed across the connections between the dyke systems and the river, and, for a time, at least in the dykes furthest from the river, substantial populations of plants, including frogbit, hornwort and water soldier reappeared. Again, isolation from nutrient-rich water seemed to have done the trick. Something rather similar also occurred at Cromes Broad on the River Ant where isolation from the river gave at least a temporary recovery of a limited flora. Overall, however, the effects of nutrient control were not very promising or were downright ineffective.

Light starts to dawn

This was somewhat disturbing to those of us involved, the paradigm of nutrient importance being so strongly established for fresh waters on a world scale. It was inconceivable that nutrients were not involved in some way, but they were clearly not the entire story. Three more sets of observations and experiments in Broadland started to throw more light on the problem, all of them with a strong element of unexpectedness that in one sense ruins the intentions of careful scientific planning, yet contributes far more understanding in the end.

The first was at Brundall Broad (Fig. 12.11). A local businessman had bought the surrounding area at the edge of the River Yare to fit out luxury boats for the overseas market and had modified the bankside. This included dredging out a basin that had been a Broad, but, close to the river, had filled in with sediment. The basin was extended a little and had a dumbbell sort of shape. There was a wide area, the Outer Broad, at the riverside, open to movement in and out of River Yare water, which was extremely rich in nutrients because of the large sewage treatment works discharging at Whittlingham, just upstream. Another wide area, the Inner Broad, was at the other end, with these two areas separated by a narrow channel. The Inner Broad was an extension of the original Broad and was dug out from the peat and separated from the river by peat balks only a few metres wide. The owner dammed it off, across the connecting

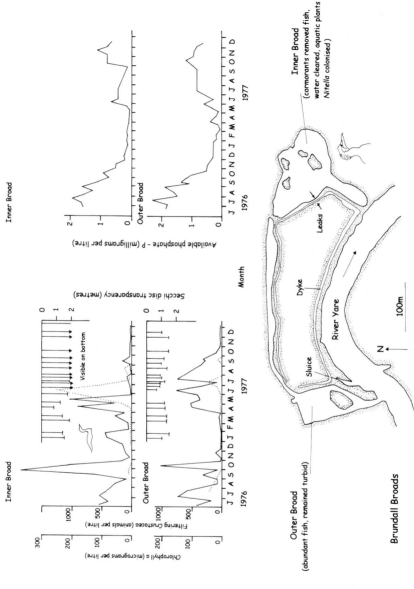

Fig. 12.11 An experiment carried out in the two basins of Brundall Broad in 1976 and 1977 did not behave as planned, but gave much more interesting results than if it had. Based on Leah et al. (1980).

channel, to form a small amenity lake, thus creating an experimental pair. One basin received ample amounts of nutrient-rich water, the other was isolated and expected to become much poorer in nutrients, in the manner of lakes elsewhere isolated from a continuous source. In such circumstances, phosphorus becomes bound in the sediments and nitrate is denitrified back to nitrogen gas. We anticipated that the Inner Broad might regain a plant population as the nutrients decreased.

In the first season of monitoring, both basins behaved similarly. They both had turbid water and there were no plants. Nutrient concentrations, however, were very high indeed in both. At this stage we discovered that the peat balks isolating the Inner Broad were not watertight and that with the quite high tides on the Yare, substantial amounts of nutrient-rich river water were entering and upsetting our experimental intentions! Nonetheless we continued monitoring and were very surprised in the second year to find that although the Outer Broad remained turbid, the Inner Broad became clear during the summer. This was despite continued high levels of both nitrogen and phosphorus, and there was even a rich development of an aquatic plant, indeed a charophyte, *Nitella flexilis*, which is associated with water richer in nutrients than others of this group.

The potential for algal growth in the water of the Inner Broad was huge, but the algae did not grow. The reason was that they were being grazed away by zooplankters, particularly a species of *Daphnia*. The *Daphnia* did not develop in the Outer Broad, which remained turbid, because it was being eaten by small fish, such as roach; this is a common scenario for *Daphnia*. In the Inner Broad, fish turned out to be very scarce. A cormorant, whose wing had been damaged so that it was unable to fly away, had been in residence and confined to the Inner Broad for the previous winter and spring. Cormorants require lots of fish, around one kilogram each day. It was an easy calculation to show that the entire fish stock of the Inner Broad could have been removed over those months by this bird, especially as other cormorants were attracted to the Broad by it and would have fed also.

At a stroke, our view of the Broadland problem began to change. Of course, algal populations could be controlled by more than nutrients and other elements of the food webs were surely involved. We were still far from a solution as to why the plants had disappeared or of the role of nutrients, but we were also off on a new line of thinking. It thus helps, at this point, to say a little in general about the relationships between phytoplankton algae, zooplankton and fish, for all of these proved to be important.

Plankton – the algae

There are many sorts of algae (Fig. 1.3). They come from several Divisions, each with somewhat different general properties, including their photosynthetic pigments, the composition of their cell walls and their propensity to produce odd substances that can sometimes be poisonous to animals. Thus there are grass-green coloured algae (for example, the green algae and the euglenoids) with chlorophylls *a* and *b* and a series of yellow or orange pigments, which though plentiful, are masked in colour by the chlorophylls. Then there are yellowish-brown algae (for example, the diatoms, yellow-green, or golden algae and dinoflagellates), still with chlorophylls, this time chlorophylls *a*, c_1 and or c_2, but in which the yellow pigments predominate. Thirdly there are blue-green algae, which are truly bacteria in their cell structure, but which have chlorophyll *a* and yellow pigments masked by a third group, the phycobiliproteins, which are red, blue or turquoise. Combinations of this pigment mixture result in blue-green algae appearing to the eye as a whole spectrum from blues to pinks.

The green algae have walls mostly of a carbohydrate, cellulose, the euglenoids have walls of strips of protein and the blue-green algae organic walls of sugars joined into chains coupled with nitrogen-containing groups. All of these walls are relatively light, but the diatoms, which have glass-like silica walls, are heavy, which means they sink rapidly and need fairly vigorous mixing to keep them in suspension in the water. Most algae are slightly denser than water and are kept in suspension by such currents, but some smaller cells have flagella and can swim to remain in suspension whilst some blue-green algae have small vesicles containing air, which allow them to float.

Among other differential features, some blue-green algae produce very powerful toxins, particularly toxic to mammals, though the biological significance of this is not yet understood, whilst some dinoflagellates and some yellow-green algae produce toxins that can kill fish. All these toxins may also have some effect on invertebrates, reducing the palatability of the algae to grazers.

Among the individual species of each of the algal groups is a range of organisation, from single cells to long, thin filaments to more globose or flat colonies, sometimes of definite shape (coenobia), sometimes of indefinite shape. These forms together have a range of size from single cells, a few micrometres in diameter to the biggest colonies, visible to the naked eye. These are a millimetre or so across – half a billion times as voluminous as the smallest. By analogy, this is essentially the size range akin to mice and elephants among mammals. Most algae, however, are in the range of 2 to 200 micrometres.

Size is very important. The larger an alga, the less vulnerable it is to being eaten by filter feeding grazers, but large size means faster sinking, so that a large alga may easily fall out of the water column and become mired in the sediments. Because algae are photosynthetic and require light and because light is rapidly absorbed by water and the organic matter dissolved in it (Fig. 7.2), staying in the water column is crucial. Small cells also divide faster than large ones, so that populations of smaller algae can be more rapidly built up in the face of factors tending to remove individuals, such as grazing, sinking and being washed through the outflow and down river. Fresh waters offer a huge range of combinations of such circumstances and the huge variety of freshwater algae can be seen as a response to this, different species thriving best at certain times of year, others later or earlier. A typical phytoplankton community might have more than 200 species appearing from time to time, much in the same way that plants grow, flower and wither in grassland.

For the population of a phytoplankton species to increase, its rate of growth must be greater than the sum of all the rates of loss – sinking, grazing, disease and washout (Fig. 12.12). Shortage of nutrients will reduce the growth rate, abundance of zooplankters may increase the grazing rate. Calm summer conditions may make it impossible for some heavy diatoms to survive, and winter washout by river floods may make it impossible for anything to increase.

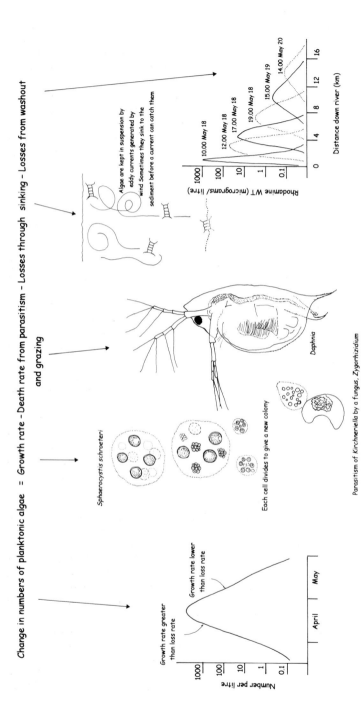

Fig. 12.12 Algal populations grow when their growth rate is greater than the rates of loss from grazing and parasitism, sinking and washout. Washout is illustrated here by the results of an experiment in which a dye tracer, Rhodamine WT was added to the River Bure, close to Wroxham Broad, and the trace followed down river for the next few days. There is generally time for algal populations to build up in the slow-flowing Broadland rivers, but the washout in many British rivers is too rapid to allow much build-up.

Change in numbers of planktonic algae = Growth rate - Death rate from parasitism - Losses through sinking - Losses from washout and grazing

Sphaerocystis schroeteri

Each cell divides to give a new colony

Daphnia

Parasitism of *Kirchneriella* by a fungus, *Zygorhizidium*

Algae are kept in suspension by eddy currents generated by wind. Sometimes they sink to the sediment before a current can catch them

Number per litre

Growth rate greater than loss rate

Growth rate lower than loss rate

April | May

Rhodamine WT (micrograms/litre)

10.00 May 18
12.00 May 18
17.00 May 18
19.00 May 18
15.00 May 19
14.00 May 20

Distance down river (km)

Plankton – the smaller animals

The same general principles apply to the nature of the zooplankton community – that of the smaller animals in the open water, which, though they can swim, are much more vulnerable to drifting in the water currents than the vigorously moving fish. There are three main groups; the rotifers, and two groups of Crustacea, the Cladocera or water fleas and the copepods. Each group of zooplankters has small and large species and each has some species that feed on small particles in the water and some that grasp and bite larger particles.

The small-particle feeders do so either by suspension or filter feeding. Suspension feeders, the rotifers, create a feeding current by the beating of a wheel of cilia, which brings a stream of water to the mouth, like mud in a bucket which moves to the centre in a vortex created by swirling the water. Filter feeders, including many Cladocera and one group of copepods, the Calanoida, strain the water through fine hairs borne on limbs, which beat rhythmically through the water. The spacing of the finer hairs determines the size of particles that can be filtered out, so that Cladocera, such as *Daphnia*, can take particles from about one micrometre to 30 or 50, whilst the copepods take those from five to 100 micrometres. The rotifers are confined to the very smallest particles – a few micrometres up to ten or so. One very important generalisation is that the effectiveness of filtration, the volume of water that can be swept free of edible particles per day, depends on the length, or rather the square or cube of the length, of the animal. Thus a small rotifer will process only a few cubic millimetres of water per day, a small cladoceran a few tens of cubic millimetres, but a large cladoceran or copepod as much as a litre each day. The entire volume of a lake can thus sometimes be swept through several times each day by a moderate population of water fleas.

In each zooplankton group there are also species that can grasp and bite large prey. Some rotifers will seize a large algal cell by the flagellum and burst it to release the granular cell contents into the feeding stream. Larger Cladocera such as *Polyphemus* feed by seizing smaller rotifers or Cladocera or large colonial algae, and among the copepods the bigger of the many species of *Cyclops* will even seize small insect larvae. Size ranges among the zooplankters are slightly more limited than among the algae, but the smallest rotifers are only 100 micrometres in size, whereas adult Cladocera and copepods can range from less than half up to several millimetres.

All zooplankters move actively through the water (as opposed to the passive drift of most algae), but movement is slow in rotifers and Cladocera, which move in jumps as they beat their antennae, followed by a relaxed fall-back as the antennae are repositioned. The copepods are capable of much faster movement with their antennae and can use a flick of the abdomen to dodge out of the way of a predator, such as a fish, which they have detected by sensory hairs on the antennae. Neither the rotifers nor the Cladocera have such devices.

Population growth rates also vary. The rotifers and Cladocera reproduce parthenogenically, which means that for most of the time only females are present, producing eggs that develop without fertilisation into new individuals over a few days or a week, dependent on the temperature. Thus population growth rates can be very high. Males are produced only occasionally and sexual fertilisation leads to production of resting eggs that await more favourable conditions of food supply or temperature. Copepods, on the other hand,

Fig. 12.13 Freshwater zooplankton communities are determined largely by the degree of fish predation. Fish quickly remove large cladocerans, but smaller Cladocera and rotifers are too small to be easily seen. The copepods can also avoid predation by moving out of the way as they sense the approach of a fish through hairs on their antennae. Scarcity of fish allows larger cladocerans to persist. Because the large cladocerans are efficient filterers whilst the rotifers are not, algal crops will tend to be higher (shading) where fish are abundant.

always reproduce sexually, with a complex life history that involves 12 stages, six of them as small nauplii which are filter feeders, six of them as copepodites, which are either filter feeders or grasping feeders. This life history, however, usually takes many weeks to complete, thus limiting the copepods' ability to compensate for the high death rates that might result from predation. Predation by other invertebrates, fish or sometimes amphibians or birds is the fate of most zooplankters. Some may die of starvation if algal growth is low. But vulnerability to predation largely determines the nature of zooplankton communities (Fig. 12.13).

Predation

The predators of zooplankton fall into two groups – those that find their prey by contact, usually the invertebrates, and those that must first see it then attack it, usually vertebrates, especially fish. The invertebrates may be insect larvae, for example, the larvae of phantom midges (*Chaoborus*), fly larvae that live by day in the sediment, but then move up into the water at night (they too are vulnerable by day to attack by fish). Or they may be other zooplankters, such as *Polyphemus* or *Cyclops*. Invertebrate predators must be able to grasp and manoeuvre their prey to eat it and will thus usually attack animals smaller than themselves – often small water fleas, rotifers and nauplii. A zooplankton community that is subject only to invertebrate predation will thus tend to be one of the bigger animals, including the predators themselves, large copepods and the larger species of water flea, such as *Daphnia* and *Simocephalus*.

On the other hand, the visual feeders, particularly young fish once they have got past the first weeks of life when they can only manage to get algae and rotifers into their tiny mouths, progressively go for the biggest prey that they can find. They have to expend energy in cruising around to find prey, then in the attack itself, so it pays to meet this investment with the biggest meal available. Thus a zooplankton community subject to fish predation will lack large animals, especially large water fleas, which cannot move rapidly out of the way of an attack, and will be dominated by rotifers and small water fleas, such as *Bosmina* and *Chydorus*. These are generally too small to be worth the fishes' effort. There will also be copepods – small ones if the fish stock is high, bigger ones if it is only moderate, for these animals can detect an attack and sometimes move out of the way.

In the Broads, the fish community is dominated by cyprinid fish: roach, bream, rudd and tench, and perch, eels and pike. The latter is a fish predator, therefore relatively scarce, and its young soon outgrow any feasibility to take zooplankters, whilst the eel completes its young stages in the sea, so is adult and feeding on bottom invertebrates by the time it reaches fresh waters. All of the others are feeders on zooplankton during their first year and sometimes later. Eventually they require such big meals that none of the zooplankters are adequate and they move to feeding on bottom invertebrates and those associated with plant beds.

The post-war loss of the plant beds had implications for the fish communities in that such invertebrates disappeared with the plants and survival of cyprinid fish and perch, which also prefers plants for deposition of its eggs, has been low. Few of these fish reach their third year in areas where the plants have gone, and since anglers like to catch large fish, the quality of the fishing has inevitably declined. Moreover, the lack of large fish, which can be predatory on their own young, means a greater survival of small fish and hence more intense predation on the zooplankton. Pike fare badly in the present state of the Broads too, for they are lurking predators, that need vegetation cover to await their prey, which they seize as it passes. With plants absent, this cover is not available and their hunting success and consequent growth and survival are also limited. Fish-eating birds may not be affected so long as they can manage on small fish and can move around to different waters where fish may be more available.

If we now put together this information on algae, zooplankton and fish, it follows that if nutrients are increased, algal populations will tend to increase (Fig. 12.12), but this potential may not be realised if grazing by zooplankton is sufficient to remove the algae as fast as they grow. This will be the case if fish predation is absent or low or ineffective for some reason (Fig. 12.13). The

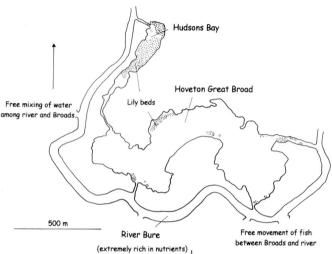

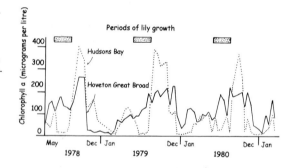

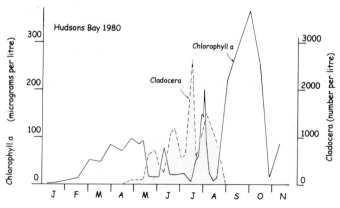

Fig. 12.14 Hoveton Great Broad and Hudsons Bay (top) are linked basins through which nutrient-rich River Bure water and fish can freely move. Hudsons Bay has extensive beds of yellow water-lilies; Hoveton Great Broad has few. The water adjacent to the beds in Hudsons Bay clears in summer, whilst that in Hoveton Great Broad remains turbid with phytoplankton (middle). The reason is that there is an abundance of large cladocerans in Hudsons Bay. There is a striking inverse relationship between numbers of cladocerans and phytoplankton chlorophyll *a* in the summer water of Hudsons Bay (lower). Based on Timms & Moss (1984).

water will then be clear. But if there are many small fish, predation will be intense, the bigger, more effective grazing zooplankters will be removed and algae will be able to take full advantage of the available nutrients and the water will be turbid with their growth.

Two more crucial experiments

This understanding of plankton communities helped to explain a set of crucial observations, made at Hoveton Great Broad, that contributed much to understanding the new situation in the Broads. Hoveton Great Broad had had extensive beds of submerged plants and lilies at least until the early 1960s, when all but a few patches of lily disappeared. Connected with the main basin of the Broad is a smaller area, Hudsons Bay (Fig. 12.14), that had retained extensive patches of lilies and a few submerged plants among them. It had only a few thousand square metres of open water in summer. Water circulated freely on the tide between the River Bure, rich in nutrients from a dozen or more small sewage treatment works upstream, and an agricultural catchment, and both Hudsons Bay and Hoveton Great Broad and the channels between them were also big enough to allow free passage of fish. Oddly, this area was clear, whilst the open water of Hoveton Great Broad was very turbid with algae (Fig. 12.15). Initially we saw it as an interesting pattern to try to explain, but it emerged as a very important key to the whole problem.

Monitoring of the algae showed that Hoveton Great Broad developed large populations of diatoms in spring, then even larger ones of a mixture of diatoms, green algae and blue-green algae in summer, followed by even greater populations of diatoms in late summer and autumn. The floods of winter then flushed out the algae as daylength and temperature reduced their growth rates to below the rates of washout. In Hudsons Bay, the spring populations grew, as did those of the autumn. But in the summer, when the lilies were in full leaf, there were virtually no algae, despite plenty of light, high temperatures, abundant nutrients and a daily injection on the tide of algae-rich water from the river and Hoveton Great Broad.

There were no algae because they were being grazed by zooplankters faster than they could grow. Among the lily beds of Hudsons Bay, huge populations of *Daphnia* and other water fleas were present. There were few in the open water by day for the fish quickly took them, but at night they deliberately moved, or more likely continued to drift out, into the open water. In the darkness, the fish could not see them, and they grazed and prevented any build up of algae in water that was otherwise very favourable for algal growth. By day, in the lily beds, they were also safe, for dense beds are shaded places where fish, even perch, which are reasonably efficient hunters in thinner beds, could not hunt effectively and preferred not to go. Dense beds are deoxygenated in the lower layers, owing to the decomposition of plant debris, and pike lurk at their edges.

It was the work of a few days to confirm that if we took Hudsons Bay water, and freed it of zooplankton, it would support the growth of large crops of algae. Conversely, when we took Hoveton Great Broad water and placed it in large bags, lacking fish, suspended in the Broad, large Cladocera were able to survive and multiply. In the loss of plants from the Broads, it was now clear that animals as much as nutrients were important. The evidence was building for a new understanding.

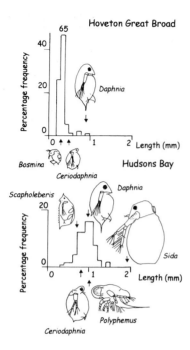

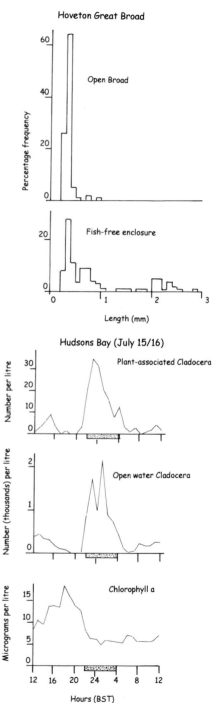

Fig. 12.15 The great contrasts between the zooplankton communities of Hudsons Bay and Hoveton Great Broad are shown above left. If fish are excluded from Hoveton Great Broad water in a large polyethylene bag, the zooplankton community acquires large animals and begins to resemble that of Hudsons Bay (above right).Yet fish are as abundant in Hudsons Bay as in Hoveton Great Broad, being able to move freely between the Broads and the river. Indeed, they feed actively by day in Hudsons Bay, but the lily beds contain huge cladoceran populations, which find refuge in their dark labyrinths from the fish by day. By night they drift out at to graze in the adjacent open water (right upper and centre panels). Phytoplankton builds up a little by day (lower right), but is grazed away from twilight onwards. Cladocerans left out in the open by day are quickly eaten, but the reserve troops in the lily beds are actively multiplying and abundant enough to replace them the next evening. Based on Timms & Moss (1984).

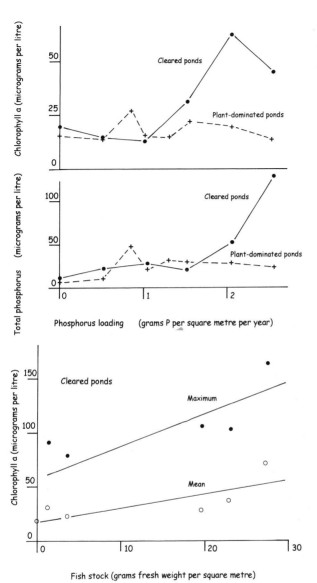

Fig. 12.16 Experimental ponds created with wooden board dams in the dykes of the Woodbastwick marshes provided valuable clues as to how these systems functioned. Based on Balls et al. (1989) and Irvine et al. (1989).

A second crucial experiment was carried out in the Woodbastwick marshes. Its original intent was to determine the threshold concentration of phosphorus at which plants would decline and be replaced by phytoplankton. The Woodbastwick marshes is an area of fen through which pass a number of parallel-sided dykes, originally dug for transport of fen products, and in which, coincident with the cleaning out of the dykes and their isolation from the river, a rich collection of submerged plants was growing. We created a series of experimental ponds along one such dyke, with hornwort, water soldier, frogbit and ivy-leaved duckweed growing in it, by installing simple dams of wooden boards (Plate 20).

Over a summer we then added a similar load of nitrate to each pond at regular intervals and stocked the ponds with a community of cyprinid fish, including roach. We divided the ponds into two series, from one of which we raked out the plants to give open water, whilst in the other we left the plants intact. Finally we gave to each pond in each experimental treatment (with or without plants) one of a graded series of phosphorus additions, from none at all to a level far above that which the Broads themselves were receiving. We expected that plants would disappear at the upper levels of phosphorus addition and that phytoplankton would take over. No such thing happened.

In the ponds where the plants had been left intact, they flourished. Phosphorus concentrations in the water remained low and steady and unrelated to the additions we were making, and the water remained clear of phytoplankton. Adding nutrients had no effects at all on the algae, but made the plants grow better! On the other hand, in those ponds where we had raked out the plants, phytoplankton did develop and phosphorus concentrations did increase in proportion to the amount we added. Furthermore, when we analysed the data in detail, the phytoplankton chlorophylla concentration was also closely related to the fish stock found in these ponds at the end of the experiment (Fig. 12.16). This was more evidence that nutrients were only part of the story.

A new hypothesis – alternative stable states

At that stage we understood that a lake could have either clear water and plants or turbid water and no plants, more or less irrespective of the nutrient concentrations or loadings. Our two sets of experimental ponds at Woodbastwick and the paired Hudsons Bay and Hoveton Great Broad and Brundall Inner and Outer Broads all showed these two different states under the same nutrient conditions. In each case, there was also a link with the animal communities, including the zooplankton in two of them and the fish in the third. And in the latter, the fish stock was inversely related to the size of the zooplankton. Shallow lakes could thus exist in two states as alternatives to one another. Work in Holland and Denmark was producing similar results and it was time to re-examine all the information and see if some general scheme might not apply. What developed is known as the alternative states model (Fig. 12.17).

At the very lowest nutrient concentrations, there was insufficient nutrient to support a very large phytoplankton community anyway, so the water would remain clear and plants rooted on the bottom would inevitably be able to grow. But as the nutrient concentrations increased, perhaps to above about 25 micrograms of phosphorus and 250 micrograms of nitrogen per litre, it was possible either to have the clear water, plant-dominated state or the turbid algal-dominated one.

The clear water state could be found even at very high nutrient levels – one lake in Cheshire investigated later had clear water and plants in a basin that was little-diluted sewage effluent, and our Woodbastwick ponds were receiving huge amounts of nutrients, yet plants persisted. There seemed to be no upper limit to the nutrient levels per se that the plants could survive. Equally, over the same range of nutrient levels there could be phytoplankton dominance with no plants, as in many of the Broads in their post-war state, our cleared ponds at Woodbastwick and in Hoveton Great Broad and Brundall Outer Broad.

If this was the case, two things also had to be true. Firstly there had to be

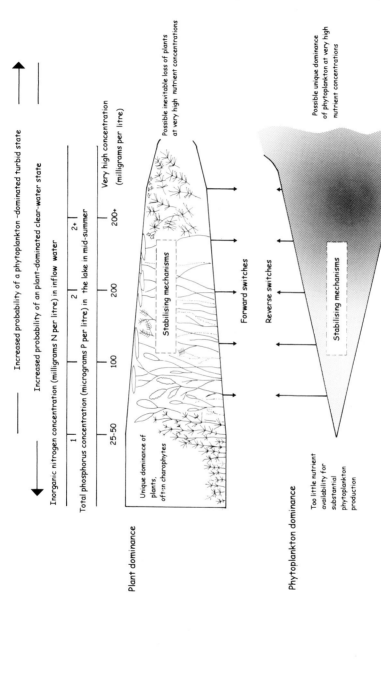

Fig. 12.17 Current understanding of ecology of shallow lakes is based on the alternative states model, in which plant-dominated, clear water states and turbid, algal-dominated states can both exist over a wide range of nutrient concentrations.

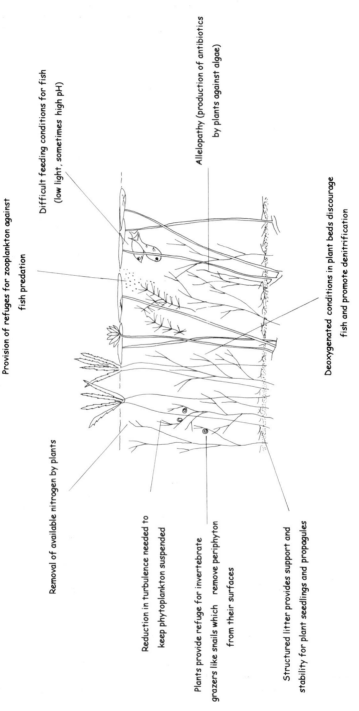

Fig. 12.18 A variety of mechanisms help to stabilise submerged plant communities once they are well established.

mechanisms that stabilised the alternative states in the face of changing nutrient concentrations or loadings – either increasing them as in our experiments at Woodbastwick, or decreasing as in the attempts to restore Barton Broad, where nothing much changed as the phosphorus supply was reduced. Secondly, if either of these states was to switch to the other, there had to be some additional mechanism, because nutrient change alone was not effective. Somehow, however, nutrients were also involved. There was too much of a coincidence between plant loss and nutrient increase on a world scale.

Buffers and switches

Plant communities cope with changing nutrients by a number of stabilising or buffering mechanisms (Fig. 12.18). Some directly involve the plants themselves, others concern organisms for which they provide habitat. Firstly, the plants can take up nitrogen compounds such as nitrate and ammonium very readily and in the oxygen-poor, dark, unstirred conditions deep in their beds, they create conditions in which bacteria denitrify nitrate to nitrogen gas. Thus although there is usually plenty of available phosphorus in the water, because of release from the sediments, nitrogen may be kept limiting to phytoplankton. The plants are able to take up nitrogen and phosphorus through their roots, direct from the sediments, which the phytoplankton cannot. Secondly, there may be allelopathy. Thirdly, the plants provide habitat, and refuge from predators, for grazers both on the phytoplankton and on the periphyton growths (including epiphytic algae) that colonise their surfaces. The phytoplankton can be readily controlled if sufficient zooplankters, particularly *Daphnia*, are present, but *Daphnia* are so vulnerable to fish predation that only if plants are abundant enough to provide a secure refuge can a sufficient reserve be maintained for more than a few days. The zooplankters may actively move out from the beds by night and back again by morning, but it is more likely that they drift out all the time, are taken by fish during the day, but can build up adequate numbers in the open water at night. The mechanism then depends on a very large swarm of animals being present in the beds and this is often the case.

Periphyton can be more deadly to plants than phytoplankton in denying adequate supplies of light and carbon dioxide to the leaf surfaces. It may form a very dense, fur-like coat, but it is readily grazed by snails, some mayfly and caddis fly nymphs and chironomid larvae. These can keep it clipped to a short turf that is not a problem for the plant. The grazers, however, are readily eaten by larger fish – tench especially seek snails – but can coexist with fish if they have refuges in the small-grain labyrinths of a plant bed, where fish cannot easily penetrate.

The very existence of the plant beds, and the larger invertebrates within them, also promotes vigorous recruitment of piscivorous fish such as pike, whose young at first feed on invertebrates. Later, the juvenile pike turn to small fish, which means that predation on the young zooplanktivorous cyprinid fish, in the months after they are born, is severe and that the pressure on the zooplankton is reduced. The plant beds are also self-maintaining because an existing bed will produce plenty of propagules – sometimes seeds, but more frequently large detached buds, called turions – that lie on the bottom during the winter and develop in spring. The presence of a tangle of plant debris on the bottom provides a sort of scaffolding structure that prevents them from being

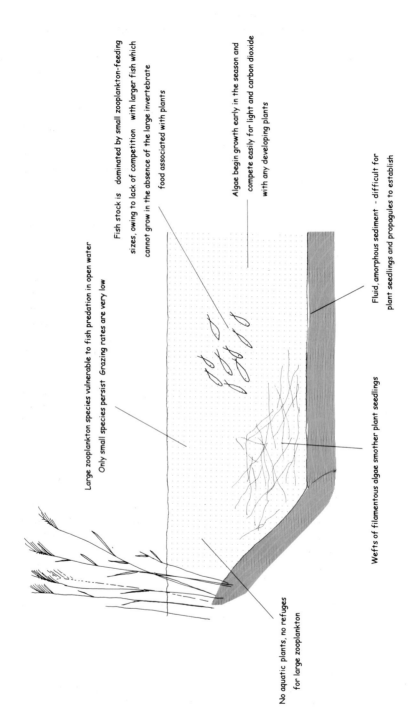

Large zooplankton species vulnerable to fish predation in open water
Only small species persist Grazing rates are very low

Fish stock is dominated by small zooplankton-feeding sizes, owing to lack of competition with larger fish which cannot grow in the absence of the large invertebrate food associated with plants

Algae begin growth early in the season and compete easily for light and carbon dioxide with any developing plants

Fluid, amorphous sediment - difficult for plant seedlings and propagules to establish

Wefts of filamentous algae smother plant seedlings

No aquatic plants, no refuges for large zooplankton

Fig. 12.19 Equally, complementary mechanisms acting in the opposite direction will stabilise phytoplankton-dominated communities.

smothered in fine sediment and possibly killed.

All of these mechanisms, acting together, form a powerful array for promoting plant persistence when nutrient levels are increased. Equally powerful mechanisms also ensure the persistence of phytoplankton once *it* has got the upper hand (Fig. 12.19). Algae, almost all of whose cells are photosynthetic when exposed to light, compared with plants, which are bulkier and have to maintain non-photosynthetic root and support cells, can begin a faster increase in late winter, at lower temperatures and light intensities than plants. Even in a lake that is plant-dominated in summer there may be a substantial algal growth in spring, but it is checked by grazing as the zooplankton develops a little later. If there are few plant propagules, or they cannot easily germinate, however, the young fish, hatching in early summer, soon decimate the zooplankton and the algae resume growth for the rest of the summer. The open water without plants is a perfumed garden for algae, a dangerous battlefield for the larger zooplankters.

The same is true of masses of filamentous algae, which can form flocs like green cotton wool in the water. They flourish when potential grazers, such as snails, are easily found and eaten by fish in the absence of protective cover from plants. In turn the filamentous algae may smother any plant propagules and grazing birds, such as coot, starved of food, will take any plant remnants available. The amorphous sediment laid down by phytoplankton, lacking the structure given by plant debris, will also make it difficult for colonising plants to make much headway in a water column now turbid with suspended phytoplankton algae. All possibilities of dislodging the algae by regeneration of the plant-stabilising buffers are thus countered. Sometimes a single season of algal dominance can undermine indefinitely the capacity for plants to regenerate.

In the featureless open water, only small zooplankters can persist because small fish become very abundant. And being abundant, they compete with one another for food and remain small and zooplanktivorous for longer. Predators are scarce. The habitat that pike need for lurking is lacking, and perch cannot reach a size large enough for them to be piscivorous because of the lack of large invertebrate prey, dependent on plants and their periphyton. By the end of the season, any scrappy plant growth that has persisted will have little energy to produce overwintering buds and the plant population will start the next season at an even greater disadvantage.

Lack of grazing by zooplankton will also have an effect on the nature of the algae in the phytoplankton. Grazers take the smaller species and one consequence is that the bigger species of algae are favoured. If grazing is low, the smaller species have an advantage in that they sink less rapidly and have a greater relative surface area over which to capture nutrients. For the same amount of algal biomass, light is more effectively absorbed by a population of small organisms than one of larger ones. By analogy, if you take a litre of water and stir into it a gram of flour, the water will be much cloudier than if you put in five dried peas, which weigh about the same. Plants attempting to grow on the bottom receive much less light if they are overlain by populations of tiny algae than if the algae are bigger.

Switch mechanisms

We thus have two alternative systems, plant dominance and algal dominance, which, once established, show formidable buffers to change. Yet change they

Fig. 12.20 Mechanisms switching the plant-dominated state to a phytoplankton-dominated state include those which destroy the plants directly (left), and those which interfere with the zooplankton grazer community (right).

do. In the 1950s and 1960s the plant-dominated systems of the Broads switched rapidly to phytoplankton. Mechanisms came into play that destroyed the effectiveness of the plant buffers (Fig. 12.20). If the plant community is severely damaged, or if the zooplankton population is markedly reduced, the various buffers can be overcome and a switch follows to phytoplankton dominance.

In our experiments at Woodbastwick marshes, we made the switch simply by raking out the plants. In the case of Zwemlust, a Dutch lake used for swimming, in which the swimmers did not like the weed, a single application of herbicide just as effectively turned the lake to phytoplankton dominance for many years. In some Dutch city canals, those with no boat traffic have clear water and plants, whilst interconnected canals used as regular boat routes have turbid water, for the boat propellers can chop up the plants.

Intense grazing on the plants can also effectively make the switch and this generally occurs with introduced alien species, whose populations, unchecked by their natural predators, can become very large. They might be invertebrates such as crayfish, fish such as common carp or grass carp, or birds such as

Canada geese. Carp are particularly damaging for they grow big and greatly disturb the bottom as they forage for invertebrates as well as directly feeding on the plants. Many city park lakes and some wetland bird reserves that have artificially high populations of ducks and geese maintained by feeding, have turbid water and no plants, for the latter cannot stand the combination of trampling and grazing. Marked increases in water level can disadvantage the plants, for which light availability at the bottom is a critical issue; so can prolonged drying out of a lake in arid areas, like many parts of Australia, which kills all the propagules.

All of the above are switches that directly affect the plants; other switches attack the zooplankton, remove the grazing potential and indirectly lead to the demise of the plants. These are perhaps the most interesting for they are not obvious. Instances have occurred where leakage of pesticides, especially organochlorine compounds, to which water fleas are very susceptible, have led to immediate increase in the phytoplankton. Dutch experiments have shown that low levels of heavy metals as well as pesticides can have similar effects. Increase in salinity to levels of above about 5 per cent of sea water can kill the bigger water fleas and reduce grazing pressure, and it is possible that differential fish-kills under prolonged ice in winter or on still nights in summer can have similar effects. Under the deoxygenated conditions that develop in both these conditions, piscivorous (fish-eating) fish are less tolerant than zooplanktivores (zooplankton eaters) and the zooplanktivore population can increase for a time – perhaps long enough for the phytoplankton to gain the upper hand.

Switches in the Broads – what could and what couldn't?

All the above gives the general case. The interesting question now is what exactly happened in the Broads in the critical period of the 1950s and 1960s. We shall probably never know exactly, for different switches could have occurred in different places and several mechanisms may act together. There is also the complication that the switches may act more readily, or more effectively, when nutrient levels increase, so that a degree of, say, bird grazing that would be sustainable at low nutrient levels, may be devastating at high. A number of mechanisms are unlikely to have occurred in the Broads. Water level changes, weed cutting, herbicides and fish-kills under ice are unlikely. (In the earlier part of this century the weather was much colder than it was in the middle part, and prolonged freezing is now not common.)

Carp are present, but not abundant. They do not breed easily at British temperatures and carp problems usually only occur when they have been heavily stocked for competitive angling, which has not been the case in the Broads. There are some feral populations of geese, including Canada geese and greylag, which do not now migrate. Their effects can currently be seen in close grazing of the grass by some of the Broads such as Salhouse, but they are too localised even now to have acted as widespread switches. An introduced mammal, the coypu, which was abundant in the 1960s, eats plants and caused widespread damage to reed beds (see Chapter 13), but does not much eat the flimsier submerged plants that are being discussed here. This leaves pesticides or other substances toxic to daphnids, boat activity, summer fish-kills and salinity as possible switch mechanisms in the Broads, though the evidence is circumstantial.

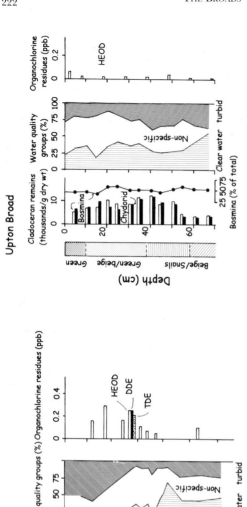

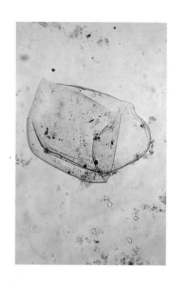

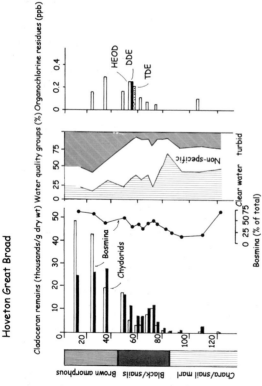

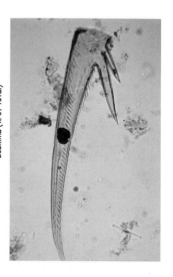

Toxic substances

Following the promotion of increasingly intensive post-war agriculture by the Agriculture Act, the range of pesticides used on the land widened. Although there are now many restrictions on their use and the hazards they pose are better understood, this was not the case in the 1950s and 1960s. They were used indiscriminately, and proper records were not kept. Even now, testing of these substances is very unsophisticated when it comes to predicting sub-lethal effects of them in complex communities. There is near total ignorance of what their effects might have been then. In a prime agricultural area such as the Broadland catchments, covering a large proportion of Norfolk, many such substances could have leaked into the waters.

There are distinct traces of organochlorines in sediment cores from Hoveton Great Broad, coinciding with changes in the remains of zooplankton in the cores (Fig. 12.21), whilst in cores from two Broads that have kept their plants, Upton and Martham, the pesticide levels are much lower. It is also possible that accumulation of pesticides in fish-eating birds and piscivorous fish could have allowed changes in the fish communities that led to increased zooplanktivory. The effects of pesticides in decreasing the numbers of bird predators during this period are among the best documented of pesticide effects.

Heavy metal pollution is rare in Broadland. There is some mercury contamination of the sediments of the River Yare below Whittlingham sewage treatment works, which has dealt with effluents from a chemical factory in Norwich, but Broadland lacks the sort of industry associated with metals such as copper, lead and nickel. Toxic effects of heavy metals can probably be discounted as forward switches in loss of the plants. But when the plants began to disappear, Ted Ellis suggested that surfactants, which were starting to replace soap in the post-war development of new detergents for washing machines, and appearing in sewage effluents, might be damaging the plants. In concentrated form they certainly do, but the presence of very healthy growths of duckweed on the secondary sedimentation tanks at various small sewage treatment works rather discounts this. But it leaves the possibility that such substances, or others present in sewage effluent, might have had effects on the zooplankters and indeed might be continuing to have such effects, for sewage effluent is now even more chemically complex. It is not just a solution of inorganic nutrients. It contains

Fig. 12.21 (opposite) Circumstantial evidence suggests that increased levels of organochlorine pesticides during the 1950s and 1960s may have acted as switch mechanisms that helped convert plant-dominated communities to plankton dominance by poisoning the cladoceran zooplankton. Cores from Hoveton Great Broad, which lost its plants at that time, and Upton Broad, which did not, have been analysed for pesticide residues (HEOD is lindane, TDE and DDE are derivatives of DDT). HEOD is quite water soluble and may diffuse down the sediment core, but TDE and DDE are not and remain located in sediment deposited at the time of their use. The peaks of these compounds at around the transition from plant dominance in Hoveton Great Broad and the lack of them in the isolated Upton Broad are suggestive. The zooplankton can be traced through fragments of their exoskeletons preserved in the sediment. Two examples, a carapace and a claw, are shown below. *Daphnia* does not preserve well, but *Bosmina* and members of a group called the chydorids do. Increase in *Bosmina* frequently accompanies declines in *Daphnia* as fish predation exerts its selective effects in turbid water. The pesticide rise is associated with a relative rise in *Bosmina* in Hoveton Great Broad, but not in Upton Broad. The change is also indicated by a change in the chydorid community from species associated with clear water to those associated with turbid water at around the same time. No such change is seen in Upton Broad. Based on Stansfield et al. (1989).

thousands of different organic residues from the huge range of household products and industrial by-products that are routed through sewage treatment works (now often called waste water treatment works to reflect this). Any number of these could potentially inhibit feeding rates, if not actually kill zooplankton grazers. Such substances might explain some instances where plants have disappeared when sewage effluent, in the absence of more obvious switch mechanisms, has been discharged to lakes.

Boats

Boats were wrongly blamed for the turbidity in the water of the Broads, but boats as direct destroyers of the vegetation need a little more attention. They certainly do break plants into pieces, but this does not necessarily destroy them; it may help disperse them, for most aquatic plants regenerate from fragments. Moreover, those, such as the lilies, that do not regenerate this way, tend to be the species that persisted longest when the plants started to disappear. There is also the objection that plants disappeared from Broads that have no boat traffic.

On the rivers, however, there is an argument that boats could have been the switch mechanism. Traffic was increasing after the Second World War. Plants persist in boat channels only where movements are very light, such as Somerton Dyke at the top of the River Thurne, and just above the limits of navigation in the Bure and Wensum (though here the build-up of phytoplankton is prevented by the high flushing rates). In Hickling Broad, plants have persisted away from the main navigation channel, but are very scarce in it. Where boats move away from the channel, they cut the tops from plants such as milfoils. Boat numbers climbed fourfold in the 1950s and 1960s to a peak around the end of the 1970s (Fig. 12.22). With the increase in nutrients adding greater stress, it is possible that boat activity could have tipped the balance in the rivers.

Rising salinity as a switch

Salinity has to rise a very great deal from freshwater conditions to be lethal to water fleas, but it was almost certainly involved as a switch in Hickling Broad

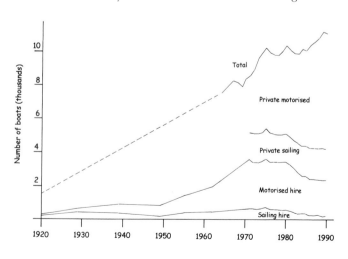

Fig. 12.22 Changes in numbers in the fleets of privately owned and hired craft in Broadland from 1920 until 1990. Based on George (1992).

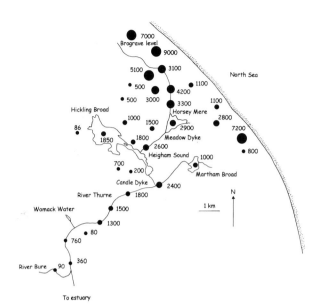

Fig. 12.23 Salinity (as chloride, mg per litre) in the Thurne system in spring 1984, based on a compilation of measurements in dykes and the main waterway. For comparison, sea water has about 19,500 mg per litre chloride, so waters in dykes on the Brograve level contained nearly 50 per cent sea water during these measurements. From Moss et al. (1991).

and Horsey Mere. These Broads are separated from the coast by only a narrow strip of land, now pump drained, underlain by peat and porous deposits of Norwich Crag. They are tidal, but the tide is physical not chemical so that their greater salinity compared with the other Broads depends on salt water sucked in from the coast by the pumps draining the surrounding land (Fig. 12.23).

At the turn of the century, the salinity in Hickling Broad was about 600 milligrams chloride per litre. Now it is around 2,000 (Fig. 12.24) and the available data suggest that the levels increased a lot in the 1960s after more powerful

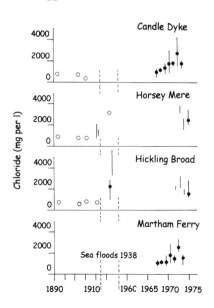

Fig. 12.24 Changes in the salinity, measured as chloride concentration, at sites in the Thurne system during the twentieth century. Open symbols are isolated data. Solid symbols are means of seasonal determinations. Vertical lines show ranges recorded. The timescale is not even. The hatched lines enclose a short period in the late 1930s following a breach of the dunes and temporary sea flooding. From Holdway et al. (1978)

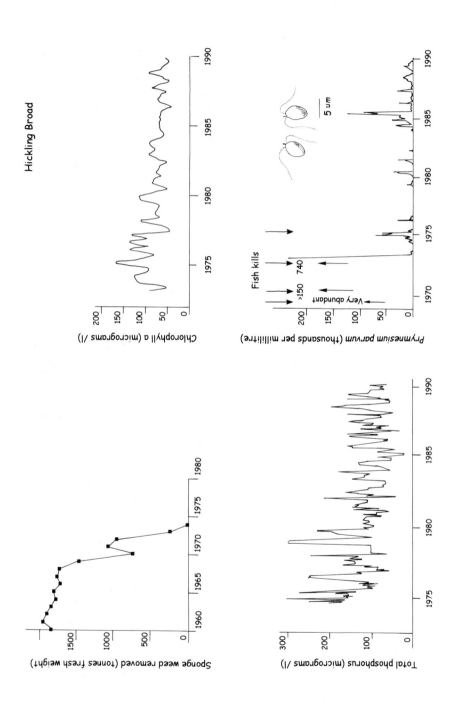

pumps had been installed. At the turn of the nineteenth century, Hickling Broad had extensive beds of charophytes, particularly the short *Chara aspera*, and clear water. The records show that as the century progressed, the plant communities changed to ones in which vascular plants became more common. The amounts of filamentous algae (largely the green alga *Cladophora*, locally called sponge weed) draped among them increased, but the water remained clear. That change I have attributed earlier to increased fertilisation by the growing roost of black-headed gulls (Chapter 10). Robert Gurney sampled Hickling Broad and his diaries show *Daphnia* and other water fleas to have been common. A range of charophytes was present, among the vascular plants and filamentous algae, at least until 1961.

With the increase in salinity in the 1960s, however, a number of changes took place (Fig. 12.25). From about 1969 onwards, there was an increase in the phytoplankton; the plants disappeared from much of the Broad, with only clumps of a few species persisting in the shallower marginal areas; there were extensive fish-kills, caused by one particular phytoplankter, *Prymnesium parvum*, which secretes toxins. Some of these increase the permeability of fish gills, allowing other toxins to penetrate and lyse the red blood cells. The zooplankton community switched from one with water fleas to one in which copepods, particularly the salinity-tolerant *Eurytemora affinis*, dominated. This was particularly significant because the fish-kills might have been expected to have had the opposite effect and to have resulted in an increase in water fleas following reduced predation. There may also have been a decline in a mysid shrimp, *Neomysis integer*, which is an omnivore, common in brackish water, feeding on zooplankton, but also scraping periphyton from plant surfaces. Large invertebrates using gills to absorb oxygen are also vulnerable to *Prymnesium* toxins.

The events were thus complex and driven by increased salinity, which facilitated growth of *Prymnesium*, a brackish-water and marine alga. *Prymnesium* kills fish, which in this case had little consequence, but also large invertebrates such as *Neomysis*. Daphnids are very sensitive to salinity and the changes in the 1960s took salinities to above the limit that most daphnids can tolerate. Removal of both daphnid grazers on phytoplankton and *Neomysis* on the periphyton seem thus to have been direct and indirect consequences of the rising salinity.

The gulls provide an extra twist, for their guano releases not only nutrients, but is also potentially a rich source, through bacterial action, of various vitamins that *Prymnesium* needs for its growth. *Prymnesium* is an interesting organism from a group of algae that evolved early and still has the characteristics

Fig. 12.25 Steady changes were going on in Hickling Broad throughout the twentieth century as the gull population increased and farming changed in the catchment, but they became suddenly dramatic in 1969 and the ensuing few years of the early 1970s. The first indications were mass fish-kills, caused by a tiny planktonic alga, *Prymnesium parvum* (bottom right). The aquatic plant population, which had had increasingly large proportions of sponge weed, a filamentous alga, *Cladophora sauteri*, was greatly reduced and the River Commissioners needed to remove smaller and smaller amounts to maintain the navigation in the main channel (top left) and ceased to bother in 1974. Chemical data are lacking for before these events, but by 1974, both total phosphorus (bottom left) and chlorophyll (top right) concentrations had become very high and certainly much increased from those which would have characterised the clear water state up to the 1960s. The salinity levels had also risen (Fig. 12.23) during the 1960s and the zooplankton community changed from a mixed community with cladocerans, to one strongly dominated by the brackish water copepod, *Eurytemora affinis*. Based on Moss & Leah (1982) and Bales et al. (1993).

associated with all plants, animals and fungi. It photosynthesises like plants, but also requires pre-synthesised organic compounds, as do fungi and animals and, if it follows many related species in its group, may even be able to ingest bacteria like animals do.

Hickling Broad and Horsey Mere, with which there is a substantial exchange of water on the tide in summer, thus offer a fascinating example of vegetation change through guanotrophy, followed by a switch to phytoplankton occasioned by the consequences of increased land drainage, reflected in increased salinity. The fish-kills were probably tangential in the saline Hickling water.

Fish-kills elsewhere – possible switches?

Fish-kills can be caused also by even greater rises in salinity, which can occur during and following storms in the North Sea. These pile up sea water under low air pressure and substantially raise the tidal levels, especially during periods of spring tides. Fish tend to run upriver ahead of the salt water as it moves further upstream than normal and can be killed if they are trapped in a side channel, boat yard or small Broad. This usually occurs in winter, however, and there are sufficient survivors to repopulate the stretches, where the kill has occurred, in time for the spawning season. Most European fish produce so many young that the subsequent population is unlikely to be affected and in any case, since piscivores and zooplanktivores are equally vulnerable to salinity, changes in the ratio that might affect the intensity of zooplankton predation are unlikely.

Fish-kills where there is a change in this ratio might be more likely candidates. They might occur on summer nights in densely weeded stretches of water through deoxygenation by the huge biomass of plants present. One of the greater myths of water gardening is that plants oxygenate the water. They do by day, but reverse the effect by night. The masses of weed described by Patterson and later authors would have provided the right conditions for severe deoxygenation and there are some early reports of fish-kills at Hickling Broad in the 1920s that might be attributed to this. There were no additional consequences there, however, and even the anecdotal evidence is silent during the critical period of the 1950s and 1960s in Broadland.

The verdict?

There are consequently many possibilities for the causes of the switch from plant to phytoplankton dominance in Broadland in the post-war period. We can be certain of their existence, for the evidence of alternative states demands their operation when states have changed. The alternative states hypothesis embraces the available evidence in a much more satisfactory way than the former hypothesis that nutrient changes had been solely responsible for the loss of submerged plants from the Broadland waterway.

The current understanding of the alternative states scheme (Fig. 12.17) takes account of the likelihood that nutrients do have a role, however, in that switch mechanisms appear to be more effective at higher nutrient levels than at low. It also recognises that, because there is considerable release of phosphorus from well-developed plant beds, nitrogen may be the more important nutrient once the change from charophytes to vascular plants, stimulated by phosphorus, has taken place. And with increasing nitrogen loading, the diversity of the plant community will decrease. In Chapter 16 we will use this model to examine what has to be done, should it be considered desirable to return the plant-dominated communities to Broadland. Before that, however, some account is needed of even more changes in Broadland – in the fen and grazing marsh communities – in the post-war period.

Further reading

This chapter contains a wide range of material, some of it concerned with research that is still very active. A list of further reading is thus necessarily long and sometimes quite technical. It is arranged in order of the topics covered. Ellis (1965) contains a series of maps showing the terrestrialisation of the Broads until the 1950s. The first technical report on the eutrophication problem was Mason & Bryant (1975), who attributed the problem to agriculture, not sewage effluent. In retrospect they were partly right, without knowing it, in view of the renewed realisation of the importance of nitrogen. The general issue of eutrophication is covered by Edmondson (1991) in a very appealing way that deals with the case of Lake Washington, including its political and human aspects. Good general references for eutrophication issues are Moss (1998) and Moss, Madgwick & Phillips (1996).

Nutrient budgets for Barton Broad may be found in Osborne (1981), for the River Bure in Moss et al. (1988a, b, 1989), and for Hickling Broad in Leah et al. (1978) and Moss & Leah (1982). Ideas on the importance of epiphytes in the demise of plants were first trawled in Phillips et al. (1978) and then developed by others including Sand, Jensen & Söndergaard (1981). The earliest survey of the relationship of boat activity to turbidity in Broadland was Moss (1977), followed by Hilton & Phillips (1982). More recent unpublished work is included in Figs 12.6 and 12.7. There is a huge literature on sediment release of phosphorus (see Moss 1998 and Marsden 1989 for reviews). Annadotter et al. (1999) gives an example of how dredging is usually ineffective in preventing it, and Moss, Madgwick & Phillips (1996) reviews the issue. The ineffectiveness of phosphorus control in Barton Broad is covered in Phillips (1984) and Phillips et al. (1999). Methods of nitrogen control are reviewed in Moss, Madgwick & Phillips (1996).

The experiments at Cockshoot Broad are discussed in Moss et al. (1986, 1996), at Alderfen Broad in Moss et al. (1990) and Perrow et al. (1994) and at Brundall Broad in Leah et al. (1980). The issues of phytoplankton, zooplankton and fish relationships command a huge literature, approachable through Moss (1998). Classic papers in the area are Andersson et al. (1978), Brooks & Dodson (1965), Hall et al. (1976), Hrbacek et al. (1961) and Hurlbert et al. (1971). The concept of plants providing refuges for grazing zooplankters and the work at Hoveton Great Broad and Hudsons Bay are contained in Timms & Moss (1984), and were developed by, for example, Schriver et al. (1995) Lauridsen et al. (1996) and Moss et al. (1998). The concept of alternative states arose from experiments carried out at Woodbastwick by Balls et al. (1989) and Irvine et al. (1989) and from theoretical work by Scheffer (1998). The idea was conveniently reviewed by Scheffer et al. (1993). Other work on buffers of the plant-dominated state includes Howard Williams (1981), Brönmark (1989), De Nie (1987) and Gross & Sutfeld (1994), but these are only a few examples of a large body of supporting information.

The role of carp in damaging vegetation is covered by Crivelli (1983), Breukelaar et al. (1994), Cahn (1929) and Lamarra (1975). That of toxic substances such as pesticides and heavy metals in reducing the effects of zoo-plankton grazing is reviewed by Stansfield et al. (1989), who adopted the idea from work by Shapiro (1980) in the USA, Gliwicz & Sieniawska (1986), Jak et al. (1996) and Sanders & Cope (1968). Salinity as a forward switch in Hickling Broad, and also the biology of *Prymnesium parvum*, are documented in Bales et al. (1993), Irvine et al. (1993), Leah et al. (1978) and Holdway et al. (1978). Instances of tidal salinity causing fish-kills in the Broads are given in George (1992). The concept of alternative states is now established in official publica-tions, including Broads Authority (1997), but in general the earlier, less sophis-ticated schemes, which talk of Phases 1 (Charophytes), 2 (Vascular plants) and 3 (Phytoplankton), tend to be used. The concept is still evolving and Figure 12.17 should replace previous versions.

13

Changes in the Reedswamps and Fens

Close to White Slea, a narrow channel at the entrance to Hickling Broad, stands a white-painted, thatched lodge. It is a substantial building, built originally in 1875, but later expanded, and much used from the Edwardian period to accommodate parties of gentlemen invited to shoot the rich bird life of the estate. From a platform built against the house a large expanse of water, reedswamp and fen can be seen (Plate 21). Between the two World Wars, on this 290-hectare estate, Lord Desborough employed seven marshmen, three or four reedcutters, a gamekeeper and two under-keepers. He was among the last of the landowners able and willing to carry on the traditional management of the wetlands.

After the Second World War, there was little labour willing to continue the intensive work of maintaining a fenland estate. Some soldiers came back to the land, other workers had been held in farming during the War, but the War had made profound changes. For a second and final time that century, the ordinary people questioned the patrimony of the hierarchy. For what had they risked life and limb? Something better, perhaps, than a desultory wage and long hours in cold and wet conditions, when a warm factory or office job beckoned.

Moreover, the subsidies provided by the Agriculture Act of 1947 promoted a move to machinery and an emphasis on food crops. New and less expensive products were becoming available to replace the reed and sedge, marsh litter, sallow and alder that had been the mainstays of a wetland estate. The market for marsh hay and litter, much of which had been sent for cab horses in London, had collapsed even earlier. The casualties of the First World War, and the advent of the motor car, left only 700 of the 13,000 hansom cabs that had plied the streets in 1900.

There was some continued demand for reed and saw sedge as the human need for status found expression in a more expensive thatched roof than a more commonplace tile one, so some fen management did continue. Many of the fens, however, were simply abandoned to plant succession. Areas that had been open for centuries quickly turned to scrubs of sallow, sweet gale, birch and alder. The vistas of reed, golden in the winter sunshine, turned to duller brown thickets and eventually to dense secondary forests. Regular cutting and removal had kept the fens relatively nutrient-poor and free of choking litter so that many smaller plants, often of great attractiveness, even rarity, had been able to survive. These began to decline.

Moreover, the shallow peat diggings, or turf ponds, of which there is evidence from maps and from the deposits of looser, wet surface peat associated with them, were filling in and not being renewed. There was an extensive system of them, at least in the Ant valley (Fig. 6.3), dug during the nineteenth century for peat. These possibly continued a tradition in which these areas had been continually dug and re-dug for centuries following the abandonment of the much deeper pits that are now the Broads. The significance of the turf ponds is that those deep in the fens and close to the upland, where nutrient levels are unaffected by river water and underlying clay, are sometimes associated with very rich plant communities.

Dykes through the fens, which had been regularly cleared and became colonised by aquatic plants, silted up and were choked by reed. Slubbing out a choked dyke was a heavy, labour-intensive job that became worse the longer the dyke was neglected. Broadland was beginning to be reclaimed by the wild-wood of 6,000 years ago for lack of the hands that had halted the natural succession since at least the Bronze Age (Fig. 13.1).

It was not quite so simple as that, however, for in the aftermath of the War there were several influences leading to more complex consequences than mere lack of labour to manage the fens. Reedswamps and stands of other emergent plants, fringing the rivers and Broads, which had not been formerly managed, were also disappearing, and bird communities changed for more reasons than simple change in vegetation. There was a more intensive approach to the management of the fens that remained; water quality was different as fertilisation rates increased in the arable catchment. More ground water was taken for irrigation and other human use, leaving less for some of the marginal fens close to the upland. There were more boats, those hired out plying for longer each year; and feral geese and an introduced mammal, the coypu, were to be reckoned. All of these combined to change the appearance and natural history of the fens, just as a complex of factors had switched the waters from limpidity to green and brown soups in the same period.

Reed loss from the rivers

Like everything else, habitats show wear if heavily used and the post-war rivers of Broadland were no exception. Even within the floodbanks in their lower courses, where they are flanked by drained grazing marshes, the rivers had had ronds – sometimes wide fringes of rooted and semi-floating reedswamp and flote grass. The undrained fens of the middle courses of the rivers had sported a gentle transition from the lilies at the edge through reedmace and bulrush to reed and the managed fen behind.

In the late nineteenth century, much of Breydon Water had also been reedswamp-fringed, though dredging of the harbour and greater penetration of salt water was putting paid to it by the early 1900s. Beyond Breydon, however, the rivers had preserved their fringing swamps despite the commercial traffic and this gave a soft and natural appearance to their edges. Sometimes the ronds were grazed and acquired swards of iris and some were cut for reed.

Much of this fringe disappeared in the decades after the Second World War. The obvious reason was that it was simply worn away by the increasing boat activity, but there were additional forces at work. In the lower reaches, boat wash undercut the peat in which the reed was rooted and the changing tide broke off weakened parts, but substantial ronds still remain in the reaches bordered by floodbanks, for boat activity is lowest in these and the rivers are wider. Further upstream, the narrower channel and the greater popularity for boating meant much greater erosion from boat passage and damage from mooring. In places the inevitable trampling by anglers, let alone their cutting the vegetation to allow easy casting of their lines, began damage that worsened once begun. The rising nutrient levels in the water may not have helped,

1958

1964

Open water

Open fen

Scrub

Carr

Woodbastwick Marshes

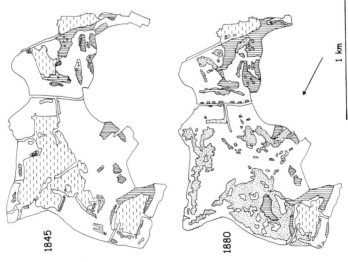

1845

1880

1 km

Fig. 13.1 Changes in vegetation cover on the Woodbastwick estate, now part of the Bure Marshes National Nature Reserve, between 1845 and 1964. The trends of encroachment on the open water of the turf ponds and from open fen to scrub and carr are clear. Based on Nature Conservancy (1965).

because bulrush and reedmace are associated with lower nutrient levels than common reed. Reed is more tolerant and though its disappearance from the Broads is probably linked with rising nutrients, the impact of erosion was probably pre-eminent in the rivers.

Along the undrained fens of the riverside, succession to alder and willow shaded the edges, and as the floating reed-fringe mats were eroded away, impeded any regeneration of them. This left much of the bank of the River Bure, for example, between Belaugh and Ranworth, a wall of trees, their roots exposed at low water by the erosion. Increasing cultivation of the upland catchment was also bringing more sediment into the rivers, shallowing the channels and bringing demands for dredging from boating interests. Sometimes this was over-zealous and carried out with scoop dredgers that made the banks vertical and even more prone to erosion and collapse, whilst the dredgings were dumped on the ronds, again not helping reed growth.

Once such decline has begun it has proved very difficult to check. Indeed, the ideas of alternative states developed in Chapter 12 apply here too. Intact reedswamp will resist disturbance by its tough and intertwined mat structure, but once this is destroyed, even a much lower rate of disturbance will prevent regeneration from replantings that are inevitably far less bulky.

Coypu

Coypu damaged reeds and floodbanks. They are interesting animals, and are not a problem when controlled by jaguar and the like in their native Argentina. In the Broads they became something of a pest. Yet again the problem was ultimately linked to social change, for coypu have a dense under-fur that can be made into coats. I well remember the icons that fur coats were to the least wealthy groups of my parents' generation. Mink and sable were so costly as to be unattainable, but coypu could have been a start, at least, on the ladder of increasing respectability. Coypu (Plate 22) were introduced to Britain in the 1930s and there were about 50 fur farms at the outbreak of the Second World War. Inevitably some coypu escaped and others were deliberately released as the farm labour was drafted into the army in the 1940s.

Coypu are large rodents, weighing up to six or seven kilograms and adult males measure a metre from snout to rump. They become sexually mature in as little as three months, breed year round, and take only five months to produce litters averaging around five. Their front incisor teeth are bright orange in colour and highly destructive to reed rhizomes, saw sedge beds, large wetland plants, such as the great water dock and cowbane, and to sugar beet. Their burrowing can weaken floodbanks. Ted Ellis recorded whole areas that had been reduced to patches of mud in the 1960s as their population in Broadland built up to a legendary 200,000, though probably only half of this in reality. Pressure from farmers and the River Board, then responsible for the river banks and flood protection of the grazing marshes, led to payments by the Ministry of Agriculture to the Rabbit Clearance Societies – informal groups largely of farmers, set up some years previously to control rabbits. The payment was half the cost of shooting the animals.

Many coypu were shot – 70,000 in 1962 – and the population was decimated by the severe winter of 1962/63, but the fecundity of coypu and the lack of natural predators, allowed easy recovery. When the Rabbit Clearance Societies were wound up, because rabbits were becoming scarce owing to the disease of myxomatosis introduced into their populations, one society continued as Coypu Control, employing trappers. A small research laboratory was established in Norwich to study the animal and investigate the relationship between population size and the impact of control measures. The costs of trapping were high, but the trapping effort was steadily increased, with declines in the population but little sign of imminent extinction.

In 1978 it was decided that ultimately the least costly option was to increase trapping intensity greatly for a few years, in order to eliminate the animal. In the early 1980s up to 200,000 trap-nights were being set each year and by 1986 only a few coypu were left. By 1989 it was likely that the coypu had been removed (Fig. 13.2). There were occasional sightings or corpses for a year or two afterwards, but there have been none in recent years. In any relationship between a predator and its prey, total extinction of the prey is disastrous for the predator. In this particular relationship, the trappers were compensated for bringing about their own extinction, following that of the coypu, by offers of substantial bonuses. Coypu may now be seen in zoos in the UK, but their paddocks must meet stringent standards to prevent escape.

Reed dieback at the fringes of the Broads

Before the Second World War it had been difficult to row across some of the Broads. This was not only because of the tangles of waterweed that had troubled Arthur Patterson, but also because rather more solid clumps of reedmace and bulrush stretched out into the open water and merged into the reed at the edge. There had been enough for bulrush, locally called bolder, to be harvested for the making of chair seats and reedmace for stuffing into horse harness collars at local factories. One of the first of the group of English ecologists, Marietta Pallis, had published a cross section of the vegetation across Barton Broad in 1911 which very clearly showed the abundance of these

Fig. 13.2 Coypu established a strong presence (right, large symbols) in Norfolk and Suffolk in the mid-1960s and was also colonising Essex, Lincolnshire and inland counties. Campaigns to eliminate it were effective only after severe winters and when the number of trappers employed had been greatly increased (left). Based on Norris (1967) and Gosling (1988).

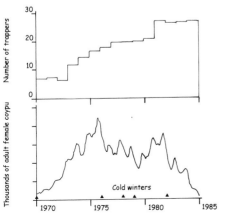
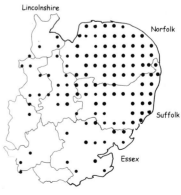

emergent plants.

Nowhere are they now abundant; indeed, the few remaining clumps are hard to find and even the remaining reed fringes of the Broads are often clean-cut walls, with very little sign of younger plants tentatively edging out to colonise the open water. The bulrush and reedmace were retreating by the late 1940s and had almost disappeared by the late 1950s; the common reed was showing distinct signs of regression in the 1960s. The retreat was not uniform, and was recorded elsewhere in Europe where human activity was also rife in the waters and catchments.

In Broadland, studies of aerial photographs and successive editions of Ordnance Survey maps give some idea of the changes (Table 13.1), with a steady advance of reedswamp into the open water of the Broads until 1946, and substantial natural succession to more solid fen between 1905 and 1946. Some reedswamp was lost, probably following damage by boats and subsequent erosion, but it was compensated by new advance elsewhere. Then, after 1946, the balance changed to loss – later in the Trinity Broads and to only a small extent at Hickling – but substantial and early in the Bure, Ant and Yare Broads.

Table 13.1 Changes in reedswamp area (hectares) in the Broads. Values are the areas of open water newly colonised by reed (second column) and of previous reedswamp becoming open water (third column) or more solid fen (last column) in the periods concerned (first column).

Period	Advance into open water	Loss and change to open water	Succession to fen
1880–1905	54.1	10.8	18.5
1905–1946	34.3	6.6	150.8
1946–1977	3.3	67.8	13.6

Much of the loss was probably due to coypu; the process was closely observed and recorded by Ted Ellis and deep in the fens recovery of the reed has occurred following control of the coypu. Some damage was probably caused by geese, swans and coot, as their preferred submerged plants disappeared. In the Yare Broads, coypu grazing led to replacement of reed by flote grass, which was less frequently eaten. Since the 1970s, and decline in the coypu, this change has reversed. The problem, however, is that coypu may not have been the only causes of the loss – it has occurred elsewhere in Europe where there were no coypu – and in Broadland, the fringing reedswamp has generally not recovered despite elimination of the coypu.

Several factors are at work and a change is not necessarily reversed by removal of the original cause. Discovery of what really happened, years after the event, is also very difficult. The loss has been called reed dieback, but this is not a helpful term for it seems to imply disease, yet there is no evidence of any debilitating outbreak. Reeds are naturally colonised, like every other living organism, by fungal parasites, and they are eaten by caterpillars and other insects. Their young shoots are also eaten by water birds, and locally, this can be quite damaging, but cannot explain the wider problem.

One clue comes from the nature of the reedswamps. Some are rooted in solid peat or clay and are called littoral reed; others are floating mats or hovers. Two of my colleagues, Caroline Crook and Rosalind Boar, spent much of 1982 probing the edges of many of the Broads to determine whether the remaining reed was of the hover or the littoral type. They then plotted this information on maps also showing the extent of reedswamp loss since the War. Most of the loss had been along shores characterised by hover; the littoral reed was relatively intact (Fig. 13.3). Hover is inherently more vulnerable to mechanical damage than littoral reed and sometimes breaks free in storms, but used to regenerate readily. Some of the Broads had floating islands of it, occupied at Hoveton Great Broad and Alderfen Broad by breeding black-headed gulls until the 1960s, when the islands disappeared.

Reed hover disappeared from Broads barred to boats as well as those to which they had access. Could something have happened to weaken the rafts of reed so that they broke up under the normal pressures of wind, water and grazing birds? The evidence is circumstantial, but the interpretation reasonable. Crook and Boar grew reed hydroponically – in water culture rather than rooted in pots – in a glasshouse under different regimes of water chemistry. The levels of nitrate proved to be particularly important. When the nitrate was increased, the reed grew more vigorously, but as the green tops flourished, the plants invested less in their root and rhizome systems (Fig. 13.4). Hover depends on a firm, intertwined mat of root and rhizome to support the growth of the shoots. If the mat was weaker and the shoots relatively bigger, there

Fig. 13.3 Common reed grows in two distinct forms, littoral and hover (left). Where fringing reedswamp has been lost, it has mostly been of the hover form. Stippling indicates reed areas in 1946. Dark shading indicates areas of reed still existing in 1982. Based on Crook et al. (1983).

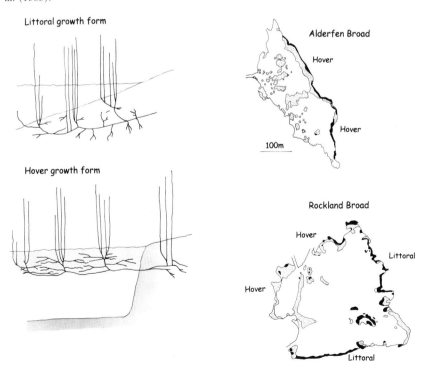

Littoral growth form

Hover growth form

Alderfen Broad

Hover

Hover

100m

Rockland Broad

Hover

Littoral

Hover

Littoral

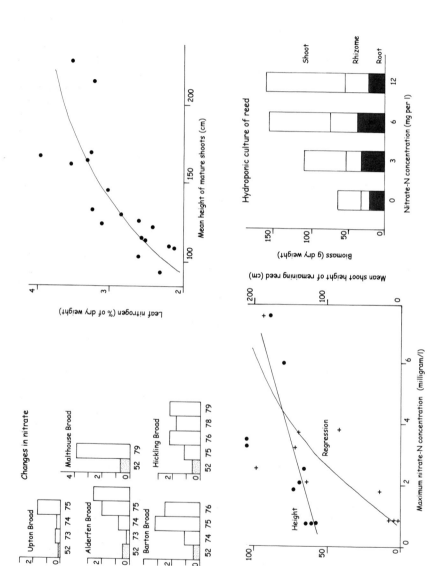

would be a greater chance of breakage, damage and even capsizing in a storm or following boat damage. Nitrate had increased in the waters of Broadland substantially in the post-war period with the intensification of agriculture (Fig. 12.8) and the work suggests a plausible reason for much of the reed loss.

However, some littoral reed had disappeared too and though lesser root and rhizome growth might be expected here also when nitrate was more available, the support given by the soil would make such reed less likely to be disrupted. There was, however, an interesting parallel in the lodging (flattening by wind) of crops such as barley when heavy nitrogen fertilisation led to softer stems with less woody supporting tissue and more soft parenchyma. Most plant stems are supported by cells called sclerenchyma fibres, full of lignin, the stuff of wood. Elsewhere in Europe, reed grown under high nitrogen conditions appeared more vulnerable to damage, though the evidence was circumstantial and not particularly convincing.

Work on Broadland reed showed that nitrogen did decrease the sclerenchyma content of reed stems, but not absolutely, only when the ratio of nitrogen to potassium in the water was high. Potassium levels in the Broadland waters have probably increased with use of fertilisers and greater penetration upriver of sea water, but certainly not by the ten or 20-fold increase in nitrogen. A role for nitrogen is thus plausible in the case of loss of littoral reed too. For the moment, therefore, we leave both the submerged plants and the fringing reedswamps in a dire state brought about by switch mechanisms operating more readily in waters whose nutrient levels were on the increase. The model of alternative states fits well in both cases and in Chapter 17, I will look at the means by which these losses might be reversed.

Changes in the area and diversity of the fens

Of the 5,000 hectares of undrained wetland that formed the vistas of the middle stretches of the rivers between the World Wars, most still remains. Little more has been drained, but the nature of the vegetation has changed. About 1,000 hectares were formerly left as mature alder carr and another 1,000 hectares of carr were coppiced to provide poles and wood. The remaining 3,000 hectares had been cut and maintained as open fen. Since the War, 1,000 of these 3,000 hectares of formerly open fen have been abandoned to succession, and very little coppicing of the carrs has taken place, so that there are now about 3,000 hectares of scrub and carr and 2,000 of still-open fen. Some of this area is cut or grazed by nature conservation organisations to maintain

Fig. 13.4 (opposite) Reed regression occurs because the reed is broken away by physical mechanisms such as erosion or bird grazing, but ultimately the reasons are more fundamental. The reed is made vulnerable to such damage by changes in water quality. Nitrate concentrations in Broadland waters increased greatly after the Second World War (top left). The extent of reed swamp regression in a series of Broads is significantly linked with the nitrate supply (bottom left). Paradoxically, the reed appears to grow better at high nitrate concentrations (bottom left) and has a greater nitrogen content in the leaves (top right). This may make it a more favoured food supply for grazers, but, especially for hover reed, which is the form that has most regressed, high nitrogen supply favours shoot growth over root and rhizome growth (bottom right). This leads to top-heavy, poorly supported mats, which more easily erode and capsize. Nitrate data from 1952 from unpublished measurements of A.C. Barry. Other information based on Crook et al. (1983).

open fen communities and to produce an income from reed and sedge sales. Some is privately managed to produce a commercial crop of reed or sedge.

The current conversion of previously open wetland to scrub and carr, about 2,000 hectares, has thus been 40 per cent of the total, half of it from alder coppice, half from open fen. In the Bure valley there are large areas of alder carr, a huge stand of which can be seen from the top of the tower of St Helen's church at Ranworth, whilst the fens around Hickling Broad are mostly open. Partly this is because of active management in a prominent nature reserve, partly because of greater exposure to salt-laden winds near the coast and introduction of pumped saline water, to which alder is not very tolerant. But in all the valleys there has been some succession to carr and scrub and in all of them there remains some active management on nature reserves or private estates.

A transformation of only 20 per cent of the original tall grass fen to scrub and woodland may not seem very serious; it represents a loss of only a third of the former cut area; two thirds remain, despite great changes in land management overall in the UK. What remains though has also changed in nature. The management is less intensive; the fens are now cut much less frequently, often by machines that compress the surface and do not provide the selectivity that grazing with stock does. The litter cannot always be removed. Management was resumed in some areas after a long gap in which litter had built up, suppressing many smaller species, and this litter is hard to move. And areas of scrub that have been cut to open up the fen, have rapidly reverted to scrub because it has not been possible to remove the tree stools, which rapidly regenerate.

The dyke systems, formerly frequently cleared out, have colonised with reed and lost their aquatic plants and associated animals and where they have not been dammed from the rivers, the influences of nutrient-rich water have been felt no less than in the Broads. At the river edges, highly competitive plants such as nettle and willowherb have taken over, promoted perhaps by nutrient-rich water. However, where management has continued and river water has failed to penetrate, remnants of the former rich flora still remain. It is difficult to quantify the change because although survey methods are now stringent, comparable surveys from the past were simply not done and we must rely on anecdotal accounts.

The fens and their fauna

The animal communities provide some indication of the change, however; there has been a long tradition of counting birds and listing insects. The invertebrates have survived well where their habitat has persisted, so that the long lists of species recorded by past naturalists have often been added to in recent years, though the overall sizes of individual populations must have declined. Of the 21 dragonflies and damselflies recorded in Ted Ellis' book on the Broads, which was compiled over the ten years prior to 1965, all but two, the downy emerald and *Coenagrion armatum* are still present, if less widely distributed. The downy emerald was last recorded in 1975 and *C. armatum* was last seen in 1956.

Some fen birds have declined in numbers, but new ones have appeared. Cetti's warbler, which favours thickets of sallow, appeared in 1974 and is spreading, with at least 60 now in the Yare valley fens. The reed, sedge and grasshopper warblers and reed bunting typical of open reedy habitats still have substantial populations and Savi's warbler, which disappeared in the mid-nineteenth century, reappeared in the 1970s around the Thurne Broads, though it is still scarce.

The bittern, however, has had very mixed fortunes. It was lost from Broadland, probably as a result of egg-collecting, in the nineteenth century, but following protection there were nine pairs in 1918, 16 or 17 in 1928 and at least 23 in 1938. In 1954/55 there may have been as many as 60 calling males, though census by this method probably overestimates numbers. There were still 27 pairs in 1970, but this had fallen to nine in 1976 and there have been even fewer, in some years none, since then. Bittern feed on small fish, amphibians and the larger crustaceans, in reed-bed dykes and reedswamp edges; they are secretive and have declined in some other places (Wales, Lincolnshire, Kent) in the UK, but not in East Suffolk or Lancashire. Reasons for the Broadland decline are thus probably local.

Disturbance from people in the tourist season has been blamed, but the much less shy grey heron has also declined from having 200 Broadland nests in the 1960s to 60 in the 1980s. The reason for the bittern decline might lie in either the lesser availability of suitable feeding habitat as dykes have filled in, or in the clarity of the water as algae have come to predominate, or in the availability of fish and frogs. We really do not know. Marsh harriers, on the other hand, are slowly increasing in numbers, as maybe are otters. The pressures of persecution in the nineteenth century by keepers, fishermen and egg-collectors, compounded by pesticide and polychlorinated biphenol poisoning in the years after the Second World War, have been relieved. Otter populations, however, are still very low.

Fig. 13.5 Feral geese, ducks and other waterbirds collect by parking areas and other places favoured by visitors who feed them. The enormous production of somewhat slimy, green goose faeces is not appreciated by visitors, whose activities nonetheless fuel the problem. The edge of Salhouse Broad is a prime example.

Two naturalised species of waterfowl have increased and may cause significant local damage to reedswamps through their grazing. The greylag goose was
introduced in 1935 and there is now a flock of over 2,500 birds, increasing
yearly by about 13 per cent. Their effects can be seen in the close grazing of
grass swards along the edge of Salhouse Broad, and near any water's edge car
park (Fig. 13.5), where they receive a rich food supply of visitors' bread and
cake. Greylag can be legally shot, but the current bag of 250 a year is insufficient to relieve the problem. Similarly, a flock of introduced Canada geese has
expanded from negligibility in the 1950s to about a thousand in Broadland by
now, with an annual increase of 8 per cent, whilst there is also a small flock of
introduced Egyptian geese. These introductions follow the development of
landed estates in the United Kingdom since the Tudor period, when the
impulse to modify nature to the flattery of the wealthy owners resulted in the
introduction of numerous species of animals and plants, many of which have
subsequently caused problems.

Fox numbers have grown. Foxes were very unusual in the 1960s, but appear
to have been attracted by the availability of coypu and the shortage of rabbits
on the uplands. It is alleged that ground-nesting birds now suffer because the
coypu have been eliminated. Finally, Chinese water deer, original escapees
from a private collection, which spend most of their time in thick, scrubby fen,
moving out to feed on arable crops, now number about 100, but are unlikely
to have had any significant effect on Broadland ecology.

Commercial reed and sedge beds

Though the market for marsh hay and litter collapsed in the 1920s, the pre-
Second World War fens had still been managed to a far greater extent than was
economic afterwards, when only the sale of reed and saw sedge underpinned
traditional management, though it was not now so traditional. Traditional
management included the cutting, with hand-held scythes, of very wet areas,
close to the rivers and Broads, as well as dryer areas further inland. Post-war
management has increasingly farmed reed in bunded areas (commercial reed
beds or reed floods) using machines.

The timing and frequency of cutting are very important. Saw sedge cannot
stand frequent cutting and is cut once every three or four years in summer.
Summer cutting suppresses reed growth and also removes much of the litter,
and its contained nutrients, from the cut areas, so these fens may be quite
species-rich. Cutting too late in the season, which can be a problem when
labour is scarce, for sedge is still cut by hand scythe, is less damaging to the
reed, which may then take over. Failure to cut at all leads to accumulation of
litter and introduction of other large 'weedy' species, and eventually scrub. For
thatching, much less saw sedge is needed than reed. The roof ridge takes about
one bundle per three inches (the trade has stolidly resisted the metric system),
or perhaps a hundred or so for a modest house. About 24,000 bundles have
been cut from sedge beds in the Ant valley (Catfield fens), the Thurne
(Braydon marshes, Hickling and Martham) and in the Woodbastwick marshes
of the River Bure, in recent years.

A few thousand, much larger, bundles of reed are needed for an average
thatched roof, so the extent of the commercial reed beds is much greater than
that of sedge beds. Reed beds are much less diverse in plants than sedge beds,
however. Reed is a very variable product. Productivity can range fivefold from

400 to 2,000 grams per square metre per year, even in a single bed, due to a subtle mosaic of growth conditions and different genetic characteristics of particular clones. A cut bundle can vary in the length of the stems, which are cut in winter when they are dead, and weathering has removed the leaves, leaving just the flowering head at the top. It can also vary in the thickness of the stems, in the cleanness of the cut at the base or butt, and in the hardness of the stems at the butt. This last reflects the woodiness of the stems and perhaps their content of silica, which many grasses absorb.

Reed cutters and thatchers are aware of these differences and of the properties of particular beds as they vary with weather and water level from year to year, previous cutting regime and management, though a rational scheme to accommodate all this information is still elusive. Cutting every two years (called double wale, 'wale' coming from an old Norse word meaning 'choice') gives stronger reed than annual cutting (single wale).

The best reed, taller and coarser, was said to have been cut from the very wet edges of the Broads and dykes, but this was not accessible even by hand-pushed machines, and sometimes not even by foot in very wet winters. Reed-bed owners have thus now favoured areas where the water regime can be managed with sluices, allowing flooding in spring and drainage for ease of access in winter. Several areas of former grazing marsh, the earliest in the 1920s at Ranworth, were embanked and sluiced. They are flooded in April, when cutting has ceased and drained down in August, ready for cutting in December.

Such control allows the bringing in of machine cutters, powered by small engines, and leads to rather more thorough coverage of the bed than hand cutting. The beds are thus more uniform and less diverse not only from their recent establishment, but also because awkward corners and slightly raised areas, surmounted by occasional bushes, are scarce. The beds are drier in winter than those in the traditional open fen. Habitat for warblers and bearded tit and wet stubble for the nesting of snipe, teal, shoveler and mallard, are thus absent or scarce. Nonetheless these reed floods have an important landscape quality, keeping areas open that would otherwise succeed to scrub.

Machine cutting has its problems. The wheels compress the peat surface and reed grows less well in the tracks. The height at which the reed is cut above the surface of the fen is also greater than in hand cutting because of the need to protect the cutter bars from tussocks and other irregularities in the ground. The butts are thus less hard than they might be, for the stems are most woody towards their bases, and more likely to be frayed. Thatchers like a hard clean cut. More litter is left by machines and the bundles, which are not only cut but also tied by modern machines such as the Olympia rice harvester, may be more infested by weeds such as pond sedge and creeping bent, especially if the beds are kept too dry. The litter build-up can eventually be a major problem, for the reed grows much less well and the only solution is to dig out the top 18 inches or so. This is a backbreaking task, not easily done by machine without risk of severe damage to the surface, and hence unlikely to be carried out. From its past practice we have inherited the term 'turfing out'.

There remains, however, a good market for reed and about 150,000 bundles, a third of the British crop, are still cut in Broadland. This is insufficient to meet demand and the industry is threatened by cheaper imports from mainland Europe, sometimes of poorer quality. There have also been allegations of declining quality and reed rotting prematurely on roofs, but these have not been substantiated. Productive beds will yield 1,200 bundles per hectare cut double wale, fewer if cut each year and a professional worker with a machine can cut 25 hectares each year. Each bundle (usually called a bunch, locally) is about 24 inches in circumference, 12 inches above the butt. There are about 2,000 stems in a bunch, so perhaps 300 million reed stems are still annually cut in Broadland. Thatching currently uses a thousand or two bunches to cover a cottage roof to 12 or 15 inches thickness and will cost much more than tiles will. Insurance costs against fire will also be greater. The roof will last for several decades, however, provide much better insulation and usually look more attractive, certainly more sympathetic to a rural landscape.

The mention of landscape introduces questions about management of the fens and the future of Broadland, to be posed in Chapters 17 and 18. Now it is appropriate, following the post-war changes in the waters and the fens, to turn to the fate of the grazing marshes.

Further reading

Early literature on the fen birds include the classic *Broadland Birds* (1924) by Emma Turner, who was among the first to carry out systematic observations, whilst also adding to the list of 'Broadland Characters', beloved of many authors of books on this area. Another was Jim Vincent, gamekeeper on the Whiteslea (Hickling) estate for several decades before his death in 1944, who kept detailed diaries, one year of which is published as Vincent (1980). Stone (1988) is a biography of a third, Ted Ellis, and Linsell (1990) gives an account of the area around Hickling Broad that is replete with anecdotes. The extent of the problem of declining management of the fens is covered in Nature Conservancy (1965), Nature Conservancy Council (1984), Ewans (1992) and Broads Authority (1997).

Boorman & Fuller (1981) chart the decline of fringing reedswamp and Boar et al. (1989) summarise experimental work on the causes of the problem. George (1992) contains much detail on the reedswamps, thatching and management. The problems caused by the coypu and their solution can be traced through Carill-Worsley (1932), Laurie (1946), Davis (1963), Ellis (1963), Gosling & Baker (1987), Gosling (1988), Gosling et al. (1988) and Smith (1995).

14

Drainage and Threats to the Grazing Marshes

In 1991, one of my students, Sarah Anderson, asked groups of children in Liverpool primary schools about their likes and dislikes among various habitats and animals. What emerged strongly was that wetland habitats, though not troubling the youngest – swamps had rather a good press in children's literature – acquired a very negative aura for the older. This antipathy is shared by many adults. Wet places, in the past, were places of danger and terror, the haunts, in the traditional literature of Europe, of trolls and water witches, sucking mud and death by drowning. They were associated with ague and fever, tracts difficult to cross; they were places to be avoided, and to be got rid of whenever possible. Perhaps not surprisingly, therefore, once the means of draining the lower floodplains of Broadland became more efficient in the twentieth century, the opportunity was grasped with enthusiasm.

There were several forces at work. The grazing marshes, like floodplains elsewhere, included soils that were potentially very fertile from the silts and clays they had accumulated, over millennia, from the erosion of the uplands. The vocation of farmers is to grow large and vigorous crops. They had the encouragement of governments, avid, in the second half of the twentieth century, to lessen the dangers of dependency on overseas foodstuffs, revealed by the submarine blockades of the Second World War. Land drainage – the very term carries with it a particular view – after all, land should be dry – has long been a holy grail for agriculture.

There was also the danger of flooding by the sea in a region where relative sea level had been rising naturally since the retreat of the glaciers. The sea had broken through the dunes near Horsey on several occasions, notably in 1938 when it had effectively recaptured its former Thurne estuary (Fig. 14.1). It had overtopped and washed out the embankments, which held in the rivers behind Yarmouth on several occasions. There was always the possibility that it would regain its former territory here too.

Floodplains, salt marshes and mud flats are part of the river bed; human occupation and development of them in such a way that they are unable to accommodate natural flooding will always bring threats and problems. Human memory of past disasters soon dulls, though, and human ambitions can often be met on shorter timescales than serious floods. All of this proved to have serious consequences for the natural history of the Broadland grazing marshes, culminating in unprecedented confrontations between groups of people involved in the 1980s.

Sea defence and land drainage

There has been a division, for some time, between two sets of responsibilities for the organisation of land drainage and the protection of Broadland from

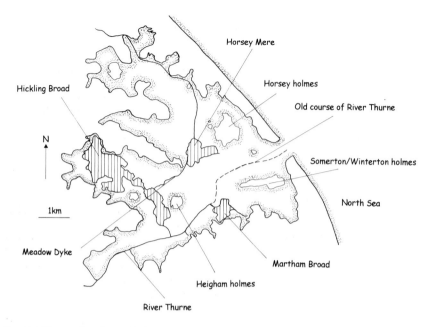

Fig. 14.1 The sea flooding of 1938 effectively showed the extent of the original estuary of the Thurne when it discharged to the nearby coast through what is now the Hundred stream. The holmes were then islands in the estuary. The location of the present Broads, deep within the estuarine limits, suggests that the entrance to the estuary was blocked, either naturally or by people, sometime between the Roman period, when the clay that floors much of the area was laid down, and the ninth century when the digging of the peat and clay pits probably began. Based on Sainty et al. (1939) and George (1992).

flooding by the sea. Defence against the sea has been regionally organised and associated also with the embankment of the main rivers. It is essentially concerned with creating a protected environment for property, which secondarily allows drainage of the levels of the grazing marshes. Land drainage is concerned with the removal of fresh water and with lowering water tables and is more locally organised. Both aspects have been strongly associated with aid from successive governments through the agriculture ministries in the post-war period to increase the productivity of the grazing marshes.

Sea flooding of Broadland is known from 1250, 1287 and 1608 when the first temporary committee, the Sea Breach Commission, was constituted to deal with its consequences. There were successive Commissions following floods in 1617, 1622, 1717, 1718, 1720 and 1791 and thereafter until a Commission was made permanent by the 1861 Land Drainage Act (Chapter 9). Its job was not small and the tools for keeping out the sea were at first puny. They were confined to re-heaping the sand and embedding bundles of faggots in the seaward face of the dune until artificial defences were engineered following the 1938 flood. Sea water had then flowed through a gap of 642 metres around the place where the natural outlet to the Thurne had been blocked some centuries previously – a somewhat vigorous chicken come home to roost. The water was up to four metres deep, leaving the ancient holmes or islands, of Somerton,

Winterton, Heigham and Horsey dry, but overtopping the embankments and flooding the grazing marshes to the north and east of Hickling Broad and Horsey Mere with salt water (Fig. 14.1).

The dunes were re-formed and strengthened with bags, filled with concrete and spiked with steel rods to hold them together. It took a year for salinity levels in the waterway to fall to the previous background of about 1,000 milligrams of chloride per litre and five years for the soils of the 3,000 hectares of grazing marshes to recover fully. There were, inevitably, widespread deaths of freshwater fish and plants after the flooding, but the more tolerant members of the community, such as fennel pondweed and spiked water-milfoil, recovered within the year.

The next flood came during a storm surge tide in 1953. It was again after weather conditions in the North Sea had been severe, with a major depression in the atmosphere allowing winds from adjacent high pressure areas to pile more sea water into the area, at a time that coincided with high spring tides. Though this was a tragic time along the eastern coast of England, with many people drowned, Broadland bore less than in 1938, and only 490 hectares were flooded when the sea broke in at the now weaker section of the coast around Sea Palling. However, the flood increased the resolve of the authorities. Because the original flood defences at Horsey were crumbling, as the steel rods corroded, a long section of coast was provided with reinforced concrete walls by 1987.

Even walls are vulnerable though, and the defences are not invincible. The beach has eroded at the foot of some sections, undermining the foundations, so rock has had to be piled at the base of one section and offshore breakwaters have recently been made in parallel lines to the shore. These are intended to increase accretion of shingle and sand on the beach. The concrete wall is partly camouflaged by blown sand, but its lip and more is sometimes exposed. The movement, in the wind, of the spiky marram grass trailing over it, traces arcs upon the concrete like the fatal writings on the palace wall of Nebuchadnezzar.

The river embankments

More often than the sea breaks through the coast, the embankments, which hold in the rivers from their former floodplains, are overtopped and broken. The flooding is then more usually fresh water, though it can be salt close to the coast. Ultimately, the flood is caused by the river channel having been made too small to accommodate the rain, especially at high tide. The greed for land to either side of the channel in the past has been too great. There was a famous flood in 1912, which covered parts of Norwich with two metres of water, and damaged bridges, buildings and culverts. It also cut through the embankment that holds in the northern edge of Breydon Water, flooded the Cobholm district of Yarmouth, drowned five people, flooded 3,500 houses and 100 workplaces and led to the evacuation of 10,000 people. River floods often follow storm surges as in 1905, 1921 and 1943 as well as 1953.

Rising sea levels increase the risk of flooding. Relative sea levels have been continuously rising in East Anglia both naturally (see Chapter 2) and because the ocean is expanding as global temperatures rise through changes in the composition of the atmosphere. There is greater penetration of the tide than would naturally be the case, partly because of dredging of the Haven for navigation at Yarmouth, but primarily by the very constraints that flood

Fig. 14.2 Large, raised embankments keep the rivers of Broadland confined to what were formerly only their summer channels and prevent the water moving over its former flood-plain. This maintains the grazing marsh landscape, but the banks are expensive to maintain and increasingly threatened by erosion to the river side and rising sea levels.

embankments make on the volume of the waterway. Water does not disappear; if prevented from spreading sideways, it must go further upriver.

The embankments (Fig. 14.2) are now old and weak. They are made of earth and they settle about three centimetres each year as the drained land sinks. The ronds, which protected them at the river edge, have been eroded by boats and the banks themselves are being undermined. They are also weakened by the dykes, called soke dykes, which parallel them at their foot on the grazing marsh level. Through these, water flows to the pumps, carrying material from the base of the bank with it. The close grassy sward that once consolidated the embankment surfaces has been replaced by less resistant thistles and nettles as farmers keep their stock away from the risks of the river's edge – litter of glass and plastic – and the vegetation changes. The Breydon north embankment was breached again in 1976 and 1,500 hectares were flooded. There is writing on the wall here too.

Land drainage

Floods of fresh water over the grazing marshes, even in summer, are no great problem for the traditional pasturage regime, provided they are not pro-longed. They are little problem at all in winter. Some flooding has been inevitable ever since the rivers were first embanked – flaps on sluices stuck, wind pumps were damaged in storms and put out of commission. Flooding became more of an issue, however, as the agriculture of the marshes began to change in the 1970s and 1980s and there was a strong tendency to plough and grow arable crops, and as the risks of flooding increased through deterioration of the embankments.

To cope with such flooding, small drainage authorities were created in the early nineteenth century following the passing of the Enclosure Acts and the 1861 Land Drainage Act, though as often as not individual landowners took their own action. The Ministry of Agriculture created a more coherent body, the East Norfolk Rivers Catchment Board, under the Land Drainage Act of 1930, to assume responsibility for the sea defences and the main rivers and to reorganise the former small drainage authorities into the Internal Drainage Boards or IDBs. These held responsibility for the drainage by pumping water from the levels over the embankments and into the main rivers. They were (and are) able to charge landowners a rate to cover the costs of new works and modification of the existing ones. They made and make payments to the Catchment Board (and subsequently its several successors, now the Environment Agency) for maintenance of the sea defences and embankments, without which local drainage would be futile. Occupiers of the land are also charged a rate to cover the services provided and to maintain the drains and pumps.

The IDBs are elected bodies. Their electors are owners of more than one hectare or occupiers of land rated at more than £35 per year in 1935, or otherwise of more than eight hectares. The number of votes per elector is approximately proportional to the area occupied and the elections are rarely contested. The Boards (Fig. 14.3) are essentially the purview of the major

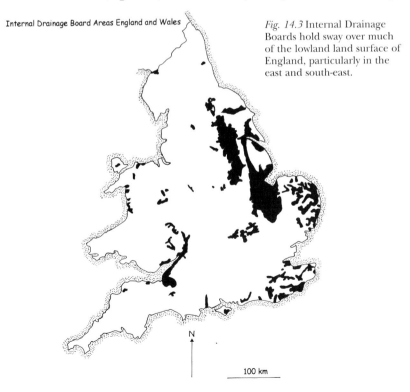

Internal Drainage Board Areas England and Wales

Fig. 14.3 Internal Drainage Boards hold sway over much of the lowland land surface of England, particularly in the east and south-east.

N

100 km

landowners of the level and, as they were intended, have a single-minded purpose to relieve the land of as much water as possible consistent with the agricultural regime desired at the time.

They do this using the system of dykes, whose water level can be regulated by removable dams to give higher or lower water tables in different sections, by main drains and by pumps. There are currently 18 IDBs in Broadland, responsible for drainage of nearly 29,000 hectares. This represents the bulk of Broadland, other than the upland catchment. The era of wind-powered drainage, related in Chapter 9, ended, with a pragmatist lack of nostalgia, when steam pumps were constructed in the 1930s. These had a brief heyday with 30 in use in 1938. The buildings of only three now remain, substantially at Strumpshaw on the Yare and Black Mill, opposite Somerleyton on the Waveney, and as a chimney at Seven Mile House on the Yare (Plate 23). Coal to fire them was bulky and had often to be brought in by river and they required frequent attention.

Steam pumps were replaced by diesel pumps, whose fuel was easier to handle, but which were almost as troublesome to run, until the invention of electrical automatic starting equipment, responsive to water levels, in the 1950s. Electrical pumps then became universal. They needed less labour, and fuel costs were reduced. They could also be much more powerful and shift much more water, more quickly, than ever before.

Farming aspirations

There was, at first, only a slow change from the traditional pasturage regime after the Second World War. Most of the marshes have probably been ploughed occasionally and either re-seeded with grass or planted with oats, wheat or mangolds. The improved drainage with the new electric pumps allowed lower water tables and more encouragement of arable cultivation, but it remained on a small scale. Land ownership remained in the hands of many different people, often with modest aspirations, and the drainage boards at the time gave great cognisance to pleasing as many as possible of the farming community.

Many owners wished to retain high water levels to provide access to cattle for drinking and to ensure secure boundaries for the stock. This meant that though stop-board dams could divide the levels into different regimes, their leakiness made it difficult to maintain very low water tables on adjacent land. As late as 1976 there were nearly 700 different owners in the IDB districts in the Halvergate triangle, with more than 300 owning less than ten hectares in a total of 21,000 hectares. Only 26 owners had more than 120 hectares. This pattern had come about partly through the traditional division of holdings, generation by generation, among the daughters of a family on death of their father.

Cattle pasturing changed somewhat after the closure of much of the railway network in the 1960s in an attempt by the Government to improve transport efficiency. It was then less easy and more costly to transport hardy cattle from the west to be fattened. Local cattle were used instead and the stock became infused by breeds such as Friesian-Holsteins, bred for high milk production under more cosseted conditions, but doing less well out on the marshes. In recent years the collapse of the beef market, following the development of bovine spongiform encephalopathy, has led to even fewer cattle and many more sheep. Dairy holdings, however, have expanded slightly, especially at the valley margins where there was early access to roads for daily collection of the milk. All of this started a change, but, until the 1970s, the grazing marshes maintained a landscape that was essentially that of previous centuries (Plates 5, 8, 17).

The landscape of the 1960s and 1970s

Local bird-watchers saw that some bird populations of the grazing marshes had decreased even with the greater drainage that followed steam and the first electric pumps. These pumps eliminated the need for temporarily flooded washland areas to accommodate the water whilst the earlier, slower pumps coped. Wigeon declined rapidly after 1947, pink-footed and white-fronted geese had virtually disappeared by 1972, but there remained a very characteristic wetland landscape with a pattern of plant communities and interesting birds. Equally important, the dykes harboured many of the plants and invertebrates that had disappeared from the Broads. The dykes at the edges were becoming influenced by some of the same problems as the Broads for they received water from the upland and were closest to human habitation. The remoter central areas of the marshes are fed mostly by rain and were to some extent protected.

The pasturage regime, although keeping many features of its earlier history, was changing, but most of the land was unploughed, except occasionally when it became infested with couch grass. Little nitrogen fertiliser was added, much less than 100 kilograms per hectare, and herbicides were not used. Dairy holdings at the edges used a more intensive regime with 200 or 300 kilograms of nitrogen added per hectare. These pastures were cut twice or three times per year for silage, and a higher stock density was maintained than on the central beef and sheep marshes, where typical densities have been 0.5 to 1.5 cattle or 3 to 10 sheep per hectare. Land maintained by owner-occupiers was better maintained than that rented out to other graziers through annual auctions. Renters inevitably attempted to cover their costs through a greater yield with heavier fertilisation and spent less effort on long-term maintenance such as dyke cleaning.

There were several sorts of grassland. The commonest was a standard grazing or hay pasture with a variety of common grasses and meadow plants. The grasses included common bent, meadow foxtail, soft brome, crested dogs-tail, cocksfoot, Yorkshire fog, meadow barley, perennial ryegrass, annual meadow-grass and associated herbs such as daisy, chickweeds, thistles, plantains, buttercups, dock, ragwort, clovers and nettles. Where this was hayed, Yorkshire fog tended to become more abundant, giving a purplish sheen to the sward from a distance. The surface of the marshes under a pasture regime was not flat but had humps and hollows caused by slumping of the soils and dumping of material slubbed out of the dykes when they were cleared. Many fields were like saucers with the mounds of material paralleling the dykes and impeding drainage a little at the centre. In these wetter places, rushes and sedges were more abundant, with marsh thistles, meadowsweet, hard and jointed rushes, ragged robbin, purple loosestrife, fleabane and tufted vetch.

In a few places, at the edges of the marsh, where spring water fed them, were small areas of very rich vegetation, approximating to fen, with reeds, iris, valerian and meadow rue in some cases. Probably these resembled the characteristic vegetation of the marshes under the former, less efficient, wind pumping.

The richer examples included bog pimpernel, quaking grass, sweet vernal grass, common and spotted-orchids, marsh orchids, meadowsweet, marsh bed-straw, soft and hard rushes, ragged robin, woodrush, yellow rattle, and in their wettest parts, marsh ragwort, kingcup, bogbean, spearworts, marsh helle-borine, twayblade, grass of Parnassus, butterwort, primrose and even the tiny adder's-tongue fern.

Where the marsh edges were more acidic, as spring water was drawn or pumped from crag deposits around the head of the River Thurne, more bog species were found – creeping cinquefoil, heath spotted-orchid, sundew, louse-wort, cotton-grass and *Sphagnum*. Overall, the richer communities were on peat soils at the fringes, the less remarkable on clay towards the main river channels, but it was not for these communities that the marshes were noted. It was for the characteristic open landscape (Plate 5), with its derelict wind pump towers, gates with sloping fences, the tapestry of subtle greens, and for the rich-ness of the dykes.

The dyke system

In the 1960s, water plants remained abundant in the dykes whilst they dwin-dled in the Broads. The richness of the dykes depended on regular manage-ment for, if left for more than a few years, they would fill up with silt and become colonised by reed, which shaded out most else. But as long as they were cleaned about once every five years (though not so rigorously as to remove all traces of the plants), and water tables were kept high (as they need-ed to be under grazing regimes), they could contain up to 20 species of plants in a 100-metre length. The most diverse communities were those away from the main rivers, where salt seepage and nutrients had a depressive effect, and away from the upland margins where yard drainage water and slurry runoff from farms was especially devastating. Sometimes there was foul-smelling black water with little but duckweed growing on it.

The richest communities (Plate 24) included water-plantain, floating pondweed, bur-reed, floating club-rush, water violet, greater bladderwort, frog-bit, arrowhead, water soldier, flowering-rush and tubular water-dropwort. Where nutrient-rich river water seeped in, there was lower diversity, more hornwort, reed canary grass and filamentous algae and a tubular green alga, *Enteromorpha*, looking like intestines. Where salinities rose above about 1,000 milligrams of chloride per litre, from seepage through the river embankments, or, around the River Thurne, because salt water was being pumped from the water table, there was often heavy growth, but only of fennel pondweed, spiked water-milfoil, sea arrowgrass, duckweed and *Enteromorpha*.

Nonetheless, in the 1970s, 57 per cent of the British aquatic flora list could be found in the dyke system, including 11 species that were nationally rare or uncommon (these terms are formally defined in terms of the number of 10 kilometre x 10 kilometre squares of the national grid in which they occur). Several pondweed species were included in this list of 11, together with the water soldier, floating water-plantain, greater water-parsnip, whorled water-mil-foil and soft hornwort. The dykes were also rich in the smaller rushes, butter-cups and forget-me-nots that are able to survive in the bare areas created in the bank by the hooves of cattle as they come to drink. There were also rare inver-tebrates, including the shiny ramshorn snail.

Agriculture continues to change – the 1970s and 1980s

There are records of ploughing of the marshes from the mid-1800s, when markets for oats, wheat and mangolds were buoyant and from just before the First World War. But it was generally short term, dependent on locally favourable conditions, where embankments were firm and drainage efficient for its time, and where machinery could be easily got onto the marsh. Mostly, arable cultivation was uneconomic, for much of the area was inaccessible except on foot and holdings were too small. In the 1950s, with increased drainage efficiency, farmers already owning land on the upland, and therefore having the machinery already available, took opportunities to buy out smaller adjacent holdings.

In the 1970s the pressure to plough increased. Beef profits were declining, subsidies provided by the Common Agricultural Policy of the European Community particularly favoured wheat, and pumps installed in the 1950s and 1960s were able to lower water tables substantially. Drainage rates levied by the IDBs were increasing with pressure to drain more deeply. More of the smaller graziers were forced to sell out to the larger units, which could afford the increased rates.

Arable cultivation gives a very different landscape and severely changes the dykes. The land is flattened by filling in hollows and old salt marsh tributaries, and bulldozing the mounds of ancient debris paralleling the dykes. It may be under-drained with pipes; modern plastic piping is much cheaper and faster to lay than the old tile drains. This means that fewer small dykes are needed and filling in the surplus increases the field size so machinery can be used more easily. Water levels are held much lower so that some dykes may dry out completely in summer, with the loss of the aquatic community. The dykes are cleaned by machinery, often comprehensively on a regular contract, so that the mosaic of dykes in different stages of colonisation, which was an inevitable consequence of hand clearing, is lost. The possibilities of recolonisation of a cleared dyke from adjacent dykes or remnants are lowered.

There are no longer cattle to provide niches in the dyke sides for small plants; the land is cultivated to the dyke edge so that grass tussocks and nesting cover for birds is lost. So too are the characteristic gates across bridges over the dykes with their sloping side rails. And there is the strident uniform bright green of heavily fertilised winter wheat to replace the subtleties of patchwork pastures managed to different aspirations. In the 1970s fields began to be increased from a few hectares to as many as 25; many smaller dykes were filled in (Fig. 14.4) and the main dykes were widened.

Water depths in the dykes were reduced from more than half a metre under grazing regimes to as little as 20 centimetres or complete dryness in summer. The bank slopes were steepened to 1 in 1.5 or even 1 in 1 from the previous 1 in 3 and became colonised with nettles, great hairy willowherb, false oat-grass and other tall overhanging species, shading out any remaining submerged plants and destroying invertebrate communities.

Ochre

Especially in the marshes of the Thurne catchment (Fig. 14.5), acidification and ochre formation are problems. These marshes, close to the sea, either now or in the Romano-British upper clay period, have been infused with sea water, which contains much sulphate. In waterlogged soils at high water tables, the

Fig. 14.4 Intense drainage by powerful pumps of some of the grazing marshes in the late 1970s and early 1980s led to great reduction in drainage dyke length and increase in field area to accommodate the machinery of the new arable regime. After Driscoll (1986).

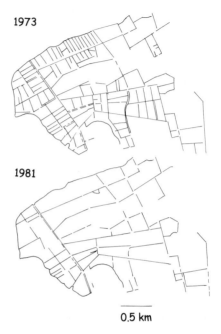

Sub-area 1 Happisburgh to Winterton Internal Drainage Board

1973

1981

0.5 km

sulphate is reduced to sulphide by bacteria, which use the oxygen contained in the sulphate to release energy from organic matter. The sulphide, which is otherwise very poisonous, reacts quickly with iron in the soils to form the intensely black precipitate of iron sulphide that is common in wetland soils (and salt marsh muds). When water tables are lowered through drainage and air penetrates, the iron sulphide is oxidised chemically and two undesirable products are formed – sulphuric acid and a mixture of rusty-coloured iron oxides and hydroxides called ochre. The drainage pumps thus suck out a rather nasty looking acidic suspension of these iron compounds, sometimes bright orange in colour.

The acid is usually neutralised by carbonates in the water when it reaches the dykes, but the ochre is precipitated out to cover the bottom and sides and any surviving plants. It reduces the diversity of the invertebrates. It may even block the navigation. Some 3,500 tons of ochre were removed from the Waxham Cut, which extends beyond Horsey Mere across the Brograve Level, to keep it navigable, but removal has now been abandoned. The marshes closer to the sea in the Halvergate triangle also have much sulphate, but here the clays are close to the surface and contain sufficient calcium for white gypsum (calcium sulphate) to be formed and insufficient iron for ochre to be prominent.

Birds

Many birds disappear from arable marshes. Improved drainage had eliminated the black-tailed godwit and the ruff soon after the Second World War. As the area ploughed increased, geese fell in numbers from 3,000 pink-foot to only a

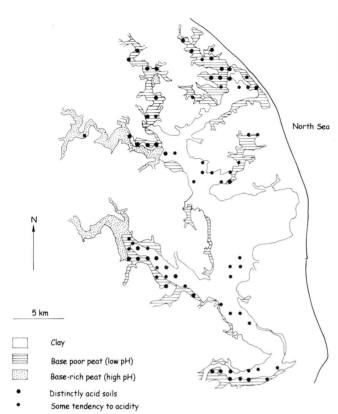

Fig. 14.5 Some Broadland soils are particularly susceptible to acidification if they are drained. They include those of the upper parts of the Ant and Thurne, the Muck Fleet and the Waveney, fed by base-poor waters from the Norwich Brickearth and the crag rocks. Drainage leads to acidity and ochre problems and is now discouraged, though this was not always the case. Based on George (1992).

North Sea

N

5 km

☐ Clay

▤ Base poor peat (low pH)

▦ Base-rich peat (high pH)

● Distinctly acid soils

• Some tendency to acidity

few, white-fronts from 2,000 to 150; the redshank has declined and there are many fewer migratory wildfowl. Snipe, which breed in the long grass of wet fields, are much scarcer; oystercatchers, lapwing and yellow wagtail have had mixed fortunes, for arable stubble favours at least their breeding if not feeding. The particular race of bean geese that clusters in the Yare valley has increased where there has been no ploughing and where shooting rights are not exercised. Bewick's and whooper swan numbers have grown through sympathetic management in reserves bought by conservation organisations, but the overall trend for the birds has been one of continued loss.

The Halvergate controversy

Trends towards more intense arable cultivation were in train in the 1960s and 1970s, but were unlikely to have permanently changed more than a small part of the marshes, because of the capital costs and the inability of most small landowners to meet them. However, the tangle of politics, economics and land use that had determined the fate of the undrained fens and waters, was to drive a sequence of events in the early 1980s that threatened to convert the Halvergate triangle, the last large remaining block of grassland in lowland Britain, into yet another insipid arable prairie. A central theme of history is that the running is made by the richest and fastest. It was so here. It was also the case in Broadland where State institutions began to take over the determination of Broadland's present, if not future, from individuals and local consortia of them. But that is an issue for Chapter 15.

The intensification of British agriculture

The roots of the Halvergate issue were laid in Parliamentary Acts of nearly half a century previously. The Marketing Acts of 1931/33 and the Agriculture Act of 1947 made provision for grants to farmers in the interests of Britain maintaining self-sufficiency in temperate foodstuffs. The Acts supported an approach to agriculture that dominated attitudes for the remainder of the century. They were reflected throughout Britain in changes that have become notorious. There has been the removal of hedgerows, the drainage of river meadows, and the elimination of the native flora of field margins and crop rows.

Predatory birds were poisoned by pesticides (though these birds are fortunately recovering owing to greater restriction of the more dangerous compounds). But there has been a marked loss of small birds through unsympathetic cultivation – ploughing of stubble immediately after harvest, and herbicide elimination of food plants. The plant variety of adjacent land has been damaged by herbicide and fertiliser drift, and the increase in fertilisation, on average nearly ten-fold, and increased cultivation of old grassland, has led to runoff of nitrates and latterly phosphates, which can be devastating to freshwater habitats.

The lowland countryside of Britain has altered much and though change is something that has been a universal feature of its history, its recent guise has not been one of replacement of one particular panoply of variety by another. It has been one of ruthless destruction of charm and the promotion of industrial dreariness. It has been inexorable and shameful and ignored by governments and their advisors trammelled into a continuation of policies that have become destructive by a powerful minority lobby that benefited greatly from them.

It is easy to blame farmers for countryside destruction, but they too can be victims of the system from which they have gained. The responsibility for countryside destruction ultimately lies in institutions far beyond the farm gate. Encouragement of more intensive agriculture and grants for equipment inevitably led to investment in machinery and materials that required part financing by the farmer. Maintenance of continued high production was the trap to meet interest payments and avoid bankruptcy. The demands of an equally powerful food processing and retailing industry, in turn, have added pressures for a high uniformity of product. This then necessitates heavy use of agricultural chemicals and nitrogen-demanding, high yield varieties of crop that cannot hope to survive without intensive use of fertiliser and crop protection chemicals.

In the face of all this, it is no surprise that exhortations towards environmental responsibility are weak and ineffective, politically hypocritical even. Entry of Britain into the European Community, now the European Union, in 1974, additionally gave farmers guaranteed prices. No longer did they have to respond to demand from consumers; the more they grew, the more they were paid, even if the crop had to be stockpiled and destroyed. It was apparently a ludicrous system. It was sensible, though, for the maintenance of small, traditional farmers elsewhere in Europe, who were vulnerable to economic and weather fluctuations, but morally corruptible, legally so, in the agricultural climate of the UK.

The Common Agricultural Policy of the EC, coupled with the prior development of crop strains that gave double the yield compared with that of the 1950s, led to a 30 per cent increase in cereal production in the UK over only ten years following Britain's accession to the EC. Wheat production doubled and the guaranteed payments, determined as a community-wide fixed fee for beef and wheat, widened the growing gap between beef and wheat profits. The number of beef animals in Britain fell from 800,000 to 500,000 in the same period and eventual restrictions on dairying, because milk also was produced in unneeded surplus, but could not easily be stored, also encouraged a move to cereal production.

Proposals to drain the Halvergate marshes

Not surprisingly therefore, the grazing marsh levels began to look, to some of their owners, like an opportunity not to be missed. They needed more intensive drainage for good wheat crops, and earlier British schemes for the award of grants for under-drainage of the fields were boosted by European schemes in the 1980s. In the 1970s, central government paid up to 60 per cent of the costs, even at a time when many drainage schemes would have been profitable, because of the guaranteed payments, without grant. There was also indirect support through the IDBs, again partly British, through the Land Drainage Act of 1976, and the European agricultural fund.

These schemes provided for replacement of pumps and other engineering work, but they did not provide all the necessary capital funds. The IDBs were not permitted by law to save money towards these improvements but had to borrow the remainder from the Public Works Loan Board. These loans had to be repaid with substantial interest and the consequence was always that drainage rates increased whenever major works were undertaken. Small landowners could less easily afford these than larger ones, and, with the selling out of more land to the latter, already powerful individuals became even more influential, even strident in their demands.

What they demanded were drainage schemes far more drastic than anything previous. Pumps were to be replaced by bigger ones, concrete roads constructed that would give easy access to the pumps in wet weather and also for farm machinery to the fields. There was to be a deepening of the main drains and a filling of the smaller ones, backed by intensive under-draining. A very low water table keeps water below the level of the under-drains and delays the process of blockage by silt; bigger main drains give temporary flood storage so that pumping can be delayed until times of day when lower, off-peak electricity prices need only be paid.

Modern pumps are immensely powerful, with a large vertical lift and capacity, and need little maintenance. The previous pumps had not been replaced sometimes for 30 years and were not up to the demands that the new proposed scheme would make. Moreover, levelling and under-draining, which would have been difficult to contemplate with hand labour in previous decades, could now be achieved easily using hydraulic excavators and mechanical pipe-layers, with a twentieth of the labour. Six hectares of land can be under-drained by machine in a day. The whole of Halvergate might take only a year for ten men to drain.

The first major schemes of this intensity emerged in the late 1970s, when the Muckfleet and South Flegg Internal Drainage District was provided with two new Archimedes screw pumps, capable of lifting 80 tons of water per minute through a vertical distance of five metres. Nine thousand metres of drains were deepened and nearly 1,000 hectares deep-drained. A neighbouring scheme increased this to 1,800 hectares and wheat and high yielding dairy farming left only a small proportion of the level for traditional grazing. Following hard on this scheme was a proposal by the Halvergate Fleet and Acle Marshes IDB to deep drain 3,625 hectares in the Halvergate triangle. The pumps were old and the Board planned a three-phase project that would transform the very heart of the grazing marshes.

It was not to happen because a new political climate was emerging and the Ministry of Agriculture had decided, as a general principle, that grants would only be given following consultation with other public bodies with concerns in the area. The newly constituted Broads Authority (Chapter 15) saw conflicts in that the characteristic landscape of the marshes would be destroyed and found support from the Nature Conservancy Council at a time when public concerns about the influences of intensive agriculture on the countryside were increasingly being voiced. Without the benefits to the farmers of the grants they could be given, the deep-drainage schemes could be shown to be unprofitable and the philosophy of production at any cost was crumbling. A concerned public was increasingly unwilling to meet the costs of destruction of traditional agricultural landscapes in the interests of a lobby of wealthy large farmers, civil engineering companies and machinery manufacturers, but of no-one else.

The whole issue, which is related in Chapter 17, emphasised the growing importance of administrative bodies in the post-war period. Before considering what can be, should be and is being done about the deterioration of the natural history of Broadland since the 1960s, we must examine the natural history of human beings and their organisations, in general and in Broadland. For it is in the nature of these that the future of the natural history of everything else may lie.

Further reading

I have drawn heavily on the detail in George (1992) for this chapter. Much of the information on the state of the grazing marshes is contained in unpublished reports to the Broads Authority and the Nature Conservancy, which he reviews in detail. Examples in the public domain are Driscoll (1984, 1986) and Doarks (1984). A general coverage of the implications of global temperature increase, including sea level rise, is Houghton (1997), whilst among many works on the general decline in the countryside, Shoard (1980), Harvey (1997) and Moore (1987) are particularly well written and among my favourites. Purseglove (1989) is very attractively produced and concentrates on wetland habitats, drainage and flooding issues. Nature Conservancy Council (1984) is equally valuable, written with the cool distance of all quasi-government documents, but with passion bursting to get out. The work carried out on perception of wetlands by children is in Anderson & Moss (1993).

Part IV

Officer, Visitor, Minister, Sage

15

The Natural History of Organisation Man in Broadland

Until the nineteenth century, it was largely the will of individuals – earls, abbots, peat cutters, small farmers, traders – that shaped Broadland and its natural history. Gradually these were joined by small organisations – the Sea Breach Commissioners, the Mayors and Aldermen of Yarmouth and Norwich and then bigger ones – County Councils – in the nineteenth century, backed by an expanding government bureaucracy in London. By the latter half of the twentieth century, organisations became the deciding factors. Individual farmers and estate owners still persist, but increasingly have to operate in a framework created by organisations, both local and national. It is these organisations that determine the present, and will determine the future, of Broadland.

Historians, especially natural historians, thrive on detail, and the number of organisations that have been created then changed, gained and lost influence, been replaced or even extinguished in the recent history of Broadland is legion. A blow-by-blow account of the last 50 years might satisfy the pedantic, but would throw little light on the processes at work. For it is the process that is most important and revealed perhaps by a different sort of approach.

Human organisations have many parallels with individual species. Species emerge into a continually changing environment, survive for a time, evolve a little by adjustment of their gene content. They do not cope indefinitely, however, but ultimately are overcome by changes too rapid to match and are outcompeted by new species. Organisations are much the same. Some account of how modern ecologists view the biological world is thus a very useful background for interpreting the roles of navigation, conservation, drainage, planning and all the other bodies that have been part of the natural history of Broadland.

The environmental theatre and the evolutionary play

One of the most important ecologists of the last century was George Evelyn Hutchinson, an Englishman and limnologist, who did most of his best work from an office at Yale University in the United States, following extensive field experience in Tibet, South Africa and Connecticut. Hutchinson created the concept of the environmental theatre and the evolutionary play. It is a revealing analogy for how living organisms evolve and the meaning of their ecology. The environmental theatre is the planet Earth and its stages the mosaic of conditions created by rocks and climate, ocean and air. Not only are the stages constantly changing, but so also the theatre is being steadily remodelled.

There are some steady and predictable changes – day and night, the seasons – but many that are quite unpredictable. Some are short term – the day-to-day weather, for example. Some are long term – the drift of the continents on the plates that make up the Earth's crust and the development of ice ages and other long-term climatic cycles. Others are disruptive and quite unexpected – earthquakes and volcanic eruption on a local scale, and on a wider one the impact of collision with meteorites and the evolution of organisms with quite unexpected properties. The emergence of the blue-green algae in the Precambrian period was the first of two such events. It resulted in the release of an extremely poisonous gas, oxygen, into a world that had been oxygen-free for three billion years and colonised only by anaerobic bacteria. The second was the emergence of our species of human, a million or so years ago.

Evolution is the way that the living system – a complex biochemistry, most features of which are common to every living organism from bacteria to ourselves – copes by manifesting itself in different forms as the environment changes. Some biologists see particular genes as the characters in the evolutionary play, others the individual organisms in which these genes are contained. Either way the characters are competing for a place on the stage and for enough material resources – energy, food, mates – to persist. At any given time some combinations of genes are better able than others to persist and reproduce. They become more common whilst other combinations become steadily less frequent and eventually disappear. Individuals are selected, for or against, by the nature of the environment at the time.

In a predictable environment, an unchanging stage, a steady specialisation takes place. Existing forms multiply, taking advantage of the near constant conditions to shine in a particular role or in occupying a particular patch of stage. At every generation they change a little, those that have been most successful in garnering resources tending to reproduce most abundantly, passing on their particular combinations of genes to meet the coming conditions. This adjustment is necessary, for even if the physical environment is relatively steady, the biological one is not.

But if, in these relatively steady conditions, organisms become very specialised and dependent entirely on a particular narrow set of circumstances, even a small change of scene – a period of wetter weather, or a series of droughts – may be disastrous. And if the stage changes a lot – prolonged unpredictable weather – there may be widespread destruction and only flexible generalists able to cope with a variety of conditions will survive. They may not have been present locally, but move in from less predictable environments elsewhere, where they have thrived. If the change is very great there may be extinction even of many of these, often in a largely random manner. And then, from the survivors, as conditions steady once more for a time, the specialisation, the fine dividing up of the resources, will begin again with a new set of species manifestations of the living system.

The play is thus about survival, which means being able to obtain sufficient resources to persist in the face of others who are also competing for these resources, whilst also coping with continuous small change until such time as the change is overpowering and survival impossible. There has only ever been a temporary, a quasi-stability. There is no balance of nature, where everything lives happily ever after. There is always disruption.

The strategies for surviving changes are many. Some organisms rely on comparative simplicity. Like the bacteria, they are small, reproduce frequently, expending few resources on maintenance, most on new production in the form of offspring, with the advantage that through sexual processes, new combinations of genes are produced every few hours or days to meet a changing environment. If some catastrophe engulfs the planet, it will be bacteria, if any-thing, that survive. The down side is that any individual bacterium has a very short life; it is the concept of the bacterium that persists, not the individual.

Other organisms take an opposite approach, investing resources in a more complex, bigger structure that is individually resilient to degrees of change short of the catastrophic. They may thus invest in structural tissues to hold leaves above those of their competitors for light, or mechanisms of tempera-ture control or of water storage to cope with climate fluctuations. They have fewer resources spare for new production – new offspring – so their chances, as a species, of surviving a severe change are much reduced. Elephants are much less abundant than mice and far more vulnerable to extinction. And mice look very precarious in comparison with bacteria.

In the course of biological evolution a huge range of species has evolved, for the theatre is very complex and the stages many. Most are now extinct, for they did not survive the frequent changes. The current cast is not permanent; the environment still changes and will continue to do so. A range of strategies for survival co-exists. Each has its advantages and disadvantages, from the single-celled, prolific bacterium, individually vulnerable but collectively invincible, to the large mammal, individually able to cope with moderate environmental change, but facing collective and complete extinction when circumstances change just a little too much.

Organisations and their fates

Human organisations and individuals are subject to much the same fates. The theatre in which they play is the same, but with an added set of unpredictable circumstances when new law, policy decisions, granting of funds or removal of them is imposed by their own activities, often with thought mostly for the pre-sent and not for the future.

Individual landowners were the former principals on the stage and deter-mined the nature of Broadland for centuries. Their individual influence was small and local, but, subject to the same changes in the natural environment, and availability of markets for their produce, they tended to act similarly. They were beholden to little in the way of imposed authority; they survived or lost according to their individual skills and were replaced by others. Like the bac-teria they are still around, and collectively they determine most of the action, but not directly so. Like the microorganisms that were the sole denizens of the Precambrian, they are no longer in the forefront, though ultimately they underlie the key processes. Like multicellular organisms, human organisations now apparently dominate. The great change occurred in the nineteenth cen-tury when the evolution of organisations accelerated. There is now layer upon layer from the local to the national and the supranational with the establish-ment of the European Union and transnational companies of the late twenti-eth century.

The earliest Broadland organisations were specialist species, developed to carry through a highly specific role without reference to any other demands. They did it efficiently in general, until the point was reached where their activ-ities began to impinge on others. As specialists they were then unable to cope and their decline began. Their focus was too narrow, they tended to be defen-sive of their interests, established under a different environment and no longer adaptive to a new one. They could adjust by acquiring new individuals as members, just as individual species acquire new combinations of genes when they reproduce. Their tendency, however, was to acquire more of the same, the safe, the committed, the trusted, and thus they could not easily evolve in their attitudes to meet the changing political environment.

Specialisation is no longer a good bet for longevity. The political environment has become increasingly unpredictable; the stage is changing much more now after centuries of comparative stability. Only generalist organisations can survive these changes and they must behave in a particular way if they are to survive. They must meet many contrasting, often mutually incompatible demands and therefore must compromise continually. They cannot therefore fulfil any one role as single-mindedly and as well as a specialist organisation, but if they fail to satisfy the demand in any one area, they too will not survive. They must be bigger, and like the elephant, as opposed to the mouse, spend more energy on their own maintenance, less on new production. Since there are inevitably several of them, they struggle to some extent for a place on the stage.

Sometimes they might secure it by amalgamation into an even more wide-reaching organisation, sometimes by acquiring less conservative members or employees who cope with continuing change by adjusting the organisation for a time. In general they will be wary, however, of departing too far from the familiar and the safe; in the end they will fail to cope and the political environment, in its wayward changes, will ensure their replacement by some new organisation. The perception of our individual short lives is often that organisations have always been there; indeed, the publicity they all put out on behalf of their own survival will give this impression. But they are all temporary and continually succeed one another, in a supposed progression, but really mostly a wayward random evolution, reacting to unpredictable circumstances.

Broadland organisations

Navigation

Navigation was the first use of Broadland that demanded organisation. The big problem was the mouth of the main estuary at Yarmouth. It opened out to the sea at the end of a long channel to the inside of and paralleling the sand bar, and it tended to shallow unpredictably and become partly blocked with sand. The town made several attempts to shorten the channel and make its entrance closer to the town, by creating breaches across the bar to the sea, in 1347, 1375, 1393, 1408, 1549 and 1558, but they tended to refill with sand. Finally, in 1555–1567, stout wooden piling was installed to make the flanges of the opening resistant to erosion. This made the town, which was heavily dependent on trading and comparatively wealthy, more vulnerable to invasion, so further cost was incurred to erect a removable boom across the river and man it. As the port developed, the town council, through an Act of Parliament, established the first navigation authority, the Yarmouth Pier and Haven Commissioners, in 1670.

It regulated the harbour and could levy charges on imports and exports to maintain the facilities. This included dredging the harbour. In an early example of protection of specific interests, the Yarmouth hegemony was not keen to dredge the channel through Breydon Water lest it ease the passage of ships to Norwich and undermine Yarmouth's trade. Eventually, in 1864, it was dredged and a low wall was constructed close to the confluence of the Yare and Waveney to deflect the current and scour out a notorious shallows. The Commissioners were responsible for the rivers up to particular limits – Hardley Cross, for example, on the Yare where the Corporation of Norwich took over responsibility – but their main concern was the haven at Yarmouth. Nonetheless, trade on the rivers was potentially lucrative and, in 1866, the Great Yarmouth Port and Haven Act set up separate sub-committees of river commissioners for the Yare, Bure and Waveney, each levying separate tolls, and for the Haven with Breydon Water. This arrangement persisted until 1989, when the long-term self-protectiveness and intractability of the Commissioners led to enforced change.

Over most of the twentieth century, the Port and Haven Commissioners saw immense changes in the Broadland navigation. Set up to ensure free physical passage for trading boats, at a time when natural movements of sediment and succession of water plants at the edges threatened to block the navigation, their clientele steadily shifted to hire boat and recreational boat owners. The steadily increasing activities of these stopped plant encroachment in the rivers through erosion, increased the wear on the banks and readily widened the navigation. This gave concern to the drainage authorities, who feared a breach and flooding of the grazing marshes, but any curbing of boat activity, beyond a modest speed limit, was resisted by the Commissioners. A major report, *The Broadland Study and Plan* was produced in 1971 by a collection of public bodies, including the Navigation Commissioners, in response to the perception that Broadland was suffering severe problems. One prominent concern was severe boat damage, but it was the Port and Haven Commissioners who dissented from attempts to control boating activity, producing a minority view, a sad little booklet tucked inside the covers of a folio-sized report.

The Commissioners responded to some of the changes. They set the first speed limits (between Wroxham and Horning) in 1931, dredged the channels and reinforced moorings with wooden piling. Boat styles changed over the years with broader beams developing so as to give greater comfort to hirers. Passing boats created wash that eroded river banks and several studies were instigated, though not by the Commissioners, to investigate the factors determining the amount of wash. These included beam, power, weight distribution within the boat, underwater profile, angle of the propeller shaft, distance from the bank and speed. Speed was particularly important, with an index of wash damage being halved for a 1-mph reduction in speed. Upper speed limits of 7 mph set in 1979 were reduced to 6 mph, but any attempt to regulate the number of boats has been resisted. It would be illegal under present legislation, but not inconceivable under new legislation had the will been there. The Commissioners required speed governors to be fitted to the engines of hire boats in 1980, but made no provision for private boat owners.

Until the 1950s the Commissioners were primarily interested in the Yarmouth Haven, their main source of revenue, but as the traffic on the rivers increased, they formed, in 1971, a powerful Rivers Committee. It had eight members drawn from local authorities, two from private yacht owners and two from hire boat owners. Boats had been regarded as a major problem in Broadland for many years, sometimes fairly, sometimes not, but by failing to recognise the concerns of others, the Commissioners, from 1984 onwards, trod a path to their own extinction and replacement. In that year the number of local authority members on the Rivers Committee was reduced to five from a previous eight, thus increasing the influence of specifically boating interests. Suggestions that parts of the waterway should be closed off to allow repair and recovery were always refused in the fear that these might be the thin ends of wedges of permanent closure. Eventually, the Commissioners had become so single-minded that they could not survive in an environment that was having to accommodate greater needs for the use of Broadland than the historic baggage of river trading.

The Norfolk and Suffolk Broads Act of 1988 transferred responsibility for navigation in the rivers to the Broads Authority and confined the original body to responsibility only for the haven as a Port Authority. Extinction is a more complex concept than usually realised, however. Many genes of a species may be transferred to new populations before extirpation. The new navigation committee of the Broads Authority inevitably embraces some of the thinking of the original Commissioners and for its survival also depends on a degree of single-mindedness in looking after the interests of boat users, which become its own interests. As the number of hire boats has declined with changes in the holiday aspirations of the public to warmer places, pressures from the private boat owners and of the 14 yacht and sailing clubs affiliated in the Norfolk and Suffolk Yachting Association have increased.

Management of the water resources

Hard on the heels of the need to regulate navigation through a dedicated organisation, was the need to prevent flooding, and the Sea Breach Commissioners, finally made permanent in 1861, was the first of an evolutionary line of bodies that took over a widening range of responsibilities. Land drainage, at first promoted in the grazing marshes by owners and occupiers, became formalised into the Internal Drainage Boards in the 1930s, and these came under the control of the Ministry of Agriculture and a succession of bodies concerned with the quantity and quality of the river waters. The first was the East Norfolk Rivers Catchment Board, with responsibilities for bank protection along the rivers. The Catchment Board's successor, the East Suffolk and Norfolk Rivers Board, acquired responsibility also for fisheries and monitored water quality from this respect. Responsibility for water supply for domestic consumption was in the hands of local authorities and small private companies, whilst the disposal of sewage was left to local authorities who maintained an increasing plethora of small sewage treatment works, sometimes in a not very efficient way.

The boundaries, on the ground, of these various bodies, were set by the jumble of history. Political boundaries still are. But the passing of the Water Act in 1973 could have represented a significant long-term improvement. The Act took control of sewage disposal, water supply, fisheries, land drainage and sea defence from the large number of small bodies previously responsible, and gave it to ten huge Water Authorities, each based on the catchment area of one or a few large river systems. Broadland was a tiny part of the area covered by the Anglian Water Authority.

The Water Authorities were very much the children of their predecessors – the gene transfer effect again. They were run for the most part by engineers. Chemists had considerable influence, but biologists comparatively little. Solutions to problems were seen very much in terms of concrete and of processes. Two main issues were to ensure adequate domestic water supply and to dispose of sewage so that it did not cause the problems of disease and gross organic pollution that had bedevilled Victorian rivers. Other main issues were to prevent sea encroachment and to maintain the river floodbanks so as to support agriculture. Engineers understood the need for production and their professional reputation was geared to new works and installations. The brass plaque commemorating Authority, engineer and local mayor on some new sewage works wall, bridge parapet or dam was the public manifestation of an inner esteem.

Ecological issues had been raised by the old Rivers Boards, especially in connection with the maintenance of fisheries, and a number of systems had been developed to assess river quality from the community of invertebrates on the bottom. But the lesser importance accorded to ecological quality, that had been no great problem when the Broadland waters still maintained high diversity and interest, was anachronistic as they deteriorated in the 1970s. The Water Authorities were poorly constituted to cope with the need for an approach subtler than that provided by concrete and pipes. There was appreciation of the problems that pesticides, heavy metals and nitrate might cause for human health, but little of what these substances might do to the natural communities.

Sewage effluent was assessed, as it had been since 1910, by its capacity to deoxygenate; its biological oxygen demand. The idea that phosphates, ammonium and nitrates, the conventional end-products of sewage treatment, might also be damaging, was anathema. This was despite a growing realisation of this problem in mainland Europe and the United States, and indeed a great deal of action there to deal with it in the late 1960s and early 1970s. The British Water Authorities were large and lumbering, too big to be able to see the detail of problems at local level, too monolithic and entrenched to be open to new ideas. And government guidance to the Authorities placed priorities on them that did not even mention conservation or ecological quality.

Large organisations, like large organisms, need to spend much energy on self-maintenance. This left little to support radical new initiatives. To contemplate additional processes at sewage treatment works to improve effluents, beyond the standards set conventionally, would have entailed expense that was not welcome. In the 1970s, local opinion held that boats were the bugbear of the Broads. The Anglian Water Authority was happy to leave it at that and it was not for several years that it was officially persuaded that eutrophication problems existed and it moved to do something about them – though only on an experimental basis.

The Anglian Water Authority became Anglian Water in 1984 following yet another Water Act. This restricted membership of the Authority to those appointed by the Government. The Authority, now no longer so-called, became more authoritarian. In a smaller, less powerful body without close government interest, these changes would have been fatal. Nonetheless the new authority was among the first to propose standards of water chemistry appropriate to particular uses – drinking water, irrigation, industrial, conservation and amenity – and these were innovative.

The legislation under which the Water Authorities operated to control water quality, however, was far from comprehensive. They had control over the discharges that came from discrete sources – factories, sewage treatment works –

and could take legal action over discrete spills of pollutants, such as pesticides, silage effluent or cattle slurry, into a river. They had no control over the diffuse leachings from the fields or urban areas, which can be equally damaging. Under the Control of Pollution Act of 1983, any operation that was deemed by the Ministry of Agriculture, Fisheries and Food as good agricultural practice was (and still is) exempt from prosecution, no matter what the consequences. A river might be turbid throughout the winter with the eroded silt of autumn ploughing, have very high concentrations of nitrate and more than trace concentrations of a shelf-full of pesticides and herbicides, but there was nothing the Water Authority could do. The similar cultures of engineers and agriculturalists, where production was the central theme, meant that the Authorities in general saw no problems with this arrangement.

The proposals for standards of water quality for particular uses were a step forward, and recognised conservation as a use. But before much could be done, more change was afoot. The Water Authorities were both gamekeeper and poacher. They were responsible for setting the standards of effluents that might be discharged to the rivers by industry, but also those discharged by themselves from the sewage treatment and waterworks that they also managed. Because of the poor state of many of the sewage treatment works, they were frequently in breach of their own conditions, but found it more difficult to prosecute themselves than they might an external organisation.

There was a culture of secrecy also, though this was not confined to the Authorities; government bodies in Britain have always felt it best not to be too informative, it is part of the investment in self-protection that any organisation makes in order to perpetuate itself in a changing world. The Control of Pollution Act made provision for data collected by the Authorities to be made available to the public, but arrangements were not put in place to ensure this for ten years after the passing of the Act. Indeed, it is still cumbersome to obtain them. The Authorities, driven by central government, also failed to make appropriate use of legislation available in European Directives that could have widely improved the water quality of Britain as a whole and particularly of Broadland. In the early 1970s the European Union had passed two Directives (on Urban Waste Water Treatment and on Nitrates), which have as yet only been used in the UK to a minimal extent, far short of the spirit of this legislation and its enactment in some other member states of the Union.

The Urban Waste Water Treatment Directive intends that waste water (sewage) treatment works beyond a certain size should have processes installed to remove nitrogen and phosphorus from their effluents, especially where the receiving rivers and lakes are at risk from eutrophication. Because eutrophication is the increase in supply of nutrients to a waterway, the logical position, taken by states such as Germany and the Netherlands, is that all of the territory is potentially vulnerable. In the UK, the Government chose to define such areas as those already seriously enriched with nutrients and designated a derisory number of such areas. Only very recently has the list climbed modestly. Many very vulnerable areas are unprotected.

On many counts the Water Authorities were becoming anachronisms even as they were still building themselves. They were lacking in their appreciation of environmental needs in a world becoming environmentally more and more degraded and in which an increasingly well-informed public was acquiring different aspirations. They had certain advantages, not least a catchment-based approach, and would probably have persisted longer than the 15 years that they did were it not for one of the unpredictable changes in their operating environment that can be as fatal to organisations as a volcano can be to a forest. In the 1980s successive governments convinced themselves of the odd notion that public services would be better run if they were done so for private profit.

Experience has shown that this by no means automatically follows. The services fluctuate in quality no less than previously whilst the charges made for them increase and are passed on as profit to the shareholders. However, in 1989, the Water Authorities were divided into those parts that supplied drinking water and treated domestic and industrial waste and those parts responsible for regulation of water resources and water quality. The poacher was separated from the gamekeeper and the reservoirs, treatment works and pipe systems were sold to private companies, which are now often part of multinational consortia, and the regulatory function passed to a new government organisation, the National Rivers Authority. The separation was wise, the privatisation perhaps not. The National Rivers Authority was not unlike the old River Boards in concept, but it was national and internally organised on the same catchment basis as the Water Authorities had been.

With regulation as its sole function and without the problems of having to prosecute itself for pollution incidents that the Water Authorities had had, it was potentially more powerful. It benefited also from new legislation, which gave greater emphasis to furthering nature conservation and amenity in carrying out its duties. It was welcomed and started to take a much broader view of the environment than any of its predecessors, though its activities were closely controlled by a central government more influenced by industrial and agricultural lobbies than by the wider views of its electorate. Just before the National Rivers Authority had been established, there had been a very warm summer. In the still conditions of one of the large reservoirs of lowland England, Rutland Water, in Leicestershire, growths of blue-green algae, usually well distributed in the water by mixing, accumulated at the surface, and washed up in the gentle breeze on the shoreline. Many blue-green algae produce quite potent toxins that affect the nerves and liver of mammals and can be fatal. Several sheep and dogs, drinking the water at the edge of the reservoir, were killed. At another reservoir, Rudyard Lake in Staffordshire, army cadets on training exercises also drank water with heavy blue-green algal growths in it (albeit unintentionally when their canoes capsized), and were hospitalised.

There was nothing new about these blooms. They had been frequent in eutrophicated British waters for at least 20 years, but had simply not been perceived as a problem worthy of consideration. Coinciding with the formation of the new National Rivers Authority, and with the British penchant for the welfare of pet animals as a spur, the 1988 blooms widened the agenda for the new organisation. It set about matching national thinking with that of environmentally more advanced countries in the EU and elsewhere. The legislation it had been given was not significantly more potent; there was still little control over agricultural operations; but it could be more stringent about consents to discharge from discrete sources. It retained responsibilities for sea defence and flood control and thus was required to work closely in the defence of agricultural interests. Its approach to the management of fisheries perhaps owed more to the lobbying of anglers than to what might have been more appropriate to the wise management of fresh waters, but creation of the Authority was a very positive step forward. But it, too, quickly fell foul of the random nuances of national politics.

In 1996 it was merged with a body responsible particularly for air pollution from factories, the Pollution Inspectorate, and with the Local Authority departments responsible for the disposal of municipal and industrial solid waste, and became the Environment Agency. Ostensibly this was another positive step forward, for air pollution and the leachates from poorly sealed waste tips are closely connected with water pollution, and the catchment organisation was retained. The Government's motives in taking this step were interesting and not necessarily laudable. The National Rivers Authority had been carrying out its role of regulation diligently, perhaps too diligently for a government concerned to support industry and the exploitation of resources for private profit and tax revenue. The new Environment Agency was trumpeted as the most powerful environmental regulatory organisation in Europe, but the legislation that set it up offered little that was new. Indeed, its responsibilities towards conservation and amenity were weakened by the wording of the Act, and its ability to regulate was progressively diminished by decreased budgets, compared with those enjoyed collectively by its previous constituent organisations. There is a general perception that its policies are more closely controlled by central government than before.

Responsibility for agriculture

Responsibility for the waters of Broadland has been that of readily identifiable organisations. Responsibility for the land surfaces of the catchments has been a more complex matter. Just as species of living organisms in a community can be grouped together as guilds of those having similar functions, we can group these organisations into those concerned with agriculture, with nature conservation and with general planning. The Ministry of Agriculture, Fisheries and Food has always been a major influence on Broadland though its local presence has not been nearly so obvious as that of other organisations.

Since the Agriculture Act of 1947, however, and with a myriad of its own schemes for grant-aiding farming and those it has administered on behalf of the European Union, the Ministry has effectively determined the major change in the face of the Broadland catchment that has taken place since the Second World War. No doubt some of these changes would have occurred anyway, but not on the scale that they have with Ministry help. The huge, windy, hedge-less and monotonous expanses of the arable fields that occupy the plateaux only a few metres above the floodplains are one manifestation, the precarious position of the grazing marshes another. Operation of many grant schemes has favoured the already large farm, the ostensibly more profitable machine-orientated approach, and the conversion of a countryside with a small grain of detail to one much more uniform and uninteresting to most eyes.

Change was slow for the Ministry, but it created an increasing number of schemes to support less aggressive agriculture in particular areas. It was a large and lumbering beast, enjoying a more steady environment, in London, than any of the local organisations. Government ministries are well-organised machines, carrying out the policies of government efficiently and well. The snags are that those policies can rarely be appropriate everywhere and therefore are rarely sensitive to local needs, and that the consequences of the policies, when they are detrimental, are rarely perceived or admitted very quickly.

Ministries really are the super-elephants of organisations. Moving through the administrative landscape they reduce trees to pulp then pass on ruminating about what they have done in retrospect, but unable to stop the process until some even larger organisation for super-elephant control confronts them. The Ministry of Agriculture in 2001, facing a crisis of foot-and-mouth disease in cattle and sheep, was unable to change its policies rapidly enough to cope with increasing use of the countryside for tourism. After the General Election of 2001, it found itself subsumed into a new Department of Environment, Food and Rural Affairs, and its future may be very different.

Apparently not nearly as important as the Government in the ultimate management of the land are the landowners. Their scope for operation is largely determined by grants and markets, the extent of which is determined in London, Brussels and elsewhere. The organisations of farmers and landowners, the National Farmers Union and the Country Landowners Association, however, have influence beyond being rallying points for their members to organise opposition when change is threatened. They have many contacts among government officials and ministers. As one junior environment minister, Lord Caithness, said in the House of Lords in 1993, when arguing against a new survey of the state of the countryside: 'We don't need all this money on research – I'll just ring up one of my chums in the Country Landowners Association'. Ultimately, landowner and tenant organisations can be particularly important in influencing the local attitudes of farmers and landowners towards other bodies, such as those involved in conservation.

The organisation of conservation

Conservation-management of the land and waterscape for its intrinsic value and that of its non-human denizens is a comparatively recent concept compared with that of exploitation of the resources they can provide for human societies.

The earliest organisations concerned with conservation in Britain were set up by concerned individuals to ensure that the provisions of the Wild Birds Protection Acts, passed in 1880, 1894 and 1899 were carried out, at least in places such as Breydon Water, where the birds were prolific, but had been shot for food or feathers for centuries. The Breydon Wild Birds Protection Society employed a watcher, whose evidence led to prosecutions. Amendments to the Acts over the years led to special protection of the Hickling Broad area and the Trinity Broads in 1895 and to increasing restrictions in general. The law attempted to protect particular species but not others, which might be shot for the pot, and contained complex provisions in which, for example, it was an offence to take birds' eggs, but not to be in possession of them. The Acts were thus difficult to enforce until much more comprehensive provision was made in the Protection of Bird Acts of 1954 and 1967.

Two local organisations became concerned about conservation in Broadland in the early period – the Norfolk and Norwich Naturalists Society (founded as a small learned society in 1869) and the Norfolk Naturalists Trust founded in 1926. Many of the same individuals became involved with both and though the former now has little influence in the management of the area, the Trust (now the Norfolk Wildlife Trust) is a substantial landowner. Realisation that conservation could only be substantially guaranteed by ownership of the land led to the formation of the Society for the Promotion of Nature Reserves and the drawing up in 1915, by Charles Rothschild, of a list of sites in Britain worthy of preservation. He listed land around Horning, Barton Broad, Hickling Broad and Upton and these sites have figured prominently in the agendas of successive organisations ever since.

The Society for the Promotion of Nature Reserves spawned the county naturalists trusts, of which Norfolk was the first, and organised a conference in 1941 that set up the Nature Reserves Investigation Committee, which drew up a longer list of desirable sites in Broadland. Meanwhile the Norfolk Naturalists Trust was acquiring, through the subscriptions of its members and legacies, a number of small sites, the first at Starch Grass near Martham in 1926 and then Alderfen Broad in 1930. Other sites were in the hands of landowners with strong aspirations to conservation, especially at Hickling and Horsey. Hickling Broad and much of the land around it was bought by the Trust in 1945, Barton Broad in 1946, and areas at Ranworth and Cockshoot were acquired in 1949 and Surlingham in 1952. The Trust expanded its holdings a great deal in the 1960s and by 1986 owned a total of 1,155 hectares at 11 sites in Broadland. Its smaller sister, now the Suffolk Wildlife Trust, also acquired a few sites, notably Carlton marshes on the south bank of the River Waveney, close to Oulton Broad. Finally, among these private organisations, the Royal Society for the Protection of Birds gained a reserve at Strumpshaw in 1975 and 147 hectares of the grazing marshes near the Berney Arms Mill in 1985/6.

The Norfolk Wildlife Trust was, for many years, a rather exclusive organisation, founded largely by the gentry so that they might continue to have access to attractive habitats for their hobbies of entomology, bird-watching and botanising. Its attitudes and management owed much to those of the land agents who managed the big farming estates and education for environmental awareness was not high on its agenda. It was a small, specialist species that functioned very well in the moderately stable conditions between the Wars when the social changes that were to come were being effectively resisted by the Establishment. It fitted comfortably onto the shooting sticks of the hospitality tent of the Country Landowners Association at the local agricultural show, and would have been reduced to a quaint museum piece had it not, in the 1980s, done what all such specialist species must do if they are not to suffer summary extinction. It acquired a few new and progressive genes in the form of young employees and council members steeped in a culture that was recognising the necessity to adjust to new ideas. Nature conservation was not going to survive by being exclusive and humble.

The Trust made all its reserves freely open to the public, rather than just to its subscribers, and moved into areas of education with visitor centres at Ranworth and, in the 1990s, at Hickling. To be sure, the displays were far from radical in a situation where the damage to Broadland has been considerable. They pandered still to an establishment which sees Broadland as a diversion from the real business of production and profit, and cast Broadland in an anodyne rosy glow, but the organisation has shown that it can evolve as its environment changes. The same is true of the Royal Society for the Protection of Birds, now the largest nature conservation organisation in the country. Since its foundation as the Society for the Protection of Birds in 1889, and its acquisition of Royal patronage in 1904, the RSPB has become an organisation that has embraced a very broad membership. This has given it a large capacity to adjust so that its views are taken seriously and are backed by a very great deal of informed expertise.

Just as the farming community has been influenced by the Ministry of Agriculture, the private conservation organisations are also manipulated by government. The influence is through small project grants or funds to acquire land, given by the statutory conservation body, English Nature. There is, however, no comparison between the Ministry of Agriculture and English Nature. The latter is small, the latest manifestation of a series of conservation organisations originally set up in 1949 and progressively weakened since, and, from the evidence of State papers, never a favourite of successive Secretaries of State. Matters began in a promising way. The influence of the Society for the Promotion of Nature Reserves and pressures for access to the countryside following the First World War led to the National Parks and Access to the Countryside Act in 1949, of which more will be said later (p.276). Protecting a representative range of the country's natural and semi-natural habitats was the lesser of the thrusts of this Act, which set up the Nature Conservancy. Its role was to identify suitable sites and promote understanding of their functioning through research and management.

The Conservancy was strongly dominated by scientists with considerable expertise and was able to acquire land for National Nature Reserves, or negotiate management agreements with other landowners for paid management of their estates to retain the conservation interest. The central mechanism for nature conservation was the designation of Sites of Special Scientific Interest (of which the National Nature Reserves were the highest grade), but the Act gave no influence over the wider countryside outside, and rather few funds to do very much to protect even these. One consequence is that freshwater sites cannot be adequately protected because their water is usually drawn from catchments outside the boundaries of the protected site. The Conservancy had to be consulted about any development proposed within a Site it had designated, but not about adjacent land or water, even though such development might, through water quality, boat yard development, agriculture, drainage or river engineering, impinge severely upon the value of the Site. In 1965 the Nature Conservancy began a major survey to review the nature conservation quality of the UK and this was published in 1977. There were seven Grade 1 sites in the Broadland floodplains, three of international importance among a total of 24. The scope for damage was thus considerable.

The Conservancy was a gentlemanly body, maintaining research stations to further its work, as well as actively managing sites it owned or leased and giving advice about others. It was strongly dominated by ecologists and geographers and indeed came under the aegis of the Natural Environment Research Council. It was the epitome of a specialist organisation and continued to be so after 1973 when it was decided to transfer its research functions to institutes of the Natural Environment Research Council and rename it the Nature Conservancy Council (NCC). This body was to be responsible for designation and management of reserves and sites and for provision of nature conservation advice throughout the UK. The NCC had a budget for the promotion of research and was the instigator, in the 1970s, of major research projects in Broadland designed to discover the reasons for the major changes that were occurring in the rivers and Broads.

For nearly 20 years the Nature Conservancy Council survived, as effective as it could be, under the weak legislation within which it had to manage. Great hopes for strengthening it under the Wildlife and Countryside Act of 1981 were dashed when legislation that was to have given much greater powers to protect sites was undermined by largely agricultural and landowning lobbies in Parliament. Many sites in the UK were being damaged, indeed still are, but the legislation merely introduced the notorious three-month rule that landowners wishing to develop a Site of Special Scientific Interest must stay their hands for three months after notifying the Council.

The Council then had to compensate the landowners for not carrying out the development, if it could not persuade them to abandon their plans. Few funds were made available for such compensation and the Act also required the Council to re-notify all the several thousand sites on its list, including contact with every landowner. This was a vast and unnecessary bureaucratic task, which might be seen as an attempt by government to clip the wings of its own new Council. Part of the task was also to draw up a list of 'potentially damaging operations' for each site, which was the basis of negotiations with the landowners when development was proposed.

There was much emphasis on the 'voluntary principle' rather than coercion by law to further nature conservation interests. Although in principle this is the way one might wish society to function, the sad fact is that at the present rate of damage, the entire array of Sites of Special Scientific Interest in the UK has about a 40-year life span before every site will have suffered significant damage. At the present rate of removal of sites from the list, because of irreparable damage, the projected longevity of the system is finite and about 300 years.

Nature conservation has never been a favourite child of government, which has been much more concerned with exploitation and development. The child was further abused in 1991, when, having overcome the obstacles put in its way by the Wildlife and Countryside Act, it was dealt a cynical blow. It was an open-minded organisation, receptive to new ideas produced by the research it funded and strengthened by the knowledgeableness of its staff, and was widely respected by other professionals concerned with ecology and conservation. It began to point out that the wildlife resources in Scotland, in particular, were under-protected and increasingly threatened. This enraged the major landowning interests of Scotland, who were starting to benefit from developments as diverse as conifer afforestation on unique blanket bog sites and ski resorts on fragile mountain-scapes. The Government, sensitive to its own political difficulties in a country that was showing strong nationalistic tendencies to become independent, whilst also providing substantial revenue to the UK through offshore oil, destroyed the Nature Conservancy Council. There had been lesser but similar difficulties in England also, particularly about scheduling of the Somerset levels as Sites of Special Scientific Interest against powerful drainage interests.

From 1991, there emerged a divide-and-rule policy, with separate statutory conservation organisations for Scotland, England and Wales and a small rump in the form of the Joint Nature Conservation Committee, which was supposed to give advice of a general nature and look after the Government's international commitments to wildlife conservation. English Nature, the English scion, has been a very different organisation from its predecessors. It has had a much smaller budget and is unable to support research projects of more than very local substance. It has been run increasingly by administrators who have not had the scientific standing that was formerly the great strength of conservation in Britain. It has seemed to be more concerned with the image it presents to government rather than to pursue as strong an offensive for conservation as other interests pursue for development.

Whereas the council members of the former Nature Conservancy were the intellectual giants of ecology of the time, councils of English Nature have fallen far short of this, with a prominence of business and management interests. As its publications have become ever more glossy, a plethora of magazines and newsletters, its influence in furthering conservation in any significant sense has become puny. In the community of organisations it is now a minor species, specialist and hanging on in a small niche where the resources it commands are too small for the competition to bother. It is like the fen orchid, a Broadland rarity, once much more abundant, now reduced to a few plants, carefully nurtured as icons, but barely influencing the functioning of the fen system. Its extinction cannot be far off unless the political environment changes greatly in its favour. If Broadland now has around 30 Sites of Special Scientific Interest, covering over 5,000 hectares, this is a monument to earlier organisations and not to recent government proposals, one of which, fortunately dropped, was to sell to private ownership even those lands that the Nature Conservancy and Nature Conservancy Council had acquired as their own.

Planning and overall management of Broadland

Broadland was recognised, even before the Second World War, as interesting, attractive and worthy of some sort of protection against unsympathetic development. Local government exerted most of its influence through the novelty of planning controls. These had originated only in the 1930s following the Town Planning Act of 1925 and the Local Government Act of 1929, which set up several separate planning committees covering Broadland. They were to draw up planning schemes, for building development largely, but were supposed also to safeguard natural characteristics and amenity and distinguished between towns and villages (development zones) and agricultural zones. The War intervened, however, and the planning committees had negligible influence.

The ravages of past development had led nationally to the founding of the Commons Preservation Society in 1865, the National Trust in 1893 and the Society for the Promotion of Nature Reserves in 1912. There was also a movement, originating in the north of England, for great swathes of upland to be made available by their owners for walking and quiet recreation, which had led to a mass trespass of the Kinder Scout moorlands in Derbyshire in 1932. In the United States, establishment of the system of National Parks had begun in 1872 and the National Park Service was founded in 1912. It was not until 1931, however, that a National Park system for Britain was openly discussed, in which the Broads were included in a list of potential areas.

A committee chaired by Lord Justice Scott in 1941 had been particularly concerned about a feared invasion of the countryside by unthinking townspeople and ways to allow access without damage. In a spectacular misunderstanding of the future, the Scott Report illustrated just how wrong the great and the good can be: '... a radical alteration of the types of farming is not probable and no

striking change in the pattern of the open countryside is to be expected ...'.
The key issue, however, was that the committee saw a separation between the
needs of countryside recreation and nature conservation and the probable
necessity for provision of separate areas for each. Thus was born the *borghetto*
of the countryside, the concept of fortress conservation where selected areas
are specially protected and the remainder of the landscape is left to be developed *ad libitum*. The key document came four years later with John Dower's
report on the provision of national parks.

Dower's key criteria were that for selected areas, characteristic features
should be preserved, access provided, wildlife and traditional buildings protected and farming maintained. The Broads were included on a list dominated by the upland areas most desired by walkers. Dower had doubts about the
suitability of this lowland area, already developing problems of boat conges-
tion, disfigured banks, inappropriate chalet development and drainage,
because of the complications these would bring. Nonetheless a further committee reporting in 1947, under the chairmanship of Arthur Hobhouse, was
enthusiastic about the Broads as a National Park, despite an even greater list
of problems, now including vegetation encroachment, organic pollution
(from boat lavatories) and the need for new holiday centres.

Locally there were also moves to consider the area more as a whole. There
were two County Councils involved (Norfolk and Suffolk), two County
Boroughs (Norwich and Great Yarmouth) and several Rural District Councils
as well as the East Suffolk and Norfolk River Board and the Great Yarmouth
Port and Haven Commissioners. The Norfolk County Council set up a committee of all these bodies that saw the key problems of Broadland as pollution
by sewage from boats, litter on the banks, increase in the number of boats,
bungalow development, dumping of dredging spoil on the banks, invasion of
the open water by vegetation, overgrowth of trees which impeded sailing, and
the decay of the drainage mills and other characteristic buildings. It thought
that a single executive authority was needed, but was deterred by the realisation that this would require a special Act of Parliament.

A conference in 1947 proposed a Broads Committee, to strengthen the powers of the River Board, the Port and Haven Commissioners and the planning
authorities, and that the committee would be more than just consultative. The
conference was discordant, however, and nothing significant was done; meanwhile the Government dropped the issue of the Broads as a National Park. It
was too difficult a problem. In 1949 yet another committee, the Broads Joint
Advisory Planning Committee, was founded by the County Councils. It did little, whilst conflicts between the navigation interests and the River Board
increased because the Port and Haven Commissioners refused to support
repair of banks eroded by the boats from which they drew tolls. But the issues
took on a low profile. The various organisations perhaps really did not want
more than cosmetic change, for anything more fundamental would have
removed some of their individual powers and hence their importance. The
community of organisations settled down into an uneasy co-habitation, each
defending its niche and its own survival.

Ten years on and the pressures continued to build. There were skirmishes
when the East Suffolk and Norfolk River Board claimed it was the best authority to take over the navigation responsibilities, because of its responsibilities for
the floodbanks. The National Parks Commission reconsidered the Broads, but

the idea of a National Park was finally dismissed by the Government in 1961. There were no regrets from local government, who did not favour a rival body which a National Park Board would mean, from the boat hire industry, which was flourishing nicely and feared any major regulation, and from the River Board and the Port and Haven Commissioners, whose existence might be totally jeopardised. There was little public support for a National Park. Norfolk has always prided itself on an independence of attitude, however imaginary, that might be the tradition, or burden, of its isolation from the Roman to the modern period.

The reasons that had been given by the Government for excluding the Broads from the list of National Parks, in the National Parks and Access to the Countryside Act of 1949, were that the Broads would be too costly to manage, because of the need to remove encroaching vegetation and sediment, and that they were bedevilled by too strong commercial pressures and a multiplicity of authorities. There was now also a doubt as to whether the grazing marshes, which constitute the greater proportion of the area of the floodplains, were really of national scenic significance. All were apparently rational reasons, but underlying them was the competition between the relatively weak environmental bodies of central government, whose wholehearted support they did not have, and the increasingly entrenched local bodies. This was a community very resistant to the invasions of new species that were delicate, if not shrinking, violets.

But there was change in the air. The 1960s saw international concern about the environment, specifically Rachel Carson's exposé of the influence of agricultural chemicals, and this heightened concerns in general. The Nature Conservancy was finding its feet. The Conservancy was particularly concerned for the future of its Sites of Special Scientific Interest in Broadland and fully realised that their protection was not possible without consideration for the area as a whole, which, of course, it was alone powerless to ensure. It managed to bring together a number of interested groups and produced its *Report on Broadland* in 1965.

The report was generally highly readable, though redolent with the usual tortured language of such reports in proposing its plan for 'unification and extension of powers, policies and practices relating to the future planning, management and development of Broadland'. It emphasised the need for control of boat pollution (through sewage disposal), activity and numbers and the provision of new waterways, for to do nothing was 'to abandon the region to erosion, conflict and decay'. It suggested a consortium of planning, river and navigation authorities to implement its proposals, develop support, create new facilities, advise on their economic implications and generally manage working liaison. It said rather little about the fundamental ecological problems in the waters – boats were still the fashionable bugbear and the telltale water chemistry that would have indicated the real problem had not then even been considered.

The report revived interest and concern for the torpor that had beset the previous decade or more, and The Broads Consortium was founded in 1966. It had four members from the Norfolk County Council, four from the East Suffolk and Norfolk River Authority, four from the Great Yarmouth Port and Haven Commissioners and one from the East Suffolk County Council. It included no ecological expertise at all. By 1971 it had, after much gathering of information, though no fundamental research, produced ... a report. The *Broadland Study and Plan* was very much a local authority planners' document rather than a comprehensive appraisal. In the period during which it was being produced, major changes in the ecosystems of the Broads were taking place or had already done so, yet there is no mention of them. They were recorded in a paper produced elsewhere in 1972.

The Consortium plan hung on to the usual problems, which it listed as the conflict between expansion of holiday and recreational facilities and the character of Broadland and conflicts between various uses for the limited water space. It concluded that more boats could be accommodated and proposed the excavation of new Broads and waterways (much like the proposed construction of more roads and car parks to solve traffic problems even now). It thought that since the northern waterways (the Bure, the Ant and the Thurne) were the most crowded, the increase should be on the Yare and Waveney, with an expansion of facilities at Great Yarmouth. There should be increased tolls to pay for it and increased rates for property owners benefiting from living by the water.

The plan's whole emphasis was on meeting the demand for more facilities, on generating employment and rateable value rather than on safeguarding the goose that laid these golden eggs. The Consortium stuck a knife in its own heart by suggesting (sensibly) that the responsibility for navigation on the rivers should be passed to a body responsible for other aspects of river management, but (not so sensibly) proposed that this should be the existing River Board. If organisations behave like organisms in manoeuvring to ensure their own survival, then it is understandable that the Port and Haven Commissioners rejected this idea and wrote their minority report. The Consortium was disbanded. In the 20 years since the passing of the 1949 National Parks and Access to the Countryside Act, the competition between organisations had ensured the prolongation of the existing community. Nothing substantial had been done to protect the Broadland system and it was now deteriorating rapidly.

Next on the environmental stage was the Anglian Water Authority, replacing the River Board. The local authorities were concerned that such a large organisation would be insensitive to the needs of what was a tiny part of its area. The Water Authority set up a token Broads Committee, whose influence, despite its having executive control over all Water Authority activities in Broadland bar flood control and drainage, was minor. It was dominated by Water Authority members and, predictably, contained as a minority group, representatives of the Port and Haven Commissioners, the Nature Conservancy Council, the Anglers Consultative Council, the Broads Society (an amenity society founded in 1956) and the private and commercial boating organisations.

But as the water management was put on a slightly more logical basis, yet another of the random changes that affect the operation of organisations came about, with the reorganisation of local government. With two County Councils and six District Councils, a Water Authority and the Port and Haven Commissioners, Broadland, in desperate need of a wide-ranging, balanced management, with substantial input of ecological expertise, was now to be run by ten organisations, compared with a previous four, and with precious little ecological input. In the evolution of organisations, as in the evolution of organisms, there is no direction, just a response to continuous change.

Tokenism waxed and waned. The Broads Consultative Committee (full of representatives of all the usual myriad organisations) was set up by the local authorities to consider planning applications in Broadland. It was purely advisory and had no powers. The Water Authority's Broads Committee could restrict itself only to Water Authority matters and its separate Land Drainage Committee had few representatives on it who were not avid to drain every last drop if they could. In 1983, a Water Act was passed in which elected local authority representation on the Water Authority was discontinued in favour of a board appointed entirely by the Government. The new board disbanded the Broads Committee entirely.

The Broads Authority – a local authority joint committee

By the mid-1970s, however, there was a lot of concern among perceptive individuals in the area. If outspoken enough, individuals can catalyse more change than organisations; indeed, history shows that organisations follow individual thinking rather than the reverse. New problems were appearing: the loss of the submerged plants, fish-kills in the River Thurne and its Broads, loss of reedswamp and coypu damage. The regional officer of the Nature Conservancy Council, Martin George, suggested the appointment at least of a co-ordinator, a Broads Officer, to try to bring some cohesion to an increasingly messy problem, and the Countryside Commission (a government body with overall responsibility for the countryside, including the National Parks) raised again the issue of a National Park for Broadland.

The Countryside Commission was the latest in a series of bodies that had been responsible for recreation in the countryside, though itself labouring nationally under the same problems with agriculture as were experienced locally in Broadland. It too concentrated on the familiar issue of boats, though by 1976 when it started to move on the issue, there was increasing evidence that water quality was of much greater importance. Boats are, however, highly visible; phosphate and nitrate are not. The Commission's immediate problem was that existing National Park legislation did not provide for control of river navigation and that to amend this legislation would create considerable problems for other National Parks. It suggested the setting up of a new authority specific to Broadland, though it did not think the Government would support it, as an alternative to new National Park legislation encompassing control over both navigation and water quality. There was the customary defending of entrenched positions by the existing organisations, but the local government authorities, perhaps mindful that the area was being damaged to the extent that a main source of revenue through tourism was threatened, made a proposal for a local Broads Authority. This would not need a new Act and, if they supported it financially, could be brought into existence more or less immediately as a joint local authority committee under the Local Government Act of 1972.

The Countryside Commission was not initially enthusiastic, for it saw nothing particularly new in this that had not already failed in the form of other committees, but it was remote enough from the area for its own survival not to be threatened by a retreat from its original stance. It decided that if it could nominate national representatives to the new committee, so that local rivalries could be tempered, it would support the idea and would contribute funding for projects to protect the area. Thus was borne the Broads Authority, with a remit to enhance wildlife and natural beauty, to protect economic and social interests and to preserve natural resources for recreation, holidays, scientific research and education.

In essence the only new ingredient was the national contribution. The Authority had no control over the key issues of water quality and navigation and there were oddities in the definition of its boundary area, which excluded the upper part of the River Thurne, reflecting a degree of nefarious influence among some of its first members. Its area included very little beyond the flood-plains. However, it thrived. The political environment had changed sufficiently to accommodate a new species with the advantages of financial resources from central government and a fortunate set of choices among its first officers.

It took over the previous local authority functions of planning, recreation, local nature conservation, ancient monuments, footpaths and bridleways. It channelled funds into projects such as the purchase of land for a new nature reserve at Carlton Colville and the rehabilitation of Cockshoot Broad by removal of the sediment that was almost entirely filling it. It also continued the tradition of the Nature Conservancy Council of funding research so that its policies would be based on new information and not only on somewhat hack-neyed presumptions. This was largely the influence of a chief executive, Aitken Clark, drawn from a research and teaching rather than an administrative back-ground – a fortunate new gene.

In 1982, the Broads Authority produced a clear strategy and management plan, *What Future for Broadland?*. This gave much more attention to habitat restoration and wildlife conservation than any previous report and inevitably was criticised by boating interests. Many of the old tensions persisted. There had been attempts at skulduggery in the compilation of the reports of one of the working groups that informed the eventual strategy and management plan. The Water Authority attempted to downgrade the water quality issue into an appendix away from the main text, but this was foiled. Fortunately, however, the new Authority was quickly presented with a flagship issue which, because it eventually successfully helped negotiate a solution, began to consolidate its influence.

This issue was the major controversy concerning the ploughing of the Halvergate marshes, the outcome of which was a Ministry of Agriculture-financed scheme to support traditional grazing on the marshes through payments to farmers instead of subsidies to grow wheat. This scheme was the prototype of a number of similar ones the Ministry now supports in 'Environmentally Sensitive Areas' and is discussed in Chapter 17. The issue was resolved after considerable acrimony and the resolution owed much to the Authority's officers.

The Broads Authority – a national body

The Countryside Commission was thus well pleased with its adopted child and set about making the Broads Authority a truly national one through new legislation that would allow much greater funding from national sources and establish the area as a National Park in all but name. The Norfolk and Suffolk Broads Act was passed in 1988 and the Broads Authority came into permanent existence, in its new form, the following year. It has been the most effective vehicle yet for improvement of the Broadland environment. Its constitution is not perfect and some cracks have been papered over, but it shows signs of persistence that none of its predecessors have displayed. It now has control of the navigation. The Port and Haven Commissioners continued to be intransigent during the years of the local Broads Authority, and the Countryside Commission, in formulating the legislation, decided that there was sufficient local impatience with these attitudes that a transfer was politically feasible. The Port and Haven Commissioners thus came close to extinction, for they failed to adapt and are now reduced to running just the Port of Yarmouth.

The problem remains that the Broads Authority's boundary, now including the upper Thurne, but omitting Fritton Lake, close to the River Waveney, because it was thought that this area had been too far developed by commercial interests, is still confined essentially to the floodplains. The Authority has no control over the catchments. It still has no control over water quality, though the body that has, now the Environment Agency, is, potentially at least, much more disposed to stringency in this respect than the former Water Authority. Also it still has to balance the often competing demands of preserving and enhancing the natural beauty of the Broads, of promoting the enjoyment of the Broads by the public, and of navigation. The Authority's membership was engineered by the Government to favour navigation and farming interests over those of conservation and it must maintain a distinct navigation committee, which to some extent is an uneasy symbiosis of many of the attitudes of the former river commissioners. Nonetheless, the principle that conservation issues should be foremost and that environmentally benign policies should be applied, has been operated.

It took nearly 60 years from the first mooting of the idea of the Broads as a National Park for the present, very positive, arrangements to be achieved, yet Broadland is still extremely vulnerable. Its present and future is the topic of the remainder of this book. Its fate is immediately mostly in the hands of two organisations, the Environment Agency and the Broads Authority. Neither are immune to the forces that may overtake any organisation that is not swift on its feet in an environment that is changing, both politically and physically, perhaps faster than at any time since the retreat of the ice 10,000 years ago. Both must ensure that they remain small enough to be productive, yet large enough to be resistant to minor vicissitudes of change. Both must be extremely open to new ideas and capable of supporting genuinely innovative research to inform their policies. And both must shun the temptation to recruit into their ranks the predictable and the safe, for the demands of changing environments are not for conformity but for radical action.

Further reading

The literature on organisations is generally of the kind known as 'grey'. It includes official documents, often unpublished reports and material that represents the final compromise of many committee meetings, position papers and informal contacts. Some of it appears as the minutes of committees of official organisations and is of questionable value in determining what really happened. Minutes are always carefully examined and adjusted before being eventually approved in anodyne form at some future committee meeting. Many government documents are not released for 30 years and even then it is impossible to be certain that all of them are made available. Any account of institutional history, however detailed, must then be only a version of the truth. I have relied also on my personal experience and perception of current organisations in coming to my conclusions, as well as the documents they produce to project their chosen images.

I have used the accounts of historians and conservationists such as Sheail (1976, 1998), Stamp (1969) and Green (1985) to trace the general history of conservation in Britain and George (1992) for the particular details relevant to Broadland. The history of National Park discussions can be followed in MacEwan & MacEwan (1982, 1987), and three relevant government reports of Scott, Dower and Hobhouse are published as Scott (1942) and Ministry of Town and Country Planning (1945, 1947) respectively. A wider view of National Parks can be obtained by looking at the American experience in Runte (1987). Countryside conflicts in Britain in recent years are reviewed in Lowe et al. (1986).

The first formal reporting of the deteriorating situation in the ecology of the Broadland waterway was Morgan (1972) and the reports that preceded it, but overlooked some key problems, were Nature Conservancy (1965) and Broads Consortium (1971). The events surrounding the emasculation of statutory conservation in Great Britain are related by Marren (1993) and the Worldwide Fund for Nature (1997). The Norfolk Wildlife Trust celebrated its 50-year anniversary with a volume that contains an account of its history to that date (Norfolk Naturalists Trust 1976). The *Nature Conservation Review* was published as Ratcliffe (1977) and the first *Strategy and Management Plan* for Broadland as Broads Authority (1982). The issue of toxic blue-green algal blooms that gave particular prominence to the National Rivers Authority is published as National Rivers Authority (1990). Finally, the ecological basis for this chapter may be found in Hutchinson (1965).

16

What Can Be Done? The Current Condition of the Waters and their Restoration

A bleak prospect?

Inexorable changes and handicapped, if willing, authorities: a bleak assessment of the waters of Broadland and the means to restore them, but true. The solutions are well understood; there are still gaps in the scientific understanding, but they are not such as to preclude action. The action necessary can be taken to some extent, and more has been taken in recent years than ever before. The two key organisations that might promote such action, the Environment Agency and the Broads Authority, but they are not backed by sufficiently comprehensive or powerful enough legislation to cope. This becomes very clear from an examination of the key documents produced by each organisation – the strategy and management plan of the Broads Authority, the *Broads Plan* 1997 and the *Local Environment Agency Plan* for the Broadland Rivers of June 2000. Both organisations make as much use as they can of the tools available, but the restrictions imposed by the need for compromise and the lack of legislation to manage the catchments are very clear. The ultimate problem is that remediation of the Broads requires wiser management of the entire catchment as well as a cluster of local solutions. The Broads Authority has limited powers but wide influence and enthusiastic motivation in its local executive area, but this is less than 10 per cent of the catchment (Fig. 16.1). The Environment Agency has potentially wide powers over point sources of pollution, such as industrial discharges and sewage treatment works for the whole catchment, but virtually none over the diffuse pollutants of agriculture, and its operations are strongly determined by national politics.

The first difficulty in restoration is that there is now pouring into Broadland, from its catchments, a quality of water that is not compatible with the diverse biological communities that are remembered from 50 and more years ago. The second is that the structure of the river ecosystem has been destroyed by the damage that boats have done in the past and which, although boat activity is better managed now, is impossible to repair without temporary, but severe, local curbs on that activity. And the third is that the ecosystems of the Broads have switched to dominance by planktonic algae. Their return to the submerged plant communities of former times requires improvement of the water quality together with *in situ* measures that also require closing Broads from boat and other access for a period of some years. None of these problems is easily solvable. All have been tackled to the extent that current possibilities allow, but progress has yet been modest and is unlikely to be hastened in the near future.

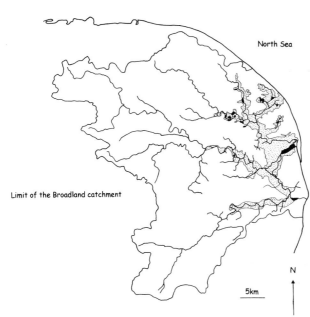

North Sea

Limit of the Broadland catchment

N

5km

Fig. 16.1 The Broads Authority's executive area, although it covers the traditional area of 'The Broads', in fact covers only about 10 per cent of the catchment that determines much of what happens in the floodplains.

Extent of the Broads Authority Executive area

The scientific background

Current understanding of the system (of both rivers and Broads) is summed up in the alternative states model discussed in Chapter 12. The key, if a more diverse, attractive system is wanted, is to switch what has become a phytoplankton-dominated, turbid water system to the clear water, plant-dominated system that characterised Broadland until the 1960s. In doing so it is also important to restrict the plant growth to somewhat less than it became in the weed-choked channels of the late nineteenth and early twentieth centuries, when sewage and its effluent promoted the great swathes of weed through which Arthur Patterson had trouble rowing. One need in doing this is to reduce the nutrient supply, but this alone (unless it were to be so severe as to allow very little human use of the catchments) will not be enough. The original plant communities could survive enormous increases in nutrients; likewise the plankton can persist even with substantial decreases.

What first has to happen is that any potential forward switches, which jeopardise the plants, are removed. These might include herbicide levels capable of killing plants or pesticides of zooplankton. They also potentially include intense grazing by geese, or physical damage by boats, wind and wave erosion, or very high salinities (Chapter 12). Switches that operated in the past will not necessarily be operating now; there may be new ones that must be identified and dealt with.

Then the nutrient concentrations have to be reduced and this probably means those of both phosphorus and nitrogen. Although nutrient reduction will not alone solve the problem, the effectiveness of the next step, called biomanipulation, increases greatly as the nutrients are reduced. Biomanipulation means changing the fish community so as to encourage the development of grazing zooplankton. The zooplankters then clear the water, creating the potential for water plants to grow.

This potential may not be achieved, however, if there are no plant seeds or sprigs remaining, so plants may have to be introduced as the next step. They are very vulnerable to bird grazing and other disturbance at this stage, and may need to be physically protected until they have started to spread. A particular problem appears to be that the sloppy sediment now being laid down provides insufficient purchase for the rather rudimentary root systems of many submerged plants. Finally, an appropriate fish community can be reintroduced and the results monitored. This strategy (Fig. 16.2) gives a framework for discussion of practical restoration in the Broads and rivers.

General approach in the rivers ...

In the rivers, it may never be possible to bring back extensive submerged plant communities without complete closure for removal of fish stocks and prevention of their return during the restoration period, but it is possible to restore some of the plant community. Restoration of the emergent plant communities – reeds and irises, reedmace and water-lilies – to re-form a more attractive wave-absorbing defence, would bring back a much more pleasant bank edge, with its associated birds and mammals, than the present eroded ugliness of many stretches.

The first step, with improvement of water quality, is the diversion of boat activity (the probable main forward switch in the rivers at present) from sections to be restored. This need not involve total exclusion, but certainly alternating one-way traffic and traffic-calming measures. There must be a regrading of the edge to a more gentle slope, where a vertical cliff has now been eroded, to provide a favourable habitat. Then appropriate species must be planted and protected from bird damage until they have begun to spread. Finally, there can be the return of the section to use by boats and anglers, though perhaps with increased thought being given to design and operation of the craft and management of the anglers.

... and the Broads

In the Broads, the general approach, again following nutrient control, is isolation so that fish can be removed and their re-entry from the river prevented for a time. Forward switches such as high pesticide ingress are less likely to be operating now, but boat damage and bird grazing are both likely. (At Hickling Broad, salinity is an issue, though this problem has been circumvented in a rather remarkable way by a severe reduction in nutrients, as will be related below.) Finally, the Broad may be reopened provided nutrient control has been general rather than local and that boat activity is initially controlled. A well-developed, tangled bed of submerged plants can effectively defend itself from boats by simply excluding them. Fish will naturally recolonise from the river. This is the theory. The next steps are to look at the techniques available for each stage.

Nutrient control

The keys to nutrient control are to minimise the intensity of cultivation and fertilisation and restore semi-natural vegetation to the catchment (Chapter 3)

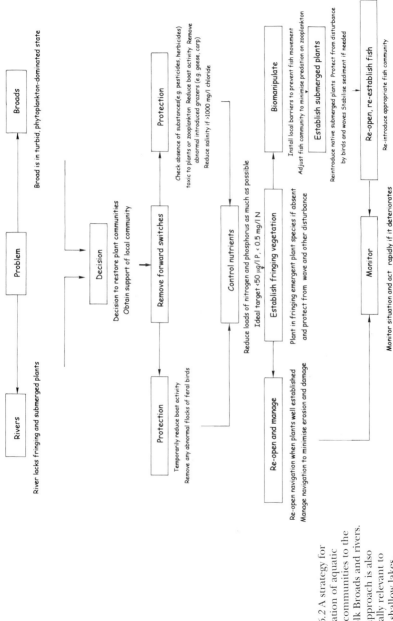

Fig. 16.2 A strategy for restoration of aquatic plant communities to the Norfolk Broads and rivers. This approach is also generally relevant to other shallow lakes.

where possible, and to intercept the nutrients that come from stock and people. Algae need both nitrogen and phosphorus to grow prolifically, and it used to be thought that control of only one would be sufficient to limit growth. Theoretically this is true. Phosphorus has been the target of most control because it enters lakes and rivers from mostly discrete (point) sources such as sewage treatment works, or farmyards. Its compounds can be more readily precipitated than the very soluble ones of nitrogen, which come in from thousands of field drains and diffuse land runoff. Often, however, when phosphorus has been controlled in point sources, there has still remained a substantial supply from release from the lake sediments or diffuse leaching from cultivated land. In many shallow lakes there has probably always been sufficient phosphorus released from the sediments to maintain a large crop of algae provided nitrogen supplies are adequate (Chapter 12).

The process of eutrophication in shallow lakes may then have been driven as much by increases in nitrogen as of phosphorus, and at different times of year either nitrogen or phosphorus may be more crucial to the algae. Moreover, if diverse communities of plants are to be restored, reduction of nitrogen is probably essential. The plants can obtain adequate supplies of phosphorus but not nitrogen from the sediment, and high nitrogen supplies in the water lead to dominance by a few or only one competitive species. In like manner, weeds such as nettles come to take over fertile soils. The most successful strategies of control for Broadland will thus reduce supplies of both elements. Therein lies the problem.

Control of phosphorus at waste water treatment works has been carried out routinely in many countries (though only sporadically in Britain) by precipitation of it from the effluent with iron, aluminium or calcium compounds. The effluent concentration can be reduced from as much as 30 milligrams of phosphorus per litre to as little as half a milligram, though more usually one or two milligrams per litre (Fig. 16.3). There is even interest in the chemical industry in extracting phosphorus from this process for re-use in industrial products such as detergents. The only problem is in precipitating it in a form that the industry can use, but this will no doubt soon be solved.

Phosphorus control from human effluent is also promoted by a European Directive (the Urban Waste Water Treatment Directive) that requires all works treating the sewage from over 10,000 people or the equivalent, including industrial effluents, to remove phosphorus to a specified level. Member states need only do it where the waters receiving the effluent are defined as eutrophic or at risk of becoming so. This allows individual governments to use the legislation fully or weakly by the way they define 'eutrophic'. The British Government has defined very few waters as sensitive, mainly those used commercially for water supply and, somewhat surprisingly, only three Broadland rivers, the Wensum, Ant and Bure, have been so defined, and then only in 1998. Nonetheless, phosphorus precipitation is carried out at works on the River Ant and some on the River Bure, as a result at first of voluntary co-operation on an experimental basis by Anglian Water and then through the system of issuing official consents to discharge by the Environment Agency. It has, however, been extremely successful in reducing phosphorus concentrations in these rivers.

Many problems remain however; there are many small works that do not fall under the Urban Waste Water Treatment legislation, yet ten works treating the

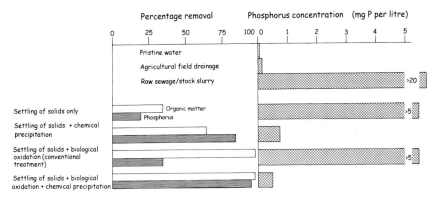

Fig. 16.3 Sewage, from humans or stock, contains much more phosphorus than water draining natural vegetation (pristine water) or agricultural land. After minimal treatment (settling and disposal of solids to land) the remaining water still contains a lot of organic matter (measured as the biological oxygen demand, or amount of oxygen that is used up by bacteria in it in breaking down the organic matter) and phosphorus. Conventional treatment, in which the organic matter is oxidised by a protozoon and bacterial community on filter beds or in activated sludge tanks at a treatment works (biological oxidation), still leaves thousands of times the concentration of phosphorus in pristine water and hundreds of times that in field drainage. Chemical precipitation by iron or aluminium salts from the sewage water removes at least 80 per cent. Full treatment (settling, oxidation and chemical precipitation) can remove more than 95 per cent of the phosphorus, still leaving ten times as much as in pristine water, but the ultimate effect is small when the effluent is well diluted in the receiving river water. Based on Gilbert & De Jong (1978).

sewage of 1,000 people each, though not covered, release as much phosphorus as one works of 10,000, which is. The Broadland catchment has nearly 200 sewage treatment works. Works that are distant from the floodplains tend to be ignored, yet phosphorus can easily travel from the headwaters to the floodplains; and phosphorus released from the large works serving Norwich on the River Yare can be transferred by the spring tides far up the other rivers. Therefore there is still a great deal of phosphorus being released into the Broadland system from sewage effluent, but legislation exists, were it to be used, to eliminate this source almost entirely.

Phosphorus from the land has been the minority component of the Broadland phosphorus budget – probably around 25 per cent in the Ant and Bure before phosphorus precipitation from works on these rivers, even less in the Yare and Waveney, where larger towns discharge to the rivers (see Fig. 12.4). It dominates the budgets of the Trinity Broads on the Muck Fleet, which receive effluent only from a few septic tanks. In the River Thurne it dominated the budget in the early decades of the twentieth century, was superseded by the excretion of black-headed gulls from the middle to the late decades and has now come to dominate again as the gulls have declined in numbers.

In the past it was accepted that rather little phosphorus ran off cultivated land, because the insolubility of its compounds leads to its being held rather tightly on the surfaces of clays and other soil components. The fertiliser industry has maintained the view that cultivation also led to little phosphorus loss on the basis that the percentage of loss, compared with what was put on the land, was very small. The problem with this is that a small percentage can be a large absolute concentration. To soil scientists, used to thinking in terms of grams of phosphorus per litre of soil, the couple of hundred micrograms of phosphorus per litre that might leach out in the water seemed trivial, but for algal growth these are huge supplies. Even so, formerly it was generally true that supplies from the land were small.

Currently, however, evidence from Northern Ireland and elsewhere is suggesting that soils, heavily fertilised since the 1950s, are becoming saturated with phosphorus, as eventually they must. The number of binding sites on the clay particles is finite; the amounts put on the land are inevitably slightly in excess of the crop needs, to ensure the crop has an adequate supply. With the vagaries of weather it is impossible to balance exactly the supply and the need and, from the farmers' point of view, sensible to err on the side of excess. Most soils probably have sufficient stocks now for them not to need phosphorus fertilisation on a regular basis. However, there is a large industry dependent on the trade, and with crop profits dependent on the yield beyond that production needed to cover costs – most of it – there is no great incentive for more parsimonious use.

The only way of controlling these diffuse phosphorus sources, other than through changing the nature of agriculture, is to attempt to intercept them before they reach the streams. Much hope has been put in buffer zones and constructed wetlands. Buffer zones are areas of semi-natural vegetation kept between the agricultural land and the streams, in which uptake by plants and retention of phosphorus-containing eroded particles might provide a barrier. They can be effective (because their wet soils promote denitrification) for nitrogen, but are less so for phosphorus. Just as agricultural soils can become saturated with phosphorus, so eventually must those of the buffer zone and the wetter soils close to the stream will likely release phosphorus (see Chapter 4).

Buffer zones must therefore be extensive for long effectiveness, and this means not just a token strip a metre or two wide along each bank of a stream. Some calculations suggest that, with current agriculture, almost as great an area of buffer zone will be needed as of agricultural land to be isolated.

Constructed wetlands are a particular form of buffer zone in which an artificial reedswamp is planted in a suitable depression and water channelled through it. Again they work well for retaining silt and decomposing nitrogen compounds to nitrogen gas, but are much less effective at phosphorus retention. Sometimes they are used for the final polishing of sewage effluent, after conventional treatment and chemical phosphorus precipitation, but, despite many hopes to the contrary, cannot cope with waters very rich in phosphorus.

Both parsimonious fertilisation and use of buffer zones depend on voluntary co-operation of landowners. There is a Code of Good Agricultural Practice produced by the Ministry of Agriculture, which promotes their use, but its suggestions are mostly confined to nitrogen and even then are mild compared with what is needed for adequate control. There are no penalties if its provisions are not followed, except where grant money for improvements is being sought and may be refused. The law does not require control of diffuse nutrients.

Stock wastes are probably a small component of the Broadland phosphorus budgets. Farming in the catchments has been dominated by arable for many decades, but dairying in the river valleys, where damp grasslands favour it, and an increasing industry in poultry and pigs, must provide quantities that will become more important as other sources are controlled. There has been a problem of piggery wastes contaminating the River Waveney with ammonium ions, which must also mean that phosphorus supply was similarly increased. The problem was small, however, and dealt with by controlling the pig slurry; storing it and disposing it on the land as fertiliser under conditions that minimise runoff. Manure spread in wet weather can release very large supplies of nutrients to the streams, for the water runs over the surface and not through the soil where there is at least some possibility of retention.

Internal nutrient supply from the sediments

Ultimately all phosphorus and most of the nitrogen comes from the catchments, but phosphorus can be stored in sediments and emerge later as an internal supply. The rate at which phosphate emerges from sediments depends on many factors, for example temperature, disturbance by invertebrates and pH of the overlying water. Despite much research it is not a very predictable process because so many influences affect it simultaneously.

Because most of the release is in summer, when water flows are lowest, and much of the phosphorus may be returned to the sediment in particles of algae and detritus before it can be washed out, this supply may be available more or less indefinitely once quantities of phosphorus have built up in the sediment. It is tempting therefore to attempt to take out the sediments rich in phosphorus to remove this source.

Sediment removal is an expensive business, however, for it is slow and the sediment must be disposed of. Three Broads, Cockshoot, Alderfen and Strumpshaw together with Pound End, part of Hoveton Little Broad, have been suction dredged by pumping a mixture of fluid sediment from them and settling it in lagoons created among the surrounding wetland. Sediment removed from Barton Broad has been settled on agricultural land then ploughed in to the soil and agriculture resumed. Sediment will have to be removed from a much greater area of Broadland in the near future if open water is to be maintained for navigation, for current sedimentation rates, measured in cores dated by lead-210 dating, are of several millimetres, even a centimetre or so, each year.

The results of sediment removal on reduction of phosphorus inputs to the water have, however, been disappointing (see Chapter 10). Perhaps this is inevitable if it is the case that all shallow lake sediments release substantial amounts of phosphorus, even under plant dominance. Results are awaited for Barton Broad where external loads have been reduced by phosphorus precipitation and effluent diversion and where phosphorus concentrations have fallen in a situation where there is a vigorous flushing of the Broad. Summer release of phosphorus appears to be reduced and overall concentrations are falling in consequence. However, the precedents are not good for long-term control.

Nitrogen control

Nitrogen is both an old and a new card on the table. It has always been understood that it was closely involved in eutrophication, but it is very difficult to control. The earliest attempts at solving eutrophication problems were in Canada, North America, Switzerland and Sweden, where the local geology was such as to make phosphorus very scarce and strongly limiting. The problem was mostly one of urban wastes affecting deep lakes, and phosphorus control alone was very successful. This conditioned the thinking about nutrient control on a much wider basis, including Broadland, but in lowland areas, covered by glacial drift, and in shallow lakes, phosphorus is much more available. Thus it may have been increases in nitrogen that have driven the eutrophication of areas such as the Broads. Moreover, the present high nitrogen levels result in much lower plant variety so that where plants have been restored the communities have the instability that is associated with such low diversity and readily collapse. The consequence is that a stepwise decrease in both nutrients is likely to be needed for nutrient control in Broadland, as opposed to the sole control of phosphorus that has pervaded the thinking so far.

Some nitrogen comes from waste water treatment, as ammonium and nitrate, but this amount is trivial compared with that which drains as nitrate from agricultural land. The two approaches of interception by buffer zones and parsimonious use on the land, already discussed for phosphorus, are as yet the only possible solutions. At least for nitrogen, buffer zones and constructed wetlands can be very successful, as in waterlogged soils, especially those whose water tables fluctuate, denitrification by bacteria is effective.

The difficulty is that the loads of nitrate now coming from the land demand quite extensive buffer zones if control is to be effective and farmers are unwilling voluntarily to give up land, on which they could be growing crops, for this use. There is legislation, under a European Directive, that could create areas, called Nitrate Vulnerable Zones, in which farming practices can be legally limited to reduce nitrate levels to below 50 milligrams per litre (ten if the value is expressed as nitrogen, as it usually is). Some 600,000 hectares of land have been scheduled since 1996 as Nitrate Vulnerable Zones, but only small areas of the Broadland catchment, at Lyng Forge, near Wroxham, and in the upper reaches of the River Waveney, have been included. All of the areas so far designated have been to protect domestic ground water supplies, though the Directive promotes use of these zones also to protect sites of value in conservation of wildlife. The British Government has chosen not to use this option, but this has been noticed by the European Community and, in consequence, Britain is threatened with prosecution in the European courts. This has stimulated some thinking, at least, about suitable areas for scheduling.

Nitrate losses from arable agriculture come from both surplus fertiliser use and ploughing of the soil, which promotes decomposition and oxidation of nitrogen-containing organic matter. The Ministry of Agriculture worked out a number of strategies to minimise the losses, which, as in the case of phosphorus, are comparatively small from the farming point of view compared with the nitrogen stored in the soil and taken off in crops. Nonetheless they are huge compared with what would run off natural vegetation into streams and lakes, whose communities thrive on extremely low levels of such nutrients.

The Ministry recommended that high yielding crop varieties be used, which remove a lot of nitrogen. Unfortunately this is a two-edged sword, for a lot of fertiliser has to be used to support them. It recommended minimising the time the soil is bare, following ploughing, by planting cover crops and sowing the seed for the next summer season early the previous autumn. It suggested calculating fertiliser requirements carefully, avoiding fertilisation in spring, when runoff is high, and putting the fertiliser on in stages rather than all at once.

And it recommended that the fertiliser be put on carefully, away from watercourses, and that irrigation take more careful account of weather and periods when uptake of nitrogen by the crop is greatest. Manure put on the surface can release a great deal of nitrogen and so it should be ploughed in, or not put on, when wet weather is expected.

These strategies can reduce nitrate losses significantly, but not prevent them entirely. The fundamental problem is that fertiliser is cheap compared with other farm costs and the profit from a crop increases markedly from the last few per cent of extra yield obtained in response to nitrogen (Fig. 16.4). There will thus always be a tendency to put on a little extra to guarantee this. Leaching losses of nitrate from arable land and vegetable crops can be high, up to 200 kilograms per hectare from brassica crops, but less from cereals, which make up the bulk of cultivated land (4.5 million hectares compared with 0.2 million for other crops in the UK). Changes in practice and increasing yields have reduced potential losses from winter wheat from about 70 kilograms per hectare in the early 1980s to about 25 kilograms per hectare (Fig. 16.4) now. However, because of the vagaries of weather and the economics of crop growing it is claimed that it is unlikely that they can be reduced by much more.

The long-term average runoff of rain (that is the total precipitation minus the evaporation) in Broadland is about 150–200 millimetres per year. Thus a leaching of say 20 kilograms of nitrogen per hectare is likely to create a concentration of 9–13 milligrams per litre of nitrate-nitrogen in general and locally much more. The likely pristine concentration from under natural vegetation would be less than 1 milligram per litre. Some of the nitrate currently leached from the land is denitrified in streams, rivers and upstream swamps before it reaches the Broadland floodplain, so that values of up to 9 or 10 milligrams nitrogen per litre (Waveney, Yare and Bure), or 3–6 milligrams per litre (Ant, Thurne and Muck fleet), are found in water entering the Broads in winter. This is still very high. It means that a combination of both improved practice and interception by buffer zones will be needed to solve the problems of the Broads. There is still some possibility of reduction by designation of the Broadland catchments as Nitrate Vulnerable Zones, but there will have to be substantial conversion of land to defensive use as buffer zones.

The future for nutrient control

Serious attempts have been made to reduce the phosphorus flows into Broadland and these have been very successful in the Bure and the Ant. And there is one instance, at Hickling Broad, discussed below, of reduction in nutrient loads without benefit of any management at all. Yet there has been little impact on the ecological state of the system overall. A much more ambitious approach will be needed.

Greater impetus may be given by the new European Water Framework Directive, agreed in 2000, which requires a whole-catchment approach and the restoration of water bodies to good ecological status, by whatever means is necessary. This can only mean restoration of clear water and plant dominance to shallow lakes and lowland rivers. There are many opportunities within the Directive for member states of the European Union to derogate particular water bodies, but nonetheless it is the first legislation on water quality based on modern understanding of the importance of the catchment.

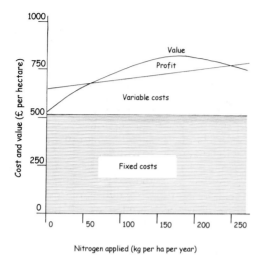

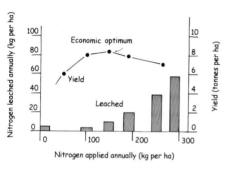

Nitrogen applied annually (kg per ha)

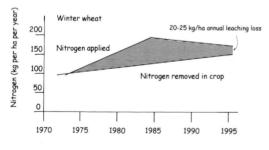

Fig. 16.4 Nitrate use for agriculture in the UK brings problems for fresh waters that must be seen in the current economic context (top). The profit (including a subsidy, the Arable Area Payment), is a small part of the overall farm costs, but the cost of the fertiliser, between nothing and £150 per hectare (in 1997) is also only a small proportion. The profit is increased with increasing fertiliser use, though not hugely. However, because the other costs are currently high, it is worth putting on ample fertiliser to make sure the maximum profit is attained. The need to meet legislative standards imposed by the European Union on nitrate concentrations in drinking water has led to much research into how nitrate leaching losses might be reduced without affecting farm profits. Long-term studies on land cultivated for wheat at Rothamsted Experimental Station (centre) show the increased loss by leaching as more nitrogen is applied. Above about 150 kilograms per hectare, which also represents the maximum profit, leaching losses increase greatly. Applications in recent years (bottom) have often been greater than this, but the encouragement of more careful practice as well as economic considerations have gradually narrowed the difference between the nitrogen applied and that removed in the crop. This difference, however, which represents the leaching losses to fresh waters, remains at 20–25 kilograms per hectare. In terms of concentration this can be up to 25 mg per litre, or 50 times that which leaches from natural vegetation. It is thought that leaching losses cannot be reduced any more than this under conventional intensive agriculture. Solution of nitrogen problems in fresh waters will thus require a much more radical reform of agriculture. Based on Ministry of Agriculture, Fisheries and Food (1999).

Restoration of the rivers

Until water quality can be improved on a catchment-wide basis it is not worth thinking of re-establishment of submerged plants in the rivers. Restoration of emergent plants is another matter and is possible. There is a variety of river edges (Fig. 16.5). On those upstream, reed fringes still occur, and occasionally water-lilies have persisted, but often past dredging and erosion have created a rather precipitous edge, rather than a gentle batter into the water, stopping any extension of the beds. Then there are those where alder growth has taken over and the edge is also steep with exposed tree roots. Both of these types front undrained fenland.

On river edges downstream, within the floodbanks protecting the grazing marshes, a part rooted, part floating rond may persist, with reed and other grasses, but often erosion has removed this and the water now extends to the floodbank. Finally, there are those sections where piling (quay heading) of wood or steel has already been inserted, because of the need for moorings or to protect property or badly eroded floodbanks. Above the tidal reaches most of the bank has a reasonably natural appearance, but within the tidal sections (around 183 kilometres, counting both banks) about 62 per cent retains something of a natural appearance, with ronds, although confined within floodbanks. Along 21 per cent the ronds have been eroded away, 9 per cent is piled and only 9 per cent retains a truly natural appearance. Everywhere there is erosion to some extent and the irregular plant-fronted edge of earlier decades has been replaced with a starker, straighter line.

Current boat traffic is incompatible with a spontaneous, natural redevelopment of fringing plant communities. Conversely, with the reduced traffic of the last decade or so, some further restrictions on speed, and with some temporary protection, new reed fringes might be established, except where piling has

Fig. 16.5 Some examples of bank protection in Broadland.

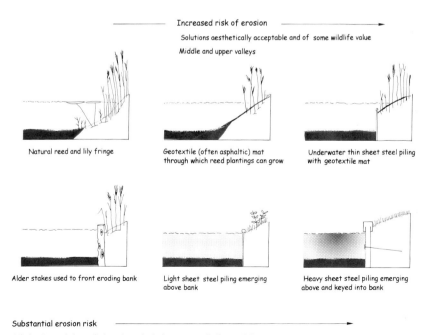

Increased risk of erosion ⟶

Solutions aesthetically acceptable and of some wildlife value

Middle and upper valleys

Natural reed and lily fringe

Geotextile (often asphaltic) mat through which reed plantings can grow

Underwater thin sheet steel piling with geotextile mat

Alder stakes used to front eroding bank

Light sheet steel piling emerging above bank

Heavy sheet steel piling emerging above and keyed into bank

Substantial erosion risk ⟶

Solutions increasingly costly, intrusive and ugly Lower parts of valleys with floodbanks

Fig. 16.6 Bank repair along the River Thurne, using geotextile matting that has been pegged over the regraded eroded bank.

excluded this possibility forever. A reed fringe not only looks better than an eroded edge, but creates habitat for mammals and birds. Only the more tolerant – moorhen, coot, mute swan, great-crested grebe, mallard – are likely to persist, but these are familiar denizens and welcome even if more unusual animals fail to tolerate even modest amounts of boat disturbance.

In the past the problem has been that attempts at restoration (Fig. 16.6) have been too modest. They have attempted the impossible compromise of establishing the fringe with no control of boat traffic or regrading of the banks. Tough 'geotextile' matting has been laid down on the steep banks, with perforations for the reed to grow through, or barriers of car tyres threaded on stakes have been used to give some protection against waves along short sections. Neither has given very impressive results and neither is attractive. Both have been the approaches of conventional engineering.

What is needed first is restriction of boat traffic to reduce disturbance for probably two to three years along substantial sections in turn. This means confining boats to a lane along the centre line and a system of alternating one-way traffic flows so that substantial protection can be given whilst the reed fringes re-establish from plantings. These will need a bank edge that has been re-contoured to a gentler slope and protected by decomposable matting during the time that the reed is establishing. There is no great conceptual problem in arranging this. It is done every day in the repair of roads, even motorways, so it is faintly odd that it should have been opposed so stolidly by the navigation interests in the past. One problem in Broadland is that alternative parallel routes for traffic diversion are generally not available, but alternating one-way traffic over a couple of kilometres at a time would pose no real difficulty for holidaymakers.

The Broads Authority, now the navigation authority, has the powers to carry out such work under such circumstances, but has hitherto been slow to use them. Its preference has been to promote development of less damaging boats, through changes in hull design. Sensible and necessary though this is, it will not solve the ultimate problem, for when edges are eroded, spontaneous recovery is impossible, even at much lower levels of disturbance than can be tolerated with an intact vegetation fringe.

Restoration of the Broads

The Broads are, in theory, less difficult propositions for restoration of clear-water, plant-dominated conditions than the rivers, simply because they can be isolated. The results of local restoration have been promising, but limited and to some extent disappointing – low diversity of plant communities and a tendency to revert – because it has not been possible to reduce the nutrient loads sufficiently.

The strategy described in Figure 16.2 was worked out in hindsight. It is an ideal that can act as a reference to assess what should be done. The first step is to remove forward switches that might disturb a plant community. The problem is that it is never possible to be certain that none are operating, especially where there might be trace toxic substances, but at present in Broadland, boat damage and grazing by birds are the most likely agents, with salinity also an issue in the Thurne catchment.

Small-scale experiments in enclosures that protect against physical disturbance in Broads along the River Bure have shown that plants can be established and grow well (Fig. 16.7). This means that chemical switches, such as

Fig. 16.7 Protection from physical damage and especially bird grazing can result in some plant growth in turbid waters, but these measures, coupled with biomanipulation, can give excellent growth. In this experiment, at Belaugh Broad, a slatted palisade of wood prevents birds from entering, whilst the flushing of the river at this point minimises phytoplankton development.

pesticides or trace toxic substances potentially present in sewage effluents, can be discounted in the Bure. This might not be the case on the River Yare, where there is a large waste water treatment works serving Norwich, which has more varied industry than elsewhere and has discharged effluents with heavy metals such as mercury in the past. However, there is a substantial plant community, mainly of water-lilies, in Rockland Broad downstream of it, so even on this river, physical damage is likely to be the switch mechanism most to be guarded against.

The second step is to reduce the nutrient loads as much as possible and this topic has been discussed above for the desirable catchment scale. On a local basis it is possible to reduce nutrients by isolation of a Broad from the river or diversion of inflow streams around it, as related in Chapter 12.

Biomanipulation

Following nutrient control, the strategy for restoration (Fig. 16.2) moves to biomanipulation. The aim is to clear the water of algae by husbanding the growth of populations of *Daphnia*, thus creating better conditions for plants to grow on the bottom. In the absence of the refuges that plants naturally provide (Chapter 12), and which allow coexistence of large numbers of *Daphnia* with substantial fish stocks, this can only be done by removing the fish that eat the *Daphnia*.

There are several ways of doing this. The first, and best, is to remove as many fish as possible, leaving only a few fish predators such as pike to hunt the fish that always remain after even exhaustive fishing. Inevitably this interferes with angling. The second is to remove only the species of fish that produce many young that feed on *Daphnia* in their early stages, such as roach and bream, but leave bottom-feeding fish such as tench, which do not form such large populations and do less damage, as well as the piscivores. This is more acceptable to anglers, but such selective fishing is more expensive. The third is to increase artificially the stock of piscivores such as pike. This is effective only if very large numbers are added and has to be done year after year, at great expense, because the young pike do not survive very well. Pike also function best among plant beds, which are, of course, absent at this stage. Adult perch are also piscivorous, but again prefer weedy conditions and their young are also zooplanktivorous.

The option of introducing exotic predatory fish such as the zander (pikeperch) is precluded under the Wildlife and Countryside Act. It would, in any case, be undesirable in principle, introduced species everywhere having created rather more problems than they have solved. The significance of zander is that it is an open-water shoaling fish, which, unlike pike, does not depend on the cover of plants for its hunting. It is native to mainland Europe and undoubtedly occurred in Britain during the interglacial periods, but the accident of history prevented its reinvasion before Britain became an island 8,500 years ago.

In Broadland the first approach, complete removal, has generally been taken, with fish removed to the main rivers. Biomanipulation has been carried out in Cockshoot Broad, Pound End (Hoveton Little Broad) and Ormesby Broad as well as in small-scale experiments of up to a hectare or so in Hoveton Great Broad (Plate 1). These have demonstrated its feasibility (Fig. 16.8) even where nutrient control has not been very great. Biomanipulation is now a

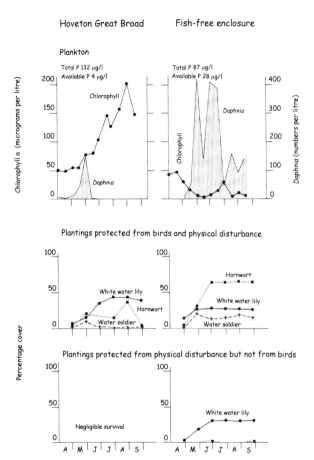

Fig. 16.8 Removing fish can have a substantial effect on the plankton in shallow lakes and thence on light penetration and plant growth. The plant growth, however, is also affected by other factors including physical disturbance by waves and by bird grazing. The experiment from which these data are taken is shown in Plate 1. An enclosure, about 1 hectare in area, was made with plastic and wood sheets, perforated by stainless steel mesh windows, in Hoveton Great Broad. These allowed free exchange of water. Fish were removed from inside the enclosure, but remained outside it in the main Broad. Plants were planted in protective structures (Fig. 16.7) inside and outside the enclosure. The protection comprised circular wooden fences with slats spaced widely enough for birds, particularly coot, to enter (protection from physical disturbance only) or narrowly to prevent such entry. The latter structures were also covered with netting to prevent birds flying in. Removal of fish allowed considerable numbers of *Daphnia* to persist (upper panels) and this had an effect on the phytoplankton, which was greatly reduced, and the water chemistry. The phosphorus content fell as particles containing phosphorus were sedimented in *Daphnia* faeces, but the available portion of it increased as the *Daphnia* excreted it but prevented, by their grazing, further uptake of it. The plant growth, measured as individual coverage of the water surface, was best and in greatest diversity when protected from birds in the clear water of the fish-free enclosure. They did not survive unprotected in the open Broad, but even there, protection from birds allowed lesser growth of white water-lilies and hornwort. The persistence of plants was thus shown to be a function of a package of circumstances. Based on unpublished data of J. Stansfield, C. Bennett, G. Phillips and B. Moss.

commonly used technique and has been employed widely in mainland Europe. Research in Broadland has contributed significantly to understanding of the technique and its limitations.

There are several conditions that make biomanipulation most effective. Firstly, there should be no more than about 1 gram of fish per square metre (10 kilograms per hectare) remaining. This compares with about 20 grams per square metre in 'normal' waters and twice as much or more in those heavily stocked for angling. In water that lacks refuges for zooplankters, even a small stock of fish can undermine the grazing potential of *Daphnia*. Methods for removing fish are generally confined to the least effective, but more ethical ones. Use of a natural fish poison, rotenone, or of gill netting are most efficient but kill the fish; electrofishing, where the fish are stunned in an electric field created between two electrodes placed in the water, or seine netting, are less efficient, but the fish survive. It is comparatively easy, though time-consuming, to fish out a small lake of only a few hectares, but much more difficult to fish out one even of only a few tens of hectares.

Fishing is best done in winter, when many small fish from the previous summer will have grown to a more catchable size or been removed by natural predation. In winter, at low temperature and high oxygen levels, damage to the fish is also minimised. Piscivorous fish are usually put back – they might control the residual population of other fish – and so are eels, which do not feed on zooplankton and will get back anyway, for they can travel overland through wet vegetation. All other British lowland fish feed on zooplankton, when they are small, though tench never breed prolifically and are not much threat and might also be returned. Roach, bream, rudd and perch all feed voraciously on zooplankton until they are at least ten centimetres in length, in their first and sometimes second year of life. Thereafter they feed on larger animals.

The second condition for the success of biomanipulation is obviously that the fish cannot return to the lake. This means isolation by some form of barrier, which means curtailment of navigation, for where boats can pass, so can fish. Cockshoot Broad was isolated by a solid dam, Ormesby Broad by a raised mound of pebbles on its small outflow that allowed row boats to be slid over it into the Broad, but that prevented fish from passing. Other forms of barrier, such as curtains of tough but flexible plastic sheet with floats at the surface that might allow boats to pass over them, are being tested (Plate 25). Fish could in theory pass over them also as the boat depresses them, but are likely to be scared away by the disturbance.

The need for isolation restricts the number of Broads that can be biomanipulated, because of the navigation issue. It may also preclude successful biomanipulation because of the effect on the algal populations through reduction of flushing. A well-flushed Broad, at current nutrient levels, has a phytoplankton dominated by diatoms and green algae in summer, with only a small proportion of blue-green algae. The latter grow slowly and develop best in water that is not flushed through very rapidly. Isolation generally means reduced flushing and greater proportions of blue-green algae.

The problem then is that blue-green algae are less palatable to *Daphnia* than diatoms and green algae. They are more rubbery in texture, harder to eat and difficult to digest. They may also produce toxins, so that the *Daphnia* reject them from their feeding grooves. Experiments in a well-flushed Broad (Hoveton Great) compared with a poorly flushed one (Ranworth) have shown that exclusion of fish leads to development of abundant, large, efficiently feeding *Daphnia* only in the former. Where blue-green algae dominate and populations are already well established, *Daphnia* fail to grow well and the larger species, which are the more efficient grazers, do not grow at all (Fig. 16.9). Sometimes, however, in shallow lakes, biomanipulation carried out over the

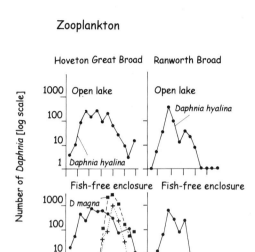

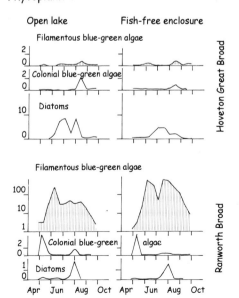

Fig. 16.9 The influence of fish removal on the development of the zooplankton may sometimes depend on the nature of the phytoplankton community. The experiments were carried out in fish-free mesh enclosures in the well-flushed Hoveton Great Broad and the poorly flushed Ranworth Broad, with their very different phytoplankton communities. Based on Moss et al. (1991).

winter can prevent the development of the blue-green algae because the *Daphnia* can sometimes, though not reliably, control the small residual populations of blue-green algae by which these species overwinter.

One theoretical solution is to pump ground water through an isolated Broad, but this has not yet been feasible for lack of adequate supply of high quality ground water. The ground water supplies in Broadland are mostly already over-committed for public supply and irrigation. Another is to make the isolation barriers permeable to water, but not to fish or their tiny larvae. This can be done by building barriers of sheet plastic, or wood, with windows of stainless steel mesh (Fig. 16.26). The windows soon clog with algae and detritus, however, and must be frequently scrubbed clean with a wire brush, but the approach might allow successive areas of a large Broad to be isolated, whilst maintaining flushing, and allowing navigation and angling over the remaining area. When a substantial proportion of the Broad has been restored, the barriers might be removed, but this approach has only yet been tried with the establishment of a single such enclosure in Hoveton Great Broad (Plate 1 and Fig. 16.8).

The third condition for successful biomanipulation is that nutrient levels should be reduced as much as possible. If the algae are severely short of nutrients and not growing well, they can be controlled by a much less active *Daphnia* population and perhaps by less severe biomanipulation. At present it is not possible to be very precise about how much nutrient reduction is needed. It is easier to get modest reductions than significant ones and hence there is a tendency to compromise at levels that are not nearly so stringent as are probably needed.

Getting the plants to grow

Biomanipulation, by promoting *Daphnia* development, clears the water so that plants can potentially grow, but it does not guarantee their growth. There may no longer be live seeds left in the sediment and vegetative fragments will usually have long disappeared. Sometimes, however, a few plants have persisted, or fragments are brought in by river flows and may establish. More often plants have to be introduced and may find it difficult to become established.

The sediments laid down under phytoplankton-dominated conditions are amorphous and fluid, lacking in the fibrous material that binds together the sediments laid down under plant-dominated communities. Small plants may easily be dislodged by water movements or uprooted by birds such as coot, foraging for invertebrate food around them to feed chicks in spring, or eating them directly later in summer. This means that plantings may have to be protected against disturbance from both waves and birds by cages, which may be prominent and unsightly, but nonetheless necessary.

Of the two whole-lake restorations yet carried out in Broadland, at Cockshoot Broad and at Ormesby Broad, the plant populations have developed much better at Ormesby Broad. There was a substantial starter population already present, which expanded considerably after biomanipulation. At Cockshoot Broad, there was no plant population left, even before sediments were removed, and plantings, which were unprotected, fared badly except in one very sheltered area that had been the dyke connecting the Broad with the river before isolation (Fig. 16.10). The main body of the Broad acquired growth of hornwort, but it never established very vigorously and its fortunes

Fig. 16.10 Following isolation and biomanipulation, the sheltered areas of Cockshoot Broad developed vigorous populations of plants, but these have not been very stable.

have fluctuated greatly from year to year. This lack of stability in the plant populations is a common feature of restoration attempts and may be linked to still high nutrient levels in the water, particularly of nitrate. Ormesby Broad has quite low nitrogen input, whilst Cockshoot Broad receives nitrate-rich Bure water several times each winter when floods circumvent the dam that otherwise isolates it from the river.

Reintroduction of fish

The next step is to reintroduce a fish population, which ideally should have predators such as pike and a range of native fish, but not introduced species such as common carp. Carp are not the problem in Broadland that they are elsewhere, where large stocks have been introduced to shallow lakes for angling, and have ruined the structure and diversity of the system by acting as forward switches. There are few carp in Broadland waters, and it would be undesirable to increase the number. Fortunately, under present climatic conditions, carp do not breed easily in Britain. It is generally too cool.

In the Broadland restorations so far there has been no deliberate restocking of fish after biomanipulation. The residual populations have been allowed to redevelop in Ormesby Broad, and the instability of the plant community in Cockshoot Broad has meant that this stage has not yet been contemplated. However, experience elsewhere suggests that a community of pike, perch, rudd and tench is most appropriate to stable plant-dominated shallow lakes, with roach and bream also normally present but not dominant, as they are in turbid waters. Bream, like carp, can be damaging to establishing plant populations because they forage in the bottom sediment.

Monitoring

The final step in such lake restorations is to monitor the results carefully and learn new lessons about what are quite complex systems. There are almost always complicating factors and the general strategy outlined above was developed on the basis of experience in hindsight. In general, in restorations of shallow lakes in Europe, results have been very good where nutrient levels were low, a residual plant population remained, and almost all fish were removed. They have been most disappointing where nutrient levels remained comparatively high, plants had disappeared entirely or fish stocks remained substantial. One Broadland restoration, at Ormesby Broad, is in the first category, the other, at Cockshoot Broad, perhaps in the second.

The scale of the problem

Lakes are parts of river systems and rivers are inseparable from their catchments. If restoration of the Broads has been slow, it is partly because the scale on which it has been tackled is too limited. Although it is possible to do something about a small lake, if it can be isolated from its catchment, it is rarely a long-term stable solution. There are many ways in which its ecology is interdependent on that of surrounding wetlands and adjacent water bodies as well as on the nature, the amount and the seasonal distribution of the water delivered to it.

One small lake in the Netherlands, called Zwemlust, which had been restored from a turbid plankton-dominated state to clear water with aquatic plants for a few years, suddenly reverted to turbid water in the late 1990s. A build-up of coot, from the ditches of the surrounding, largely drained land, concentrating on an attractive new food source, overgrazed the plants and switched the lake back to a turbid state again. Formerly such lakes, like the Broads, were part of whole river-floodplain systems where the larger-scale availability of food and habitat precluded such concentrations of birds. The potential restoration of the Broads and rivers is thus best looked at in terms of the river catchment units – the Ant, the Thurne, the Muck Fleet, the Bure, the Yare and the Waveney. A geographic tour will reveal the possibilities and problems.

The River Ant

The Ant (Fig. 16.11) is a small river, with a catchment that is less intensively farmed than those of the Yare and Bure, but more than that of the Thurne, lying close by, to the east. In one stretch it was straightened and deepened to form a canal in the late nineteenth century, with locks at North Walsham and Honing. The valley floor is largely of fen, carr and reedswamp, with the result that the high nitrate concentrations draining from the distal arable lands of the catchment are much reduced, though still significant. A waste-water treatment works serving Stalham discharges effluent, and there is also some food factory effluent entering through the Smallburgh Brook. Much of the phosphate has been removed from these by precipitation and the nutrient loads entering the floodplain stretch are now lower than formerly.

Tributaries, including the former Stalham and Sutton Broads, which are now confined to channels through the infilled reedswamp and fen, join the river before it enters one of the larger of the Broads, Barton, still bordered by

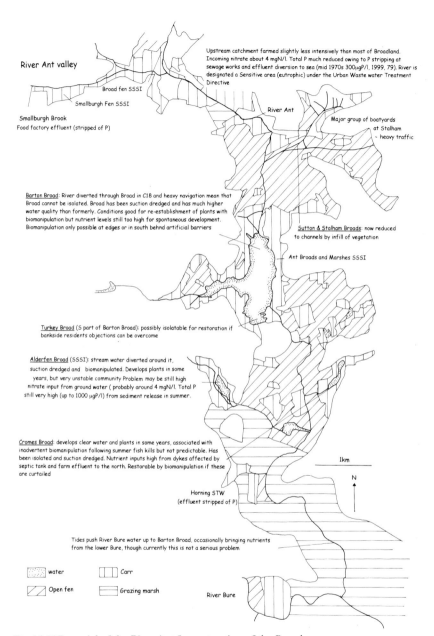

Fig. 16.11 Potential of the River Ant for restoration of the Broads.

extensive wetlands on most sides. The river once flowed around the Broad in a channel still discernible from the pattern of the ditch system in the Catfield fens to the east of the Broad, and in the winding line of the Parish boundary. This immediately puts the Broad at a disadvantage for local restoration, for it is now part of the main navigation of the River Ant, with large boat yards situated at Stalham.

Below Barton Broad, at the edges of the valley, are two small Broads, Alderfen and Cromes. These also are flanked by wetland, though it is limited in extent. The river then becomes embanked in its lower reaches and the wetland has been drained to grazing marsh, the topmost fringe of the extensive sward that reaches down to Halvergate and Yarmouth.

Barton Broad figured prominently in the early thinking that the solution to the problems of the Broads lay primarily in the reduction of phosphorus in its inflows. The loads from the point sources have been reduced to about a third since the early 1980s and there has been a parallel decrease in the concentrations (Fig. 12.7) but there has been no return to clear water or plant colonisation of the Broad.

Further reduction of the phosphorus supply by removal of sediment thus was apparently a sensible strategy, though experience elsewhere is that there is inevitably sufficient supply left, after removal of what is practicable, to make rather little ultimate difference. A major dredging programme has been carried out at Barton Broad in an attempt to reduce the internal supply, as well as to deepen the water to improve the navigation. The Broad is now approaching a state where a restoration of aquatic plants is likely to be successful if biomanipulation could be carried out. Nitrate levels are modest in the upstream river (3–4 milligrams nitrogen per litre) and become reduced by denitrification as water moves into the Broad. A substantial plant population in the northern part of this large Broad would cause further reduction so that stable, diverse communities could develop in the southern section.

Alas, biomanipulation of such a large Broad, on a major navigation route, is extremely difficult; in fact currently impossible. There is also the risk of a new forward switch as tides sometimes push saline water up the river and into the Broad. Salinity has not yet reached the sorts of levels that would threaten *Daphnia*, but rising sea levels and greater tidal surges might do this in the future.

Alderfen Broad and Cromes Broad lie on small tributaries. That serving Alderfen Broad was diverted easily around the Broad in 1979 and that action gave rise to temporary euphoria when a modest crop of hornwort developed. Its fortunes fluctuated and in some years it dwindled and algae grew to abundance (Fig. 12.10). Phosphorus concentrations were high, despite isolation, because of release from the sediment and, despite sediment removal in 1994, they have remained high. The lake has also suffered fish-kills as well as deliberate experimental biomanipulation. It still has a fluctuating plant population, but it is becoming increasingly difficult, with such a diverse management history, to sort out cause and effect.

Cromes Broad, isolated from the river in 1992, has had better fortunes following sediment removal in 1988, but it is equally difficult to say why because it has not been extensively monitored. It has not been biomanipulated, but there is anecdotal evidence of summer fish-kills in 1999, which may indicate that the fish community has been subject to similar events in previous years. These may have reduced the fish community sufficiently for plants to have become more securely established and able to cope with intervening years of greater fish survival. The plant community is again more or less confined to hornwort, but the fish community, though it fluctuates greatly, may be less dominated by zooplanktivorous fish at present than in the past. It has a greater proportion of piscivores such as perch and pike, which are associated elsewhere with maintenance of clear water conditions. One problem, however, is that drains to the north may still be bringing in large loads of nutrients from farms and septic tanks. They were extremely rich in phosphate and ammonium when monitored in the 1980s.

The dykes deep in Reedham Marsh, the wetlands to the west of the River Ant, have a rather more diverse flora. They are isolated by tortuousness and distance from the river and well protected by wide fens from the agricultural land and, towards the centre of the area, have very low nutrient levels and rich plant communities. In contrast, the three Broads considered here, Barton, Alderfen and Cromes, are all still subject to close influence from diffuse sources of both nitrogen and phosphorus. Much has been done in attempts to restore the Ant system, but the intentions are dogged by an inability to tackle the wider problems of the catchment's diffuse nutrient sources, an underlying theme throughout Broadland. There are, too, the problems of biomanipulating a Broad such as Barton, particularly the internal problems of compromising between ecological restoration and navigation, which will prove to be a second overarching theme.

The Thurne and its Broads

The medieval bridge at Potter Heigham (Fig. 16.12) forms a notional gateway to the Broads of the River Thurne (Fig. 16.13). It is low and narrow, infinitely more attractive than the ugly new concrete bridge that crosses the river to its north, and restricts the flow upstream of tidal water from the lower reaches of the Thurne and the Bure to the Thurne Broads. This is important, for the

Fig. 16.12 Potter Heigham bridge forms something of a gateway to the Thurne system, probably minimising, with its narrow openings, inputs upstream of nutrient-rich river water on high tides.

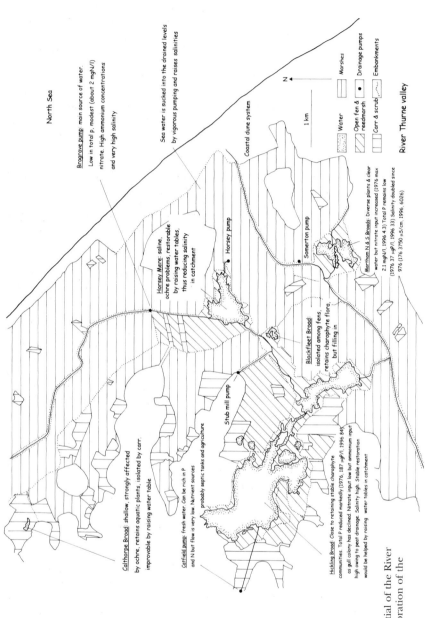

North Sea

Brograve pump: main source of water. Low in total p, modest (about 2 mgN/l) nitrate. High ammonium concentrations and very high salinity

Sea water is sucked into the drained levels by vigorous pumping and raises salinities

N ←

Coastal dune system

1 km

Water

Open fen & reedmarsh

Carr & scrub

Marshes

Drainage pumps

Embankments

River Thurne valley

Horsey pump

Somerton pump

Horsey Mere: saline, ochre problems, restorable by raising water tables, thus reducing salinity in catchment

Blackfleet Broad: isolated among fens, retains charophyte flora, but filling in

Martham N & S Broads: Diverse plants & clear water but nitrate input increased (1976 low (1976 37 µgP/l, 1996 33) Salinity doubled since 976 (176 3750 µS/cm. 1996. 6026)

Calthorpe Broad: shallow, strongly affected by ochre, retains aquatic plants, isolated by carr, improvable by raising water table

Catfield pump: fresh water. Can be rich in P and N but flow is very low. Nutrient sources probably septic tanks and agriculture

Stub mill pump

Hickling Broad: Close to retaining stable charophyte communities. Total P reduced markedly (1976, 187, 1987, µgP/l, 1996 84) as gull colony has declined. Nitrate input low but ammonium input high owing to peat drainage. Salinity high. Stable restoration would be helped by raising water tables in catchment

Fig. 16.13 Potential of the River Thurne for restoration of the Broads.

Bure water is rich in nutrients whilst the Broads of the Thurne remain the least eutrophicated of all Broadland. There are no sewage treatment works discharging into the system above Potter Heigham bridge, though a modest works, serving Ludham, discharges into Womack Water, a tributary three kilometres below the bridge. Some, but probably not much, of this water may move upstream on the tide. To the north-west and west the catchment is of arable land, but the area is small, and the bulk of it lies to the north and east, bordered by the North Sea, and is mostly of low-lying grazing pasture. An area close to Horsey Mere and Martham Broad has been more intensively cultivated for cereals in recent years, however. Most of the water entering the main Broads, Martham, Horsey Mere and Hickling, is pumped from these levels up into the waterway, which is held in by embankments (Fig. 16.13).

A very small Broad, Calthorpe (Fig. 16.14), lies isolated to the north, surrounded by alder carr, and is heavily vegetated with yellow water-lilies and some remaining submerged plants. It is a good example of the process of filling-in by encroachment of vegetation and now has very little open water. Robert Gurney, who once owned it, records in his diaries from the 1920s that he spent much time trying to clear out lilies to delay the process and maintain open water.

In 1970, following earlier increases in the intensity of drainage of the adjacent level, Calthorpe Broad became very acid (pH 3) as peat in its surrounding wetlands dried and oxidised, producing sulphuric acid and ochre (Chapter 14). When heavy rain washed more acid into the Broad that winter, there was a fish-kill and deaths of three species of freshwater mussel (*Anodonta cygnea, Anodonta anatina, Unio pictorum*) that had been common, and of toad eggs and frogspawn the following spring. There was a similar event in the dry year of 1976 and pH values now frequently fall to 5.5, whereas previously they had always been above 6. Though Calthorpe Broad is still dominated by plants, it has fewer species than previously, and is dosed with chalk from time to time to counteract the acidity. This is a palliative measure; the fundamental solution would have to be the raising of the water table.

Close to Calthorpe Broad, the New Waxham Cut, a long, straightened channel, flows between embankments and receives water pumped from a swathe of land separated from the sea by a thin line of dunes, which its course parallels. It turns south into Horsey Mere, bringing with it water that is heavily loaded with ochre and salt (Fig. 12.23). The salinity in Horsey Mere rises to about 20 per cent of sea water, much higher than it was earlier this century. What the salinity might have been prior to that, when the Thurne system was an estuary discharging through what is now the Hundred stream close to Martham Broad, is not known.

The Broads in this area have the familiar characteristics of peat or clay pits and could only have been excavated following blocking off of the Thurne estuary at the outlet to the present Hundred stream. The picturesque restored Horsey Mill (Plate 17), close to Horsey Mere (Fig. 16.15), presides over a Broad that no longer has the clarity of former times, but which is turbid with colloidal ochre and phytoplankton. The net flow from Horsey Mere is through Meadow Dyke and into a Broad, called Heigham Sound, which is effectively a widening of the river. Water is ponded back in the system on the rising tide that forces water from Horsey Mere into Hickling Broad, and sometimes vice versa in summer. On the falling tide, the flow from Meadow Dyke into Heigham

Fig. 16.14 Calthorpe
Broad lies at the top
end of the Thurne
system, in a peat fen
that is relatively base
poor. Drainage of
the land to the east
has reduced water
levels around it and
resulted in severe
ochre and acid pro-
duction. In 1970, pH
fell to 3 and fish
were killed. Because
drainage in the area
has remained
intense, the Broad
(upper panel) con-
tinues to be vulnera-
ble especially in dry
summers and pH
often fell to 3 or 4 in
adjacent dykes in the peat
in the 1970s (central
panel). The marginal dyke
receives water from the
upland and is, to some
extent, protected (lower
panel). In the late 1970s,
following dry summers in
1977 and 1978, ground
chalk was added to the
Broad to neutralise the acid
and improve conditions for
the freshwater community.
This is just a treatment of
symptoms, however, and the
Broad no longer has the
plant and invertebrate community it formerly had; the
cause remains, its solution
ultimately resting in the
nature of agriculture in the
catchment.

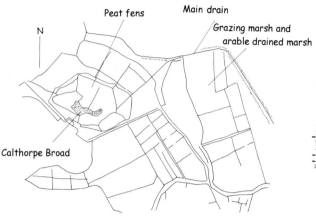

Calthorpe Broad

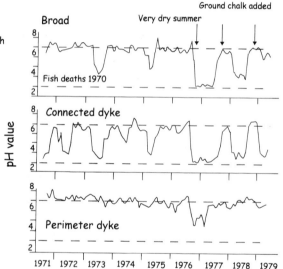

Sound and down to the Thurne can often be seen from a boat because of the
different colours of the Meadow Dyke water and that upstream of it at White
Slea and in Hickling Broad.

Some water comes directly into Hickling Broad, through Catfield Dyke, from
the catchment to the west, and is not saline, but the flow is low for the area is
small. It is in general richer in nutrients, however, than that coming in from
Horsey Mere. The net effect of these inputs is that Hickling Broad is much less
well flushed than Horsey Mere, and saline, but at around 10 per cent of sea
water, less so than the Mere. The recent history of Hickling Broad has been
very dramatic. It has changed from a clear-water Broad earlier this century to

Fig. 16.15 Horsey Mill presides over a Broad, Horsey Mere, which suffers from high salinity and ochre problems. It is, however, potentially restorable through a move back to high water table pasture agriculture in its catchment.

a turbid one between 1970 and the late 1990s, a very clear one in 1998 and 1999 and in 2000 is turbid again. The story of these events is intricate.

The self-restoration of Hickling Broad

The eutrophication problem that Hickling Broad has suffered was due to the development of the large roost of black-headed gulls described in Chapter 12. This problem has not affected Martham Broad, which is isolated at the top of the River Thurne. Martham is one of the three Broads (the others being Upton Broad in the Bure valley and Blackfleet, close to Meadow Dyke) that still retain very clear water and communities of charophytes and the rare holly-weed. Blackfleet and Upton Broads are both isolated from river flows by extensive fens.

In Martham, as in Upton Broad (there is little information on Blackfleet Broad), the phytoplankton is likely to be limited by phosphorus. These Broads have concentrations much lower than 50 micrograms of phosphorus per litre and they are positioned, in the alternative states scheme (Fig. 12.17), in the space at the upper left where nutrient concentrations are low enough to give unique dominance of plants. There is simply not enough phosphorus or nitrogen to support sufficient phytoplankton or periphyton to create a problem for the plants. Hickling Broad and Horsey Mere, however, although they are close to both Martham and Blackfleet Broads, have undergone major changes.

The water pumped into them, through the Waxham New Cut from the Brograve Level, rose in salinity in the middle part of the twentieth century as pumping intensity increased. The nutrient contribution from the gulls also rose and resulted in the events related in Chapter 12, including loss of most of the plant biomass (Fig.12.24).

The symptoms were at their worst in the 1970s, but there was continuing change in the 1980s. The plants never entirely disappeared and clumps of three species could always be found even in the 1970s – fennel pondweed, spiked water-milfoil and mare's tail. Hickling Broad and Horsey Mere are linked by Meadow Dyke and, with the daily pulse of the tide, water can be moved between them upstream and downstream, especially when the flows pumped in from the catchment are low or lacking in summer. The chemical effects of the gulls could thus be transferred to Horsey Mere even though the gulls generally did not roost there.

Fig. 16.16 Neomysis integer, a mysid shrimp versatile in both its salinity and food requirements, has played an important role in the changing ecology of Hickling Broad.

Fig. 16.17 Hickling Broad changed greatly in an almost cyclic fashion in the twentieth century. This and Figs 16.19 and 16.22 summarise the relationships between the main components of the system. This figure shows the workings of the system as it would have been seen by the Reverend Bennett at the turn of the nineteenth century (upper). The lower part shows it as it slowly changed until the middle of the twentieth century through build up of the gull roost, and a small intensification of agriculture. This resulted in a slight rise in salinity, which probably had a negligible effect. Based on Bales et al. (1993).

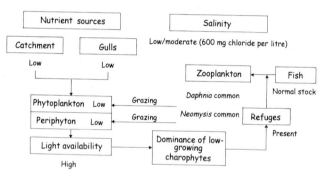

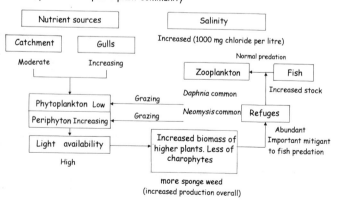

In the 1980s there was a small but progressive recovery of the plants, which accelerated in the 1990s. This recovery was associated with a reduction in the phosphorus concentration of the water. The gulls were decreasing in numbers, apparently as the local waste tip near Martham village was covered over and provided less daytime attraction for them. The plants may have been able to persist because one of the common salt-tolerant crustaceans in the Thurne, a mysid shrimp, *Neomysis integer* (Fig. 16.16), is an omnivore, capable of scraping periphyton from the surfaces of the plants and thus improving the amount of light able to reach their surfaces. This shrimp has been very abundant in the Broad, following possible setbacks caused by the *Prymnesium* toxins, to which it is vulnerable. Figure 16.17 shows the relationships within the Broad prior to and during the 1970s.

The 1980s saw a progressive extension of the area covered by plants in Hickling Broad and even of some charophyte species and hollyweed. The water remained brown, despite a decrease in the phytoplankton, because of the ochre both in suspension and adherent also to the mucilaginous wall of the dominant blue-green alga, *Aphanothece clathrata*. Conditions were clearly improving, however. The gulls continued to decline, but there was still a substantial reserve of phosphorus available in the surface sediments in the form of gull excreta yet to decompose. The early 1990s saw further increases in the area of plant cover in Hickling Broad (Fig. 16.18), less in Horsey Mere, possibly because of the greater ochre problem, possibly because nitrogen levels are higher there, it being closer to the catchment sources. The plant densities became great enough for the local sailing club to have difficulty getting through the beds in summer and the weed had to be cut – for the first time since the early 1970s.

Fig. 16.18 In the 1980s and 1990s, Hickling Broad began to recover its plant populations (left). In 1998, recovery had reached a stage by which charophytes, particularly the rare *Chara intermedia*, had come to dominate. Based on Bales et al. (1993) and Eaton (1999).

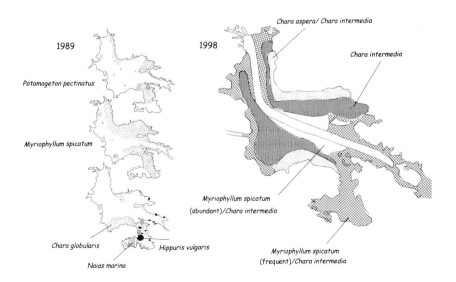

Fig. 16.19 In the
1970s (upper),
Hickling Broad
changed greatly.
Nutrients from
the gull roost
reached a peak,
agricultural
changes had
increased the
nineteenth-centu-
ry salinity three-
fold. The gulls
not only provided
inorganic nutri-
ents, but their
guano was a rich
source of organic
compounds that
may, with the ris-
ing nutrients and
salinity, have stim-
ulated the large
populations of
the toxic phyto-
plankter,
*Prymnesium
parvum.* This alga
caused fish-kills
and possibly also
kills of large
invertebrates such
as the mysid
shrimp, *Neomysis
integer.* The high
salinity removed
daphnids and the

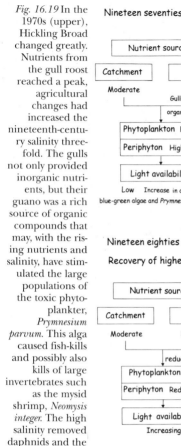
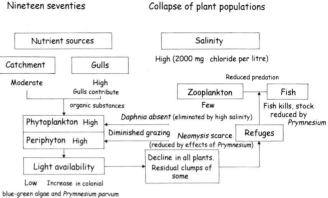
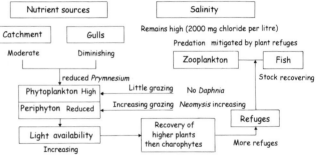

consequences were much less grazing on phytoplankton and periphyton. Turbidity became
    high and most of the plants disappeared. However, as the gull roosts and their imported
    nutrients declined in the 1980s and 1990s (lower) the *Neomysis* recovered, the algal crops
    began to fall and the plants slowly returned. Daphnids remained very scarce because salinity
        had not changed, however, and the water remained quite turbid, the plants benefiting
            mostly from a reduction in their periphyton burden. Based on Bales et al. (1993).

No management had been carried out in the Broad or catchment that can
explain these events. They simply followed from the decline in the gull roost
and movement of the birds elsewhere, perhaps because of the closure of the
waste tip where they had been feeding, but this is unlikely to be the entire
cause. The excreta of the gulls we had studied in the 1970s included parts of
contraceptive sheaths which suggested they had been feeding also at sewage
treatment works and they feed on the land also. Many charismatic photographs show gulls following the plough. Bird flocks sometimes show changed
behaviour for no obvious reason and the birds now roost on Breydon Water
and the sea.

At this stage it seemed likely that Hickling Broad would stay a somewhat tur-

Fig. 16.20 In the 1990s, the populations of charophytes steadily increased in Hickling Broad, culminating in dominance over much of its area by a rare species, *Chara intermedia*, in 1998 and 1999. Despite its rarity, it grew very vigorously in the Broad.

bid water with beds of vascular plants such as the water-milfoil and pondweeds, for *Daphnia* remained scarce and grazing pressure on the remaining phytoplankton low (Fig. 16.19). The plants benefited from grazing over their surfaces by *Neomysis*, but any major increase in the clarity of the water seemed unlikely as long as the salinity remained high enough to exclude *Daphnia*. Reduction in salinity would have meant changing the agricultural regime of the catchment, where it had been converted to arable agriculture, and raising the water tables. There was no prospect of this.

Rather surprisingly, therefore, in 1998, the waters cleared and huge growths of charophytes appeared, including a predominant *Chara intermedia*, but also several other species, and this situation persisted in 1999 (Fig. 16.20). *Chara intermedia*, though no shrinking violet, for it grows vigorously, is nonetheless a very rare species, growing in only a handful of other locations in the UK and apparently nowhere else. The annual flow-through of water must have flushed out the critical last tranche of gull-provided phosphorus that had been left in the sediments and brought nutrient concentrations low enough to give the charophytes the advantages they apparently have at very low nutrient levels. The sheer biomass built up may also have reduced the phosphorus levels further for they dipped below 50 micrograms per litre in the summers of 1998 and 1999 (Fig. 16.21). Events may be tentatively put together as in Figure 16.22.

The renewed clarity of the water is something of a mystery, for the brown ochre colloids are still being formed in the catchment and still enter the system and colour the water in Horsey Mere and in winter in Hickling Broad. Charophytes, however, produce organic substances that may suppress algal growth and that may also flocculate fine particles. Hickling Broad, without benefit of learned opinion or practical intervention, had recovered to close to

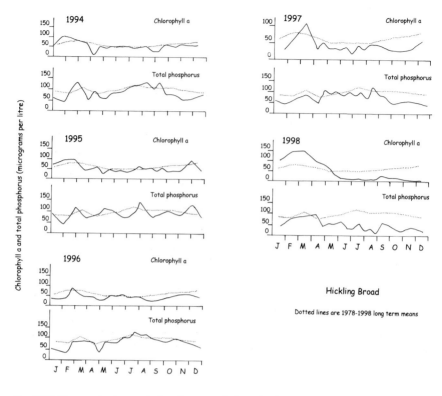

Fig. 16.21 Changes in the total phosphorus and phytoplankton chlorophyll *a* concentrations in Hickling Broad between 1994 and 1998. Data are shown in each year in comparison with the long-term mean (1978-98). The marked fall in concentrations of both chlorophyll *a* and total phosphorus in the summers of 1997 and particularly 1998 is clearly shown. Data from the registers of the Environment Agency, published in Eaton (1999).

the state it had been in the late nineteenth century when the Reverend Bennett described its great swards of charophytes.

There was no universal rejoicing, however. The conservation bodies, English Nature and the Norfolk Wildlife Trust, were extremely pleased. The members of the local sailing club were not. A European Directive, the Habitats and Species Directive, had been passed in 1992, which required the Government to schedule sites of great conservation interest as Special Areas of Conservation (SAC), for which a target state for maintenance or improvement had to be set. Hickling Broad had not finally been scheduled as an SAC, but it was on a list of sites awaiting this distinction and was treated as if it had been finally scheduled. Its target state was a clear-water lake with predominant charophytes and this had been achieved, with the additional piquancy of a very rare species.

The conservation status of Special Areas of Conservation is to be regarded as pre-eminent in the face of possible development. The conservation bodies were thus opposed when the Broads Authority, as the navigation authority, proposed to cut a substantial area of the charophytes in the centre of the Broad

1998 and 1999
Dominance by tall Chara

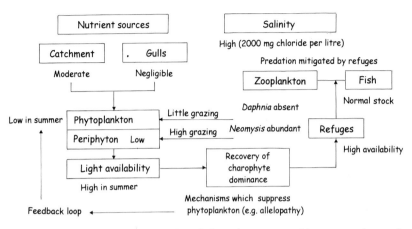

Fig. 16.22 In 1998 and 1999, Hickling Broad charophyte communities recovered strongly. The nutrient source from the gull populations was by then negligible and the charophytes, which had been recovering slowly in the 1990s, gained dominance over vascular (higher) plants. The Broad has not yet quite attained the conditions of the late nineteenth century (Fig. 16.17) with low-growing charophyte species. The current charophytes are rank and aggressive, perhaps because nutrient levels from the pumped water are higher than they would have been then (nitrate and ammonium concentrations are relatively large) and partly because salinity levels remain high. Daphnids have not reappeared.

to permit competitive sailing. The sailing club had blossomed in the years of open water between the 1970s and 1990s and the sailors had become accustomed to no impediment to their progress. The charophytes were very much in the way and there were strong demands for the cutting. English Nature and the Norfolk Wildlife Trust, which owns the land surrounding the Broad, but which do not have responsibility for the navigation, feared that cutting might permanently damage the charophytes and switch the Broad back to a more turbid state with mostly vascular plants. The Royal Society for the Protection of Birds feared that the increases in coot, gadwall and other herbivorous birds, which depended on the plants, especially in the winter when charophytes persist as perennials, would be reversed.

The Broads Authority was caught in the dilemma of having to fulfil its duties under the Broads Act as the navigation authority and its duties under the Habitats Directive to achieve the target status for a Special Area of Conservation. Its constitution demands it be all things to all men. Clearly this was impossible, especially with a strong Navigation Committee. In such circumstances the Habitats Directive demands an appropriate enquiry by an independent panel. The panel, in 1999, decided that a lesser regime of cutting than had been proposed was unlikely to cause permanent damage and was necessary to assess the effects of cutting so that future decisions could be made on a rational basis.

An area was cut that might allow sailing races (though in fact was not, in the end, very convenient), but would not affect most of the *Chara* beds, and the results were that such limited cutting, and perhaps rather more, would not seriously jeopardise the state of the Broad. The tensions that the issue has raised, though, are indicative of the continuing problem of trying to maintain the multiple uses of Broadland, a position that is not often possible whilst also retaining high quality of use in any respect. Multiple use means universal mediocrity.

The Hickling story is not yet over, however. In 2000 the *Chara* grew much less well and most peculiarly, the pondweed and milfoil appeared to be dying. They had survived 20 years of previous turbid conditions. There was also a small resurgence in growth of *Prymnesium parvum* (Chapter 12) which had caused fish-kills in the 1970s. Cutting of the plants for navigation reasons was not necessary and tensions subsided, but the circumstances of plant decline in 2000 are odd and not easily explained by the natural changes in the environment of the Broad.

If a stable charophyte community is to be retained in Hickling Broad and if Horsey Mere is to be restored to clear water, the solution probably now lies in a reduction in pumping and a rise in the water table in the catchment. This will have the multiple effects of reducing ochre formation, reducing the input of nutrients from the catchment and decreasing the salinity. At present, neither Broad has cladoceran zooplankton capable of grazing phytoplankton very efficiently, though formerly, when salinities were lower (perhaps a third of present values) Hickling Broad, at least, certainly did. The evidence comes from the meticulous field notes kept by Robert Gurney and preserved in the Castle Museum in Norwich.

Martham Broad

Martham Broad, or Broads (Fig.16.13) if you care to distinguish the section north of the dyke from that to the south, is well known and probably the most diverse of the Broads in its plant populations. It is favoured by having a small catchment and by lying at the top end of the system where it is better flushed by water draining through gravity from slightly higher land to the east and south. Like Hickling Broad and Horsey Mere, it has no sewage treatment works in its catchment. It has, however, doubled in salinity from around half that in Hickling Broad (1,000 milligrams chloride per litre) in the 1970s to similar values (1,800 milligrams per litre) from the 1980s.

This increase in salinity arose because the owners of the nearby land in the Somerton Level decided to deep drain and plough the former grazing marshes in the early 1980s. The result was an increase in ochre as well as salinity, for the Level has frequently been flooded by the sea and has sulphate-rich soils. The ochre, although it precipitated phosphate from the water and reduced total phosphorus concentrations to 20 micrograms per litre, unprecedented for modern Broadland, threatened to smother the plants and invertebrates. Negotiations between the Internal Drainage Board and the then Nature Conservancy Council led to relocation of the main pump from above the Broad to the Hundred stream, effectively now parallel with it, and a weir was installed to contain the ochre, which is periodically dredged out. The increased salinity remains, however, because of tidal back flow of some of the Hundred stream water and because a smaller pump still operates above the

Broad. The Broad has retained its quality, however, and even Somerton Dyke, above the Broad, is rich in plants, despite its popularity for boat mooring. Conservation of water and ecosystem quality in Martham Broad needs no particular action, merely protection of its present favours.

The Muck Fleet

The third of the smaller rivers of Broadland and also, like the Ant and Thurne, a tributary of the River Bure, is the Muck Fleet, which discharges six kilometres below the confluence of the Thurne and the Bure. It has a sluice where it enters the Bure so that water cannot pass up it on the tide from the Bure, and is headed by a complex of Broads: Ormesby North and South, (Little) Rollesby, Lily and Filby, collectively called the Trinity Broads (Fig. 16.23). They receive water from a largely arable catchment that contains several villages. The villages are served by a sewerage system that removes effluent to well outside their catchment, so there is no problem with point sources of phosphorus, apart from a few septic tanks serving isolated cottages and farms.

The water quality is not as poor as that of the Broads on the main rivers, but it is not without nutrient problems, the origins of which have been difficult to pinpoint. Ormesby and Rollesby Broads, the larger of the group, have generally clear water and have retained some aquatic plant communities. These Broads are slightly deeper than most others so light penetration to the bottom is lower than in shallower waters and it is the combination of agricultural eutrophication and greater depth that disfavours the plants. Ormesby Broad has been biomanipulated, which improved the water clarity and extent of the plant populations considerably.

Lily Broad now has rather few lilies and quite a large phytoplankton population and Filby Broad is also phytoplankton-dominated. Filby is hemmed in by a number of houses and a village and may receive more septic tank effluent than the others in the group, whilst the small stream entering Lily Broad from arable land with some cottages is also poor in quality. Ormesby Broad, which is also used as a water supply for Yarmouth, is at the head of the system with few houses very close and this correlates well with its having the best water quality of the group.

There are well-developed reed fringes around most of the group and from time to time Ormesby has become very clear, in years when fish recruitment has perhaps been poor and *Daphnia* populations have increased. The combination of circumstances in this group is such that, with some attention to sources of nutrients, substantial improvement could be possible. Some septic tanks may leak to the surface waters more than necessary if they were functioning at their best, and could be improved. An extension of the alder carrs that fringe most of the inflowing streams into more substantial buffer zones, and ensuring that the water diffuses among the wetlands rather than passing directly through, could also help. Biomanipulation has made a considerable difference to Ormesby Broad and this suggests that the nutrient threshold for making the improvements stable is not too far below the present state.

The River Bure

The Bure is the epitome of the Broadland system for the holidaymaker, and a nightmare for ecological restoration. It is a large system (Fig. 16.24), though smaller than those of the Yare and Waveney, draining a large catchment of

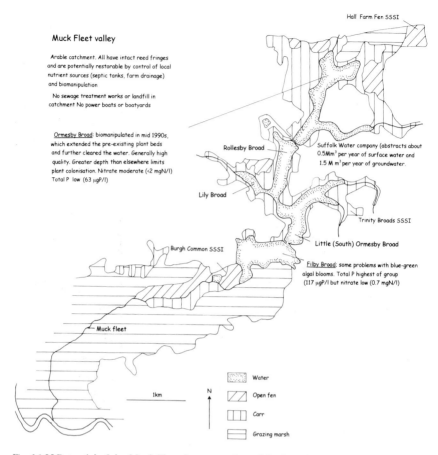

Fig. 16.23 Potential of the Muck Fleet for restoration of the Broads.

intensive arable agriculture. It bears several substantial villages and small towns – Aylsham, Buxton, Coltishall, Wroxham and Hoveton and Acle – all with sewage treatment works discharging to the river. It is tidal to around Wroxham and bleak between its embankments in the lower reaches, which are bordered by grazing marsh. It has many Broads, with all but Burntfen and Upton linked to the river by wide dykes, mostly open to navigation. And it is the most popular area for tourists and boating, with attractive wooded sides in the upper reaches and the amenities of villages, pubs and churches in the middle, where the Broads are situated. It also has poor water quality and is plankton-dominated almost throughout.

Upton Broad is the best placed. It is one of the few Broads to retain reasonably clear water and an aquatic plant community containing charophytes and hollyweed and is protected by thick belts of carr and fen. It is connected by a dyke system to the surrounding fens and receives some water from the upland arable catchment to the south, but it is isolated from the river by a thick belt of grazing marshes separated from the fens by an embankment. Some

River Bure valley

Catchment large and intensively farmed (nitrate winter values up to 9mgN/l) Many small STW Phosphate removed at larger STW. Total P reduced from 200µgP/l in the 1980s to less than 90 in 1996. Designated a Sensitive area (eutrophic).

Burntfen Broad: receives water from nutrient-rich stream (septic tanks, farm drainage) but has residual plant population. Receives main river water rarely on high tides but easily isolatable by a one-way sluice. Potentially restorable by local nutrient control and biomanipulation

Ranworth & Malthouse Broads: Malthouse Broad is heavily navigated and not isolatable. Ranworth, although closed to boats, is difficult to isolate because of large tidal changes (15cm) and shots of downstream nutrient rich water are frequently injected. Total P levels have been reduced a little but remain high (1980, 180 µgP/l. 1996 130). Nitrate about 4 mgN/l because of upstream and downstream supplies. Not restorable on an individual basis

Hudsons Bay/Hoveton Great Broad: potentially restorable by isolation and biomanipulation. Not navigated and not fished. Phosphorus high in summer owing to sediment release but overall mean now much reduced (100µgP/l) compared with 1980 (300 µgP/l). Nitrate high (up to 5 mgN/l) but likely to decline on isolation due to denitrification

Hoveton Little (Blackhorse) Broad: western part (Pound End) has been suction dredged and isolated and temporarily improved by biomanipulation. Nutrient levels still high. Main Broad widely used for navigation and not restorable on an individual basis

Upstream movement of water from the lower river and Breydon Water on very high tides containing effluent from distant sewage works. Evidence of slowly increasing salinity since at least the 1950s owing to rising sea levels and increased tidal penetration

Upton Broad: High quality owing to isolation at edge of grazing marshes and protective fringe of carr. Clear water, charophytes and hollyweed. Total P is low (1980 29 µgP/l. 1996 37) Moderate nitrate (max 1980 1.7 mgN/l. 1996 1.6). One of only three Broads remaining close to pre-C19 conditions.

Cockshoot Broad: isolated, suction dredged and biomanipulated. Restoration has been successful but unstable owing to bird damage to plants, and still high nitrate concentrations owing to overtopping of dam by river water in floods Phosphorus levels high owing to release from sediments despite dredging

South Walsham Broad: heavily navigated and subject to high tide injection of downstream nutrient rich water Also received effluent from a small STW. Very high nutrient concentrations (Total P 250 µgP/l maximum nitrate 4 mgN/l. Not restorable on an individual basis

Belaugh Broad: suction dredged, well flushed. Phytoplankton low and submerged plants present

Bridge Broad: a widening of the river, not individually restorable

Decoy Broad: potentially restorable by isolation and biomanipulation. Max nitrate around 4 mgN/l. Lies in Bure Broads and Marshes NNR and is not navigated. Isolation would need to be sufficient to cope with winter floods and angling club may object to biomanipulation

Snapes Water: capable of restoration by isolation from river and biomanipulation

Wroxham & Salhouse Broads: essentially widenings of the river because of short connecting dykes widened by boat erosion. Not individually restorable because not isolatable owing to heavy boat traffic and sailing club. Total P levels now <100 µgP/l compared with 170 µgP/l in 1980)

Water
Open fen
Carr
Grazing marsh

N

1 km

Fig. 16.24 Potential of the River Bure for restoration of the Broads.

additional nutrients reach it from the upland, but the problem can probably be contained by diffusing the water through the carrs rather than allowing free passage through the dykes. This might simply mean putting dams on the inflows to force the water out over the carr and allow the carr to act as a nutrient filter.

Cockshoot Broad is next in quality for it has been the subject of intensive research and experimental restoration for 20 years. The beginnings of this story were related in Chapter 12. When it was thought that nutrients alone were the problem in the Broads, Cockshoot Broad was dammed from the river and much of its sediment was removed. There was an immediate improvement; the water cleared and *Daphnia* were very abundant, but progressively they declined and the phytoplankton increased before aquatic plant populations could become well established. Lilies that had been planted flourished and hornwort also, especially in the area that had been the dyke, but not in the main basin to any extent. What appears to have happened is that the noise of the suction dredging had scared most fish out to the river and they had not been able to return because of the dam. There had thus been inadvertent biomanipulation as well as isolation from nutrient sources and this had led to the increase in *Daphnia* and the clearing of the water (Fig. 12.10).

The residual fish population, however, soon recovered. The *Daphnia*, lacking much refuge from the fish, were decimated and the phosphorus concentrations also increased as a result of release from the remaining sediment. In the winter of 1987/88 the fish were deliberately removed and the Broad immediately cleared again and remained clear because, each winter, for the next several years, fish that had persisted were removed. Plants grew, though not in great quantity except in the sheltered dyke area, and not in great diversity.

The reasons for this may be that they were unable to withstand the grazing of coot and other water birds and never exceeded the threshold that would allow them to establish and withstand grazing, and also that nutrient levels remained quite high. Much phosphorus was released from the sediment, shots of high-nitrate water reached the Broad from the river when the dam was bypassed by winter floods and the nitrogen supply from the remaining southern stream may have been substantial despite the carrs through which it passed.

The best plan for Cockshoot Broad would therefore seem to be to improve its relative isolation, to diffuse the inflow water from the southern stream more, to plant in a rather large inoculum of plants capable of growing rapidly enough to keep ahead of coot grazing, and to continue biomanipulation until this plant population is substantial. This, however, is a piecemeal solution that might maintain one rather small Broad in an interesting state, but does nothing for the greater problem of the river as a whole.

The wider Bure problem

Above Belaugh, the Bure is a river, for the rate of replacement of the water is rapid enough for there to be insufficient time for much phytoplankton to develop before the water passes downstream. It is clear and plants develop on the bottom. But below Belaugh there are almost no plants and a succession of phytoplankton communities develops. The Bure from that point 'works' not as a river with a set of associated lakes, but as a single convoluted lake. Understanding this is crucial to its restoration.

The individual Broads are like bays of this single lake and the river itself flows so slowly that it develops as much phytoplankton as any of its Broads and thus acts as the main basin of the lake. Water rich in nutrients enters at the upper end; tides pond the water back and cause it to be retained for quite long periods and also bring nutrients upstream from the sewage works in the lower reaches. There was also a small sewage treatment works discharging directly to South Walsham Broad.

As the valley widens below Wroxham, Broads start to appear – close to the river at first but more distant from it downstream. This effect of distance, and therefore of different degrees of isolation from the river, means that water is flushed out of the Bure Broads more rapidly upstream, but retained in them on average for longer downstream. This can be discovered by adding tracer dyes to the water and following their progressive dilution, or by doing the same thing by measuring chloride dilution after a shot of sea water has been injected following a storm surge tide. The different flushing times lead to different phytoplankton communities upstream and downstream (Fig. 16.25). Upstream, with water being retained only a month or less in the Broads in summer, diatoms tend to develop, with only a few blue-green algae. But in the downstream Broads (Fig. 16.25), with water held for several months in summer, filamentous blue-green algae come to dominate. This all has implications for restoration.

A restoration strategy on this part of Broadland will only work if it concerns the whole river. It is not possible to do the job Broad by Broad because it is not legally possible to isolate any of them from the river. There is a long-standing right of navigation on tidal waters and all but Belaugh Broad and possibly Burntfen Broad, which lies distant from the main river on a small side stream, are tidal. Boats regularly enter most, and those that are closed to boat entry from the river by their owners for all or part of the year (Hoveton Great Broad, Hudsons Bay, Hoveton Little Broad, Decoy Broad, Ranworth Broad) have substantial tidal exchange of water with the river. Isolation might prove illegal if challenged in the courts.

If the restoration strategy (Fig. 16.2) is applied, therefore, a major obstacle is in reducing the nutrient loading to the river as a whole. A start has been made on this by installation of chemical phosphorus stripping at four sewage treatment works, Briston, Aylsham, Coltishall and Belaugh, whilst at Acle the effluent is passed through a reed bed in an attempt to improve it, though not very successfully. The effluent from the small works at South Walsham Broad has also been diverted. The phosphorus stripping has been effective and has reduced total phosphorus concentrations in the upper reaches from more than 200 to less than 100 micrograms per litre in the last few years, but this is still too much to result in spontaneous return of clear water and aquatic plants. A substantial proportion of phosphorus must now come from agriculture (it was about 25 per cent in the 1980s, before phosphorus stripping) equivalent to about 50 micrograms of phosphorus per litre in terms of its contribution to the concentration. If current thinking about the importance of nitrogen is correct, the problem becomes formidable, for nitrate inputs from the catchment are very high.

In the lower reaches, the comparatively large works at Acle provides a lot of nutrients to the middle section of the river. Water is pushed back upstream and into South Walsham, Ranworth and Malthouse Broads, at least, from this

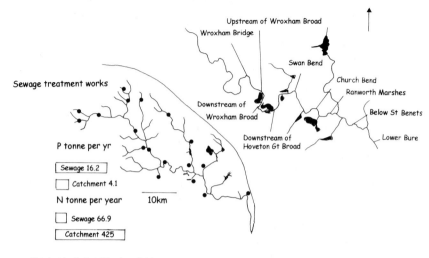

Nutrient budget at Wroxham Bridge

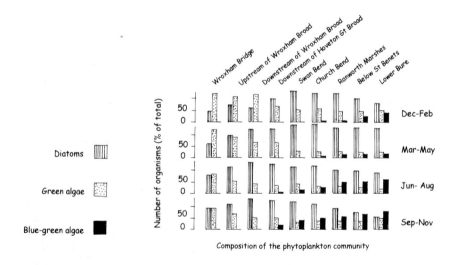

Composition of the phytoplankton community

Fig. 16.25 The algal communities of the River Bure change steadily down river, as do those of the associated Broads. As retention times increase (i.e flushing rates decrease), blue-green algae become more prominent, especially in the low flows of late summer and autumn. The River Bure is influenced by a large number of small sewage treatment works, and a few large ones. Before processes to remove phosphorus were installed at four of the latter, the nutrient budgets for nitrogen and phosphorus at Wroxham Bridge were as shown. Sewage effluent dominated the phosphorus budget and agriculture that for nitrogen. Currently effluent contributes probably around half of the phosphorus whilst the budget for nitrogen is unchanged. Based on Moss et al. (1984).

source, whilst the tides also bring the even more nutrient-rich water that the
Yare provides to Breydon Water into the lower reaches, and sometimes perhaps even the middle reaches of the Bure. Estuarine animals such as *Neomysis
integer* sometimes appear in winter as far up as Cockshoot Broad.

On the positive side, much of the Bure floodplain upstream is not built on
and could be reinstated with wetland to encourage nutrient removal and much
could be done about the many smaller sewage treatment works that discharge
to the tributary streams in the upper part of the Bure. However, ultimately,
nothing but a major change in land practices will restore the Bure to a stable
state of clear water. Prior to that, there are still problems with forward switches. Birds and boats, however, are the most obvious.

There are flocks of feral geese, especially greylag and Canada geese, which
graze the turf around Salhouse Broad to a lawn of garden height (Fig. 13.5)
and would certainly make inroads into any starting population of aquatic
plants in the shallows. This area of Broadland is also the most popular by far
for boats. Any restoration plan would have to restrict boat access temporarily,
Broad by Broad, whilst biomanipulation was carried out.

The big problem, however, is that biomanipulation would have to be done
on a huge scale more or less simultaneously unless all the Broads were separately isolated and closed to boat traffic for several years. In doing this, flushing times would be affected. If the nutrient loading is not reduced considerably, the potential for growth of large phytoplankton crops will remain and
with reduced flushing, blue-green algae will be favoured. Blue-green algae are
not readily consumed by *Daphnia*. One way around this problem, in principle,
is to isolate the Broads from fish entry by barriers with mesh windows (Fig.
16.26) that allow water but not even the smallest fish larvae to pass.

Under the present constraints, the Bure system will mostly remain a turbid

Fig. 16.26 Areas of large Broads can be isolated by mesh window barriers, which allow circulation of water and continued flushing, whilst preventing re-entry of fish after biomanipulation. This barrier was used to separate Pound End, part of Hoveton Little Broad. The mesh
windows, covered by stainless steel, are visible at the waterline. In tidal conditions they must
be frequently brushed clear of periphyton or they may clog and the subsequent difference
in water levels may result in undermining of the barrier by water currents.

phytoplankton-dominated system, except for a few showpiece sites: Cockshoot Broad, Pound End (a small part of Hoveton Little Broad that has been isolated) and perhaps Hoveton Great Broad and Decoy Broad. The latter two have not been sailed on for some time and might be amicably completely isolated and biomanipulated. Given the present difficulties of substantial nutrient reduction, especially of nitrate, perhaps these only can be restored and maintained, though with continuous intervention, as lakes with plant communities of low diversity – small victories in an unwinnable war.

The River Yare

The Yare is Broadland's biggest river, with its substantial tributaries, the Wensum and Tas and the smaller Tud, converging around Norwich, below which the main floodplain begins (Fig. 16.27). There are several Broads – Wheatfen, Surlingham, Brundall, Strumpshaw, Rockland, Buckenham and Hassingham – though all but Rockland are small. Of the others, filling-in by vegetation has reduced most to little more than widenings of the fen dyke system so that Brundall, Strumpshaw and Buckenham and Hassingham have been dredged out to increase the area of open water. The Broads cluster along a short stretch below Norwich, for the land beyond is very low lying and the clay deposits become thick not far below Rockland Broad. The river is then embanked and the valley floor covered by grazing marsh, which merges into that of the Halvergate triangle. The water is extremely rich in nutrients, largely because of the sewage treatment works at Whittlingham below Norwich. Effluent from the next largest towns of Dereham and Fakenham, which are far upstream on the Wensum, the main tributary of the Yare, is now phosphate-stripped in an attempt to improve that river, which is ecologically of perhaps the highest quality in Broadland.

The flow of the main Yare is high and the tidal rise considerable, so that retention times in the Broads are short. Phytoplankton has much less time to develop than in the Bure and Ant and Rockland Broad has retained reasonably clear water and stands of lilies and some other plants, though, from the writings of Christopher Davies and others, it was evidently much clearer in the nineteenth century.

None of the other Broads has a diverse population of plants and only a major reduction in nutrients is likely to improve the situation. The strongly tidal nature of the river means that such reduction needs to involve all the sewage treatment works discharging downstream, even to Breydon Water. Thus improvement of ecological conditions in the Yare means improvement of all of the Broadland system. For this reason there has been little pressure to install phosphorus stripping in the Yare sewage treatment works. This river has the lowest priority of all.

The River Waveney

The Waveney (Fig. 16.28) is perhaps the least damaged of the three main Broadland rivers, for its boat traffic is light, except in Oulton Broad, but it has few Broads. It winds down the Suffolk/Norfolk border, skirting higher land around Beccles and Bungay so that its floodplain lies largely to its south, then, as it turns north-west towards Breydon Water, the floodplain switches to the left bank. Along the first stretch there is only the small Broad, Barnby, filling in with vegetation, but with a residual aquatic plant population, and three small

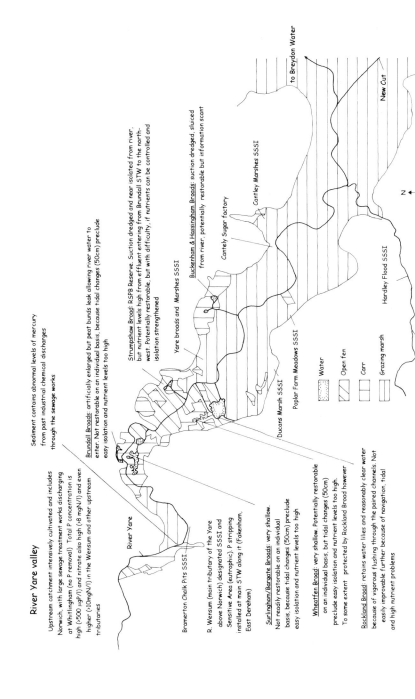

River Yare valley

Upstream catchment intensively cultivated and includes Norwich, with large sewage treatment works discharging at Whitlingham (no P removal). Total P concentration is high (>500 µgP/l) and nitrate also high (>8 mgN/l) and even higher (>10mgN/l) in the Wensum and other upstream tributaries

Sediment contains abnormal levels of mercury from past industrial chemical discharges through the sewage works

Brundall Broads: artificially enlarged but peat bunds leak allowing river water to enter. Not restorable on an individual basis, because tidal changes (50cm) preclude easy isolation and nutrient levels too high

Strumpshaw Broad: RSPB Reserve. Suction dredged and near isolated from river, but nutrient levels high from effluent entering from Brundall STW to the north-west. Potentially restorable, but with difficulty, if nutrients can be controlled and isolation strengthened

Buckenham & Hassingham Broads: suction dredged, sluiced from river, potentially restorable but information scant

Bramerton Chalk Pits SSSI

R. Wensum (main tributary of the Yare above Norwich) designated SSSI and Sensitive Area (eutrophic). P stripping installed at main STW along it (Fakenham, East Dereham)

Surlingham/Bargate Broads: very shallow. Not readily restorable on an individual basis, because tidal changes (50cm) preclude easy isolation and nutrient levels too high

Wheatfen Broad: very shallow. Potentially restorable on an individual basis, but tidal changes (50cm) preclude easy isolation and nutrient levels too high. To some extent protected by Rockland Broad however

Rockland Broad: retains water lilies and reasonably clear water because of vigorous flushing through the paired channels. Not easily improvable further because of navigation, tidal and high nutrient problems

River Yare

Yare broads and Marshes SSSI

Cantley Sugar factory

Cantley Marshes SSSI

Ducans Marsh SSSI

Poplar Farm Meadows SSSI

Hardley Flood SSSI

River Chet

Water

Open fen

Carr

Grazing marsh

to Breydon Water

New Cut

N

1km

Fig. 16.27 Potential of the River Yare for restoration of the Broads.

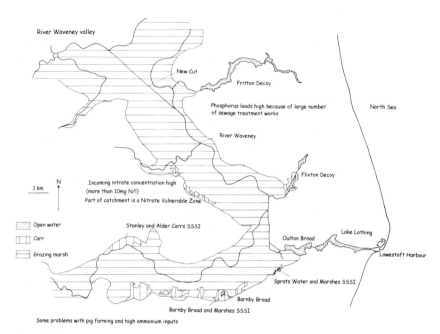

Fig. 16.28 State of the River Waveney valley.

pools at the edge of the valley in the Carleton Marshes Nature Reserve, which may be of medieval origin, but are probably more recent.

Oulton Broad is much modified and connected to the Waveney by Oulton Dyke at one end and at the other, through locks, with Lake Lothing, which is linked to Lowestoft harbour. It is heavily developed with marinas and shoreline buildings, has turbid water and is influenced by effluent from the Waveney coming downstream from Beccles and Bungay and upstream from Breydon Water.

Finally, there are two long, thin Broads associated with small side streams along the stretch of river north-west of Lowestoft; Flixton Decoy and Fritton Decoy. Little is known of their limnology, but they appear to be eutrophicated by agricultural water and have statuses not unlike the Trinity Broads. Attention to nutrient flows in their catchments could pay dividends, for they have residual aquatic plant communities. Barnby Broad is likewise salvable, for it is nearly isolated, but there is little to be done about Oulton Broad short of major modification of the catchment. The river itself still retains quite diverse banks, doubtless affected by the nutrient levels, but less damaged by boat activity than those of the Bure and its tributaries.

Overview

The potential for lake and river restoration in Broadland is currently limited, but conceivably substantial. Significant progress can only be made by reduction of the nutrient sources from the whole catchment. It is increasingly likely that phosphorus sources from agriculture will need to be controlled and unlikely that stable diverse plant communities can be regained without control of nitrates from the catchment also.

There is also the unexpected to be considered. The facility and frequency with which people and boats and other forms of transport can now move between countries is increasing the problem of exotic species. The coypu was a very significant influence on Broadland until it was exterminated. Further alien species will turn up in the future. The small Asiatic clam, which forms dense beds that can filter large quantities of water and also build up masses of shell in a mucilaginous matrix that attracts sediment to it, has appeared in the River Chet and is extending its Broadland range. There is little chance of controlling it, for it spreads readily by tiny larvae and we have no concept at present of whether it will have profound ecological impacts or remain, like some other introduced species, a local curiosity. We shall also face extreme weather events as the atmosphere adjusts to a changing climate. We might expect severe winter floods, intense droughts, extreme gales. The effects of these can be pivotal. They might change entire landscapes to unpredictable extents and obviate all manner of previous restoration work or achieve more in a week than has been possible over a generation.

The underlying philosophies of restoration ecology also are changing and widening. Increasingly it is seen that merely restoring a chunk of vegetation to some target conjured from its past history is ultimately futile if the human society, with which the environment is linked, is not fully attuned to values that favour a less exploitative approach to natural resources. Some would even say that, in turn, this needs the individuals of that society to reappraise their own aspirations and values. A ruthless exploitation of resources is what is predicted from the behaviour of man as yet another animal; history gives us plenty of evidence for this and Broadland is no exception. The test for the future is whether humans can overcome their own innate natural history. Until then the future seems bleak for the natural history of Broadland in general. We shall have to be content with isolated nuggets of high quality in a bedrock of mediocrity.

Further reading

The art and science of restoring lakes ultimately needs a thorough grasp of the whole of limnology. The scope is large, the literature equally so. Firstly there are general works on restoration of fresh waters, including Ryding & Rast (1989), Cooke et al. (1993), Eiseltova (1994) and Moss, Madgwick & Phillips (1996). The latter is particularly relevant to the Broads (and very readable!). The restoration strategy on which this chapter hangs is detailed in it. Jeppesen et al. (1999) and Van der Molen & Boers (1999) give useful accounts of the approaches taken in Denmark and the Netherlands, two of several countries in Europe that take lake restoration very seriously.

Wilson (1999) and Wilson et al. (1995) consider the available legislation in the UK and Europe, and the Environment Agency (2000) presents an 'official' strategy for coping with eutrophication, which confirms most of the problems alluded to in this chapter. Recent reviews of nutrient problems include Ministry of Agriculture (1999), Johnes et al. (1996), Schindler (1978) and of the links between nutrient control and fish and zooplankton ecology, Carpenter & Kitchell (1994) and Moss et al. (1994). Shapiro (1990) is a stimulating review of what controls blue-green algal growth and Foy et al. (1995) was one of the first papers to indicate an increasing role for increased phosphorus release from agricultural soils.

Biomanipulation is now a very well-established technique and may be reviewed through Shapiro et al. (1975), Benndorf (1987), Hosper (1989), Moss (1992), Reynolds (1994) and Phillips et al. (1996). Giles (1992) is a very interesting case study of the restoration of gravel pits using biomanipulation. Irvine et al. (1990) explored the possibility of installing artificial substrates to simulate plant growth during the early stages of restoration, but found it to be practicably unworkable. As in many aspects of life, there is no substitute for the real thing. Hammer (1989) and Vought et al. (1994, 1995) give leads into the areas of constructed wetlands and buffer strips respectively. Van Donk & Gulati (1995) and Klinge et al. (1995) concern themselves with the restoration of small lakes in the Netherlands and discuss the issues of scale. Issues concerning sediment release and the efficacy of sediment removal are covered by Marsden (1989), Osborne & Phillips (1978), Phillips et al. (1994), Bjørk (1994), Annadotter et al. (1999) and Moss, Madgwick & Phillips (1996).

For studies on specific areas of Broadland, there has been a prolific recent literature, but there is still a lot of very valuable information effectively lost because it is in obscure semi-official documents and not in the formal scientific literature. Papers on the River Ant and Barton Broad include Osborne (1980, 1981) and Phillips et al. (1999). An account of recent developments is in Moss, Madgwick & Phillips (1996). Cromes Broad is discussed in Perrow et al. (1999) and Alderfen Broad in Moss et al. (1986, 1990), Cryer et al. (1986) and Perrow et al. (1994).

The acidification of Calthorpe Broad is documented in Gosling & Baker (1980). Papers on Hickling Broad and the upper Thurne include Holdway et al. (1978), Bales et al. (1993), Irvine et al. (1993, 1995) and Moss & Leah (1982), but the very recent events of the late 1990s, though well documented in unpublished reports, are not yet properly published. The report edited by Eaton (1999) is, however, available from the Broads Authority. Insights into Hickling ecology can be obtained from studies on comparable brackish lakes elsewhere (Moss (1994), Jeppesen et al. (1994), Simons et al. (1994)). Studies on Cockshoot Broad include Moss et al. (1986), Moss (1990) and Moss et al. (1996) and on the Bure in general, Moss & Balls (1989), Moss et al. (1989, 1991) and Clarke (1990). The Trinity Broads are dealt with in Clarke (1973) and Hameed et al. (1999). Information on the Yare and Waveney is less detailed, for restoration of these has not been seriously contemplated. George (1992) includes most of it. Baker & Lambley (1980) is a survey of the upper Wensum. The first published hints of a potential problem with the Asiatic clam came in a short 'Wildlife report' in *British Wildlife*, February 1999, p.207.

17

The Present State and Management of the Fens and Grazing Marshes

The nature of nature conservation

Nature conservation in the United Kingdom (Fig. 17.1) is the well-informed keeping of the isolated departments of a diffuse museum. It tries to maintain semi-natural plant and animal communities, created by treasured and traditional ways of managing the land that are now defunct. Museums vary. There are those that preserve artefacts in an orderly collection and those that seek to recreate experiences of the past through media like film and play-acting as well as displays of objects. All are islands of interest amid a sea that is often dull in appearance or nature.

Most nature reserves are traditional museums, where the collections of artefacts, in this case species and sub-communities of them, are the *raisons d'être*. The management plans of most nature reserves talk of safeguarding the mosaic of plant and animal communities and conserving rare and local species; this is understandable, for the organisms are of great interest, the surrounding landscape is increasingly a dreary assemblage of aggressive weeds, uniform crops or even concrete. But the reserves cannot preserve the natural ecological functions of the ecosystems any more than conventional museums can maintain the functioning societies commemorated in them. The reserves are far too small for this and the managers are not encouraged to think in those terms, or much helped by legislation to do so. There is an element of museum modernity, though. Voluntary labour is often key to maintaining the collections through a participatory play-acting of the work of former times.

The conservation museum has a lot of neglected rooms that are not actively curated, for the costs are high. Until recently visitors have not been much encouraged, for the contents might be disturbed; Hellenic vases are delicate.

Fig. 17.1 Nature conservation in Britain has a strong scientific and naturalist base to inform practical management often carried out by volunteer labour.

This is changing, but an aura of separateness, of elitism and of importance is given by many official designations of the rooms – Sites of Scientific Interest, Special Protection Areas, Special Areas of Conservation, National Nature Reserves, Local Nature Reserves, Ramsar Sites – under various pieces of legislation and international agreements, but usually it is the same sites that have multiple such designations. They are not proof against damage, but sometimes only ciphers that are sops to political convenience rather than giving real support and protection; the curators have lots of tarnishing medals on the mantelpieces of their offices, lots of dusty certificates on the wall.

There is also a sense of order given first by use of the National Vegetation Classification, which allows the ordering of the communities and the designation of targets to be set for maintenance of this or that community or restoration of another. There are also books, the Red Data Books, of no official standing, but widely used to list and publicise rare and declining species. Nature conservation attempts to run in the same efficient way as necessary for a business with a product, biodiversity in its case, to display.

But like almost all museums, nature conservation is in trouble. Firstly, it is subversive; it may enshrine values that are not convenient to current intentions for society. It does not pay its way in an economy that values only those organisations that do. Its product, though cherished passionately by many, is not widely valued by most of the community – not necessarily for lack of fundamental interest, but because other needs are much more pressing. Nature conservation produces few jobs, is not seen to provide the opportunities for quiet recreation that are the attractions of the National Parks, and cannot, in Britain, offer the appeal of large and spectacular mammals. Yet it does guide the lives of a sizeable minority who see, in the maintenance of the museum, a loyalty to past values and perhaps a hope that in the future they might be extended. Nostalgia, a reaction to the imposition of authoritarian uniformity, an appreciation of detail, passionate interests in particular groups of animals or plants, are all involved. The hopes might be false, they might be valid but misdirected, but they are to be respected. They underlie the current management of most of the Broadland fens and marshes.

Fens and reedswamps

The fens and grazing marshes dominate the Broadland valleys; the open water is the minority component, for all its appeal, but that is a false comparison. The system is ultimately one, even if it currently must be artificially managed as separate compartments. The statistics are confusing because of the different ways they may be used to illustrate particular points, but let us start with 303 square kilometres of Broadland floodplain. Roughly a tenth of this (including the estuary) is open water, a fifth is undrained carr, fen and reedswamp and 70 per cent is grazing marsh. Now take the 20 per cent undrained wetlands. There remain 1,945 hectares of open fen and reedswamp, and about 3,800 hectares of carr woodland and scrub, which has extended by a fifth since the Second World War because open fens have been abandoned.

Of the 1,945 hectares of still open fen, 1,285 hectares are classified under various pieces of legislation as of international importance for they harbour 23 nationally rare or scarce plant species and at least 230 similarly vulnerable invertebrates, 50 of them characteristic of the Broads. They provide refuges for the harvest mouse, water shrew, water vole, marsh harrier, bearded tit and bittern, species that are the Broadland equivalents of the charismatic elephants of Tsavo and the polar bears of Hudson's Bay. The problems of maintaining the fen communities are those of inadequate water quality and quantity, neglect, because of tight economic margins for any produce that might be harvested, difficulties of access, handling and transport of such harvests, and dwindling markets, except in the case of reed and sedge for roofing. The 3,800 hectares of carr woodland are barely managed at all, though 2,135 of them are listed as of great importance. Of the 1,945 hectares of open fen and reedswamp, only 460 hectares (1.5 per cent of the floodplain) are now still actively managed, about 200 of them commercially for reed and sedge, about 150 for commercial cattle grazing and around 100 for direct conservation purposes. Most of the latter is done by volunteer groups, organised by the Broads Authority and the Norfolk Wildlife Trust and some by employees of these bodies and English Nature. There is now some financial assistance, for maintenance of fen habitat, from the Department of Environment, Food and Rural Affairs under an Environmentally Sensitive Areas Scheme, which otherwise covers maintenance of the grazing marshes, and is discussed below, but shortage of labour is what ultimately limits maintenance of open fen. In the battle to maintain it, the army is tiny.

Managing the fens

The remaining undrained fens and carrs lie in four main blocks, each around the main groups of Broads, in the valleys of the Rivers Thurne, Ant, Bure and Yare. There are scattered smaller areas elsewhere, notably on Burgh Common and around the Trinity Broads, around Upton Broad in the Bure valley and at Carlton marshes and around Barnby Broad in the Waveney valley. Much of the habitat is not as species rich as it probably once was, not only because it is not regularly managed, but also because the water that reaches it, or at least its fringes, is now highly eutrophicated. The fragmentation of the fens compared with formerly means that the fringe habitat comprises much of the area.

There are also concerns about water quantity, not so much for the main blocks, but for the small spring-fed fens at the margins of the valleys, where water abstraction from the ground water (for drinking water supply and particularly for crop irrigation) has reduced the flow. There are still many questions about the requirements of particular species, as with most habitats, but the key requirements for maintenance of the open fens, if that is what is wanted, are clear and form part of a general fen strategy drawn up by the Broads Authority. The strategy is supported by the *Broads Plan*, required of the Authority and updated every five years, which illustrates its general approach (Fig. 17.2) and the scope of what it is able to do (Table 17.1).

The Broads Authority expresses its intentions with admirable clarity, especially in comparison with the opaque documents of most government organisations and not a little of the scientific literature, but fine words do not butter the parsnips. The practical problems frustrating the strategy are considerable, largely because of the labour needs and the inability to reduce nutrient loading and increase water flows, for the same lack of usable legislation that poses problems for the open water.

Nonetheless the strategy is a sensible one and comprises three prongs: use of grazing by cattle and ponies (Plate 26) (and potentially other large grazing mammals); encouragement of commercial reed and sedge harvests; and development of new

Table 17.1 Formal policies of the Broads Authority with respect to fens and carr. Extracted from the current *Broads Plan* of the Broads Authority.

Aim 8 The Broads Authority will work with English Nature and other conservation bodies, wetland experts, landowners and managers to seek to maintain and improve the quality of the fen resource in the Broads area

Policy 33 Management agreements
The Broads Authority will work with English Nature to establish management agreements for all significant unmanaged fen areas in the Broads

Policy 34 Management assistance
The Broads Authority and English Nature will provide landowners with advice and management assistance to maintain the existing open fen and to restore degraded fen areas in the most appropriate way

Policy 35 Retaining important fens
Where advice and management assistance are not sufficient to ensure the retention of important fen areas, the Broads Authority will seek to purchase or lease the area, either by itself or by providing financial assistance to an appropriate agency

Policy 36 Scrub clearance
The Broads Authority will continue to expand its practical programme of fen restoration in accordance with the fen management strategy. Priority will be given to removing recently invaded trees and scrub, the clearance of fen dykes, the restoration of reed and sedge beds and the maintenance of species-rich litter marshes

Policy 37 Commercial fen products
The Broads Authority will work with the British Reed Growers Association, landowners and others to investigate ways of ensuring that reed and sedge growing, and harvesting, remain viable

Policy 38 Turf ponds
The Broads Authority and English Nature will develop a programme for the restoration and creation of shallow peat diggings as part of the overall fen management strategy

Policy 39 Eutrophication
The Broads Authority will encourage and support research into eutrophication of fens. Where problems are identified, appropriate solutions will be sought.

Policy 40 Reedswamp
The Broads Authority will establish a programme of research and experimental management to restore reedswamp at the margins of Broads

Aim 9 The Broads Authority will encourage the protection and appropriate management of carr woodland

Policy 41 Managing woodlands
The Broads Authority will, through consultation with the Forestry Authority, encourage the appropriate management of woodlands in the Broads area to benefit wildlife and landscape

uses for materials cut from the fens, such as fuel for power generation or, chopped up, as animal feed supplements. First, however, much of the overgrown fen must be cleared of woody plants.

Scrub clearance

Clearance of fens that were open but have now become colonised by scrub is not easy. It has been done in the past by hand because the peat surfaces will be damaged by heavy machines. It must be done outside the main bird breeding season in spring, but is impossible in winter because of high water levels and arduous in summer because of uneven, tussocky land, high summer humidity and lots of biting insects. New machines have been made that operate from one spot and use long arms to pull out scrub and even macerate it to chippings on site. They can clear areas faster than hand labour, but there are presently few of them. At present, availability of money from sources such as the Lottery Heritage Fund makes use of them by professional contractors profitable and it is likely that clearance will increase greatly in the next decade.

The scrub not only has to be cut and burnt, but the stumps removed or ground flat to the surface and killed by herbicide, otherwise willow and alder regenerate very quickly. Physical removal of stumps is difficult, but applications of the herbicides 2-4-5T on birch and alder and krenite or garlon on these and sallow, can be effective. It takes about 100 person-days for professional hand labour to clear one hectare of alder carr (lighter scrub takes less time, of course) and about three times as long for volunteers. There are, however, many more volunteers than employed staff so much of the clearance has been done by them with about 8,000 person-days a year currently available, equivalent to about 25 full-time employees. Nonetheless, even such a force could clear only about 25 hectares a year of scrub and carr, were all of it used on clearance. Cleared fens must subsequently be maintained by cutting and there are other necessary tasks, such as dyke maintenance. With all this to be considered, it would take perhaps a hundred years to re-clear the thousand hectares of open fen that have become colonised by scrub since the Second World War. The development of customised machines, however, might speed this.

Fig. 17.2 The Broads Authority has hitherto shown considerable tact, taste and imagination in carrying out its functions. It presents a forward-looking image through its signs and logo, not that some of its predecessor organisations did not present a certain archaic charm.

Fen maintenance

Maintenance of the fen, once it has been cleared, is easier. Cutting and removing the litter is the favoured method. It is important that the cut material is removed and burned away from the site, so as to prevent build-up of a thick litter mat rich in nutrients. Litter and nutrients favour tall competitive species such as great hairy willowherb, yellow loosestrife and meadowsweet, which oust the smaller species, such as bog pimpernel, lesser spearwort, marsh helleborine and adder's-tongue fern. Small, wide-tyred machines have been mostly used for cutting, but require professional operators and are relatively slow.

The Broads Authority and several partner organisations, using European Union grants and a very sympathetic and resourceful engineer, Nick Ash, have developed the 'New Fen Harvester' that can cut much greater areas in a short time than hand-pushed machines or hand labour. The Harvester (Plate 27) has caterpillar tracks that give a ground pressure less than half of that of human feet, and a wide cutter bar that allows the ground to be covered quickly. The machine cuts then chops the vegetation and stores the material in a bunker mounted to the rear. When the bunker is full the load is transferred to another, larger store from which air blowers can move it through pipelines (irrigation pipes can be used) to a lorry or other transport on the nearest road, which may be two or three kilometres away. The design has also been kept mechanically robust and simple. In general, if it breaks down, the machine has to be repaired on the spot! The Harvester thus neatly solves problems of damage, labour and access.

Burning the fen may sometimes be used as a substitute, although too hot a fire may cause considerable damage and sallow seedlings sometimes proliferate after a fire. Burning was not apparently a usual method of managing fens in the past, so does not result necessarily in the mosaic of traditional communities intended. Grazing, on the other hand, offers a means of reducing the biomass that is not labour intensive and that is a traditional means of management. Past grazing was mostly by cattle and some horses and these are the animals most used at present. To minimise costs, hardy breeds such as Galloway cattle, Welsh and Konic ponies (Plate 26) are favoured.

The latter, in particular, can be left without daily inspection, but conversely are difficult to handle by conventional British methods. New ways, developed in the United States, which depend on understanding of herd psychology and dominance relationships within the herd, may be more appropriate. Even then, the concept of leaving herds semi-wild to roam over the fens without daily attention is difficult to accept for a community of horse-lovers observing the process. Grazers, particularly horses, are selective and can maintain a varied terrain, creating niches for a variety of plants, but because timing of grazing, intensity of grazing and the weather conditions at the time all interact, predicting the ultimate outcome is not a precise science. Grazing does not produce the same communities as cutting, partly because nutrients are recycled rather than removed. But it does add an element of interest to fens which, when only cut and left, may seem desolate and uninteresting to the visitors whose appreciation is an essential element to maintaining support for conservation.

Some of the most diverse fen communities have been created in shallow peat cuttings (30–100 centimetres) in particular locations. The richest vegetation in the Ant valley was found to overly such 'turf ponds', dug out, presumably for fuel or to regenerate commercial sedge beds, in the nineteenth century. One of the Broads Authority's policies is to dig out new ponds. This is expensive and must be on peat, with clay not near the surface, in places where the water supply is neither nutrient rich, nor saline, nor too acid, and preferably close to existing rich communities for rapid colonisation. There have been several experiments, at Broad Fen, Dilham, at Hands Marsh near Horning and Reedham Marsh near How Hill on the River Ant. The technique has proved very successful in creating communities of marsh cinquefoil, greater spearwort, marsh lousewort, bog pimpernel, lesser water-plantain, charophytes and bladderwort, but the labour costs are so high that the total area thus excavated is still only a fraction of one hectare.

The dykes in the fens need also to be maintained, to keep them open for access as well as for their own conservation value. Slubbing-out (the local term for removal of mud) is a time-consuming and labour-intensive process, if done by hand, as it must be for the narrower dykes. The wider ones can be cleared by a pump, mounted on a boat, which sucks sediment from the bottom and sprays it over the surrounding fen. Such equipment can slub about 150 cubic metres of sediment per hour and clearance of dykes in the Woodbastwick marshes resulted in restoration of submerged plant communities in previously heavily silted dykes deep in the fens. Results were less good in dykes close to the River Bure, perhaps because nutrient-rich water leaked in despite damming of the system from the river. The fens need water from the river, however, so total isolation is counterproductive, whilst incomplete isolation results in communities of low diversity. Without catchment nutrient control, the results will inevitably be disappointing.

Commercial harvests

Encouraging commercial harvests is the second prong in the Broads Authority's strategy. There is certainly a demand for the products, but the market is subject to several limitations. First there are competing, cheaper supplies to be imported from eastern Europe; there have been worries (unconfirmed by investigation) that Broadland reed was declining in its durability on roofs; and few people wish to work at cutting and preparing the reed and thatching roofs. Cutting in winter is arduous, and thatching is physically hard work. Moreover, there are conflicts between nature conservation and commercial harvesting.

Commercial harvesters want only to cut beds giving high quality reed (long and hard), in areas where water levels can be carefully controlled, such as the embanked reed floods, which are the least diverse of the reed beds for other species. There is little incentive to cut most of the open reedswamps because of the poorer quality commercial product, though greater biological diversity if they are cut. Ornithologists prefer cutting to be infrequent (say once in five to ten years) so that there is a little colonisation of scrub to provide perches and nesting sites, and want no cutting after mid-March so as not to interfere with nesting. Neither of these is compatible with commercial harvesting.

The third prong is the concept of 'new wetland harvests', a logical extension of the history of use of the fens. Fens produce a lot of biomass, alder carrs as much in the more convenient dense form of wood. Both can be burnt in small power stations to generate electricity that is neutral in terms of the change in carbon dioxide composition of the atmosphere, as opposed to the burning of fossil fuels that results in a net increase. The principle is excellent, the practice more difficult. Fen litter is bulky and hence expensive to transport; likewise the costs of taking alder wood from difficult terrain are high if it has to be moved by road. Power stations are built at present to cope with large quantities of single fuels as opposed to small quantities of varied fuel.

Use of fen and carr biomass as fuel really needs a change in the policy of power generation, which is not immediately likely. Likewise, the development of chopped marsh hay, produced in abundance by the new fen harvester, as a component of packaged animal feeds, is in principle very sensible. Against it is an agricultural food industry geared to large quantities of highly concentrated foodstuffs, rather than small amounts of cellulose-rich bulk material, and an agriculture that has discouraged animal husbandry in the Broadland catchments in favour of arable. There is no real shortage of hay from more conventional sources and a tendency to favour silage, which requires less stringent conditions of storage and is produced locally on the farm, thus invoking no transport cost.

Overall the strategy for maintaining an extensive system of Broadland fens faces formidable difficulties. The fens are very much a museum of plant communities whose products are no longer in such demand as they were when the fens were incidentally maintained by the local economy. The past is a key element of any culture and aspects of it should be maintained, at a cost to society, just as the more obvious artefacts of human creativity are preserved in conventional museums. But Greek vases require much less curation than hectares of open vegetation.

Managing the grazing marshes

It is in the huge area of grazing marshes, however, that the issue of preservation of cultural landscapes, a less pointed description than museum departments, provided one of the major environmental controversies in the British countryside. The economic pressures on agriculture led to increased drainage and ploughing of grazing marsh for arable cultivation from the 1960s onwards (Chapter 14). This stimulated designation of greater areas of the grazing marsh as Sites of Special Scientific Interest by the then Nature Conservancy Council. From 120 hectares in 1972, the designated area increased to 580 hectares by 1981, but this was a small safeguard in the face of the threat that thousands of hectares would be ploughed during the 1980s. Areas of grazing marsh were included in reserves owned by the Norfolk Wildlife Trust, the Suffolk Wildlife Trust, the Royal Society for the Protection of Birds and sympathetic landowners, willing to enter into management agreements with the Conservancy at Hickling, Horsey, Strumpshaw, Ludham, How Hill and Carlton Colville.

These have been managed in traditional ways to maximise the diversity of the sward and particularly the dykes. Cattle are grazed, there is no liming and only moderate fertilisation. Herbicide use is confined to spot treatment of thistles, nettles, ragwort and other tall weeds. A high water table is maintained in the bird breeding season for snipe and black-tailed godwit to be able to probe soft wet depressions for invertebrate food and for redshank to be able to rear young. The marshes are not grazed until late May or June to avoid trampling of nests and are not cut for hay until early July. The dykes are kept full, free of slurry and regularly slubbed out.

During the mid-1980s, however, such a regime was increasingly unlikely in the main bulk of the marshes. The characteristic grazing landscape of these marshes, the bulk of the area of Broadland, was about to disappear. The changes had been long establishing. Since the 1930s, about 25 per cent had been converted to arable, concrete roads and machinery sheds. Overhead cables were increasingly evident. A very ugly overhead power line still crosses the Waveney valley marshes south-west of Belton, a monument to the insensitivity of a whole generation of engineering.

Nonetheless, matters began to worsen considerably in 1980 when the Lower Bure, Halvergate Fleet and Acle Marshes Internal Drainage Board (IDB) sought grant aid from the Ministry of Agriculture for four very powerful pumps. It also wanted the deepening of 20 kilometres of drains and construction of five kilometres of concrete road to convert 2,024 hectares in the main block of the Halvergate marshes, including the Acle/Tunstall, Seven Mile/Berney and Manor House levels (Fig. 17.3) to arable.

This area included areas of prime significance for landscape in particular, and for nature conservation. The grant, if given, would cover between half and a third of the farmers' costs and would make conversion to arable profitable. Indeed, it would double the land values and increase profitability several fold, as well as replace 40-year-old pumps that were at the end of their useful life.

Fig. 17.3 Major features of the scheme proposed in 1981 for the deep drainage of part of the Halvergate triangle on behalf of the Lower Bure, Halvergate Fleet and Acle Marshes Internal Drainage Board. This scheme was never established, but was the stimulus for the eventual establishment of the Broads Environmentally Sensitive Area.

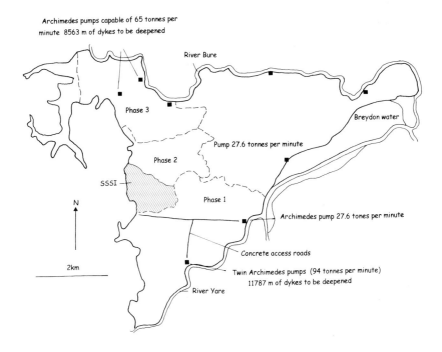

On the other hand it would involve a public subsidy of about £4,000 per hectare and the replacement of a characteristic landscape that was deemed of much greater interest than an arable landscape. This was also at a time when the crops to be grown were not needed, and indeed would attract further public subsidy under the arrangements of the European Common Agricultural Policy. Without the public subsidies, the conversion was far from capable of making a profit for the private farmers concerned.

Following the changes wrought by a previous scheme of the Muck Fleet and South Flegg IDB (Chapter 14) the Ministry of Agriculture had introduced a policy of notifying local authorities of applications for drainage grants. The Broads Authority was thus consulted and objected to the scheme, which might otherwise have been routinely approved, on grounds of its potential damage to the landscape. The grant was withheld whilst some acceptable solution was found to the problem, but this proved by no means easy because of the complex confusion of interest on all sides.

The Halvergate marshes controversy

The Broads Authority, new in its role (it had been formed only in the previous year), found itself in a difficult position. It wanted to maintain good relations with all its constituents, comprising several farmers among its ranks, and had far too few funds to compensate the farmers not to plough. It made its objection, but without too much conviction at the time to see it through. Its promoters, the Countryside Commission and its allies, the Council for the Protection of Rural England, Friends of the Earth and the Nature Conservancy Council, could afford to be more forthright, however, not having to pay so much attention to local sentiment.

Under pressure from these, the Broads Authority, by a narrow margin, formally resolved that the changes would be unacceptable and that a public enquiry should be held if the drainage grant was offered. It offered some compromise with a concern particularly about 445 hectares near the Berney Arms, which it considered to be of the highest landscape value and to which it would brook no change, but for the rest was happy to offer voluntary agreements with some compensation.

Its allies were less than happy about this. Over 7,000 hectares of similar marshland were at similar risk of conversion by schemes that could not even be contemplated without public subsidy. The compensation could be over £1 million per year, and the farmers would settle for no less. Such compensation was not available from countryside budgets and it was foreseen that there could therefore be few management agreements and the grazing marsh landscape would be lost. A new compromise was proposed in summer 1981. Compensation was offered at £150 per hectare (compared with the £500 previously mooted) and no objection would be made to drainage of the Tunstall/Acle level, which had already been substantially converted to arable, if the Manor House level was withdrawn from the scheme.

This might have been accepted, but the farmers were insisting on index linking of the compensation. The Countryside Commission advised the Broads Authority to await the passing of the new Wildlife and Countryside Act and the Authority contemplated buying the prime land involved and leasing it back for traditional farming. This would be costly, but would not involve continued compensation.

By early 1982, there was no progress. The Wildlife and Countryside Act had been passed, including an obligation on the parts of Internal Drainage Boards to further conservation in their activities, but this seems to have inflamed rather than improved matters. The IDBs would not countenance differential rates for traditional graziers who required less intensive drainage than arable converters and who could not afford the higher rates and would thus potentially be forced to sell out to the larger arable farmers. One farmer legally ploughed nine hectares of a Site of Special Scientific Interest, because he had not then been formally notified that the land was to be re-scheduled. However, he cannot not have known informally that it was to be so, in view of the controversies of the time.

In September 1982, the Broads Authority considered purchase of 178 hectares of the core area at £3,000 per hectare and reselling it at £1,500 per-hectare with restrictive agreements to farm it traditionally if the proposals for a new pump and access road to the Berney marshes were withdrawn. It could not afford the cost, however, without a major contribution from the Countryside Commission, which demurred, and continued to push for a public enquiry. In London, the Government began to be more concerned, as its policy for local voluntary solutions to environmental and conservation issues would be undermined by a public enquiry.

There was clearly a degree of manoeuvring in Whitehall, for two months later, the Government indicated it would depart from established rules. It would fund a pump of increased capacity for the Acle/Tunstall level, one of replacement capacity only for the Berney/Seven Mile level and none for the Manor House level. All this would be done under the provisions of Section 48 of the Wildlife and Countryside Act, which requires furtherance of conservation in land drainage schemes. This first ever refusal of grant aid for agriculture without a public enquiry, however, met with little approval all round.

Farmers argued that they were being compelled to look after the natural heritage at cost to themselves and could not obtain a reasonable return from their land. The Broads Authority's allies pointed out that £1 million would be spent to obtain only limited protection of the landscape. The benefit would be to the larger farmers only, and the road to be built, as part of the package, to service the Seven Mile pump, would open up large areas for conversion to arable even with no increased drainage capacity of the pump. Matters were still at a stalemate.

During the next season, in 1983, five farmers notified the Broads Authority that they would convert 301 hectares of the Seven Mile/Berney level if they did not receive compensation. Such compensation would amount to a third of the Broads Authority's total budget, even with the Countryside Commission paying three-quarters of it and the Authority only a quarter, with a further huge area still potentially at the same risk of being proposed for conversion. Several of the farmers were temporarily bought off at £125 per hectare, but two of them indicated that they would plough 150 hectares in June 1984. One was compensated, the other not, because his land was adjacent to already ploughed land. Effectively the Broads Authority had agreed to his ploughing, which he carried out.

Meanwhile another farmer at Limpenhoe proposed to drain and plough 40 hectares of more significant land and refused a compensation proposal. He was effectively stopped by use of Article 4 of the Town and Country Planning

Order of 1977, which, although it could not prevent ploughing, could be used to require Ministry of the Environment sanction for the digging of the necessary drains and other necessary engineering work. The Broads Authority asked the Ministry for refusal of sanction and was successful. A year's holding payment of £10,000 was agreed, but relationships between the conservation bodies and the farming bodies were steadily worsening.

In 1984, even the House of Lords became involved. Two of its committees criticised the Government for a failure to co-ordinate its agricultural and environmental policies. The Broads Authority was threatened with bankruptcy if it had to pay out the likely compensation payments. The Ministry of Agriculture, already obliged elsewhere in the country to pay subsidies on crops that were not needed, was realising that arable conversion would cost it further subsidies of £250 per hectare – perhaps £500,000 or more a year if the grazing marshes were substantially converted. Only a handful of farmers would benefit. Everyone else would be disconcerted and the Ministry's stock, already in decline among the public at large for its support of destructive farming elsewhere, was hardly likely to benefit.

The Broads Grazing Marshes Conservation Scheme

A solution emerged in which the substantial resources of the Ministry of Agriculture might be used to maintain the traditional farming patterns and the landscape, without undermining the Broads Authority, and with at least some financial compensation to all of the farmers, not just the more aggressive ones. Under Section 40 of the Wildlife and Countryside Act, the Countryside Commission could promote schemes of countryside management for conservation purposes. What emerged was one of these, a three-year experimental 'Broads Grazing Marshes Conservation Scheme', funded jointly by the Ministry of Agriculture and the Countryside Commission. The scheme would pay farmers to maintain traditional grazing practices in the central grazing marsh area, with a standard compensation of £125 per hectare, and an upper limit of spending of £1.7 million per year.

The area first had to be designated under Section 41 of the Wildlife and Countryside Act, so that any intended change in farming practice had to be compulsorily notified to the Broads Authority, but then compensation was payable provided certain conditions were kept. These included restrictions on the number of animals, the cutting of hay, the construction of roads and buildings and the use of fertilisers and herbicides. The scheme began in 1985, and by 1986 more than 92 per cent of the eligible area, 6,260 hectares, had been entered into the scheme. There was little further loss of land to arable cultivation.

The scheme was a major innovation. Critics have suggested that purchase of key areas of land and selective management agreements would have had the same effect and been less costly, but the reality was that most of the available funding had to come from the Ministry of Agriculture, which was restricted in the way it could spend its funds. It was not able, under government regulations, to buy land and transfer it to the Broads Authority, or to lease it back to farmers. All this is an artefact of politics, which is not always very logical or farseeing, but which constitutes the environment of the time, to which organisations must adapt if they are to survive.

The scheme was planned as a temporary arrangement pending measures to obtain European funding to further its aims. A European Regulation of 1985 (797/85), concerning grant aid for agriculture, promoted the support of farming beneficial to the environment in areas of high conservation value and this provision was incorporated into the Agriculture Act of 1986. Such areas had to be of national environmental importance, discrete, coherent, their value dependent on the nature of the farming and be threatened with detrimental change. The Broadland fitted this description well and was designated an Environmentally Sensitive Area (ESA) in July 1986, the first of 43 such schemes to be established in 33,770 square kilometres of Great Britain and part funded by the European community (Fig. 17.4). The ESA scheme began in 1987 and was reviewed in 1992, when its provisions and the area to which it applied were extended, and in 1997, when the area to which it applied was further increased. It now covers the floodplains of the upper parts of the Broadland rivers as well as the middle and lower floodplains.

The Broads Environmentally Sensitive Area scheme

As with all ESA schemes, entry is voluntary, but on acceptance of an application, the owner-occupier or tenant of the land undertakes to carry out particular practices (and refrain from others) in return for payments that are greater where the farming more favours conservation and is consequently less profitable. The payments are reviewed every two years and may rise or fall dependent on the farming economics of the time. Agreements are made for ten-year

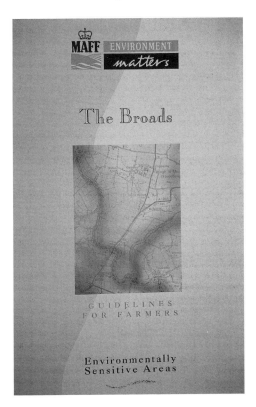

Fig. 17.4 Application forms for entry into the Broadland Environmentally Sensitive Area scheme stipulate the required management in considerable detail.

periods with a review and option to withdraw on either side after five.

In Broadland, there are three main levels of support, or tiers, with some additional provisions. Tier 1 (Permanent grassland) essentially maintains the land as permanent grassland, without much attempt to increase its conservation value, and currently attracts £130 per hectare each year. Farmers must not plough, level or re-seed the land, take no more than one cut of hay or silage each year and must put stock on the land to graze the aftermath. This keeps a short sward that increases the plant diversity and may attract geese in winter. Fertilisation is limited to previous levels and must not exceed 125 kilograms (100 units) per hectare of nitrogen per year and 75 kilograms each of phosphate and potash. The use of pig slurry or poultry manure is banned and applications of other manure are restricted to less than 30 tonnes per hectare each year. Insecticides may not be used and herbicides only to control nettles, spear thistle, dock and ragwort by spot application. Further drainage is banned and dykes must be slubbed out, in rotation, every five to eight years. Mid-channel water depths must be maintained at least 30 centimetres in winter and increased after 1 March.

Tier 2 (Extensive grassland) brings £225 per hectare, for which all the provisions of Tier 1 must be maintained, but also water levels in the dykes must be held at not more than 45 centimetres below marsh level, with a mid-channel depth of 60 centimetres in winter. There must be no mechanical operations (e.g. rolling or chain harrowing) between 31 March and 16 July, no grazing between 31 December and 1 April, no silage cutting, and hay cutting only after 16 July. Nitrogen fertilisation is limited to 45 kilograms per hectare and phosphate and potassium must not be added, nor must manure, nor lime nor slag to reduce soil acidity. Dykes must be slubbed carefully to conserve aquatic and marginal vegetation and given gentler slopes when re-profiled to create further niches for plant species.

For Tier 3 (Wet grassland), the additional provisions, for £310 per hectare, are that the water table must be at marsh level in winter and no more than 45 centimetres below it in summer. There must be no fertilisation at all, no stock grazing between 1 November and 15 May, mandatory grazing between 16 May and 31 October and no more than one bovine per 0.75 hectares before 30 June. All of this is to maintain a species-rich sward that is neither under- nor overgrazed. There are additional payments for even higher water tables in Tiers 2 and 3 and for reverting existing arable to permanent grassland, maintaining six-metre wide grassland margins along the dykes bordering arable fields, and creating new public access.

There is also a Fen Tier, which encourages maintenance of open fen by grazing by cattle or sheep (but not horses, which are no longer 'agricultural') or cutting, provided there is no fertiliser, lime or pesticide, herbicide or fungicide use. This pays £150 per hectare per year, enough for minimal management and also one-off payments of up to £500 per hectare for scrub clearance. This latter is not nearly enough, however, fully to support scrub and woodland clearance from abandoned fens, where up to 100 person-days of labour may be needed per hectare. There are also contributions (mostly between 50 and 80 per cent) to the costs of creating features such as wader scrapes, sluices, herb-rich meadows, traditional wooden gates and their sloping fences, tree pollarding, stiles and wind pumps for water level management.

Assessment of the scheme

The success of the scheme in maintaining the nature of the landscape is hard to assess, because no-one can know what might have happened without it. There has been a steady erosion of the once very generous grants for farming, and without grant aid, the only appropriate and profitable farming on the marshes would normally be extensive grazing. At present, even that would not be profitable. Take-up in the Broads Environmentally Sensitive area has been much higher than in other ESA schemes, suggesting that profitable independent farming was not really an alternative.

It would likely have been true that much land could have been ploughed without the Broads Grazing Marshes Conservation Scheme, though it is not certain. Most farmers were rather easily discouraged by modest payments at the time and would have been less likely to plough subsequently. There is always the concern that offering payments not to do things encourages landowners to propose activities they might never have otherwise contemplated. From the Ministry of Agriculture's point of view, the establishment of ESA schemes allowed it to cope with rising public concern about intensification of agriculture, whilst also maintaining its flow of funds, and hence power and influence in the governmental machine.

What can and has been done, however, is to assess the extent of change in various indices of landscape and conservation value in the area covered by the ESA scheme. The Ministry commissioned a series of reports on the scheme up to 1995, which were published in 1996. It had stated a number of objectives for the scheme and assessed the degree to which these had been achieved. There were five objectives. The first was to maintain and enhance landscape quality by retention of existing grassland and increase in the total area of grassland. The second was to maintain and enhance the wildlife conservation value of the permanent grassland, and the third was to do the same for the dykes and ditches. Maintenance of the characteristic landscape elements and of archaeological and historical features were the fourth and fifth objectives.

By and large the assessment concluded that the quality and features had been maintained, but not greatly enhanced. This is a harsh judgement, however, for the restoration of elements such as diversity and wildlife interest is not something that can be expected to occur rapidly. What has taken centuries to build up can be destroyed much more quickly than it can be restored. The target for maintenance was that 50 per cent of the eligible area should be entered under Tier 1 and by 1995, 48 per cent was included. For Tier 2 the target was 32 per cent and the achievement 37 per cent, for Tier 3, 3 per cent and 2 per cent and for reversion of arable to grassland, 5 per cent and 4 per cent. Overall these targets were close to achievement, but the target that 30 per cent of applications should include plans (conservation plans) for enhancement of features promoting wildlife was undershot at only 11 per cent. Objective 1, however, was substantially met in its maintenance element, and 1,051 hectares of former arable land were converted back to grassland, albeit inevitably of low conservation interest. In the time available the sward could simply reflect the composition of the simple seed mixes used for sowing.

Targets for enhancement included an increase in wet grassland vegetation, an upward trend in numbers of breeding waders (particularly snipe, lapwing and redshank) and that 5 per cent of eligible arable fields (those bordered by

dykes) should have grassland margins reinstated. In these there was less success. There were no clear trends in wet grassland vegetation diversity, no
increase, indeed some decline in wader numbers, attributed to national trends
and weather, and only 23 fields, out of 1,397 eligible, acquired grassland margins. The target was 70.

The dyke system was maintained, but barely enhanced. There was, in general, a deterioration attributed to increased salinity, outside the control of the
ESA scheme. This increased salinity reflects the increased leakiness of the river
embankments and the steadily rising sea level. In some areas, however, particularly areas converted from arable, dyke floras became more diverse, but there
was no overall trend. And objectives for increase in characteristic landscape
features were also not met. Rather few new wooden gates have been erected,
and a negligible number of willows pollarded or archaeological and historical
sites further protected or enhanced. In recent years, since the 1995 assessment,
grant has also been available for increasing public access, but again there has
been very little take-up. Likewise, the Fen Tier has largely attracted the conservation organisations, together with those other owners who were previously
still reed- and sedge-cutting.

The picture is one of a farming community for the most part taking the
grants on offer to carry on much as before, but not much embracing the spirit of enhancing the appeal of the area. Perhaps this is to be expected. Farmers
farm; they do not generally want to run theme parks, tourist attractions or
museums. One has a sense of impermanence, of waiting to see what might happen next, for it is clear that neither in the fens or grazing marshes are the present solutions viable in the long term. These habitats are artefacts of history
and history has changed.

It may also change again. Sea level rise is now acknowledged as a continuing
and inexorable process. There is a Broadland Flood Alleviation Strategy, drawn
up by the Environment Agency, which involves the strengthening, raising and
sometimes setting back of the floodbanks, with allowance being made for predicted sea level rises over the next 50 years. The general thinking among the
authorities responsible for Broadland is that tidal flooding would be disastrous, both for the traditional agriculture and arable agriculture of the levels,
and for the middle sections of the valleys where salt water might penetrate the
undrained fens and Broads. Both the Broads Authority and Environment
Agency are committed to minimising flood risk to both people and property.

It is proposed to spend around £50 million in modification and repair of the
floodbanks over the next several decades, though original thoughts of building
flood barriers across the Yare at Yarmouth or across the Bure above Yarmouth
have been set aside because they cannot be justified economically. Flood alleviation planning is to a large extent based on calculations of the chances of a
flood of a particular height occurring and banks are built typically to cope with
a flood arising once every 10, 50, 100 or 200 years, dependent largely on the risk
to life and property. Currently it is envisaged that the Broadland banks be raised
by up to 40 centimetres to meet the highest risks. The problem, however, is that
the calculations assume that we live in steady times and that the flooding risks
of the past will be those of the future. The flooding in north-eastern and southern England, experienced in the autumn and winter of 2000, when supposed 1
in 100 year floods recurred several times in two months, suggest that current
planning calculations are themselves now the stuff of history.

Further reading

A useful explanation of the various legal designations of conservation sites in the UK is given in Joint Nature Conservation Committee (1998), which perhaps wrote it because it was as confused as the rest of us. General issues of conservation philosophy are discussed in Green (1985) and Moss (1999a, 2000). Current management of the fens is included in the book on Hickling Broad by its former warden (Linsell 1990) and discussed by George (1992). Wheeler (1983) persuasively argues the case for re-establishment of turf ponds in the fens. The general situation in the fens is clearly stated in Broads Authority (undated and 1997) and in the several volumes of the Broadland Fen Resource Survey, available from the Broads Authority. The Halvergate controversy is related in very great detail in a chapter by O'Riordan in Lowe et al. (1986) and even greater detail by George (1992), who was closely involved in the events concerned. Ewans (1992) provides an account intermediate in detail between the latter and mine. Reports on the operation of the ESA scheme are available on the World Wide Web at the Ministry of Agriculture's site.

Postscript

'It was the best of times, it was the worst of times, it was the age of wisdom, it was the age of foolishness, it was the epoch of belief, it was the epoch of incredulity, it was the season of Light, it was the season of Darkness, it was the spring of hope, it was the winter of despair, we had everything before us, we had nothing before us, we were all going direct to Heaven, we were all going direct the other way ...'

Charles Dickens, *A Tale of Two Cities*, Chapter 1

'I think I see a solution; that is, I see the dilemma is false. The only way I can take no part in the fight is to show two versions of it. That leaves me with only one problem: I cannot give both versions at once, yet whichever is the second will seem, so strong is the tyranny of the last chapter, the final, the 'real' version.'

John Fowles, *The French Lieutenant's Woman*, Chapter 55

The epoch of belief

The cyclone that had wrecked northern France, Belgium and south-eastern England in 2025 and devastated London and Brussels, was still remembered in 2050 but distantly. It was just one of the bouts of extreme weather that had affected the globe as temperatures increased more and more rapidly in the twenty-first century. Little had been done about the causes, for that would have meant too severe a disruption of the economic interests of the richest nations. Their policies had been to invest in protective structures, both political and physical, and the problems faced by the poorer world had given welcome opportunities to extend their influence. The large increase in population in Africa and Asia had seemed a threat at first, with attempts at mass emigration from the poorer to the richer world, but this had been solved simply by creating a powerful military barrier around the national boundaries of those who could afford it. Personal and corporate taxation was an increasing burden, but there was little choice.

Twice the average annual rainfall had fallen over southern England and the adjacent parts of mainland Europe in just five days in 2025. By coincidence it was about the same amount as had fallen during the cyclone that had hit Mozambique in 2000, though less than those that had repeatedly been reducing the cities of the Atlantic seaboard of the USA to permanent states of emergency. The failure of the flood barrier on the Thames had been tragic. Very high tides, coupled with a river level 20 metres above normal, had submerged its control systems. Most of central London had been covered by ten metres of water for two weeks. Many people had been drowned. What remained of the Government had moved to Manchester. At first the intention was to return, but the costs of reinstating London were so great that it had essentially been abandoned as a major centre. In the aftermath, however, Gross National Product had risen greatly with the rebuilding work that was necessary over a huge area and Southeast Asian investment funds had reaped huge rewards for the companies concerned.

It had been a devastatingly wet year in Broadland, but the influence of the cyclone had been reduced north of Cambridgeshire. The rivers had risen very high, but fortunately the floodbanks in the lower reaches of the Yare had quickly breached and a huge washland, that had been the Halvergate triangle, was able to take much of the water. Damage in Norwich and Yarmouth, although not minor, was much less than it might have been. Sea levels had continued to rise in the decades before the cyclone, but fortunately little had been done. It had not been economically feasible to raise or rebuild the banks or to create a flood barrier in the depressed state of British agriculture. That itself had been the consequence of the pervading market economy and the lack of confidence engendered by successive abuses of technological farming. Had the river floodbanks been strengthened, central Norwich would have been destroyed by backed-up river water, and Yarmouth, by the sea. But this was not widely recognised.

The cyclone had changed much. The Manchester Government had decided that much more investment was necessary to guard against future environmental disasters. The advice of international engineering companies from the Netherlands had been taken and a dramatic reinforced concrete embankment now bordered the Norfolk coast and extended on either side of the tidal sections of the lower rivers and in the towns. It was a pity that Norwich no longer enjoyed the riverscape that had linked the cathedral and the medieval city into a pleasing panoply. However, 'the wall' was so prominent that it had been vigorously marketed as a tourist attraction anyway, with its visitor centre and the new shopping mall ('Gateway to the Broads') that combined information on the Broads Heritage Area with ample opportunities to buy souvenirs and luxury goods.

The need to generate enormous national income, to maintain both the environmental defences and the military, had meant that most people had greatly reduced incomes. There was, however, still a coterie of the very well-off benefiting from the changes, and able to afford the delights of exclusive boutiques and the opportunities for cultural pleasures that their mobility afforded. Air travel had become very expensive. Fuel prices had risen as oil reserves were clearly dwindling. There was also a need to minimise the possibilities of illegal movements from those parts of the world that had failed to stem their rising populations early enough to prevent a near doubling from the six billion at the turn of the twenty-first century. The previous popular holiday destinations had also become less attractive as climate had changed, or too dangerous as the impacts of population increase and economic exploitation had left millions of desperate people whose only recourse was crime.

This had meant that holiday areas had had to be improved in Britain. There were problems in doing this. Much of the countryside had had to be converted to very intensive agriculture and industry because of the need to finance the defensive works and guard against the breakdown of supplies of food and goods. These had been seriously interrupted by climatic change, and particularly the chaos that increasing population had brought to much of the world. The wider countryside of Britain was, frankly, increasingly unattractive, even ugly. The trends of the late twentieth century had continued and, particularly away from the hills of the north and west, there were few areas where the vista was not dominated by roads and buildings, interspersed with highly mechanised agricultural installations. River quality had also deteriorated with greater

isolation of the nation from European influences, something reflected perhaps in the re-birthing (their term) of the former Environment Agency as the
National Business Environment Agency. The new title more accurately reflected the Government's intentions and removed some confusion on the part of
the Agency's staff who had perceived it as an environment protection agency
and been somewhat frustrated in their work.

The solution had been virtual reality centres for the less well-off and the creation of rigorously preserved Heritage Areas for those who could afford them.
These could no longer be so large as the former National Parks and the many
small Sites of Scientific Interest and National Nature Reserves had had to go,
but that was a trend already showing up even before 2000. But they *were* exquis-
ite. Expensive to visit perhaps, but artfully managed to take the visitor into a
vision of the past that was unsurpassed elsewhere. The British genius for organisation, for the theatrical, and for the apparently eccentric defence of the interests of the underdog, particularly if a rare species, had all come together.

Broadland had been a natural choice. It had all the right features. Late in
the twentieth century it had been described by a local naturalist, Ted Ellis, as
'a place for the cure of souls' and this had become part of the logo of
Broadland Heritage, which had replaced the former Broads Authority. The
area had a long history, beginning with the ice age and the filling of the valleys
with peat and clay from successive invasions of the sea. That it had survived
these gave comfortable reassurance at a time when such threats had again
been realised. The successive waves of Dark Age invaders from abroad were
played down for they echoed the less comfortable present threat of environmental refugees. Broadland also celebrated the origins of industry in the digging of the peat pits, which had become the basins of the Broads, for fuel. It
was an epitome of how the beauty of the English landscape had been shaped
by the hand of man to reflect a basic goodness and love of the soil.

There was a welter of literary references quoted in the displays of the
Norwich visitor centre and the information stations, which were centred in the
remaining villages. Arthur Ransome, John Betjeman, George Crabbe,
Wentworth Day and Ted Ellis were all used to their fullest effect to maintain
the ambience. Sales of beautifully produced souvenir books, masterpieces of
the new information technologies, which used a deep understanding of lin-
guistics with the possibilities of computer manipulation of digital photographs
to create exactly the right image, were booming. Indeed, the department concerned with this in Broadland Heritage was perhaps the most influential, both
in determining how the area was managed as well as the publicity that brought
in the funds to maintain the business. It was usually just called the 'image'
department.

A healthy income was very important, for maintaining the past was not
cheap. It had been realised that Broadland would always suffer a problem of
water quality. The intensification of the agricultural catchment had increased
rather than decreased. The solution had been to create a series of compartments in Broadland, some of which could be completely isolated and maintained much as they had been early in the twentieth century, whilst other areas,
where water quality was poor, were devoted to recreation. The conservation
areas were centred around the Trinity Broads on the Muck Fleet and the
Thurne Broads. These had small adjoining catchments, which Broadland
Heritage had been able to buy in their entirety, following the flooding of 2025

and the bankruptcy of the previous owners, so that catchment use could be highly controlled.

A discrete fence, buried in hedges, carefully planted to simulate ancient hedgerows, surrounded each catchment, and in the Thurne, the water tables had been raised. The electric pumps had been removed and the eighteenth-century wind pumps fully reinstated. They were manned by information operatives, who dressed in turn-of-the-nineteenth-century dress and gave daily demonstrations of pump operations whilst relating the history of the area. In the Muck Fleet, a new Broad was being excavated by hand on Burgh Common, with operatives creating a feeling of the tenth century. Enormous attention had been given to authentication, with the land grazed by close replicas of ancient domesticated breeds of stock re-created by genetic manipulation from the starting point of some of the remaining rare breeds.

In these two conservation catchments, effort had also been concentrated on re-establishing the diverse plant communities of the fenlands, again using hand labour and traditional grazing for the most part. Broadland Heritage was a major employer and its image department had become skilled in the selection of employees who combined the right sort of appearance with an outgoing personality receptive to paying visitors. A week's stay, with access to the conservation areas, was not cheap. Only a limited number of country house hotels, mostly developed from existing old houses close to the catchments, had been permitted. In the long tradition of British hotels, a stay was inordinately expensive, which confined the opportunity to the well-off. Land transport within the conservation areas was by foot, horse or cart (Plate 28) and trails had been built that were very natural in surface appearance, but which were underlain by new composites that resisted erosion and rutting in wet weather. There were boat trails too and visitors could either be rowed by information operatives who acted as guides or could hire a small sailing boat, though the sails were kept stowed, and the boat was discretely powered by batteries recharged nightly.

Foot and boat trails led to artfully hidden locations where the visitor could be close to populations of rare fenland plants and flocks of birds or the reintroduced otters and European beavers. The fen orchid had been saved by artificial propagation and although climatic conditions did not really favour it, its numbers could be boosted from glasshouse stock in years when the outdoor population disappeared. For the most part, however, hand cultivation had been able to maintain a range of communities specified as typical of the area from the work of fenland ecologists since the 1970s. The vegetation at the edges of the Broads was carefully monitored and cut back to give a natural-looking edge, but to prevent any serious encroachment on the open water. Research had produced management formulae so that it was now possible to guarantee sightings of bitterns feeding in the reed beds at dawn and marsh harriers nesting in the fens. Discrete wing-clipping and artificial feeding had helped maintain spectacular flocks of duck and geese year-round.

Hickling village had been transformed, with houses that concealed modern accommodation at the rear with historic accommodation at the front. It allowed visitors to move, over the course of a day, from life as it was in the Bronze Age, through Viking, Saxon, medieval, Elizabethan, Georgian, Victorian and Edwardian settings, complete with more information operatives who, by being also the tenants of the houses, gave a particular historic connectivity ... in the words of the image department.

Care had also been given to the rest of Broadland to create the best possible appearance and facilities. The recreation area was much bigger than the two conservation areas, and generated much of the income that was needed to support the latter and maintain a very high quality experience in it. It had not proved possible to reduce the nutrient flows in the Bure, Yare and Waveney and although Broadland Heritage had made a little headway with the Ant, its inability yet to purchase the catchment meant that for the time being this river was still largely used for recreation. With the exclusion of Hickling Broad and the Trinity Broads from all but conservation activities, it was in any case necessary to keep the water open in Barton Broad for competitive sailing and the popular re-enactment of the eighteenth-century 'water frolics'.

A philosophy of quiet recreation had prevailed, however, so that speed boating was prohibited except in a new reservoir area covering part of the Halvergate triangle. The new flood wall had been used partly to enclose a deep flooded area, close to Yarmouth, where a vigorous boating industry had developed, serving both the coastal and freshwater zones. The near collapse of the holiday boating industry early in the twenty-first century had led in any case to a rethinking of the future, but it was the restriction on foreign travel that had saved it. The rather ugly fibreglass boats had been replaced by traditional wooden ones, or rather by ones made of new unrottable plastic composites that resembled wood so closely that it was necessary to look at a microscopic section of the material to confirm that they were not. The boats were also powered by electrical batteries, and moved more slowly than the previous diesel boats. Although ultimately the energy had to be generated by some means that was potentially environmentally damaging, the net damage was believed to have been reduced.

All boats were hired by the day. Visitors stayed in high quality land accommodation built in the waterside villages, again to traditional specifications. Much of it was thatched and took the produce of the conservation areas. There were few local residents, for properties had been bought up for conversion into holiday accommodation. Commercial traffic, necessary for essential supplies and restocking of the heritage shopping areas developed in the villages, was led in and out by short routes and not permitted to cross the region. Traffic on the roads was thus kept light and the usual pattern was for visitors to hire a boat for the day on one of the rivers, having driven to one of the regional recreational centres to pick it up. This had had the effect of confining the visitors by night to a few such centres, where the accommodation was also located and adding to the image of remoteness of the waterway, though in reality it remained very busy.

Special attention had been given to maintenance and restoration, even relocation, of traditional properties, even churches. This had required a special Act of Parliament and was well overdue. The age embraced organised religion to no great extent and the churches' role was mostly as important landscape features. The parsons of the churches around the Muck Fleet and Hickling were mostly still genuine despite their period costume, but their income came mostly from Broadland Heritage. One proposal of the image department had been that even the staff at its headquarters, centred in Norwich, should be uniformed in period dress, but the Chief Executive and Controller had vetoed this. The company was now listed as one of the 100 most successful British companies and his photograph regularly appeared on the financial pages of the remaining national broadsheet newspaper. It was certainly not in *his* image to discard his business suit.

By and large the river banks had been improved. The change from holidays afloat to shore-based visits using day boats had increased the ease by which sections could be closed, and a programme of regrading and planting had been carried out. Ugly eroded edges had been eliminated. The development of a genetically modified clone of reed, which would establish quickly almost anywhere (genes of couch grass had been inserted) had helped. The danger now was that it would spread to the conservation areas, but fortunately it had been engineered to be sterile and for its rhizomes to be very resistant to fragmentation, so the problem was as yet seen only as a potential one.

Alongside the Bure and Yare it had been possible to isolate and restore a few Broads as examples of the former waterscape. Boat entry from the river was not allowed for it was necessary to keep these Broads entirely isolated and to pump in ground water to maintain their flushing rates, but the installations were highly concealed and soundproofed and the fantasy was not adulterated by them. Visitors were able to leave their electric boat in a camouflaged parking area, transfer to a rowing boat, pulled by an information operative if they wished, and dangle their hands among the lilies in the manner of an Emerson photograph, an image widely used by the company. At Hoveton Great Broad, a row across the water brought them to a wonderful small teashop, where the tables were graced by vases of flowering-rush and the cream teas came from the produce of authentic cattle breeds kept, and hand milked, in the conservation areas.

The grazing marshes had been a huge sheet of water following the cyclone and many people had doubted that they could ever have been recovered. For some ten years they had not, but the increased winter flooding of the early twenty-first century had stimulated the invention of new, very powerful pumps and processes of concrete construction that meant that very large structures could be quickly and relatively cheaply made. A barrier had been installed at Yarmouth to guard against storm surge tides, which were now to be expected more frequently, and to support this, nearly 2,000 hectares of grazing marsh had been enclosed as a reservoir, whose level could be regulated, alongside Breydon Water. In summer it was used as a huge area for sailing, water-skiing and power boating – it was, after all, 20 times bigger than any area that had previously been available for sailing and the size muffled noise problems in the flat lowland landscape. In winter the level was lowered so that there was a large emergency storage for flood waters. That having been constructed, the company had turned its attention to restoration of the grazing marsh.

The floods of 2025 had posed major problems for the marsh. Some people had felt that it was not worth trying to recover land from under several metres of water. The cost was very high and the farming that was likely to be possible was unprofitable without grants from the State. On the other hand, it was argued, if not openly, there was a principle at stake. In a country where the landscape entirely bore the shaping hand of man and had done so for generations, it was unthinkable that nature, even manipulated inadvertently by man, should be allowed to take its course.

The Broadland grazing marshes had been a historic landscape; historic landscapes were more interesting and attractive than the urban and intensive agricultural landscapes that had been imposed by the market economy since the early 1980s. The governments of that period were now reviled by the bulk of the community, but nothing had been done to reverse their effects, for policy was not determined by the people, but by the powerful multinational consortia who owned most of the country. Historic landscapes, furthermore, could be profitable if managed in the right way. The new heritage companies, created soon after the storm, when the military government that had taken over in the chaos that had destroyed central London handed back responsibility, at least apparently, to an elected government, were keen to invest.

It had been difficult to build the new river walls with so much water about, but no worse than creating a polder from the sea in Holland. The reservoir was quickly created and the rest of the land returned to a drainage regime equivalent to that before the Second World War. There was a mixture of wind pumps, restored to working order, and a couple of steam pumps. Broadland Heritage felt that diesel pumps did not have quite the appeal of wind and steam and did not reinstate these. It skilfully re-created those wind pumps that it did not fully restore to the romantic ruins that, set against a sunset, had been the very marrow of Broadland photography for decades. Its attention to detail was faultless. Gates with their sloping wooden rails across the dykes were made of the same virtually indestructible wood substitutes that were being used for boats, and cattle were kept as they had been for generations.

It was more difficult to 'sell' this landscape than those of the conservation and recreation areas, but it had helped to call it simply the 'Windmill Heritage'. A few small touches – the heritage farm at Ash Tree where salt was prepared by the evaporation of sea water on peat fires by information operatives, the opportunity for children to mingle with cattle, even bulls, specially engineered to be very docile, and the working pumps – helped a great deal. Cart tours in the area were now a substantial earner for the company.

Indeed, all was proceeding very well. Broadland Heritage's share value on the stock market had risen steadily and this was attributed to the care it had taken to provide what the market really wanted. Escape from the tribulations of a society showing many signs of distress was perhaps the most valuable commodity that could now be marketed. The world overseas was increasingly threatening and most people did not begrudge the additional levy placed on visitor fees and accommodation in heritage sites so that the defences could be maintained.

There were some disturbing signs. The spate of arson in the Hickling historic village was perhaps one, and the repeated mysterious problems with the computer telemetry system, which told the company's headquarters staff exactly where every information operative was at any time, was another. This was particularly irksome, for the system also gave information on the position of every boat, cart and horse at every moment, displayed it on screens in the control room deep in the heart of medieval Norwich and analysed it. The company was thus able to keep track of which features of Broadland were proving most attractive and under what conditions of weather and current fashions. The image department was then able to adjust the marketing and publicity output to emphasise less popular features, redistribute the visitor load and maintain the impression of remoteness although at any one time in the main season there would be a quarter of a million people within the controlled area.

On a wider scale there was considerable unrest, and not only in the crowded estates of the poorer areas of the cities. But then, that was a normal feature of history and the image department had produced a splendid book showing the parallels between the current problems and those of the thirteenth and seventeenth century and how these had eventually been solved in ways that had given bucolic countryside and rejoicing people. There was even a virtual reality exhibition in the magnificent nave of the Cathedral at Norwich where people could experience something of the terrors of these periods and then be soothed into the pleasures that were to come in the late twenty-first century. They left with the recorded reassuring voice of a British Prime Minister of the mid-twentieth century, that they had 'never had it so good'.

The spring of hope

The cyclone that had wrecked northern France, Belgium and south-eastern England in 2025 and devastated London and Brussels was still remembered in 2050. Its lesson had been immediate, in a way that reports of disasters abroad had never been, to a populace treated nightly to the sanitised images on their television screens. It was quickly recognised as yet another example of the extreme weather that had affected the globe as temperatures increased more and more rapidly in the twenty-first century. Little had been done to remove the causes for that would have meant disruption of the economic interests of the richest nations. But physical devastation in the seats of economic power was a new reality that had to be faced. It brought home the difficulties that increasing populations of the Third World had been facing for decades. It, and similar cyclones affecting Washington and New York, triggered a response among people who had been uneasy about how society was managed, but had not been able to articulate it collectively in the face of a barrage of propaganda, subtly imposed by the advertising and the public relations departments of government and multinational corporations.

The failure of the flood barrier on the Thames, when very high tides coupled with twice the annual rainfall that had fallen on the catchment in just five days in 2025 had submerged its control systems, had been tragic for most of central London. It had been covered by ten metres of water for two weeks. Many people had drowned. What remained of the Government had had to move to Manchester, at first with the intention of returning. The costs of reinstating London were so great, however, that its centre had essentially been abandoned. That had been the pivotal event, for it broke the structures that had prevented change in society and had maintained an economic system that could not have been sustained indefinitely anyway. It had hitherto been maintained by building up a debt of environmental and social costs not only in Europe and North America, but in the poorer countries, which had been made increasingly poor, as their populations steadily increased, by the hegemony of the West.

There was a wealth of ideas available that had been denigrated by the economic interests of the late twentieth and early twenty-first centuries, but that could now be tested as those interests were discredited by the catastrophic consequences of their actions – brought to such immediate attention by the cyclone. The lessons of history had always been that change was often dramatic, fast and unexpected and the aftermath of 2025 was no exception. One old man in his nineties, then retired to the remote west of Wales, outside the main path of the storm, pointed out a parallel with the workings of ecological systems that he had drawn late in the twentieth century. Societies and systems could exist in very different states. They were maintained for long periods in one of these states by all sorts of stabilising mechanisms, but could be switched by catastrophic events to another, very different one. The cyclone had effectively made such a switch in British society and similar events had triggered parallel changes in other countries too.

His ideas had been formed, among many sources, from research into the ecology of the Broadland in Norfolk and it is thus interesting to document what had begun to happen in the management of this area following the storm. It had been very wet that year in Broadland, devastatingly so in some ways, but the influence of the cyclone had been reduced north of Cambridgeshire. The Broadland rivers had risen very high, but fortunately the floodbanks in the lower reaches had quickly breached and a huge washland, that had been the Halvergate triangle, was able to take much of the water. Damage, although severe in Norwich and Yarmouth, was much less than it might have been. Sea levels had continued to rise in the decades before the cyclone, but fortunately little had been done. It had not been economically feasible to raise or rebuild the banks or to create a flood barrier in the depressed state of British agriculture that had been the consequence of the pervading global market economy and the lack of public confidence engendered by successive abuses of technological farming.

The philosophy of management in Broadland was that used to determine policy throughout the country and increasingly abroad. It rested on several principles. First, because exploitation of fossil fuel reserves had changed the composition of the atmosphere and brought about unpredictable and devastating changes, there should be much more caution in future exploitation of all resources. It could never be certain that any particular activity would be ultimately beneficial to society, so a taxation system had been instituted that minimised environmental disruption by recovering the real costs of associated environmental damage. This had immediately stopped the production of many goods and curbed many activities. It had not, however, had the depressive effect that its twentieth-century critics had scornfully predicted. Ways were found to reuse many materials and the durability of manufactured goods had been increased many fold. Concepts such as planned obsolescence were themselves obsolete and good design, with lasting value, had replaced the fripperies of annually changing fashion.

Matters were helped also by changes in taxation that favoured use of labour rather than of materials. Costs of manufacture were assessed in terms of labour and materials and value-added tax rates increased greatly as the ratio of material to labour costs increased. This had resulted in a move back towards skilled labour and greater employment. It had also resulted in a greater evenness of income and in contentment in the working environment. Many social problems, which had begun to develop in the latter half of the twentieth century and greatly worsened in the two decades prior to the storm, were now much eased.

There had also been a great decline in managerialism. A further change made by the first of the post-emergency governments had been that many decisions should be made locally so that they could be appropriate to local conditions. Most of the former centralised bureaucracies became redundant, whilst the success of an organisation, and hence its future viability, was determined by the support of the workforce as a whole. An organisation wasteful of talent and materials became unprofitable very quickly. The taxation system had also resulted, as had been intended, in an improvement in conditions abroad, especially in the Third World. The costs of imports had increased greatly on account of the high environmental damage tax on air transport and on produce grown by inappropriate intensive cropping systems on tropical soils. Many Third World countries were increasingly able to cope with their rising populations once relieved of the burdens imposed by international economics and the influence of the former multinational corporations, which were dwindling fast. In general they had relied on high turnover of disposable goods and exploitation of cheap labour and they were unable to compete in the changed economies.

The new economy, as it spread worldwide, would gradually lead to a greater atmospheric stability, to fewer threats from globally damaging pollutants, and from such events as the cyclone. The populations, even of that most gullible of nations, the United States, had begun to realise how the propaganda of the previous economies had exploited them in the guise of a 'good life' that was ultimately a slavery to powerful marketing interests.

Broadland was managed in a very different way from that which had ever been foreseen. It had changed greatly, and had returned to being a working environment rather than just a museum of the past. The first changes had been felt with the breaching of the floodbanks during the storm. It had been very clear that the capacity of the Halvergate triangle to accommodate water had prevented complete disaster in Norwich and Yarmouth. Some people had nonetheless advocated the re-draining of the floodplains and a return to the grazing marsh landscapes of the past.

However, this would not only have been very expensive, but pointless when the marshes could only be maintained with economic subsidies that were now unacceptable. Loss of the capacity for flood storage under the present climate, when floods could be expected quite often, was a cost that had to be set against the potential profits, if any, of an agricultural regime on the floodplain. There were other ways of using the area that were more sensible. The lower river valleys were allowed to remain as a tidal estuary. At first the water was deep over the whole area, even at low tide, for the former estuarine sediments had shrunk and wasted under several centuries of drainage, but gradually the tides and rivers were bringing in silt and salt marshes were extending at the margins, backed by reedswamps.

Sheep and cattle were proving to be very profitable at the edge of the estuary, for the more hardy breeds, though less productive than some of the highly bred strains of the intensive former systems, required much less in the way of veterinary attention. They thus incurred much lower penalties in terms of tax on the use of antibiotics and other drugs formerly used. Philosophies of increasing agricultural production at any cost were now greatly outmoded and the waste that had been a concomitant of much of the food-processing and retailing industries was eliminated through the taxation system. The ultimate health consequences of former intensive systems had been treated as an environmental cost for taxation purposes and this was resulting in a population much less vulnerable to viral and bacterial diseases or those of unbalanced diet and obesity.

Moreover, the estuary was proving a magnificent area for recreation, being big enough, even at low tide, for a range of boating activities that had been impossible previously for lack of water space. It was windy and could be rough, but that provided a greater interest and excitement. There were funds now to provide very good safety coverage as the costs of other social services such as health and social security had fallen. Of course, in the coming century, the area of open water would decrease as the area of marshes and mud flats increased. They were already providing habitat remote enough to attract back burgeoning wildfowl populations. But projections suggested that when these processes were complete, there would still be a very substantial area of open water.

Attitudes to the land and waterscape had now adjusted to the idea of continuing steady change even without severe human influence, and of adjustment and wise management of the opportunities the change might give. This contrasted with the previous attempts to maintain the status quo of recent memory. For that reason too, there had been no attempt to rebuild those wind pump ruins that had survived the storm. A few were reasonably intact and were made safe and remained as reminders of past history. There was no desire to eliminate history, but to see it in the context of change and adjustment. No longer was it seen as a past golden age, or ideal, and equally the concept that all change induced by human activity was progress had been seen to be false. In one thesaurus of the early twenty-first century, 'progress' and 'marketing opportunity' had been presented as synonyms.

The second major change in Broadland had been seen in the catchment. There had been a major rethinking about agriculture, for most of its previous practices had been of uncertain long-term value. On the one hand, its use of energy was considerable and fossil fuels had become very expensive as the environmental-damage taxes on their use were high; its previous widespread use of pesticides was also no longer acceptable. Their ultimate health and environmental hazards were considerable, and following the twentieth-century concerns over animal welfare, bovine spongiform encephalopathy and genetic modification, the public was far more discerning than it had been before. The demise of the processing industry had also meant that there was much more emphasis on locally produced and marketed products and much less pressure for high yields at the expense of quality and safety. This had meant that mechanisation had decreased somewhat and that there was greater emphasis on cultivation skills and human labour.

The energy problem had been eased by local generation from renewable sources and quite large wind farms were located offshore just over the horizon whilst small wood- and litter-fed power stations provided much of the rural demand. Energy saving measures had also reduced demand considerably, now that the unit costs of electricity and other energy sources increased rather than decreased, as formerly, with individual annual usage.

The ultimate effect was that rather less land was required for agriculture, that it could be worked much more wisely, that mixed farming systems with both crops and stock had returned, and that transport costs were reduced. There was much more sympathy for the agricultural sector from the public at large, who were now much better informed about the problems of farming in a naturally changing environment. Land was now available to provide wide buffer zones along the rivers and the catchment headwaters and greater involvement of very skilled labour had revolutionised the sophistication of nutrient control within farms.

Stock wastes were treated alongside village sewage and the effluents used for irrigation of crops. Biological control methods, knowledge of crop and weed ecology, crop rotations and use of less productive, but more resistant crop strains had minimised pesticide need to rare emergencies. The water draining from the fields was much lower in nutrients and crop protection residues than it had been for a century. The taxation system had also meant that the water and sewage companies were obliged to find ways of extracting many substances from their effluents, which were regarded as their products, for reuse. They had been obliged to return to a system of small local works to adjust for the variety of substances that came from different areas, rather than having the few, very large, works formerly regarded as profitable, but in fact subsidised by the unpaid costs of considerable environmental damage.

With a less intensive land use, river flows had returned to a more even seasonal pattern and the water quality was much improved. It became feasible to convert the rather worn appearances of the river banks and the formerly turbid waters of Broadland to more diverse and attractive systems. There were some problems in doing this, for return of the former vegetation would hasten the filling-in of the Broads. This was a process that had been going on apace in the early twentieth century, but had been stopped by the combination of eutrophication and boat erosion in the latter part. Filling-in would obliterate basins that had historic significance. On the other hand, the floods of 2025 had opened up considerable areas of water in the floodplains and the topography of the system was no longer entirely what it had been. The basins had sometimes been widened, as rafts of peat had been forced up by the water and carried downstream, whilst in some other places deposition had filled in parts of the basins. The system was now perhaps a little like what it had been some thousands of years ago when the annual floods had created, then removed lagoons, as natural lakes, in the floodplain.

The Trinity Broads, with their small catchment, had changed least. It was decided that they should form the nucleus of an open-air museum that would reflect the story of the Broads and that with judicious cutting at the edges they should be delayed in their eventual succession to wetland. The Thurne system had changed beyond all recognition when the sea broke through the dunes close to Martham Broad at the height of the storm and had returned to an estuary. It was left for much the same reason that the Halvergate estuary was left and now provided a sheltered large inlet where recreational sailing was very popular.

The tides were pushing silt up the new River Thurne and starting to block it a little beyond Potter Heigham Bridge, whose medieval masonry had survived, largely by submergence in deep water, where other more modern and higher bridges had been demolished by floating debris washed from upstream. The bridge was now still partly submerged at high tide and reappeared at the lowest tides. A decision had to be made whether to dredge the blockage or not, but this would have had to be done repeatedly and was perceived as futile opposition to natural processes. Alternatively, the Bure could have been reconnected to the Thurne, as it would have been in all probability at some time in the past, and the increased flow used to prevent the blockage. The consequences of doing this, however, were hard to predict, so on the grounds that so much damage had been done in former centuries by engineering in ignorance, it was decided that the Bure should be left. The Thurne became a separate river and its estuary one of the most delightful quiet spots on the coast. It was surrounded by salt marshes and backed by reed beds and fens, where before there had only been mildly salt and freshwater fens, and was one of the richest areas for wildlife in the region.

The floodplains of the Bure, Yare and Waveney were wetter than formerly. The remaining artificial basins of the Broads were just about discernible, but now had much less distinct edges as vegetation succeeded. By 2050 they were extremely attractive, with great swards of lilies and flowering-rush, but it was accepted that within decades they would be covered by fen and carr. There was considerable controversy about their future and also that of the open fens. These had been formerly maintained artificially by cutting, sometimes for reed, but usually to maintain their 'conservation value' by exotic machines, volunteer labour and grazing. There had been a philosophy of conservation that particularly emphasised maintenance of particular communities of plants according to a classification system, the National Vegetation Classification, which recognised particular combinations of species loosely associated with particular conditions.

Much effort had formerly been invested in re-creating or maintaining these communities in nature reserves, with targets and timetables, much as in the running of a business or administrative organisation. It meant that some areas, listed as Sites of Special Scientific Interest and a welter of other designations based on a plethora of legislation, were isolated for 'conservation' amid a countryside that was rapidly degrading. It became known as 'fortress conservation', began in the mid-twentieth century and failed from the beginning. By 2000, the downward trend in 'value' of these sites was clear and calculations showed that most of the 9,000 or so such sites would be severely damaged within 30 or 40 years. It had been a popular system with government, however, for the renovation of such sites, or individual charismatic species, could become the foci of major publicity gains at minimal cost. In the meantime the wider countryside became more damaged, more uniform, less interesting and increasingly vandalised and littered.

The reserves were too small and too isolated for maintenance of diverse communities, without immense attention that amounted to gardening and zoo keeping. Where fresh waters were concerned, it was impossible to manage them because there was no control over the catchments from which their water supplies came. The European Water Framework Directive of 2000 had promised significant change and indeed had done more than any legislation previously. It had prescribed that 'high' ecological quality should be characterised for lakes and rivers and then a series of lesser categories defined – good, moderate, poor and bad – dependent on the water quality and nature of the ecosystem, for damaged sites. Within 15 years, all sites had, in theory, to be restored to 'good' quality and this meant that national legislation should have been necessary to control catchment use. The problem was, however, that many derogations had been allowable under the Directive so that very few water bodies had been included by the Government as subject to it. It had then been easy to delay new legislation indefinitely, especially with the need for Parliamentary time to counter the increasing social problems that were besetting the country.

Fortress conservation disappeared as a concept after 2025 with the realisation that, indeed, 'all things were connected' (a well-known tenet, attributed to a nineteenth-century American Indian chief, though actually written by a twentieth-century scriptwriter, but nonetheless apt). It was perceived that a diverse and interesting landscape could be better maintained incidentally to wise use of the land as a whole. Some species would inevitably decline, even disappear, but many more would flourish and the philosophy became one of sustainable use, rather than preservation of museums. Sustainable use, or as it was generally expressed, 'sustainable development' was another twentieth-century slogan manipulated by powerful interests to mean continued exploitation. It was not until 2025 that its real meaning was widely understood. Central government administrative bodies that had previously had sectoral interests in, for example, agriculture or conservation or waste management or water quality on a national basis were disbanded and replaced by single catchment-based organisations charged with sustainable management of their areas. They were of moderate size, sometimes covering a single large catchment, sometimes covering several adjacent smaller ones. The Broadland Catchment Authority was one such.

The Broadland catchment was seen as capable of supporting both farming and tourism in a sustainable way that would also maintain a varied and interesting landscape for casual recreation. The Ant and Bure valleys had had increasing amounts of carr woodland in the late twentieth and early twenty-first centuries as the natural vegetation succession had proceeded, following abandonment of grazing and cutting after the Second World War. Some of the fens in the Ant valley, however, had been maintained as open communities and were regularly cut for reed or maintenance of conservation interest. Much of this land use still existed, but for different reasons. The increasing requirement for locally produced food and for husbandry methods that were less intensive than formerly meant that the fens again became grazing pasture in summer.

Water buffalo had been introduced, alongside native cattle, for there was an increasing market for their products in a society that had become increasingly interested in variety that could not now be so readily supplied by imports. Reed was still cut, indeed the areas of reed bed were being extended because the costs of roofing tiles had increased, because of the energy demands for their production and transportation. Reed was a product with a high labour to materials ratio and hence was subject to very low tax. The carr woodlands were now also more actively managed, because local generation of electricity from non-fossil fuels was decidedly cheaper (Plate 29).

Felling created openings that allowed new successions to occur and this maintained a more varied mosaic of habitats than in the past, whilst the Catchment Authority had created a system of management that screened the disturbed areas very skilfully among other compartments that were allowed to remain untouched. Electrically-powered barges were widely used to transport the wood to the power station, where their motors were recharged nightly and this kept open a system of waterways that was of great value to the tourist industry.

Tourism had changed quite markedly. There were still many visitors, for the attractions of sailing and boating on the huge Breydon estuary and on the quieter but still large Thurne estuary were considerable. The particular appeal, however, was the enormous area of attractive countryside for walking, riding and boating that the catchment as a whole offered. Gone were the somewhat tedious holidays when boats moved quickly along river stretches because there was little to hold the interest along eroded banks, or embankments that occluded the view. Speeds were much lower simply because the plant beds and wallowing water buffalo prevented more than a careful manoeuvring in the rivers, but the open waters of the estuary allowed a contrasting opportunity for those who enjoyed the experience (most) to let rip much faster.

Because Broadland had now become a working landscape again, there was much to be seen and a real sense of continuity with the past, which had, paradoxically, been interrupted in the doldrum years between 1960 and 2025. Then its management had largely been one of frantic attempts to preserve items of interest against forces that were inexorable and destructive. Perhaps most important was the acceptance that the global environment was still changing, indeed had always been changing, and that it was generally sensible to work with these changes rather than oppose them all the time. And perhaps most significant was the fact that society as a whole was more settled, more supportive of its own need for stability and contentment and with little use for the baubles that had been the pseudo-rewards for the exploitation that had marked the previous half century or so. It was even the case that the Director of the Broadland Catchment Authority, despite considerable responsibilities, was so well supported by an enthusiastic staff, that she could spend a day every week, out in the fens or on the water, with parties of children truly interested to know about the countryside and how it worked.

Epilogue

AD 34300. The ice was melting back and the archaeologists of the Eurasian Historical Foundation at Valencia in southern Spain had begun their annual summer field work season in the moraines now occupying what had been eastern England. One of the students called over the excavation supervisor to show him some peculiar square blocks of flint, about eight centimetres on edge that seemed to have been chipped into shape. There were three of them, joined by a calcareous mortar that also would prove to have been man-made nearly 33,000 years previously. It was some time before they were identified, because in the upheaval that had brought waves of northern peoples southwards ahead of the ice, almost all of the paper and electronic archives had been destroyed. The southern libraries still held good collections, though, and the blocks turned out to have come from a building, perhaps a Christian church, probably one built by a wealthy patron, sometime around AD 1400. Indeed, in the library there was a good photograph of similar blocks set at the base of a church tower in an area that had been called 'The Broads' in a twenty-first-century book of that name.

Bibliography

Anderson, S. & Moss, B. (1993). How wetland habitats are perceived by children: Consequences for children's education and wetland conservation. *International Journal of Science Education*, 15, 473–485.

Andersson, G., Bergren, H., Cronberg, G., & Gelin, C. (1978). Effects of planktivorous and benthivorous fish on organisms and water chemistry in eutrophic lakes. *Hydrobiologia*, 59, 9–15.

Annadotter, H., Cronberg, G., Aagren, R., Lundstedt, B., Nilsson, P-A. & Srobeck, S. (1999). Multiple techniques for lake restoration. *Hydrobiologia*, 395/396, 77–85.

Baker, R. & Lambley, P. (1980). The River Wensum (2). *Transactions of the Norfolk and Norwich Naturalists Society*, 25(2), 65–83.

Bales, M., Moss, B., Phillips, G., Irvine, K. & Stansfield, J. (1993). The changing ecosystem of a shallow, brackish lake, Hickling Broad, Norfolk, U.K. II Long-term trends in water chemistry and ecology and their implications for restoration of the lake. *Freshwater Biology*, 29, 141–65.

Ball, P. (1999). *H₂O A Biography of Water.* Weidenfeld & Nicholson, London.

Balls, H., Moss, B. & Irvine, K. (1989). The loss of submerged plants with eutrophication. I. Experimental design, water chemistry, aquatic plant and phytoplankton biomass in experiments carried out in ponds in the Norfolk Broadland. *Freshwater Biology*, 22, 71–87.

Barringer, J.C. (1989). *An Introduction to Faden's Map of Norfolk.* The Larks Press, Dereham.

Barringer, J.C. (1998). *Bryant's Map of Norfolk in 1826.* The Larks Press, Dereham.

Benndorf, J. (1987). Food web manipulation without nutrient control: A useful strategy in lake restoration? *Schweizerische Zhurnal der Hydrologie*, 49, 237–248.

Bennett, A. (1884). Plants new to Norfolk, with notes on other species. *Transactions of the Norfolk and Norwich Naturalists Society*, 3, 633–636.

Bennett, A. (1910). *Najas marina*, L and *Chara stelligera*, Bauer, as Norfolk plants. *Transactions of the Norfolk and Norwich Naturalists Society*, 9(1), 47–50.

Bennett, K.D. (1983). Devensian Late-Glacial and Flandrian vegetational history at Hockham Mere, Norfolk, England: 1. Pollen percentages and concentrations. *New Phytologist*, 95, 457–487.

Betjeman, J. (1984). *Collected Poems.* John Murray.

Bjørk, S. (1994). Restoration of lakes through sediment removal – Lake Trummen, Sweden. Pp. 130–140 in Eiseltova, M. (Ed.) *Restoration of Lake Ecosystems, a Holistic approach.* International Waterfowl and Wetlands Research Bureau, Publication 32, Slimbridge.

Boar, R.R., Crook, C.E. and Moss, B. (1989). Regression of *Phragmites australis* reedswamps and recent changes of water chemistry in the Norfolk Broadland. *Aquatic Botany*, 35, 41–55.

Boorman, L.A. & Fuller, R.M. (1981). The changing status of reedswamp in the Norfolk Broads. *Journal of Applied Ecology*, 18, 241–269.

Boulton, G.S., Cox, F., Hart, J. & Thornton, M. (1984). The glacial geology of Norfolk. *Bulletin of the Geological Society of Norfolk*, 34, 103–122.

Breukelaar, A.W., Lammens, E.H.R.R., Klein Breteler, J.G.P. & Tatrai, I.

(1994). Effects of benthivorous bream (*Abramis brama*) and carp (*Cyprinus carpio*) on sediment resuspension and concentrations of nutrients and chlorophyll *a*. *Freshwater Biology*, 32, 113–121.

Broads Authority (undated). *Fens for the Future. The Management of Broadland Fens.* Broads Authority and English Nature, Norwich.

Broads Authority (1982). *What Future for Broadland? A Draft Strategy and Management Plan.* Broads Authority, Norwich.

Broads Authority (1997). *Broads Plan 1997.* Broads Authority, Norwich.

Broads Consortium (1971). *Broadland Study and Plan.* Norfolk County Council, Norwich.

Brönmark, C. (1989). Interactions between epiphytes, macrophytes and freshwater snails: a review. *Journal of Molluscan Studies*, 55, 299–311.

Brooks, J. L. & Dodson, S. I. (1965). Predation, body size and composition of plankton. *Science*, 150, 28–35.

Cahn, A.R. (1929). The effect of carp on a small lake: the carp as a dominant. *Ecology* 10, 271–274.

Campbell, J. & Middleton, C. (1999). *The Man who Found the Broads.* Hamilton publications, Gorleston on Sea.

Canter-Lund, H. & Lund, J.W.G. (1995). *Freshwater Algae. Their Microscopic World Explained.* Biopress Ltd, Bristol.

Carill-Worsley, P.E.T. (1932). A fur farm in Norfolk. *Transactions of the Norfolk and Norwich Naturalists Society*, 13(2), 105–115.

Carpenter, S.R. & Kitchell, J.F. (Eds) (1994). *The Trophic Cascade in Lakes.* Cambridge University Press, Cambridge.

Carvalho, L. (1994). Top-down control of phytoplankton in a shallow hypertrophic lake: Little Mere, (England). *Hydrobiologia*, 275/276, 53–63.

Chatwin, C.P. (1961). *East Anglia and Adjoining Areas.* British Regional Geology Series, HMSO, London.

Clarke, K.B. (1973). The unusual clarity of the Ormesby Broads during 1971. *Transactions of the Norfolk and Norwich Naturalists Society*, 22, 254–260.

Clarke, K. (B) (1990). Salt water penetration into the upper Bure. *Transactions of the Norfolk and Norwich Naturalists Society*, 28(5), 329–408.

Clements, F.E. (1928). *Plant Succession and Plant Indicators.* Carnegie Institute, Washington.

Coles, B.P.L. & Funnell, B.M. (1981). Holocene palaeoenvironments of Broadland, England. *Special Publications of the International Association of Sedimentologists*, 5, 123–131.

Cooke, G.D., Welch, E.B., Peterson, S.A. & Newroth, P.R. (1993). *Restoration and Management of Lakes and Reservoirs.* Lewis publishers, Ann Arbor, Michigan.

Cotton, K.E. (1963). The coypu. *River Boards association Yearbook*, 11, 31–39.

Crivelli, A.J. (1983). The destruction of aquatic vegetation by carp, *Cyprinus carpio*: a comparison between southern France and the USA. *Hydrobiologia*, 106, 37–41.

Crook, C., Boar, R. & Moss, B. (1983). *The Decline of Reedswamp in the Norfolk Broadland: Causes, Consequences and Solutions.* Broads Authority Research Series 6.

Cryer, M., Peirson, G. & Townsend, C.R. (1986). Reciprocal interactions between roach, *Rutilus rutilus*, and zooplankton in a small lake: prey dynamics and fish growth and recruitment. *Limnology & Oceanography*, 31, 1022–1038.

Darby, H.C. (1983). *The Changing Fenland.* Cambridge University Press, Cambridge.

Davies, G.C. (1883). *Norfolk Broads and Rivers.* Blackwood, London.

Davies, G.C. (1912). *Rivers & Broads of Norfolk and Suffolk.* Jarrold, Norwich.

Davis, R.A. (1963). Feral coypus in Britain. *Annals of Applied Biology*, 5, 345–348.

De Nie, H.W. (1987). The decrease of aquatic vegetation in Europe and its consequence for fish populations. EIFAC/CECP Occasional Paper 19.

Doarks, C. (1984). *A Study of Marsh Dykes in Broadland.* Broads Authority Research Series 9. Broads Authority, Norwich.

Dobson, M.J. (1980). 'Marsh fever' – the geography of malaria in England. *Journal of Historical Geography,* 6, 357–389.

Driscoll, R.J. (1984). The dyke vegetation at Oby and Thurne: a comparison of late 19th century and recent records. *Transactions of the Norfolk and Norwich Naturalists Society,* 26 (1), 43–49.

Driscoll, R.J. (1986). The effect of changes in land management on the dyke fauna at Somerton and Winterton. *Transactions of the Norfolk and Norwich Naturalists Society,* 27(3), 215–220.

Dugan, P. (Ed.) (1993). *Wetlands in Danger.* Mitchell Beazley, London.

Dutt, W.A. (1903). *The Norfolk Broads.* Methuen, London.

Dutt, W.A. (1906). *Wildlife in East Anglia.* Methuen, London.

Dymond, D. & Martin, M. (1999). *An Historical Atlas of Suffolk.* Third Edition. Suffolk County Council and Suffolk Institute of Archaeology and History, Ipswich.

Earwaker, J. & Becker, K. (1998). *Literary Norfolk. An Illustrated Companion.* Chapter 6 Publishing, Ipswich.

Eaton, J.W. (Ed.) (1999). *Assessment of the proposed cutting of aquatic plants in Hickling Broad.* Final Report of the Assessment Team. Broads Authority, Norwich

Edmondson, W.T. (1991). *The Uses of Ecology, Lake Washington and Beyond.* University of Washington Press, Seattle & London.

Eiseltova, M. (Ed.) (1994). *Restoration of Lake Ecosystems, a Holistic Approach.* International Waterfowl and Wetlands Research Bureau, Publication 32, Slimbridge.

Ekwall, E. (1960). *The Concise Oxford Dictionary of English Place-Names.* Fourth Edition, Clarendon Press, Oxford.

Ellis, E.A. (1935). Wheatfen Broad, Surlingham. *Transactions of the Norfolk and Norwich Naturalists Society,* 13(5), 422–451

Ellis, E.A. (1963). Some effects of selective feeding by the coypu (*Myocastor coypus*) on the vegetation of Broadland. *Transactions of the Norfolk and Norwich Naturalists Society,* 20(1), 32–35.

Ellis, E.A. (1965). *The Broads.* Collins, London.

Eminson, D. & Phillips, G. (1978).. A laboratory experiment to examine the effects of nutrient enrichment on macrophyte and epiphyte growth. *Verhandlungen Internationale der Vereinigung Theoretische und Angewande Limnologie,* 20, 82–87.

Environment Agency (2000). *Eutrophication Management Strategy.* Bristol.

Etherington, J.R. (1983). *Wetland Ecology.* Arnold, London.

Evans, M. (1992). *The Battle for the Broads.* Terence Dalton Ltd, Lavenham.

Foy, R.H., Smith, R.V., Jordan, C. & Lennox, S.D. (1995). Upward trend in soluble phosphorus loadings to Lough Neagh despite phosphorus reduction at sewage treatment works. *Water Research,* 29, 1051–1063.

George, M. (1992). *The Land Use, Ecology and Conservation of Broadland.* Packard Publishing, Chichester.

Gilbert, P.A. & De Jong, A.L. (1978). The use of phosphate in detergents and possible replacements for phosphate. Pp. 253–268 in *Phosphorus in the Environment.* Ciba Foundation Symposium 57 (new series) Elsevier, Amsterdam.

Giles, N. (1992). *Wildlife after Gravel: Twenty Years of Practical Research by the Game Conservancy and ARC.* Game Conservancy, Fordingbridge.

Giller, K.E. & Wheeler, B.D. (1986). Past peat cutting and present vegetation patterns in an undrained fen in the Norfolk Broadland. *Journal of Ecology*, 74, 219–247.

Gliwicz, M. S. & Sieniawska, A. (1986). Filtering activity of *Daphnia* in low concentrations of a pesticide. *Limnology and Oceanography*, 31, 1132–7.

Godwin, H. (1978). *Fenland: its Ancient Past and Uncertain Future.* Cambridge University Press, Cambridge.

Goodey, C. (1978). *A Century of Broadland Cruising.* Loynes, Wroxham.

Gosling, L.M. (1988). A history of coypus in Britain: 1929–1988. Norfolk Mammal Report for 1987. *Transactions of the Norfolk and Norwich Naturalists Society*, 28(2), 154–157.

Gosling, L.M. & Baker, S.J. (1980). Acidity fluctuations at a Broadland site in Norfolk. *Journal of Applied Ecology*, 17, 479–490.

Gosling, L.M. & Baker, S.J. (1987). Planning and monitoring an attempt to eradicate coypus from Britain. *Symposia of the Zoological Society of London*, 58, 99–113.

Gosling, L.M., Baker, S.J. & Clarke, C.N. (1988). An attempt to remove coypus (*Myocaster coypus*) from a wetland habitat in East Anglia. *Journal of Applied Ecology*, 25, 49–62.

Green, B. (1985). *Countryside Conservation.* Allen & Unwin, London.

Green, S. & Walker, E. (1991). *Ice age Hunters.* National Museum of Wales, Cardiff.

Griffiths, B.M. (1927). Studies in the phytoplankton of the lowland waters of Great Britain. V. The phytoplankton of some Norfolk Broads. *Journal of the Linnean Society. Botany*, 47, 595–612.

Gross, E.M. & Sutfeld, R. (1994). Polyphenols with algicidal activity in the submerged macrophyte *Myriophyllum spicatum* 1. *Acta Horticultura*, 381, 710–716.

Gurney, E. & Gurney, R. (1908). The Sutton Broad Freshwater Laboratory. *Annales Biologie lacustre*, 3, 1–12.

Gurney, J.H. (1904). Coot shooting on Hickling Broad. *Transactions of the Norfolk and Norwich Naturalists Society*, 7, 267–273.

Gurney, R. (1904). The fresh- and brackish-water Crustacea of East Norfolk. *Transactions of the Norfolk and Norwich Naturalists Society*, 7(5), 637–660.

Gurney, R. (1911). The tides of the River Bure and its tributaries. *Transactions of the Norfolk and Norwich Naturalists Society*, 9(2), 216–243.

Hall, D.J., Threlkeld, S.T., Burns, C.W. & Crowley, P.H. (1976). The size and efficiency hypothesis and the size structure of zooplankton communities. *Annual Review of Ecology and Systematics*, 7, 177–208.

Hameed, H.A., Kilinc, S., McGowan, S. & Moss, B. (1999). Physiological tests and bioassays – aids or superfluities to the diagnosis of phytoplankton nutrient limitation? A comparative study in the Broads and Meres of England. *European Phycological Journal*, 34, 253–270.

Hammer, D.A. (Ed.) (1989). *Constructed Wetlands for Wastewater Treatment.* Lewis Publishers, Chelsea, Michigan.

Hardy, A.C. (1950). Obituary. Dr Robert Gurney. *Proceedings of the Linnean Society of London*, Session 162 1949–50, (1) 118–120.

Harvey, G. (1997). *The Killing of the Countryside.* Jonathan Cape, London.

Haslam, S.M. (1972). Biological flora of the British Isles: *Phragmites communis* Trin. *Journal of Ecology*, 60, 585–610.

Hilton, J. & Phillips, G.L. (1982). The effect of boat activity on turbidity in a shallow broadland river. *Journal of Applied Ecology*, 19, 143–150.

Holdway, P.A., Watson, R.A. & Moss, B. (1978). Aspects of the ecology of *Prymnesium parvum* (Haptophyta) and water chemistry in the Norfolk

Broads, England. *Freshwater Biology*, 8, 295–311.

Holmes, D. (1998). *Back to the Broads.* Sutton Publishing, Stroud.

Hosper, H. (1989). Biomanipulation, a new perspective for restoring shallow, eutrophic lakes in the Netherlands. *Hydrobiological Bulletin* 23, 11–19.

Houghton, J. (1997). *Global Warming.* Cambridge University Press, Cambridge.

Howard Williams, C. (1981). Studies on the ability of a *Potamogeton pectinatus* community to remove dissolved nitrogen and phosphorus compounds from the water. *Journal of Applied Ecology*, 18, 619–637.

Hrbacek, J., Bvorakova, K., Korinek, V. & Prochazkova, L. (1961). Demonstration of the effect of the fish stock on the species composition of the zooplankton and the intensity of metabolism of the whole plankton association. *Verhandlungen internationale der Vereinigung theoretische und angewewade Limnologie*, 14, 192–195.

Hurlbert, S.H., Zedler, J. & Fairbanks, D. (1971). Ecosystem alteration by mosquito fish *(Gambusia affinis)* predation. *Science*, 175, 639–41.

Hutchinson, G.E. (1965). *The Environmental Theatre and the Evolutionary Play.* Yale University Press, New Haven.

Huxley, T.H. (1967). *On a Piece of Chalk.* Edited and introduced by L. Eiseley. Charles Scribner's Sons, New York.

Hynes, H.B.N. (1979). *The Ecology of Running Waters.* Liverpool University Press, Liverpool.

Irvine, K., Moss, B., Bales, M. & Snook, D. (1993). The changing ecosystem of a shallow, brackish lake, Hickling Broad, Norfolk, U.K. I. Trophic relationships with special reference to the role of *Neomysis integer. Freshwater Biology*, 29, 119–39.

Irvine, K., Moss, B. & Balls, H.R. (1989). The loss of submerged plants with eutrophication. II.

Relationships between fish and zooplankton in a set of experimental ponds, and conclusions. *Freshwater Biology*, 22, 89–107.

Irvine, K., Moss, B. & Stansfield, J. (1990). The potential of artificial refugia for maintaining a community of large-bodied Cladocera against fish predation in a shallow eutrophic lake. *Hydrobiologia*, 200/201, 379–389.

Irvine, K., Snook, D. & Moss, B. (1995). Life histories of *Neomysis integer*, and its copepod prey, *Eurytemora affinis*, in a eutrophic and brackish shallow lake. *Hydrobiologia* 304, 59–76.

Jackson, M.J. (1978). The changing status of aquatic macrophytes in the Norfolk Broads. *Transactions of the Norfolk and Norwich Naturalists Society*, 24(4), 137–152.

Jak, R.G., Maas, J.L. & Scholten, M.C.Th. (1996). Evaluation of laboratory derived toxic effect concentrations of a mixture of metals by testing fresh water plankton communities in enclosures. *Water Research*, 30, 1215–1227.

Jeppesen, E., Søndergaard, M., Kanstrup, E., Eriksen, R.B., Hammershoj, M., Petersen, B., Mortensen, E., Jensen, J.P., & Have, A. (1994). Does the impact of nutrients on the biological structure and function of brackish and freshwater lakes differ? *Hydrobiologia*, 275/276, 15–30.

Jeppesen, E., Søndergaard, M., Kronvang, B., Jensen, J.P., Svendsen, L.M. & Lauridsen, T.L. (1999). Lake and catchment management in Denmark. *Hydrobiologia*, 395/396, 419–432.

Johnes, P., Moss, B. & Phillips, G. (1996). The determination of total nitrogen and total phosphorus concentrations in freshwaters from land use, stock headage and population data: testing of a model for use in conservation and water quality management. *Freshwater Biology* 36, 451–473.

Joint Nature Conservation Committee (1998). *Nature Conservation in the UK. An introduction to the Statutory Framework,* JNCC, Peterborough.

Jones, R.L. & Keen, D.H. (1993). *Pleistocene Environments in the British Isles.* Chapman & Hall, London.

Klinge, M., Grimm, M.P. & Hosper, S.H. (1995). Eutrophication and ecological rehabilitation of Dutch lakes: presentation of a new conceptual framework. *Water Science & Technology,* 31, 207–218.

Lacey, R. & Danziger, D. (1999). *The Year 1000. What Life was Like at the Turn of the First Millennium.* Little Brown & Co., London.

Lamarra, V. (1975). Digestive activities of carp as a major contributor to the nutrient loading of lakes. *Verhandlungen Internationale der Vereinigung fur theoretische und angewande Limnologie,* 19, 2461–8.

Lambert, J.M. (1951). Alluvial stratigraphy and vegetation succession in the region of the Bure valley Broads: III – classification, status and distribution of communities. *Journal of Ecology,* 39, 149–170.

Lambert, J.M. & Jennings, J.N. (1951). Alluvial stratigraphy and vegetation succession in the region of the Bure valley Broads: II – detailed vegetational-stratigraphical relationships. *Journal of Ecology,* 39, 120–148.

Lambert, J.M., Jennings, J.N., Smith, C.T., Green, C. & Hutchinson, J.N. (1960). *The Making of the Broads: a Reconsideration of their Origin in the Light of New Evidence.* Royal Geographic Society Research Memoir, 3.

Lambert, J.M. & Smith, C.T. (1960). The Norfolk Broads as man-made features. *New Scientist.* March 31 1961, 775–777.

Lauridsen, T.L., Pedersen, L.J., Jeppesen, E. & Søndergaard, M. (1996). The importance of macrophyte bed size for cladoceran composition and horizontal migration in a shallow lake. *Journal of*

Plankton Research, 18, 283–94.

Laurie, E.M.O. (1946). The coypu (*Myocaster coypus*) in Great Britain. *Journal of Animal Ecology,* 15, 22–34

Leah, R.T., Moss, B., & Forrest, D.E. (1978). Experiments with large enclosures in a fertile shallow brackish lake, Hickling Broad, United Kingdom. *Internationale Revue der Gesamten Hydrobiologie,* 63, 291–310.

Leah, R.T., Moss, B. & Forrest, D.E. (1980). The role of predation in causing major changes in the limnology of a hypereutrophicated lake. *Internationale Revue der Gesamten Hydrobiologie,* 62, 223–253.

Leopold, L.B. (1974). *Water, a Primer.* Freeman, San Francisco.

Lilljeborg, W. (1982). *Cladocera Suecica III.* Almquist & Wiksell International, Stockholm.

Linsell, S. (1990). *Hickling Broad and its Wildlife.* Dalton, Lavenham

Long, S.P. & Mason, C.F. (1983). *Saltmarsh Ecology.* Blackie, Glasgow.

Lowe, P., Cox, G., MacEwen, M., O'Riordan, T. & Winter, M. (1986). *Countryside Conflicts. The Politics of Farming, Forestry and Conservation.* Gower, Aldershot.

MacEwan, A. & MacEwan, M. (1982). *National Parks: Conservation or Cosmetics.* Allen & Unwin, Boston.

MacEwan, A. & MacEwan, M. (1987). *Greenprints for the Countryside: The Story of Britain's National Parks.* Allen & Unwin, London.

Malster, R. (1993). *The Broads.* Phillimore & Co., Chichester.

Manning, S.A. (1980). *Portrait of Broadland.* Hale.

Margeson, S. (1997). *The Vikings in Norfolk.* Norfolk Museums Service, Norwich.

Margeson, S., Ayers, B., & Heywood, S. (1996). *A Festival of Norfolk Archaeology.* Norfolk and Norwich Archaeological Society, Norwich.

Marren, P. (1993). The siege of the NCC: Nature conservation in the eighties. pp 283–300 in Goldsmith, F.B. & Warren, A. (Eds) *Conservation*

in Progress. Wiley, Chichester.
Marsden, M.W. (1989). Lake restoration by reducing external phosphorus loading: the influence of sediment release. *Freshwater Biology,* 21, 139–162.
Mason, C.F. & Bryant, R.J. (1975).. Changes in the ecology of the Norfolk Broads. *Freshwater Biology,* 5, 257–270.
McIntosh, R.P. (1967). The continuum concept of vegetation. *Botanical Reviews,* 33, 130–187.
Middleton, C.S. (1978). *The Broadland Photographers,* Wensum, Norwich.
Ministry of Agriculture, Fisheries and Food (1999). *Tackling Nitrate from Agriculture. Strategy from Science.* MAFF Publications, London.
Ministry of Town and Country Planning (1945). *National Parks in England and Wales.* Report by John Dower. Cmnd 6628. HMSO, London.
Ministry of Town and Country Planning (1947). *Report of the National Parks Committee (England and Wales).* Chairman Sir A. Hobhouse. Cmnd 7121. HMSO, London.
Moore, J.A. (1986). *Charophytes of Great Britain and Ireland.* Botanical Society of the British Isles, London.
Moore, N.W. (1987). *The Bird of Time. The Science and Politics of Nature Conservation.* Cambridge University Press, Cambridge.
Morgan, N.C. (1972). Problems of the conservation of freshwater ecosystems. *Symposia of the Zoological Society of London,* 29, 135–154.
Moss, B. (1977). Conservation problems in the Norfolk Broads and rivers – phytoplankton, boats and the causes of turbidity. *Biological Conservation,* 9, 95–114.
Moss, B. (1978). The ecological history of a medieval man-made lake, Hickling Broad, Norfolk, United Kingdom. *Hydrobiologia,* 60, 23–32.
Moss, B. (1979). Algal and other fossil evidence for major changes in Strumpshaw Broad, Norfolk, England in the last two centuries.

British Phycological Journal, 14, 256–273.
Moss, B. (1980). Further studies on the palaeolimnology and changes in the phosphorus budget of Barton Broad, Norfolk. *Freshwater Biology,* 10, 261–279.
Moss, B. (1983). The Norfolk Broadland: experiments in the restoration of a complex wetland. *Biological Reviews,* 58, 521–561.
Moss, B. (1987).. Classic sites – The Broads. *The Biologist – Journal of the Institute of Biology,* 34, 7–15.
Moss, B. (1988). The palaeolimnology of Hoveton Great Broad, Norfolk: Clues to the spoiling and restoration of Broadland. In: *The Exploitation of Wetlands,* Symposia of the Association for Environmental Archaeology, pp. 163–191.
Moss, B. (1990). Engineering and biological approaches to the restoration from eutrophication of shallow lakes in which aquatic plant communities are important components. *Hydrobiologia,* 200/201, 367–377.
Moss, B. (1991). Robert Gurney and the founding of the Freshwater Biological Association. *Freshwater Forum,* 1, 20–24.
Moss, B. (1992). The scope for biomanipulation in improving water quality. Pp. 73–81 in D.W. Sutcliffe & J.G. Jones (Eds) *Eutrophication: Research and application to water supply.* Freshwater Biological Association, Ambleside.
Moss, B. (1994). Brackish and freshwater shallow lakes – different systems or variations on the same theme? *Hydrobiologia,* 275/276, 1–14.
Moss, B. (1998). *Ecology of Freshwaters Man and Medium, Past to Future.* Third Edition. Blackwell Science, Oxford.
Moss, B. (1999a). The seventh age of freshwater conservation. A triumph of hope over experience? *Aquatic Conservation: Marine and Freshwater,* 9, 639–644.
Moss, B. (1999b). British Phycological

Society Presidential Address 1999. From algal culture to ecosystem, from information to culture. *European Phycological Journal* 34, 193–204.

Moss, B. (2000). Conservation – of freshwaters or of the status quo. *Verhandlungen internationale der Vereinigung theoretische und angewande Limnologie*, 27, 88–96.

Moss, B., Bales, M. & Irvine, K. (1991). Food web and water quality relationships in the saline broads of the River Thurne, Norfolk. *Memorie dell'istituto italiano di idrobiologia*, 48, 345–362.

Moss, B. & Balls, H. (1989). Phytoplankton distribution in a floodplain lake and river system. II. Seasonal changes in the phytoplankton communities and their control by hydrology and nutrient availability. *Journal of Plankton Research*, 11, 839–867.

Moss, B., Balls, H.R., Booker, I., Manson, K. & Timms, R.M. (1988a). The River Bure, United Kingdom: Patterns of change in chemistry and phytoplankton in a slow-flowing fertile river. *Verhandlungen internationale der Vereinigung theoretische und angewande Limnologie*, 22, 1959–1964.

Moss, B., Balls, H.R., Booker, I., Manson, K. & Timms, R.M. (1988b). Problems in the construction of a nutrient budget for the River Bure and its Broads (Norfolk) prior to its restoration from eutrophication. In Round, F.E & Talling, J.F., (Eds), *Algae and the Aquatic Environment*, 311–338. Biopress, Bristol.

Moss, B., Balls, H., Irvine, K. & Stansfield, J. (1986). Restoration of two lowland lakes by isolation from nutrient-rich water sources with and without removal of sediment. *Journal of Applied Ecology*, 23, 391–440.

Moss, B., Booker, I.R., Balls, H. & Manson, K. (1989). Phytoplankton distribution in a temperate floodplain lake and river system. I. Hydrology, nutrient sources and phytoplankton biomass. *Journal of*

Plankton Research, 11, 813–838.

Moss, B., Forrest, D.E. & Phillips, G.L. (1979). Eutrophication and palaeolimnology of two small medieval man-made lakes. *Archiv fur Hydrobiologie*, 81, 1–17.

Moss, B., Kornijow, R. & Measey, G.J. (1998). The effects of nymphaeid (*Nuphar lutea* L.) density and predation by perch (*Perca fluviatilis* L.) on the zooplankton communities in a shallow lake. *Freshwater Biology*, 39, 689–697.

Moss, B. & Leah, R.T. (1982). Changes in the ecosystem of a guanotrophic and brackish shallow lake in Eastern England: potential problems in its restoration. *Internationale Revue der Gesamten Hydrobiologie*, 67, 625–659.

Moss, B., Madgwick, J. & Phillips, G. (1996). *A Guide to the Restoration of Nutrient-Enriched Shallow Lakes*. Broads Authority, Environment Agency & EU Life Programme, Norwich.

Moss, B., McGowan, S. & Carvalho, L. (1994). Determination of phytoplankton crops by top-down and bottom-up mechanisms in a group of English lakes, the West Midland Meres. *Limnology & Oceanography*, 39, 1020–1030.

Moss, B., Stansfield, J. & Irvine, K. (1990). Problems in the restoration of a hypertrophic lake by diversion of a nutrient-rich inflow. *Verhandlungen internationale der Vereinigung theoretische und angewandte Limnologie*, 24, 568–572.

Moss, B., Stansfield, J. & Irvine, K. (1991). Development of daphnid communities in diatom- and cyanophyte-dominated lakes and their relevance to lake restoration by biomanipulation. *Journal of Applied Ecology*, 28, 586–602.

Moss, B., Stansfield, J., Irvine, K., Perrow, M. & Phillips, G. (1996). Progressive restoration of a shallow lake – a twelve-year experiment in isolation, sediment removal and biomanipulation. *Journal of Applied*

Ecology, 33, 71–86.

National Rivers Authority (1990). *Toxic Blue-Green Algae.* Water Quality Series 2, National Rivers Authority, HMSO, London.

Nature Conservancy (1965). *Report on Broadland*, HMSO, London.

Nature Conservancy Council (1984). *Nature Conservation in Great Britain.* NCC, Shrewsbury.

Nicholson, W.A. (1904). Sir Thomas Browne as a naturalist. *Transactions of the Norfolk and Norwich Naturalists Society*, 7 (1), 72–89.

Norfolk Naturalists Trust (1976). *Nature in Norfolk – A Heritage in Trust.* Jarrold, Norwich.

Norris, J.D. (1967). A campaign against feral coypus (*Myocaster coypus* Molina) in Great Britain. *Journal of Applied Ecology*, 4, 191–199.

Osborne, P.L. (1980). Prediction of phosphorus and nitrogen concentrations in lakes from both internal and external loading rates. *Hydrobiologia*, 69, 229–233.

Osborne, P.L. (1981). Phosphorus and nitrogen budgets of Barton Broad and predicted effects of a reduction in nutrient loading on phytoplankton biomass in Barton, Sutton and Stalham Broads, Norfolk, United Kingdom. *Internationale Revue der Gesamten Hydrobiologie*, 66, 171–202.

Osborne, P.A. & Moss, B. (1977). Palaeolimnology and trends in the phosphorus and iron budgets of an old man-made lake, Barton Broad, Norfolk. *Freshwater Biology*, 72, 13–233.

Osborne, P.L. & Phillips, G.L. (1978). Evidence for nutrient release from the sediments of two shallow and productive lakes. *Verhandlungen internationale der Vereinigung theoretische und angewande Limnologie*, 20, 654–658.

Pallis, M. (1911). The river valleys of east Norfolk: their aquatic and fen formations. In Tansley, A.G., *Types of British Vegetation*, pp. 214–244. Cambridge University Press, Cambridge.

Patterson, A.H. (1902). John Thomas, punt gunner. *Transactions of the Norfolk and Norwich Naturalists Society*, 7, 339–345.

Patterson, A.H. (1920). *Through Broadland in a Breydon Punt.* H.J. Vince, Norwich.

Peglar, S.M., Fritz, S.C. & Birks, H.J.B. (1989). Vegetation and land-use history at Diss, Norfolk, U.K. *Journal of Ecology*, 77, 203–222.

Perrow. M.R., Jowitt, A.J.D., Stansfield, J.H., & Phillips, G.L. (1999). The practical importance of the interactions between fish, zooplankton and macrophytes in shallow lake restoration. *Hydrobiologia*, 395/396, 199–210.

Perrow, M.R., Moss, B. & Stansfield, J. (1994). Trophic interactions in a shallow lake following a reduction in nutrient loading: a long term study. *Hydrobiologia*, 275/276, 43–52.

Phillips, G.L. (1984). A large-scale field experiment in the control of eutrophication in the Norfolk Broads. *Water Pollution Control*, 1984, 400–405.

Phillips, G., Bramwell, A., Pitt, J., Stansfield, J. & Perrow, M. (1999). Practical application of 25 years' research into the management of shallow lakes. *Hydrobiologia*, 395/396, 61–76.

Phillips, G.L., Eminson D.F. & Moss, B. (1978). A mechanism to account for macrophyte decline in progressively eutrophicated freshwaters. *Aquatic Botany*, 4, 103–126.

Phillips, G.L., Jackson, R., Bennett, C. & Chilvers, A. (1994). The importance of sediment phosphorus release in the restoration of very shallow lakes (The Norfolk Broads, England) and implications for bio-manipulation. *Hydrobiologia*, 275/276, 445–456.

Phillips, G.L., Perrow, M. & Stansfield, J. (1996). Manipulating the fish-zooplankton interaction in shallow lakes: a tool for restoration. pp 174–183 in

Greenstreet S.P.R & Tasker M.L. (Eds) *Aquatic Predators and their Prey*, Blackwell Science, Oxford.

Pitts, M. & Roberts, M. (1997). *Fairweather Eden.* Century, London.

Poore, M.E.D. (1955). The use of phytosociological methods in ecological investigations. I. The Braun-Blanquet System. *Journal of Ecology*, 43, 226–244.

Purseglove, J. (1989). *Taming the Flood. A History and Natural History of Rivers and Wetlands.* Oxford University Press.

Ransome, A. (1936). *Coot Club.* Cape, London.

Ransome, A. (1940). *The Big Six.* Cape, London.

Ranwell, D.S. (1972). *Ecology of Salt Marshes and Sand Dunes.* Chapman & Hall, London.

Ratcliffe, D.A. (1977). *A Nature Conservation Review. The Selection of Biological Sites of National Importance for Nature Conservation in Britain.* Cambridge University Press, Cambridge.

Reynolds, C.S. (1994). The ecological basis for the successful biomanipulation of aquatic communities. *Archiv fÜr Hydrobiologie*, 130, 1–33.

Rodwell, J.S. (1995). *British Plant Communities. Vol 4. Aquatic Communities, Swamps and Tall-Herb Fens.* Cambridge University Press, Cambridge.

Runte, A. (1987). *National Parks. The American Experience.* University of Nebraska Press, Lincoln.

Ryding, S.-O. & Rast, W. (1989). (Eds) *The Control of Eutrophication of Lakes and Reservoirs.* Man & Biosphere Series Vol 1. UNESCO, Paris & Parthenon Publishing, Carnforth.

Rye, J. (1991). *A Popular Guide to Norfolk Place-Names.* The Larks Press, Dereham.

Sainty, J.E., Mosby, J.E.G, Buxton, A, & Ellis, E.A. (1939). The Norfolk sea floods. *Transactions of the Norfolk and Norwich Naturalists Society*, 14 (4), 334–390.

Sanders, H.O. & Cope, O.B. (1968). Toxicity of several pesticides to two species of cladocerans. *Transactions of the American Fisheries Society*, 95, 165–169.

Sand-Jensen, K. & Søndergaard, M. (1981). Phytoplankton and epiphyte development and their shading effect on submerged macrophytes in lakes of different nutrient status. *Internationale Revue der Gesamten Hydrobiologie*, 66, 529–52.

Sapwell, J. (1960). *A History of Aylsham.* Rigby Printing, Norwich.

Scheffer, M. (1998). *Ecology of Shallow Lakes.* Chapman and Hall, London.

Scheffer, M., Hosper, S.H., Meijer, M.L., Moss, B. & Jeppesen, E. (1993). Alternative equilibria in shallow lakes. *Trends in Ecology and Evolution*, 8, 275–279.

Schindler, D.W. (1978). Factors regulating phytoplankton production and standing crop in the world's freshwaters. *Limnology and Oceanography*, 23, 478–486.

Schriver, P., Bøgestrand, J., Jeppesen, E., & Søndergaard, M. (1995). Impact of submerged macrophytes on the interactions between fish, zooplankton and phytoplankton: large scale enclosure experiments in a shallow lake. *Freshwater Biology*, 33, 255–270.

Scott, Mr Justice (1942). *Report of the Committee on Land Utilisation in Rural areas.* Cmnd 6378, HMSO, London.

Shapiro, J. (1980). The importance of trophic-level interactions to the abundance and species composition of algae in lakes in Barica J. & Mur L.R. (Eds) *Hypertrophic Ecosystems.* Junk, The Hague.

Shapiro, J. (1990). Current beliefs regarding dominance by blue-greens: the case for the importance of CO_2 and pH. *Verhandlungen internationale der Vereinigung theoretische und angewande Limnologie*, 24, 38–54.

Shapiro, J., Lamarra, V. & Lynch, M. (1975). Biomanipulation: an ecosystem approach to lake restoration. Pp.

85–96 in Brezonik, P.L & Fox, J.L. (Eds) *Water Quality Management through Biological Control.* Report Env 07-75-1, University of Florida, Gainsville.

Sheail, J. (1976). *Nature in Trust. A History of Nature Conservation in Great Britain.* Blackie, Glasgow.

Sheail, J. (1998). *Nature Conservation in Britain. The Formative Years.* The Stationery Office, London.

Shoard, M. (1980). *The Theft of the Countryside.* Temple Smith, London.

Shoard, M. (1987). *This Land is Our Land.* Paladin, London

Simons, J., Ohm, M., Daalder, R., Boers, P. & Rip, W. (1994). Restoration of Botshol (The Netherlands) by reduction of external nutrient load: recovery of a characean community with *Chara connivens. Hydrobiologia,* 275/276, 243–253.

Smith, S. (1995). The coypu in Britain. *British Wildlife,* 6, 279–285.

Snelling, J.D. (1971). *St Benet's Abbey, Norfolk.* Privately published. Printed by F. Crowe, Norwich.

Southwell, T. (1889). Notes on some ancient customs and regulations with regard to the fresh-water fisheries of the County of Norfolk. *Transactions of the Norfolk and Norwich Naturalists Society,* 4(4), 433–446.

Sparks, B.W. & West, R.G. (1972). *The Ice Age in Great Britain.* Methuen, London.

Stamp, D. (1969). *Nature Conservation in Britain.* Collins, London.

Stansfield, J., Moss, B. & Irvine, K. (1989). The loss of submerged plants with eutrophication. III. Potential role of organochlorine pesticides: a palaeoecological study. *Freshwater Biology,* 22, 109–132.

Stevenson, H. (1879). Memoir of the late Rev. Richard Lubbock. *Transactions of the Norfolk and Norwich Naturalists Society,* 2, 292–306.

Stone, E. (1988). *Ted Ellis. The People's Naturalist.* Jarrold, Norwich.

Strong, R. (1998). *The Story of Britain. A*

People's History. Pimlico, London.

Suffling, E.R. (1887/1892). *The Land of the Broads.* Benjamin Perry, Stratford, Essex.

Tansley, A.G. (1939). *The British Isles and their Vegetation.* Cambridge University Press, Cambridge.

Teal, J. & Teal, M. (1969). *Life and Death of the Salt Marsh.* Little Brown & Co, Boston.

Timms, R.M. & Moss, B. (1984). Prevention of growth of potentially dense phytoplankton populations by zooplankton grazing in the presence of zooplanktivorous fish, in a shallow wetland ecosystem. *Limnology & Oceanography,* 29, 472–486.

Tooley, B. (1985). *John Knowlittle. The Life of the Yarmouth Naturalist Arthur Henry Patterson, A.L.S.* Wilson-Poole Publishers, Norwich.

Turner, E.L. (1924). *Broadland Birds.* Country Life, London

Turner, P. & Wood, R. (1974). *P.H. Emerson. Photographer of Norfolk.* Gordon Fraser, London.

Van der Molen, D.T. & Boers, P.C.M. (1999). Eutrophication control in the Netherlands. *Hydrobiologia,* 395/396, 403–409.

Van Donk, E. & Gulati, R.D (1995). Transition of a lake to turbid state six years after biomanipulation: mechanisms and pathways. *Water Science & Technology,* 32, 197–206.

Vincent, E.A. (1980). *A Season of Birds: A Norfolk Diary 1911.*Weidenfeld & Nicholson, London.

Vought, L.B.-M., Dahj, J., Lauge Pedersen, J. & Lacoursiere, C. (1994). Nutrient retention in riparian ecotones. *Ambio,* 23, 342–348.

Vought, L.B.-M., Pinay, G., Fuglsang, A. & Ruffinoni, C. (1995). Structure and function of buffer strips from a water quality perspective in agricultural landscapes. *Landscape & Urban Planning,* 31, 323–331.

Wade-Martins, P. (Ed.) (1994). *An Historical Atlas of Norfolk.* Second edition. Norfolk Museums Service, Norwich.

Wentworth Day, J. (1967). *Portrait of the Broads.* Hale.

West, R.G. (1961). The glacial and interglacial deposits of Norfolk. *Transactions of the Norfolk and Norwich Naturalists Society,* 19, 365–375.

Wheeler, B.D. (1978). The wetland plant communities of the River Ant valley, Norfolk. *Transactions of the Norfolk and Norwich Naturalists Society,* 24, 153–187.

Wheeler, B.D. (1980a). Plant communities of rich-fen systems in England and Wales. I. Introduction. Tall sedge and reed communities. *Journal of Ecology,* 68, 368–395.

Wheeler, B.D. (1980b). Plant communities of rich-fen systems in England and Wales. II. Communities of calcareous mires. *Journal of Ecology,* 68, 405–420.

Wheeler, B.D. (1980c). Plant communities of rich-fen systems in England and Wales. III. Fen meadow, fen grassland and fen woodland communities and contact communities. *Journal of Ecology,* 68, 761–788.

Wheeler, B.D. (1983). *Turf Ponds in Broadland.* Broads Authority Research Series 5, Norwich.

Wheeler, B.D. & Giller, K.E. (1982). Species richness of herbaceous fen vegetation in Broadland, Norfolk, in relation to the quantity of above-ground material. *Journal of Ecology,* 70, 179–200.

Whittaker, R.H. (1967). Gradient analysis of vegetation. *Biological Reviews,* 47, 207–264.

Williamson, T. (1997). *The Norfolk Broads.* Manchester University Press, Manchester.

Wilson, H. (1999). Legislative challenges for lake eutrophication control in Europe. *Hydrobiologia,* 395/396, 389–401.

Wilson, H.M., O'Sullivan, P.E. & Gibson, M.T. (1995). Analysis of current policies and alternative strategies for the reduction of nutrient loads on eutrophicated lakes: the example of Slapton Ley, Devon.

Aquatic Conservation, 3, 239–252.

Worldwide Fund for Nature (1997). *A Muzzled Watchdog?,* Godalming.

Wright, J.F. (1995). Development and use of a system for predicting the macroinvertebrate fauna in flowing waters. *Australian Journal of Ecology,* 20, 181–197.

Wright, J.F., Blackburn, J.H., Gunn, R.J.M., Furse, M.T., Armitage, P.D., Winder, J.M. & Symes, K.L. (1996). Macroinvertebrate frequency data for the RIVPACS III sites in Great Britain and their use in conservation evaluation. *Aquatic Conservation: Marine and Freshwater Ecosystems,* 6, 141–167.

Wright, J.F., Furse, M.T., Gunn, R.J.M., Blackburn, J.H., Bass, J.A.B., & Symes, K.L. (1992). *Invertebrate Survey and Classification of Rivers for Nature Conservation.* SNH Research, Survey and Monitoring report No. 1, Scottish Natural Heritage, Edinburgh.

Index